Impossible Project

Impossible Project

The Story of Russian Ballet and Its Survival

DARIA KHITROVA

OXFORD
UNIVERSITY PRESS

Oxford University Press is a department of the University of Oxford.
It furthers the University's objective of excellence in research, scholarship,
and education by publishing worldwide. Oxford is a registered trade mark of
Oxford University Press in the UK and in certain other countries.

Published in the United States of America by Oxford University Press
198 Madison Avenue, New York, NY 10016, United States of America.

© Oxford University Press 2025

All rights reserved. No part of this publication may be reproduced, stored in a retrieval system, transmitted, used for text and data mining, or used for training artificial intelligence, in any form or by any means, without the prior permission in writing of Oxford University Press, or as expressly permitted by law, by license or under terms agreed with the appropriate reprographics rights organization. Inquiries concerning reproduction outside the scope of the above should be sent to the Rights Department, Oxford University Press, at the address above.

You must not circulate this work in any other form
and you must impose this same condition on any acquirer.

CIP data is on file at the Library of Congress

ISBN 9780197653050

DOI: 10.1093/9780197653081.001.0001

Printed by Marquis Book Printing, Canada

The manufacturer's authorized representative in the EU for product safety is
Oxford University Press España S.A., Parque Empresarial San Fernando de Henares,
Avenida de Castilla, 2 – 28830 Madrid (www.oup.es/en).

To Yuri and Vari

Contents

List of Figures	ix
Acknowledgments	xi
Introduction: How Ballet Histories Are Made	1
1. The Shadow of Noverre: Ballet in a Narrative Perspective	21
2. Modern Specters, or Body Politic to Body Balletic	77
3. Ballet as a Verbal Art: Apostasy and Theodicy	177
Epilogue	256
Notes	261
Bibliography	279
Index	289

Figures

2.1. Maria Petipa in her "Little Peasant Man [*Muzhichok*]" costume   90

2.2. Ivan Vsevolozhsky, "The Preparatory Class for the Theater Administration, according to the Syllabus of Professor Skalkovsky"   115

2.3. Nicolas Lancret, *La Camargo Dancing*   119

2.4. Olga Preobrajenska and Pavel Gerdt in *The Trial of Damis*   121

2.5. Ivan Vsevolozhsky, "Kontrol'naia kletka" (The Comptroller's Cage)   134

2.6. Ivan Vsevolozhsky, a caricature featuring Virginia Zucchi on a pedestal and Aleksandr Frolov worshiping her as a deity   136

2.7. Ivan Vsevolozhsky, "La Tentation de Saint Antoine" (The Temptation of St. Anthony)   140

2.8. Ivan Vsevolozhsky, Princess Aurora, a costume design for the first production of *The Sleeping Beauty*   143

2.9. Ivan Vsevolozhsky, "La Table de Nuit de La Belle au Bois Dormant" (Sleeping Beauty's Nightstand)   146

2.10. Ivan Vsevolozhsky, "Les cloches de Corneville" (The Bells of Corneville)   147

2.11. "Evil Genius of Russia"   149

3.1. Aleksandr Benois, "Ballerina," a costume design for *Petrushka*   200

3.2. Tamara Karsavina as Ballerina in *Petrushka*   201

3.3. Aleksandr Benois, "The First Street Dancer," a costume design for *Petrushka*   202

3.4. Aleksandr Benois, "The Second Street Dancer," a costume design for *Petrushka*   203

3.5. Aleksandr Benois, "The Barrel Organ-Grinder," a costume design for *Petrushka*   204

3.6. Enrico Cechetti as Magician in *Petrushka*   205

3.7. Enrico Cechetti in class with Anna Pavlova   206

3.8. Léon Bakst, "The French Doll," a costume design for *The Fairy Doll*   209

3.9. Léon Bakst, "The Postman," a costume design for *The Fairy Doll*   212

3.10. Léon Bakst, "The Officer's Servant," a costume design for *The Fairy Doll*   213

3.11. Léon Bakst, set design for the first scene of *The Fairy Doll*   214

3.12. Aleksandr Benois, set design for *Petrushka*   215

Acknowledgments

I would like to express profound gratitude to Norman Hirschy and the OUP team who made the acquisition, editing and publication process as pleasant and productive as possible. Many thanks to Judith Hoover for her careful copyediting.

I am grateful to Avram Brown, that wizard of words, for helping me make my prose more readable.

I have been blessed to be a part of a friendly circle of fantastic scholars researching Russian ballet, whose work has always inspired me: Lynn Garafola, Elizabeth Kendall, Irina Klyagin, and Tim Scholl.

I am grateful to Marta Tonegutti for her early interest in this book.

My warm thanks go to colleagues who helped me with research: Elena Bespalova, John Bowlt, James Browning, Maya Garcia, Pavel Gershenzon, John. A Goodman Jr, Robert Greskovic, Al'bin Konechnyi, Maria Kotova, Kseniia Kumpan, Roman Leibov, Anastasia Makarova, Oleg Minin, Natalia Serdyuk, Roman Timenchik, Casper Tybjerg, Artemis Willis, Natalia Yakovleva, and the archivists of the Manuscript Division of St.-Petersburg Theater Library.

As always, I thank my parents and my brother for everything they taught me and for their endless support.

I dedicate this book to my beloved family, my husband Yuri and our daughter Vari. Much of it was written during the pandemic, a time of pain and isolation around the world. I feel guilty to admit I enjoyed every minute of it, because I spent it together with them, the best companions, intellectual and otherwise, who, as I came to understand then, literally mean the world to me.

Introduction

How Ballet Histories Are Made

Who is to blame for the regrettable fact, asks Jean-Georges Noverre philosophically in his 1760 *Letters on Dancing and Ballets* (*Lettres sur la danse et les ballets*), that next to nothing is known about the work of great ballet masters of the past—whereas the masterpieces by Corneille and Michelangelo, admired in their time, live on in ours? Noverre's speculation on the subject, found in the opening of his "Letter XVII," harbors two ideas—one perfectly obvious, the other uncommon and quite Noverrian in spirit.[1] The obvious one blames the fleetingness of ballet as a medium: unlike words on a page or traces of paint on a canvas, artworks (*ouvrages*) created by a dancer or a mime "last but for an instant, and vanish almost concurrently with the impression they produce; hence, no vestige remains of the sublime spectacles once staged by the likes of Bathyllus and Pylades."[2]

The other, less obvious idea has to do with the importance of reflection. The fact that the Roman *pantomimi* dancers, for all their popularity in the Augustan Age, failed to bequeath a lasting legacy, reasons Noverre, cannot be ascribed solely to the peculiarities of dance as a medium. The "likes of Bathyllus and Pylades" themselves are also to blame: "Knowing that they were powerless to transfer to posterity any of their fugitive tableaux, those great choreographers [*compositeurs*] should at least have communicated to us their ideas and the guiding principles of their art. Had they committed to recording the laws of the art form they had founded, their names and writings would have traversed the immensity of ages, and their pains and vigils would not have been consigned to the glory of the moment."[3]

A visionary rather than a historian of ballet, Noverre was more concerned with the future than the past. Viewed retrospectively, however, his own posthumous fame corroborates his point. Besides having been (and been seen as) an illustrious ballet master, Noverre was, just as famously, the man of *Letters*; were he not, his name would hardly have appeared on this page.

Impossible Project. Daria Khitrova, Oxford University Press. © Oxford University Press 2025.
DOI: 10.1093/9780197653081.003.0001

2 IMPOSSIBLE PROJECT

Compressed from his eighteenth-century French, Noverre's postulate may be rephrased as follows. A durable choreographic tradition—or, to reverse the chronological perspective, a robust historiographic model—sees dance in conjunction with *reflections on dance*. The only ballet a ballet historian knows firsthand is that of their own generation. Everything else we know vicariously—from film footage and video recordings of various twentieth-century ballets, and from still photographs, engravings, and drawings from ballet's earlier ages. The most informative of all such media, however, remains, as Noverre reminds us, the medium of words. Words may be less apt than pictures at capturing every little movement, but it is via verbal texts alone that we get a sense of the changing values that define ballet's history at large.

Crucial for this book, therefore, will be what I term *ballet lore*: contemporary interviews and reviews; preliminary ideas and posteriori reminiscences; grand treatises on and trite manuals of dance; letters—official, philosophical, or private; works in prose featuring a fictional dancer; and works of poetry.

In other words, in order to get a better grasp of old ballets, a ballet scholar will tap into every ballet-related source they can lay their hands on. That said, the kind of lore we select, and the use we make of it, will shape (and be shaped by—cause and effect being difficult to sort) the kind of history we write. It makes sense, therefore, to pause and consider the relationship between ballet-as-a-show and ballet lore, and how this relationship is portrayed in our historical writings on ballet.

Ballet History: Process or Progress?

Assuming that thoughts or texts about ballet—in broader terms, ballet lore—are as integral to ballet's history as productions or pas, are we entitled to say that this or that history of ballet is but a manifestation of ballet lore? The short answer is yes. Do we always realize when we read a history of something to what extent this particular picture of the past is predicated upon this particular historian's preferences for the present? A historical history is always two things in one: a factual record and a historical document—a period piece of ballet lore.

Consider Vera Krasovskaia's *Russian Ballet Theater* (*Russkii baletnyi teatr*)—one of the most competent, cohesive, and complete histories to date to have traced the Russian trajectory of ballet from its beginning in

INTRODUCTION   3

eighteenth-century St. Petersburg to its early successes in twentieth-century Paris. A classical dancer by training (Agrippina Vaganova's class of 1933) and experience (ten years in the Mariinsky, aka Kirov, corps de ballet), by the time she undertook her four-volume study (first published consecutively in 1958, 1963, 1971, and 1972) Krasovskaia knew her ballet intimately—in the round, not only from the front.

As a historian, Krasovskaia is as much at home with ballet's past, owing to her formidable knowledge of ballet lore. Following her argument in *Russian Ballet Theater* at times feels almost like entering a time warp. Every so often when citing a period review, Krasovskaia intervenes in a period controversy, upholding some critical views ("As Kudrin *correctly* points out . . ."[4]; "as the critic A. P. Ushakov remarked with *understandable* bewilderment . . ."[5]), while disagreeing, at times vehemently, with others. It is instructive to take a closer look with whom, and why.

Most of the writings we find irking Krasovskaia happen to have been authored by balletomanes, a subculture of ballet regulars remotely reminiscent of enlightened patronage in the fine arts. Being a proper balletomane— someone who would seldom miss a ballet performance, God forbid a premiere—meant to possess insider knowledge and have backstage leverage with dancers and, on occasion, with the Directorate of Imperial Theaters. "Never without their binoculars," recalled Prince Peter Lieven of such seasoned Petersburg balletomanes as Nikolai Bezobrazov, Aleksandr Pleshcheev, and Konstantin Skalkovsky, "[t]hese people were known to the artistes behind the footlights, who knew and expected their criticism."[6] Whether united in opinion or split into feuding factions, balletomanes were a force to reckon with.

In volume 2 (*The Latter Half of the Nineteenth Century*) of her *Russian Ballet Theater*, we find Krasovskaia especially displeased with the writings of Sergei Khudekov, a fixture of Russian ballet criticism for over fifty years and the owner-cum-editor of the *Petersburg Gazette* (*Peterburgskaia gazeta*), the urban daily Krasovskaia refers to as a "refuge for balletomane wisecrackers" (*pribezhishche baletomanov-ostroslovov*),[7] a hotbed of "balletomane windbaggery" (*pustozvonstvo*),[8] and so on. Distrustful of Khudekov's day-in-day-out balletic reviews, Krasovskaia is particularly unhappy about our critic's end-of-life achievement: the four-volume *History of Dances*, printed between 1913 and 1918, which Krasovskaia mockingly refers to as *History of Dances from All Epochs and Nations* (*Istoriia tantsev vsekh vremen i narodov*).[9] Here is a Soviet ballet historian critiquing her pre-Soviet predecessor—a unique

4 IMPOSSIBLE PROJECT

example of two overlaid layers of historiographic lore that warrants closer scrutiny.

Krasovskaia's criticism of Khudekov's dance history comes down to two points: its author's anything-goes approach to sources (which "lumps together hard facts with apocrypha and legends") and, no less important, the absence of "the historical process" from his book.[10]

In part, what Krasovskaia says is well deserved. Most of the time, Khudekov's *History of Dances* remains anecdotal rather than analytical and indeed relies on secondhand sources. Most of the time—but not entirely. Khudekov's *History* has a cone-like structure. Following a well-trodden path, volume 1 begins with ancient China, India, and Egypt and ends with a closer look at dancing in classical Greece and Rome; volumes 2 and 3 guide us through the Renaissance to the France of Louis XIV, and from the age of Noverre to that of romanticism in Europe. Up to this point, this, indeed, is hardly more than a survey, now sweeping, now slowing down a bit, but always panoramic. In volume 4, however, Khudekov's *History of Dances* homes in on nineteenth-century Russia, a terrain close to its author's home and heart.

As soon as Khudekov's historical odyssey finally reaches his native shore, the scholarly optics of his book changes from telescopic to close-up (or, from Krasovskaia's standpoint, myopic). Much of what we read here is no longer based on preprocessed information; rather, it sounds like an eyewitness account. Sergei Khudekov lived a long life, much of it spent in the stalls of the Mariinsky, watching ballet upon ballet, week after week. "Everything our book says about the Petersburg ballet of the latter half of the nineteenth century results from our personal observations," he declares with modest pride in his foreword to volume 4. "We only wrote down what we saw [*chto my videli, to i zapisyvali*], adhering in our judgement of every artiste's talent to utter objectivity."[11]

But fifty years in the same chair do not make one a historian of ballet; we must give Krasovskaia that. The status of eyewitness—Khudekov's assurance notwithstanding—is likewise no guarantor of impartiality. Yet this is also why we as ballet historians cannot afford to write off contemporary observers like Khudekov, even when what they say sounds like, to use Krasovskaia's epithet, "windbaggery." People of Khudekov's chosen role, with their ballet-omane routine (ever present and taking notes; joining in the backstage palaver; hunched late at night over a review to be published in a newspaper in the morning; and next week the same thing all over again) were not just observers of but also participants and players in ballet's history—unless, of course, we decide to restrict this history to the however-many square meters of the stage itself.

And participants they remained, even in those cases when one balletomane or another would come forward with a historical survey, such as Khudekov's *History of Dances*, Skalkovsky's 1882 *Ballet: Its History and Place among the Fine Arts*, or Pleshcheev's 1896 *Our Ballet (1673–1896)*. Such books have typically served two muses: Clio as a historical record and Terpsichore as a period exhibit of ballet lore. This rule—call it the rule of divided loyalty—applies equally to definitive, academic, thoroughly documented ballet histories like Krasovskaia's *Russian Ballet Theater*, an epic portrayal of previous epochs and, in the way she frames said portrayal, an accurate snapshot of her own.

Consider the notion of "the historical process," which, per Krasovskaia, Khudekov disregards in his *History of Dances*. What kind of "process" does Krasovskaya have in mind, precisely? If attending to the historical process boils down to giving a sense of history's continuities and changes, Khudekov's opus does a decent job, particularly when it comes to Russia. In line with the historiographic tradition of his time (as of ours), Khudekov divides nineteenth-century ballet in Petersburg into four ages, depending on the ballet master then in charge; traces changes within and between each of the ages as far as libretti, choreography, and staging;[12] and subdivides the age of Petipa into subperiods, before and after 1888, singling out a trend peculiar to each.[13] In a word, Khudekov's history appears quite process-oriented.

Was Krasovskaia, then, simply being unfair to Khudekov and his history? By her own standards, she was not. According to Soviet historiographic doctrine (which, to judge by *Russian Ballet Theater*, Krasovskaia made very much her own), "the historical process" was not just a matter of continuity and change; conveying it meant satisfying a number of additional conditions. The historical process had to be shown to be *heading* toward something; it had, moreover, to be presented as a *struggle*, with its ups and downs, between various forward-looking and, by contrast, retrograde tendencies and forces. In other words, the historical process in the Soviet sense was supposed to be conceived in terms of historical progress.

What this requirement entailed for ballet was that its history in Russia would be told from the standpoint of this ballet's historic triumphs. "[T]he struggle between the advanced and the backward, the truly new and the new only in appearance, went on unremittingly in Russian ballet theater, leading the latter to its artistic pinnacles, opening wider horizons, charting a path toward its future," writes Krasovskaia in the glibly phrased preface to her rich and rewarding, if not unbiased, Khrushchev-era account of nineteenth-century ballet. "Difficult and contradictory as it was, this struggle defined the substance of Russian ballet history in the latter half of the nineteenth century."[14] That Krasovskaia never hesitates to take sides in this century-old struggle makes her book an invaluable ballet-related document of its time and place—or, to rephrase, a brilliant, if biased, piece of historiographic lore.

Arguably, an unbiased history is a historiographic figment. We are blessed to be biased toward Mozart over Salieri and toward Pushkin over Faddei Bulgarin—as long as there exists a modicum of humaneness to our endeavors in the humanities. For that matter, the fact that Tolstoy's idiosyncratic diatribes against ballet are better remembered today than, say, Petr Boborykin's compassionate musings about the hardships of balletic life must be because historians are no more immune to great prose than other readers.

Some of Krasovskaia's prejudices and predilections appear easy to relate to. On page 1 of her *Russian Ballet Theater* (volume 2), she presents a list of four balletic titles she considers the pinnacles of nineteenth-century ballet: *The Nutcracker, Sleeping Beauty, Swan Lake*, and *Raymonda*.[15] Can it go uncommented, then, when Bezobrazov's 1893 review in the *Petersburg Gazette* calls your beloved *Nutcracker* a "boring nonsensical spectacle [which] ballet regulars cannot wait to finally vanish from the playbill,"[16] or when an inveterate wisecracker like Skalkovsky dubs *Sleeping Beauty* a "masterpiece of tailoring"? When no contemporary review turns out to have done justice to Lev Ivanov's choreography in *Swan Lake*, all that remains is to solace the reader with the impending remedy of hindsight: "Time has corrected their mistake."[17]

At the same time, as one goes through Krasovskaia's history, one occasionally stumbles upon a judgment whose roots and purpose may not be immediately obvious. Between 1885 and 1892, for instance, Petersburg theatergoers used to rally round the Italian guest ballerina Virginia Zucchi, whose performances in Russia, every historian admits, not only brought down houses from the gods to the stalls, but also won over many a local dancer. Krasovskaia, too, pays tribute to Zucchi's mastery and sway—only to dismiss these, on the same page, as in effect a mere eddy in the historical process by which Russian ballet flowed toward its epochal destination.[18]

But why? To judge by her book, Krasovskaia nurtured none of the nativist sentiments and protectionist persuasions of the kind that moved, for

INTRODUCTION 7

instance, the balletomane-turned-ballet-historian Khudekov to blame visiting Italian ballerinas for Russian talents' subsequent inclination to caper *all'italiana*. Indeed, Krasovskaia disavows such a viewpoint, crediting Carlotta Brianza, Pierina Legnani, and particularly the danseur and pedagogue Enrico Cecchetti for stirring Russian ballet theater from the sleepy routine into which it had reportedly sunk. Why then deny this to Zucchi, whose impact on Russian dancers, including such male idols as Pavel Gerdt, Krasovskaia readily admits?[19] To get a sense of Krasovskaia's retrospective discontent with Zucchi's triumphs in late nineteenth-century Russia, one needs to posit her *Russian Ballet Theater* not as a mere historical account but as a story of ballet's past told with an eye to its future. That is, as a project.

History as a Project: The Case of Noverre's Reform

To get a fuller sense of Krasovskaia's unwillingness to embrace Zucchi's stunning success on the Petersburg stage, we need to return to Jean-Georges Noverre, whose complaint about ballet history—or, rather, the absence thereof—I quote above. Noverre held, we recall, a historical grudge against the famous Roman *pantomimi* Pylades and Bathyllus for not having theorized and recorded the method by which they expressed in dance, without uttering a word, a mythological or heroic action. Frustrated by this silence of the ancients, relates Noverre, one night he summoned the shades of three Augustan *pantomimi* to visit him in a dream—a necromantic consultation between the present and the past that he hoped might lead to some kind of mutual rapport. Noverre's was, one must add, a boldly Orwellian idea: for want of historical past, there is always a stopgap solution of dreaming it up.

Three shades appeared, and Noverre posed his questions: Was how they danced in antiquity similar to the way one danced in modern days? Did Bathyllus and his confreres, in their time on earth, ever perform the cabrioles, entrechats à six et huite, and seven-turn pirouettes that the Paris of Noverre's time found so enchanting? The shades shrugged, then burst into laughter; emboldened by their mortal-like manner, reports Noverre, he asked his second question: What means did the Roman *pantomimi* use to intelligibly express, in the language of gestures, such concepts as past and future tense? Unhelpfully (if, from their viewpoint, logically), the shades, whose entire eloquence resided precisely in body language, replied by gesturing with their arms and hands. And so their answer was lost on their would-be interlocutor.

8 IMPOSSIBLE PROJECT

On the face of it, Noverre's consultation with the dead proved to be a frustration. There was laughter and shrugging, he recounts, followed by a comic display of mimic noncommunicability. Yet frustration was precisely what Noverre must have planned for when cooking up his imaginary meeting with the dead. His lifetime project had always been to reroute ballet from being a medium of empty entertainment to becoming a vehicle of classical—and classy—mimic drama. The work Noverre needed the long-dead Pylades and his ilk to do was to shame and deride the pointless pirouettes modern ballet dancers indulged in; by the same token, modern dancers, including the ballet master himself, were shown to have lost the noble tongue of ancient pantomime. In other words, Noverre invoked—indeed, invented—ballet's historical past only to demonstrate an assumed rupture between the present and the past. This is more or less how all project histories are made: by shaping the past so that it helps us shape the future.

That the language of ancient Roman pantomime was no longer recoverable did not discourage Noverre from seeing his cherished reform through: what could not be passed on could be invented anew. "I have, I daresay without conceit, resurrected *the art of pantomime*," he writes in yet another *Letter*, "which had been buried under the ruins of antiquity, reclaimed neither by the epoch of the Medici, nor in the reign of Louis XIV."[20]

The last (1807) antemortem edition of Noverre's *Letters on Dancing and Ballets* came out under a new, more expository heading: *Letters on Imitative Arts in General, and on Dance in Particular* (*Lettres sur les arts imitateurs en général et sur la danse en particulier*). The title laid bare, from the outset, the train of thought that had led Noverre to his discovery. Ballet can do better than just constitute an assortment of eye-pleasing dances. Ballet, Noverre contends, represents a little brother (*frère puîné*) born into the noble family of arts whose specialty is imitation. (In the framework of eighteenth-century aesthetics, art imitating someone or something harbored none of the disparaging connotations the notion would accrete in the two centuries to follow.) Painting imitates nature; tragedy, per Aristotle, is the imitation of an action. For the art of ballet to come into its own, dancers must learn to imitate—that is, enact. Hence *danse en action*—dance-in-action—the watchword of the Noverre-engendered creed. A skilled dancer and God-given tragedienne in one body, for many a Russian Noverrian the Divine Virginia was a living embodiment of their idol's daydream.

Noverre's project proved an agonistic one. That the shades Noverre had once summoned in from his dream could not help laughing at the mere mention of the cabrioles, entrechats, and pirouettes *très à la mode* in the Paris of this time foreshadowed and, in a sense, preshaped two centuries of ideological ballet battles, between the advocates of action and those who saw nothing wrong in entrechats. In Russia, diehard Noverrians, to Krasovskaia's retrospective desperation, never ceased slamming Tchaikovsky's *Nutcracker* or *Sleeping Beauty* for lacking Noverrian virtues; in addition, there were half-hearted Noverrians who, while applauding strong librettos, had nothing against enjoying dancing for dancing's sake; and neo-Noverrians, sick and tired of light-minded (aka "brainless") *féeries*. And, for good measure, there were those who frequented *Esmeralda* solely to experience, once again, the harrowing emotions induced by Zucchi's dramatic genius. And on the other side of the aisle, there were those sick and tired of anything Noverre.

In the main body of my book, I analyze the course of these battles in some detail; for the purpose of this introduction, it may suffice to quote a brief description of the opposing forces by Konstantin Skalkovsky in 1896—that is, at a time when the end of the century was already in view. The balance of power between the two parties, observes Skalkovsky, remains precarious: "Pantomimic ballets have reigned for a century and a half now, the craze for miming resulting, at times, in pure mimodramas." Growing vitality is seen, meanwhile, in a counterforce: "[I]n recent times, pantomime has been increasingly deemed boring; in its stead, fairy ballets [*féeries*] have come to the fore, and the [pre-Noverre] genre of opera-ballets would be revived."[21] Himself a weathered balletomane and prolific critic, Skalkovsky registers not only what had changed on the balletic stage since the time of his illustrious predecessor but also the ripples those changes caused in what I am calling ballet lore: "In the relatively short time span [between Noverre and now], ballet lived through a number of metamorphoses dictated by new fads, by shifting tastes, and by competition on the part of concurrent stage shows. And each time such a metamorphosis would occur, critics and dilettantes would bewail it as the ultimate downfall of ballet as such; nevertheless, on the whole, ballet and dances kept evolving, though there is decisively no telling what ballet's future fate will be."[22]

Skalkovsky's comment reflects a paradoxical transformation that befell the Noverrian idea of ballet during its century-plus-long tenure in Russia. The drawing power of Noverre's ideology was that it was all about the future: what ballet *should* be like, what ballet masters should *become* apart from being mere dance teachers (the short answers: erudite scholars, sublime thinkers, inspired poets); what had to be banished from ballet's future

10   IMPOSSIBLE PROJECT

republic and what needed to be brought in for it to flourish. In eighteenth-century France, Noverre's was an ideology of becoming; in late nineteenth-century Russia, it evolved into a culture of bewailing.

Conceived as a project rather than a mere record of things past, history serves as a tool of prediction no less than a form of cognition. When it comes to Russian ballet lore, the predictions are mostly melancholic if not outright eschatological. As I show in this book, the story of Russian ballet as seen from within is a story of survival. "O, poor Terpsichore," ironized Aleksandr Pleshcheev in a preface to the 1899 edition of his 1896 book-length chronicle *Our Ballet (1673–1899)*, "will ever various dilettantes cease lamenting you and burying you alive?"[23] ("Dilettante" was, essentially, a balletomane's term for another balletomane with whom one disagreed.)

Ironically, the "bewailing of ballet" that diehard Noverrians hastened to perform any time they saw self-sufficient choreography gain the upper hand over a dramatic plot—the very rite of such bewailing—relocated Noverre's idea of ballet from a utopian future to the idealized past: the "Golden Age" of Noverre and Charles-Louis Didelot. Yet, Pleshcheev wonders, is not our image of the past conditioned by our insufficient knowledge of it? "Of the golden days of the Petersburg ballet in the epoch of Charles Didelot and even of [Marie] Taglioni and Jules Perrot, most have only read in books or heard from their grandmothers; not many remember those times, and, should they return, our balletomanes would hardly be ecstatic."[24]

As I examine in depth in the third chapter of this book, the discursive mood around and within ballet that worried Pleshcheev and Skalkovsky in the last decade of the nineteenth century transformed it in the first decade of the twentieth. Instead of there being the one and only balletic ideology—Noverre or bust!—there now were two, each with its own vision and version of ballet's future.

One ideology, advanced by Michel Fokine and Aleksandr Benois, went under the name "the new ballet." On the face of it, their idea of *the new* stood on the shoulders of old Noverrian values. The ballets Fokine staged in his heyday (1907 to 1912) in Petersburg and Paris were invariably mimetic, whether of French rococo fantasies, fairground puppetry in Russia, or deadly passions of "the Orient." And, like Noverre, Fokine had little tolerance for stand-alone choreographic tours de force. The difference was that, unlike the orthodox Noverrians whom Skalkovsky and Pleshcheev dismissed as "dilettantes," Fokine and Benois saw themselves as *neo*-Noverrians, hence

INTRODUCTION 11

the epithet "new" before "ballet." With them, Noverre's time-honored principles acquired a modernist inflection.

An alternative plan for a new ballet came from the pens of modernist-minded intellectuals impatient with the very idea of mimesis in art: initially from Fokine's regular nemeses, the reviewers Akim Volynsky and André Levinson, and, in the early 1920s, from cultural theorists at large like Viktor Shklovsky. Ballet's artistic potential, in this view, inhered in choreography as such, unalloyed with histrionic emotions and unburdened by dramatic obligations. In practice, de-emphasizing the dramatics in ballet entailed more emphasis on music—arguably the least mimetic of all arts.

Re-enter Krasovskaia, the Dancer Turned Historian

This brings us back to Krasovskaia's vision—now prejudiced, now proud—of the historical process that, according to her *Russian Ballet Theater*, led nineteenth-century ballet to its heights. As a dancer-turned-dance-scholar, Vera Krasovskaia lived through two successive trends in Soviet ballet that, at the time, left no one uninvolved—especially since both were politically colored. Her years in corps-de-ballet coincided with the reign of *drambalet*, a Soviet redaction of choreodrama tweaked to dovetail with the doctrine of socialist realism. Whatever Krasovskaia the dancer may have thought of the classical pas being upstaged by "dancified [*otantsovannye*] pantomimes" or having to master the Stanislavsky acting system alongside exercising at the barre, her heart as a scholar lay elsewhere. Writing in 1971, Krasovskaia dismissed the dance-dramas of the 1930s and 1940s as an attempt on the part of "various vulgarizers . . . to translate the language of classical dance into the language of univocal actions."[25]

The two "nineteenth-century" volumes of Krasovskaia's tetralogy came out in 1958 and 1963, the apex of the post-Stalin liberalization in arts and cultural policy immortalized as the Khrushchevian Thaw. During the Thaw, the once-rigid ideology of *drambalet* melted into its near opposite, the loosely defined idea of "choreo-symphonism," which downplayed the role of dramatic scenarios without scrapping them altogether. The dramatic element was not gone from the philosophy of symphonism in dance; it was merely displaced. Rather than taking after acting, choreography was expected to interact with the dramatic character of symphonic forms.[26]

12 IMPOSSIBLE PROJECT

Formulated and tested (with mixed success) in the 1920s, the symphonism thesis, to repeat, gained currency in the 1950s and 1960s. Not only did Krasovskaia share it; she turned the quest for symphonism into a master plot of ballet's history in Russia. Amid the fine and constantly changing meshwork of tendencies and influences within nineteenth-century choreography revealed in *Russian Ballet Theater* with characteristic precision and perspicacity, Krasovskaia juxtaposes two styles of performance, one defined as "depictive" (*izobrazitel'nyi*), the other as "instrumental." The depictive tradition (Noverre would have called it *imitateur*) leans toward painting, sculpture, and drama; the instrumental style, like the instrumental music from which the term derives, relies on virtuoso performance.[27]

Nowhere in her book does Krasovskaia claim an inherent superiority for one tradition over the other; rather, she begins by saying that in the art of major Russian ballerinas, the two used to "collide and interlace"[28]—a somewhat balletic trope meant to evoke the conflict and unity of opposites. In the same Hegelian spirit, however, Krasovskaia endows the instrumental tradition of choreographic performance with a perspective she denies the depictive one. Her idea of the historical process is predicated on the notion of the historical clock preset by "time itself."

According to Krasovskaia, the preordained hour for the Russian ballet theater's discovery of its true symphonic self was its encounter with Petr Tchaikovsky—not in 1877 in Moscow, when and where "choreography was yet unripe"[29] to live up to the symphonic treatment of Tchaikovsky's score for *Swan Lake*, but later in the century in Petersburg, when and where the choreographers Marius Petipa and Lev Ivanov were ready to "discern the voice of time in Tchaikovsky's music."[30] Either way, what Krasovskaia calls the "symphonization of classical choreography" was, in her view, "historically inevitable [*neminuemo*]."[31]

With its destination so clearly defined, a historical process acquires the semblance of a collective pursuit, some of its participants deemed more forward-looking than others, some shortsighted, and some, while brilliant, knocking the whole procession off the designated route.

This is where the Zucchi conundrum comes in. Soon upon her arrival in Petersburg, Zucchi gained laurels for her virtuoso technique ("Without a single stumble, a smile endlessly changing on her face, [Zucchi] could have walked Nevsky Prospect end to end on pointes,"[32] rhapsodized Khudekov in the 1918 volume of his *History of Dances*), for her compelling miming and impetuous dramatic temperament (Khudekov again: "The last variation

INTRODUCTION 13

of Zucchi's pas d'action . . . always ended with her hairdo disheveled, which earned her the nickname 'mop-head' [*stepka-rastrepka*]"[33]). Zucchi's impact was not confined to fellow dancers; in his memoirs, Stanislavsky remembers a masterclass (as we might call it nowadays) that Zucchi agreed to conduct on their home stage as formative for him as a future dramatic actor and director.[34]

Krasovskaia acknowledges all this—and yet, in her book Zucchi's presence on Russian balletic stages is presented as an untimely if brilliant distraction: "Russian ballet was unswervingly [*neuklonno*] approaching one of its most important tasks—the symphonization of balletic action. Zucchi's artistry was not a positive factor in this historically progressive process. . . . Splendid as Zucchi's art of miming was, it failed to bring Russian ballet closer to its historic encounter with the symphonist composers."[35]

Change over time, no doubt, is the canonical subject of any historical study. There is no requirement, however, that in this change, agency should be ascribed *to time*. Once this or that balletic development becomes an "artistic task set by time itself,"[36] it can seem almost like a plot point in a suspense screenplay. Being "in step (or out of step) with time,"[37] trailing behind or "being ahead of time"[38]—even if the word "time" in such stock phrases often stands for some larger concept, the historical process thus described shades into a race against (or of) time.

Untenable as Krasovskaia's "Whiggish" or "march of progress" approach may appear from the viewpoint of modern-day historiography, her account harbors an intriguing internal contradiction that echoes, mutatis mutandis, turn-of-the-century concerns about the future existence of ballet. If choreography's fateful encounter with symphonic music was, indeed, as "inevitable" as Krasovskaia paints it, and progress toward this encounter so "unswerving," what would be the harm if the train of history were to make a brief halt (a few years, in this analogy) so that its passengers and engineers might enjoy the "divine" if "mop-headed" Zucchi? What's the hurry? It almost sounds as if Krasovskaia were reliving the history of ballet the way we rewatch a favorite suspense movie: even knowing full well the protagonist wins out in the finale, we cannot but wish away every obstacle on their way toward it. Little wonder if Zucchi in Krasovskaia's "period scenario" is cast as almost a seductress *malgré soi*, and Skalkovsky (owing to whose lobbying power Zucchi had been invited to dance at the Mariinsky—over the initial reluctance on the part of the first ballet master and the Directorate)[39] and his ilk, if not as villains, then as buffoons afflicted with "a typically balletomaniac

14   IMPOSSIBLE PROJECT

incomprehension of the nature of melodic dramaturgy in general and of Tchaikovsky's and [Lev] Ivanov's symphonism in particular."[40]

Ballet: A Moribund Medium?

At the same time, Krasovskaia's impatience with history's too rambling pace dovetails well with balletomanes' misgivings about the future of ballet. She and they were alike aware of the double jeopardy that menaced ballet as an art form in the latter half of the nineteenth century in Russia. On the one hand, the democratic press decried ballet as socially and aesthetically irrelevant. On the other, individual hits notwithstanding, ballet as an institution was running at a loss. Would ballet as a stand-alone spectacle stand, or slide back into what it used to be before Noverre: a sideshow to operas and dramas? Particularly since, in Paris, the downward curve was already in sight? As everyone involved knew only too well, ballet could be virtually "abolished" any moment by an executive petition approved by His Imperial Majesty, out of whose treasury ballet was being financed.[41]

Triumphalist as Krasovskaia's history may sound, it is, in fact, less of a success story than a story of survival. Had not classical choreography espoused the symphonic principle, we are told, ballet in Russia would have "broken down, becoming a mere number in a music-hall review, or devolving into a vacuous [*pustoporozhnii*] fairy show, or, as it happened in some well-to-do theaters in Europe, transformed into a semblance of a museum exhibit—an art unfamiliar with struggle, development, and growth."[42] Ballet's survival, per Krasovskaia, was nothing short of miraculous, in her telling sounding almost like a last-minute rescue in a thriller: "[At the time] when Russian ballet theater experienced the acutest of crises, when it came to decide whether it would live or die, great Russian composers lent ballet a saving hand."[43]

This narrow-escape denouement sounds familiar if we recall the incessant "bewailings of ballet" and "burials alive of Terpsichore" we heard about from Skalkovsky's and Pleshcheev's 1896 and 1899 accounts. Dissatisfied as she was with the perceived shortsightedness of late nineteenth-century balletomanes, Krasovskaia's historical narrative was driven, if in retrospect, by the same kind of existential angst as *their* writings had been. Granted, the several commentators' emphases differed. Skalkovsky admits his uncertainty as to ballet's status in the future—a natural position to take, given his

INTRODUCTION 15

public profile at the time as one of the few to stand up for ballet's continued existence. Pleshcheev puts his trust in the money: his *Our Ballet* begins by heaping praise on the Directorate of Imperial Theaters for its "lavishness in subsidizing new productions" (a true statement) and its "generosity in maintaining the troupe" (which is less accurate) and for showing such steadfastness in the face of "the outcry [*vopli*] in the press and public about the decline of ballet on the Petersburg stage."[44] Krasovskaia, for her part, sees ballet as having been rescued by music. Yet, as much as these accounts differ, they all represent answers to the same question: How would (or how did) ballet survive—against all odds?

This is not necessarily a country- or period-specific question. Forebodings about ballet's viability are ubiquitous, cropping up now in Denmark or Russia, now in Italy or France. Such anxiety could indeed be called innate to the art form itself, considering the origin myth (or dream) Noverre provides in his 1760 *Letters on Dancing and Ballets*, in which, we recall, Noverre the dreamer summons the shades of Roman *pantomimi* in an attempt to learn the lost secrets of ancient *danse d'action*—to no avail. Ballet is dead; long live ballet as reinvented by Noverre on stage and page! As will be discussed in chapter 2, this idea of *succession as immortality* is a medieval one and remains at the heart of ballet's continuity and change.

Continuity and change are interlocked constituents of any historical process. Philosophical intuition compels us to link continuity to stasis, and change to dynamism; however, in the *non*intuitive universe of ballet, this is not always the case. Here, to quote the Red Queen from Lewis Carroll's *Through the Looking-Glass*, it takes all the running you can do to keep in the same place. Let us recall, in particular, Noverre's definition of dance as an art that vanishes simultaneously with its production. Within this instantly perishable sign system, the sole form of constancy is repetition, and in ballet, any repetition—of a pas or of a production, the next day or after many years, by one and the same performer or by their successor—is also an act of re-creation, creation anew. No wonder if, in ballet lore, the continuity of ballet is more often than not described not as stasis but as a dynamics of perpetual rebirth.

Much of what I explore in this book has to do with the complex dynamics of ballet—the dynamics of change in tandem with the dynamics of changelessness or, as Carroll might have had it, running out of breath to keep ballet in the same place, alive and breathing. To comprehend this dynamics in all its complexity and inconsistency, I posit, we as ballet historians must not

16 IMPOSSIBLE PROJECT

underrate its verbal component—the various genres of ballet lore, which I treat in this book on a par with pas and mime.

Ballet lore is often viewed as "just talk," a mere mirror—truthful or crooked—of opinion. Khudekov's scathing reviews of *Sleeping Beauty* could be dismissed as the carping of a bystander along Petipa's road to immortality. But it would be more fitting to situate them in the dynamic rapport—now friendship, now jealousy—between the ballet master and the balletomane whose writings were more often proactive than reactive, representing, as Yuri Slonimsky described Khudekov's artistic outlook, "prescriptions for the revitalization of ballet."[45] It was precisely the lack of such prescriptions with which Noverre charged Bathyllus and Pylades. Deprived of the verbal tradition, the art of ballet would not survive. Ballet equals ballet plus reflections on ballet; on this, I am in agreement with Noverre.

From Here to There, or How Ballet Histories Are Mapped

Our image of a history's dynamics depends on whether we happen to have lived through this history. If we have, the dynamics of history appears erratic, tentative, and subject to chance. If, however, we have no personal experience with the particular history, it can easily appear directional and telic, like a trail that, however tortuous, unmistakably leads from then to now. No wonder retrospective histories overwrite and override lived ones; the former wield the overweening authority of knowledge. And yet, somehow, history viewed from within and history as examined by future historians are not two mutually exclusive stories; it is one and the same history, just captured in two complementary projections. Ideally, we should keep an eye on both—as they keep each other honest.

When it comes to historical dynamics, most retrospective histories of ballet (to include here, alongside fundamental histories like Khudekov's and Krasovskaia's, tangential and doctrinal excursions into dance's past made by dancers and dance reformers, from Noverre to Blasis, from Duncan to Fokine) tend to follow an established pattern. Typically, the author highlights a specific moment in the past, a point on the timeline that becomes a point of virtue or tipping point—or even the date of birth of dance as art. Thus in his 1995 study on the affinity between dance and military drill, the historian of Western civilization William H. McNeill is very specific about the genesis of ballet. It happened, he claims, after 1674, when Louis XIV, at age twenty-six, stopped practicing every day and withdrew from dancing the lead roles in festive ballet performances. "Thereafter professional dancers took over, developing what we know as classical ballet. But the king continued to take part in ballroom dances and expected his courtiers to do the same."[46]

For McNeill's purpose, the moment is well chosen. First, the embryonic connection between ballet and military exercise is real and consequential. Louis XIV appears to have believed that dance was useful for, among other things, "developing prowess in using weaponry," as the Sun King (or his ghost writers) put it in the 1661–62 "Letters Patent for the Establishing of l'Académie Royale de Danse."[47] And as we will see, the parallel between choreography and troop parades turned out to be culturally and aesthetically productive in nineteenth-century Russia. Second, the moment in historical time when the concept of "ballet," understood as a professional show, split off and drifted away from its mother-concept of "ball," indeed precipitated an avalanche of other transformations, which will be my focus in the first section of chapter 1, devoted to a comparative analysis of seventeenth- to nineteenth-century editions of *Dictionnaire de l'Académie française*.

On the other hand, McNeill's chronology must raise a few eyebrows among the community of ballet historians, balletomanes, and ballet reformers who have other moments or events on the timeline of which they too are eager to say "Here is where ballet came into its own." Some would point to choreography's felicitous encounter with symphonic music; to some, the moment of truth had to do with Marie Camargo's balletic outfit reforms; to others, with Marie Taglioni *sur les pointes*. For the entire nineteenth century in Russia, the undisputed founder of ballet remained Noverre, who, however, himself gave this credit to Bathyllus and Pylades.

The question is not whether one agrees or disagrees with particular historical scenarios of this sort, but whether one accepts the tacit assumption that underlies them all. When McNeill speaks of "the path by which ballet had shifted from participatory activity to public spectacle at Louis XIV's court,"[48] ingrained in the very language he uses is the image of history as a "path" on which, at this or that moment in time, ballet had "shifted" into the shape familiar today.

A path, a road, a trajectory. In the world of ballet, with its flocks of errant ballerinas and periodically migrating population—now from Renaissance Italy to the French court, now from France to Imperial Russia, now from Soviet Russia to the West—such terms might better serve to refer to ballet's geographical rather than historical dynamics. "Path" implies directionality,

18 IMPOSSIBLE PROJECT

a chain of ballet-related events hewing to an itinerary from here to there. But the unknown nature or even unknowability of start and end points is what lends the study of history its particular thrill. Why embark on research if you already know where you are heading, the literary historian Boris Eikhenbaum asks rhetorically in the preface to his 1928 book on Tolstoy, adding, "[Historical] science is not a ride with a ticket pre-booked to this or that station or destination."[49]

That said, a study of the studies claiming knowledge of from where and to where ballet is heading could in itself constitute an instructive historiographic project. According to the famous theorem of silent film editing known as "the Kuleshov experiment," it takes no more than two shots to engender narrative. Take three identical close-ups of a man's face, and splice each to a shot showing a plate of soup, a baby playing, or a young woman in a coffin; our reading of what the face expresses alters—from hunger to endearment to mourning. Mutatis mutandis, historical narrative is a matter of connecting two dots.

At times, where precisely this or that ballet history is heading becomes clear from the title on its cover. In the France of the 1930s, for instance, all roads appeared to lead to Serge Lifar, whose rise to fame and power coincided with a surge of Lifar lore. In writing upon writing, Lifar stands as classical ballet's final destination. Following the majestic trajectory plotted for it by Julie Sazonova in her 1937 *Life of Dance: From Ballet Comique de la Reine to Icare* (*La vie de la danse: Du Ballet Comique de la Reine à Icare*), French ballet begins in Paris in 1581 at the court of Catherine de' Medici, finds refuge in nineteenth-century Russia, and returns to Paris "ultimately transfigured" in Lifar's 1935 *Icare*.[50]

The itinerary we find in André Schaikevitch's 1939 *Ballet Mythology from Viganò to Lifar* (*Mythologie du ballet de Viganò à Lifar*) is shorter. The year of departure is 1801, when, in Vienna, Salvatore Viganò staged *Les Créatures de Prométhée* to a score by Beethoven; in this self-reflexive ballet, Prometheus uses the stolen fire to mold the human race from clay and breathe life into it, much as his human compatriot Pygmalion did to his beloved sculpture. Schaikevitch's destination is 1929, the year in which Viganò's libretto and Beethoven's music were reclaimed and restaged at the Opéra National de Paris with Lifar in the title role. Schaikevitch's is more than a story of a modernist revival: under his pen, Lifar becomes a mythopoetic Prometheus, the trickster Titan of contemporary ballet. Whatever a conversation might have

INTRODUCTION 19

been about—antiquity or contemporaneity, France or Russia, classical or modernist choreography—it would likely wind up being about Lifar.

The magnum opus of Lifar lore—Lifar's own (and his ghost writers') historical treatise on ballet—came out in 1938 in three languages under two different titles. While the Russian edition, *Tanets: Osnovnye techeniia akademicheskogo tantsa* (*Dance: Fundamental Trends of Academic Dance*), aims at shoehorning dance into an academic tradition, the title of its English (via French) translation, *Dance: Traditional to Modern*, points in the opposite direction. The choice of a title for a book is more often than not a matter of marketing, and Lifar's translator into English, Cyril Beaumont, was, after all, himself a publisher and owner of a bookstore in London. But above all, Beaumont was a balletomane keen to support the budding British ballet, which may have been enough of a reason for him to tamper with Lifar's title.

Lifar traces the history of classical dance as a royal heir might their own lineage. Focal to his story is continuity: from the seventeenth century to Didelot to Petipa to Diaghilev and down to Lifar's own "reign"—a reign built to last, given that at the end of Lifar's book, the reader is presented with a selection of Lifar's yet-to-be-staged libretti. In the decade when Beaumont translated Lifar's book and wrote his own magnum opus, *Complete Book of Ballets* (1940), ballet in Britain, unlike its counterparts in France and Russia, had no classical tradition of its own to either pick up or turn against. Not that Beaumont experienced this absence as a lack: as Tim Scholl observes, "In his *Complete Book of Ballets*, Cyril Beaumont devotes nearly half his introduction of the Petipa ballets to an indictment of nineteenth-century Russian ballet production and performance practices."[51] With three U.K.-born ex-Diaghilev dancers known by their French or Russian stage names—Ninette de Valois, Anton Dolin, Alicia Markova—already at work building Britain's own ballet, there seemed to be less need to borrow from the past. The tradition was in the making. British ballet belonged to the future.

Traditional to modern: remarkably, Lifar's book and Lifar as a figure lent themselves to be read as part of either, and both. When yet another Lifar encomium came out in 1938, authored by Aleksandr Pleshcheev (the same Pleshcheev who, forty years before, had published *Our Ballet*, the historical overview of ballet in Russia bookended "1673–1899"), its title, *Serge Lifar: From the Old to the New* (*Sergei Lifar': Ot starogo k novomu*), served to bridge rather than separate the epochs the octogenarian balletomane had lived to see. "Your quest is for the eternal, no matter its age [*ne schitaias's ego*

20   IMPOSSIBLE PROJECT

vozrastom]," Pleshcheev explains in the first chapter, titled "A Letter to Sergei Lifar." "While what you create is uniquely yours, you also value the treasures of the past."[52]

The historical narrative Pleshcheev spins around Lifar appears to be fueled by two contradictory—and, one may argue, complementary— impulses. The author is prone, in part, to confident assertions. The pedigree Pleshcheev posits as leading to "the epoch of Lifar" sounds proud and as- sured: "Beginning from the mid-nineteenth century, the pinnacles of world choreography have been Petipa, his disciple M[ichel] Fokine, and, finally, Lifar."[53] At the same time, behind the assuredness of this geneology, one discerns a note familiar from many a writing on ballet: sublime anxiety. The opening of Pleshcheev's book on Lifar sounds in part like a martyrology, or even a mayday call: "Dear friend! . . . Three great misfortunes have befallen Russian ballet abroad: Nijinsky has quit the stage, Diaghilev has passed away, Anna Pavlova has died. . . . Pavlova is no more. . . . Yet another powerful and original talent has burst into bloom. . . . It is you, Lifar."[54] The old man knew what he was talking about. Ballet must go on. "Pavlova is no more. It is you, Lifar" is a medieval principle of apostolic succession whose import for the survival of ballet I detail in the second and third chapters of this book.

* * *

History's vistas vary depending on where one is and what one is looking at. When we look at ballets of the past from the perspective of its future—that is, *our* present—what catches the eye first is a process, a road from here to here or, more habitually, from *there* to here. An alternative—and, as I in- tend to show in this book, complementary—model of history's dynamics is to think of it in terms of crossroads or, to borrow an image from Jorge Luis Borges, a constantly expanding garden of forking possibilities. To those who turn around to look back, history looks like a road; for those on the road, it's always a crossroads. Noverre or Taglioni, Fokine or Balanchine, name any game-changer across ballet's history—what these people really introduced were not new changes but new choices.

1

The Shadow of Noverre

Ballet in a Narrative Perspective

Like any evidence clad in words, ballet lore can be deceptive. Before we decide whether we can rely on them, even the most transparent terms—in fact, *especially* the transparent ones—must be, so to speak, historically and semantically vetted. To illustrate this point, let me take a brief excerpt from a perfectly ordinary press comment and examine it as a verbal text, that is, from a philological point of view.

In November 1885, in a review of *Pharaoh's Daughter* starring his protégée Virginia Zucchi, Konstantin Skalkovsky used the following argument to counter those few who would rebuke Zucchi's manner as wanting in "classical" deportment: "[P]urely classical ballets stopped being written fifty years ago, and the public would die of boredom were one to be performed [today]."[1]

From our modern perspective, Skalkovsky's remark may sound baffling. Lovers of old-time ballets will now readily stand in line (or go online) to book a seat for the latest, period-notation-based reconstruction of the 1890 *Sleeping Beauty*, and do so precisely because they know they are going to see a pure classical ballet. Why "boredom," and whence the "fifty years ago," if, in the year Skalkovsky wrote this, what we call classical ballet was on the rise toward some of its most exciting achievements?

Ballet lore can be misleading in two ways: as a statement—always somebody's—and as far as its language is concerned. When it came to polemics, Skalkovsky could err as easily and fib as willingly as any nineteenth-century balletomane pushing their aesthetic agenda, but in this particular case his point made total sense. The devil is in the lexis. What terms like "classical" or the very word "ballet" refer to often depends on historical semantics. To work out what Skalkovsky may have had in mind by consigning "classical ballet" to the distant past, a brief retrospective excursion is in order.

Impossible Project. Daria Khitrova, Oxford University Press. © Oxford University Press 2025.
DOI: 10.1093/9780197653081.003.0002

Classical Ballet: A History of a Notion

French being the lingua franca of ballet, a good place to start is the *Dictionnaire de l'Académie française*, whose nine consecutive editions enable a researcher to trace how the meaning of the word "ballet" has been defined and redefined from the late seventeenth century till now. The 1694 edition defines ballet as a "dance of mask-wearing persons who execute certain figures and assume certain attitudes as they dance, and who represent something."[2] Crucially, the word "represent" (*représentent*) here agrees grammatically with "persons," not with "dance." The minimum requirement for the dance to qualify as ballet is therefore that each dancer represents "something" (*quelque chose*)—which, presumably, could be *anything*, from Venus (the goddess or the celestial body) to warriors and werewolves. As worded in the 1694 *Dictionnaire de l'Académie*, the definition of ballet could as well serve as a definition of a masquerade, out of which ballet is known to have historically developed; it is hardly by chance that here "Ballet" is not yet a stand-alone entry, but appears in the bosom of the entry "Ball" ("Bal").

The umbilical cord between "ball" and "ballet" was cut in the 1718 edition, in which the latter is awarded a separate entry. Eighteenth-century editions of the *Dictionnaire* introduce two important amendments to the meaning of the term. The first concerns representation. It is no longer the dancers themselves who represent something, but their "figures and poses"; in other words, the burden of signification has been shifted from costumes and masks to elements of dance. The definition of the signified has changed as well. Instead of each dancer per se representing a nebulous *quelque chose*, in all the four eighteenth-century editions (1718, 1740, 1762, and 1798) their figures and poses *représentent quelque sujet particulier*,[3] the word *sujet* (topic, subject, theme) having been imported into ballet lore from the language then used to describe literature and painting.

The other amendment relates to mask-wearing. In the fourth (1762) edition of the *Dictionnaire*, the modifier *masquées* is removed from the definition.[4] By this point, the habit of wearing a mask while dancing had dwindled to zero, for which, in a footnote to the 1807 edition of his *Letters*, Noverre credits the anti-mask crusade he had waged in his book: "After this work came out [in 1760], I witnessed the masks I rose so strongly against, disappear; this reform is one of the greatest services which I flatter myself I have done to my art. And this, in my eyes, is the best and most adequate reward."[5]

The first (1835) of the two nineteenth-century editions of the *Dictionnaire* revises, once again, what ballet is and what it represents. If in all previous editions, ballet had been defined as a subgenre of dance (*espèce de danse, danse figurée*, and the like), the 1835 edition includes the definition of ballet as a subgenre of theater: "*Pantomime ballet*, or simply *ballet*: a theater piece in which action is represented solely by dancers' gestures and attitudes."[6] Note that the term *sujet*, which in 1718 had replaced 1694's *quelque chose*, here gives way in turn to the more active "action"; the clause "solely [*n'est ... que*] by gestures," moreover, highlights the now codified ban on the spoken word. All these adjustments echo the language used in Noverre's *Letters*. And it is in this edition that Noverre is first mentioned, as an example of usage: "*Ballet de Noverre. Ballet de Gardel.*" By 1835, the era of choreographic authorship, which Noverre predicts in his *Letters*, is underway.

Leaping two editions, 1878 and 1935, we land in 1992 to find the meaning of the word "ballet" markedly reconfigured. Disguised as an example of a usage is a mini-canon: "*Coppélia* and *Swan Lake* belong to the most famous ballets." A sense of diachrony is added to the notion, with three periods in ballet's history covered in a triple jump: "Louis XIV loved to take part in court ballets. *Sylphide* was one of the first romantic ballets. *Les Ballets russes* have innovated the aesthetics of ballet." To understand what ballet is, we have to know what it once was.

Most important, the eternal question, raised in each of the first eight editions, of what ballets represent (*quelque chose? sujet?* action?) is sidestepped in the ninth, evidently to accommodate nonfigurative choreography: "[Ballet is] a musical spectacle in which action or feelings are translated into evolutions, gestures and attitudes [performed] by dancers." Interpretive definitions (*a* represents *b*) have been replaced by a generative definition (*b* begets *a*). Ballet is glimpsed through its own eyes, in lieu of an outside observer's.

Notably, none of the entries for "ballet" in any of the editions of the *Dictionnaire de l'Académie française* includes the modifier "classical." "Classical ballet" and "classical dance" are phrases native to the Russian ballet-related language.[7] Today the two expressions sound interchangeable, but in the period when Skalkovsky wrote his review of Zucchi in *Pharaoh's Daughter*, they were not. To get a sense of what "classical ballet" and "classical dance" meant in 1885, we'll need to take a closer look at Skalkovsky's line of argument.

24 IMPOSSIBLE PROJECT

The unnamed Zucchi skeptics with whom Skalkovsky quarrels found the Italian ballerina lacking in the peculiar discipline of style called, in French and Russian, *danse d'école* or *shkola*. *Shkola* (the school, *école*) is what makes a stage dancer easy to tell from a ballroom dancer, however skilled and talented the latter might be. "How does one know a 'good school danseuse' when one sees one?" Skalkovsky asks, and outlines the following set of hallmarks: "Strict harmony between all parts of the body must be constantly maintained in every dance; the assuredness of movements; perfect balance; every posture of her dance must be so natural and full of taste that any moment of it could serve as a model for an artist or a sculptor. Apart from this, she must also know how to conceal her mastery, how to make her efforts invisible. M-me Zucchi meets all the above conditions."[8]

From today's perspective, the model *danseuse d'école* as sketched by Skalkovsky falls within the category of "classical" dance—provided, of course, that she keeps to the "alphabet" of steps and poses codified by Pierre Beauchamp circa 1680 and catalogued by Carlo Blasis in 1828. At least, this is how the phrase "danse d'école" is defined in the modern-day edition of the *Merriam-Webster Dictionary*: "ballet that adheres to traditional rules: classical ballet."[9] Apparently, from the late nineteenth-century perspective, the situation was more equivocal. According to Skalkovsky, for all the undeniable balance and poise of Zucchi's dances, some still denied them a place among the "classical." Why?

When we read that a *danseuse d'école* must fill her every moment with enough nature and taste to inspire a painter or sculptor to copy her frozen in it, we know that Skalkovsky never meant this literally. However, if we reverse Skalkovsky's adage, it ceases to be a mere figure of speech. Painters inspired by a dancer, or dancers by a painter? From early on, ballet people were encouraged to study and copy masterpieces of fine art. Paradoxically, but not illogically in light of Noverre's ideas, Charles-Louis Didelot, the mastermind of the Russian ballet school between 1804 and the early 1830s, believed that a ballet dancer should learn to imitate nature vicariously—by imitating *arts imitateurs*: "The manner in which a danseuse controls her muscles must replicate a good picture or statue—because these, in turn, imitate nature with anatomical accuracy."[10]

Didelot's pedagogical practice remained in force throughout the nineteenth century. As Aleksandr Shiriaev recalls, classical dance as taught at the school under Petipa entailed "a cold, sculptural [*skulpturno-zakonchennyi*] style of performance."[11] Sculptural coldness was an integral property of the dance aesthetics known as "classical" or *danse d'école*.

In the critical parlance of the epoch, a dance could be deemed "classical" or not depending on where it fell on the scale from the sculptural to the human. This was not, Skalkovsky would have entrenched purists understand, a vertical, value scale but rather a horizontal, genre scale, a scale of choice. On this scale, Zucchi's manner was, indeed, all too human to qualify as classical. "They reproach M-me Zucchi the vivacity and ardor [*ogon'*] of her dance," writes Skalkovsky, "saying that [these qualities] are 'unclassical' [*eto ne 'klassicheski'*]."[12] Not that Skalkovsky, a critic as sensitive to the period understanding of "classical dance" as any of his contemporaries, was trying, against his better judgment, to push his *préférée* into the classical category. His reasoning is more supple. The secret of Zucchi's success, Skalkovsky contends, is that she dares to use nonclassical style in the parts that traditionally presupposed classical aloofness and restraint: "That M-me Zucchi dances with certain freedom is because she is a demi-character dancer."[13]

Here I must, once again, interrupt Skalkovsky's thought in order to delve into historical semantics. In the beginning, the term "demi-character" stood for one of the three Academy-approved balletic genres, each marked by a mood. The descriptors "earnest" and "comic" speak for themselves; a "demi-character" dance, meanwhile, meant one with a natural setting (whether mythological, allegorical, or merely rural), which was to evoke in a seventeenth- and eighteenth-century theatergoer the (no longer extant) "pastoral" mood. By the Ballet Academy's rules, balletic entrées were performed between acts within the framework of tragedies, comedies, or operas, all three genres represented in an established order and with an established number of dancers participating in each.

In his *Letters*, Noverre embraces the Academy's generic triad and moreover translates it into the language of his and his century's aesthetic preferences. Noverre's signature method was to match balletic to dramatic and pictorial genres. To make ballet meaningful rather than "mechanical" (Noverre's go-to pejorative for dancing he disapproved of), to render its language "more or less sublime (*élevé*)," ballet masters should match their art to the imitative arts. In speaking of balletic genres, Noverre conjures a tripartite analogy between ballet, spoken theater, and wordless painting.[14] Turning to theater, he matches "serious dance" (which, before the age of Noverre, looked more like orchestrated mask-and-costume pageants) to tragedy, comic dances to

26 IMPOSSIBLE PROJECT

physical comedy, and "mixed and semi-serious dances, usually referred to as *demi-character*, to noble comedy, also called the *haut-comique*."[15] And, turning to painting, Noverre points to three of his favorite painters. "Serious ballets ought to be staged in the image of the historical canvases by the famous [Charles-André] van Loo";[16] comic dances whose *sujets* derive from "rough peasant life" (*l'etat grossier et rustique*) should take their cue from the incomparable genre painter David Teniers; and "gallant" Rococo-style painter François Boucher, with his satin-dressed maidens in groves blushing over pigeon-brought *billets-doux*, should serve as a model for demi-character dances.

Noverre's pictorial parallel explains his generic vision perfectly. Unlike all those freakish feasting peasants by Teniers, and unlike Alexander the Great, who in van Loo's canvas *The Victory of Alexander over Porus* looks like an equestrian statue of himself, Boucher's self-ironic modern-dress bucolics give centerstage to all-too-human feelings: love, hope, embarrassment, or empathy. And so did demi-character ballets.

A teacher as well as a choreographer and ballet theorist, Noverre thought of the three balletic genres in terms of individual dancers—primarily of their physique. His advice for tall dancers was to try their luck in serious ballets, and for shorter ones to specialize in comic entrées, where the ability to spin fast and jump high was paramount; accordingly, the demi-character genre was custom-made for dancers of medium height. Noverre called this casting principle *emploi* (the French and also Russian word for actors' typical roles, e.g., "romantic lead" vs. "character actor"), admitting he borrowed the concept from spoken theater.[17] In the latter, however, the *soubrette*, the *jeune premiere*, the heavy parent, and, say, a moralizer interact in the space of one and the same play. Noverre did not see balletic *emplois* distributed this way. When, in one of his *Letters*, he proclaims that "variety must be every ballet master's motto,"[18] he means to call, not for a diversity of dances within the framework of a ballet, but for ballet masters to master a diversity of genres. When it came to individual genres themselves, Noverre was a purist.

We can see, for instance, his frowning on the violation of generic purity in his reaction to the influence of the "high-spirited" Antonio Rinaldi, an Italian comic ballet dancer. Rinaldi's nickname, Fossano or Fusano, was allegedly derived from *il fuso* (Italian for "spindle"), hinting at Rinaldi's acrobatic spins and jumps. In Italy, the land of commedia dell'arte, slapstick ballets were more physical—hence more popular—than elsewhere in Europe. Noverre was generally impressed by Rinaldi. When, however, he toured France in

THE SHADOW OF NOVERRE   27

1733 (two years prior to landing in St. Petersburg), Fossano, reports Noverre, "turned Terpsichore's students' heads: everyone wanted to copy him, even those who never saw him dance. The sublime genre surrendered to the trivial one. . . . [E]veryone lapsed into jumping and forceful spins [*tours de force*]."[19]

What worried Noverre was that the Fossano craze might engulf or contaminate the other genres of ballet—especially his pet genre, the serious pantomime ballet. In another *Letter*, a remarkable analogy is drawn between the language of dance and natural language. Here, Noverre the purist of dance reveals himself likewise a language purist:

> In my understanding, the spirit of dance is seriousness [*le sérieux*]; it is the base and fundament of ballet. . . . To fully devote oneself only to the beaten path of peasant ballets, which have become boring after Fossano—that excellent comic dancer who brought to France the rage for jumping—would mean missing the whole point of ballet. I compare the sublime dance to our mother tongue; and the mixed and corrupted genres that divert from it to the barely comprehensible patois that mutate in proportion to the distance between their region and the capital, where the purified [*épuré*] language reigns.[20]

A tireless purifier of ballet, someone who dared to liken its wordless vocabulary to Corneille's, Noverre feared that meaningless jumps would push ballet backward from being a language to being a show. Ballet's survivals, however, are seldom a matter of either/or. By the mid-nineteenth century, the purity policy had gradually given way to that of controlled diversity. The new normal was to integrate the less serious genres of ballet with what now counted for *le sérieux*—which notion, in the wake of the French Revolution and triumphs of the romantic theater, expanded to embrace, alongside myths and heroes, a weak-hearted peasant girl, an Indian temple dancer, and a French Gypsy.

What was meant by "comic" (aka "character") dances changed as well. Noverre's grotesque peasants à la Teniers gave way to picturesque ethnic dances, arguably in conjunction with the rise of national romanticism, Romantic exoticism, and the ethnic paternalism cultivated in multinational empires like Russia. A round dance performed to the waltz in *Giselle* signaled that the action is set in a German village. The czárdás was believed to reflect the sporty Magyar spirit; the mazurka, refined Polish manners. However thin their narrative motivation, character and demi-character dances were

28 IMPOSSIBLE PROJECT

now a legitimate part of overarching plots. Mid-nineteenth-century ballet prided itself on offering "something for everyone."

This brings us back to Skalkovsky's defense of Zucchi. Viewed from 1885, purity was a bygone virtue. Zucchi's manner categorizes her as a demi-character danseuse. So what? Nowadays, Skalkovsky insists, you see ballerinas dancing lead parts "in character" (as opposed to statuesque beauty) everywhere (*v svete*). The cult of stylistic and generic purity is a thing of the past, of the epoch of "purely classical ballets."

When Skalkovsky asserts that "classical ballets" have not been written for fifty years, he means "classical ballets" in the narrow sense. In this usage, the word "classical" signaled that the ballet in question was set in classical antiquity—much as the collocation "classical gymnasium" referred to schools in which Latin and Greek were taught. In Russia, classical ballets were primarily associated with the name of Charles-Louis Didelot, the master of the Ovid-derived *Apollo and Daphne*, *Zéphire et Flore*, and *Acis et Galatée*—works greatly admired in the first third of the nineteenth century but which, specifies Skalkovsky, would have killed the public of his own time with boredom.

The latter assumption deserves another comment. Classical ballet in Skalkovsky's sense was not only a set of ballets on a common set of themes; they also had a structural peculiarity in common. Unlike most of the ballets to which the Russian public was accustomed by the end of the century, classical ballets were supposed to be homogeneous. No cachucha or czárdás was allowed to punctuate the story of Apollo's belatedly requited love for the tree that once was Daphne. The public, however, was fond of character-dance inserts—all too fond, in the opinion of certain stringent critics and Noverre-nostalgic balletomanes. As Noverre in his time discovered to his dismay, the public loved senseless jumping, and so did dancers who loved to please that public.

In the epoch of Marius Petipa, classical ballets were virtually out. Of all Petipa's ballets Skalkovsky covered, *Le Réveil de Flore* and *The Adventures of Peleus* were the only two the critic categorized as "classical." *Le Réveil* was the balletic equivalent of occasional poetry: an Anacreontic allegory staged in 1894 to celebrate the wedding of a grande duchesse. As for *Peleus*, critics were genuinely intrigued. "In the staging of his new work," writes Skalkovsky in his review of *Peleus*'s 1876 premiere, "Mr. Petipa acts as if the ballet had never been affected by the romantic revolution of the 1830s, and returns to classicism, pure and simple."[21] That Petipa set his new ballet in ancient

Greece, Skalkovsky ponders in a later review of the same work, must be in order to appease those critics who'd earlier accused him of overpadding balletic plots with character dances.[22] On the other hand, despite the perfectly Olympian nature of this story of the marriage of the Greek water goddess Thetis and Greek hero Peleus, Petipa's choreography, in Skalkovsky's view, does not always rise to the occasion: "Mr. Petipa makes concessions to the spirit of [his] time by inserting, here and there, [bits of] the cancan, particularly conspicuous in the 'General Olympic Dance' performed toward the end of the fourth [out of five] scene."[23] The jolly spirit of Fossano was alive—and kicking.

As one critic reports, by the tenth performance of Petipa's *The Adventures of Peleus*, "much of its novelty interest faded away, and the ballet was paired with the demi-charactère one-acter *Graziella*, choreographed by [Arthur] Saint-Léon."[24] Evidently, even spiced up with the cancan, Petipa's belated attempt to resurrect the genre of classical ballet fell short of enthusing the public.

In the first years of the twentieth century, a slippage occurred. The phrase that, in the epoch of Petipa, used to evoke the age of Didelot, came to evoke the age of Petipa. As Bronislava Nijinska observes in the 1918 notes for her unfinished treatise "School and Theater of Movements," the transformation occurred right before everyone's eyes: "Due to some historical misunderstanding, the ballet of Petipa's epoch has, for some reason, become known as 'classical.' The word 'classical' evokes the dances of Greek antiquity, which were not about difficulty, but about plasticity, primal things, the beginning of dance. For some reason, these days the term 'classical' is applied to dances that are artfully acrobatic."[25]

The slippage appears to have been owed to the emergence, in the course of the 1900s, of the "new ballet"—the artistic ideology I touched on briefly above and will speak of at some length later. It was in this first decade of the new century that the word "classical" acquired partisan connotations. Adherents of the new ballet had as little patience for the artifice of nineteenth-century ballets as had in his time Noverre for the then-craze for cabrioles, entrechats, and pirouettes. "Relegate to the archive the pointe, battements, fouettés, and such tricks,"[26] enjoins the Moscow champion of the new ballet Sergei Mamontov in his rave review of *Salammbô*, a bold exercise in the new ballet aesthetics staged in 1910 by the reformist Aleksandr Gorsky.

In the same review, Mamontov quotes this allegedly overheard conversation: "In the smoking room during the entr'acte, a certain respectable general

30   IMPOSSIBLE PROJECT

voiced the opinion unequivocally shared by diehard [istye] balletomanes regarding Salammbô: It is not ballet. This is the pursuit of new forms in art, for which there should be no place on the imperial [kazennaia] stage. Let private enterprises pursue new forms, but the imperial theater must devote itself to classical prototypes."[27]

In the unnamed general's smoking-room lore, "classical prototypes" stood for the familiar, for things he'd enjoyed last week, last month, or last century at the Bolshoi or Mariinsky—in other words, the balletic status quo. Conversely, to the likes of Mamontov, "classical" spelled timeworn. Two weeks after his review of Salammbô, Mamontov published a theoretical essay titled "Plasticity and Stage" ("Plastika i stsena"), in which he proclaimed classical ballet not just passé, but actually dead: "Let the devout first-row regulars fulminate anathemas on me, but I will say this: classical ballet is a gone goose [pesenka klassicheskogo baleta speta]. Where free creativity is replaced by dry techniques, art ceases to be art and becomes a craft. And yet, the diehard balletomanes expend all their ardor on worshipping a steely pointe, a record number of fouettés. . . . The gift and the living soul of an artiste does not interest them. Muscles are all they care about; they all stare at [the danseuse] as one might at a horse—a trotter or courser [skakun]."[28]

In the critical parlance used by Mamontov and his contemporaries, the phrase "classical ballet" no longer evoked a spectacle set in the classical past, as it had in Skalkovsky's time, but rather the specific alphabet of balletic pas and poses canonized on imperial stages by the end of the Petipa epoch. The meaning of "classical dance" experienced a similar expansion. In the nineteenth century, the phrase (normally used in the plural) had referred to the inventory of dances appropriate to serious ballets, as opposed to character and demi-character ones; in the twentieth century, the "classical dance" (now used in the generic singular) came to signify a full-fledged system of choreographic movements—a system unashamed of its muscular mechanics and armed with its own artistic ideology.

This is how we understand "classical dance" to this day. Mamontov's 1910 prediction proved premature—as used to happen each time someone or other declared the death of the balletic tradition. Classical dance proved more resilient than Moscow's herald of the new ballet had hoped. Not because those "first-row regulars" and stick-in-the-mud "respectable generals" stood their ground (although they did), but rather because the new-ballet ideals—soul versus muscle, gait versus steps, nature versus turned-outness—wore out sooner than the new ballet advocates could expect. In 1910, as Mamontov would soon discover, a new cohort of critics and theorists at large was already in formation, poised to reconceptualize classical dance as a sui generis art form, no matter what story, if any at all, was used as its "excuse."

This, to reiterate, continues to be our default understanding of what *the* classical dance is all about. All the more careful, then, should we be in our excursions to the balletic past, lest we supplant the period understanding of things with our own.

Complementary Stories

The phrase I use as the title of this book, *Impossible Project*, comes from a nineteenth-century writing on ballet printed in the *Moscow Telegraph* (*Moskovskii telegraf*) in 1829. The journal credits Noverre with recovering the long-lost secrets of ancient pantomime and adapting the latter to the modern craft of dance: "[Noverre's] intention has been to transform bodily movements and jumps into an expressive language, and he has succeeded in this difficult, apparently impossible project."[29]

In 1829, the phrase "impossible project" was used to play up Noverre's success against all odds. I take the liberty of reassigning the epithet, using it to describe, not Noverre's project per se, but rather its effect on the subsequent history of ballet. This effect could be likened to fission. Before Noverre, ballet was thought of as a collective entity, centering on dance as defined and codified by the Academie Royale de Danse. Noverre's ideas split the body of ballet into binaries interacting with and within and counteracting each other. Ballet became an unending project impossible to either steer or stop.

Hindsight offers illusory comforts for ballet historians, especially the phantom solace of a single "story of ballet." A *single* story, I would emphasize, but not the *same* story. That of Vera Krasovskaia, as I have shown in the introduction, is one of a battle between benign and baleful tendencies—a battle culminating in the inevitable triumph of the former. More pedestrian histories, like Pleshcheev's, offer simple, one-thing-after-another stories; the dance history authored by Liubov Blok in the late 1930s is a story of ballet's continuous discovery of its true classical self; and so on. Stories vary. But however triumphalist or essentialist, pedestrian or entertaining a ballet history may be, it is invariably about one story, *the* story. There is one point of view that explains it all, and this viewpoint is mine.

32   IMPOSSIBLE PROJECT

My approach in this book is different. Ballet has always been too many things at once for a single story to do justice to all. Following in the footsteps of literary scholars who borrow from modern understandings of physics, I find it useful to think of ballet history in terms of the "complementarity principle," a concept according to which mutually contradictory descriptions of an object do not exclude but complement one another. Certain phenomena—whether of nature or culture—cannot be amply understood unless described from two opposing vantage points. To our current thinking, *The Nutcracker* is an unquestionable masterpiece; when it first appeared, critics considered it an embarrassment, a boring and absurd toy story (per the *Petersburg Gazette*) set to poor music (per Skalkovsky), a spectacle that seasoned ballet-goers (e.g., Nikolai Bezobrazov) could not wait to see gone from the bill.[30] One could, of course, chuckle over these long-forgotten misassessments, as Krasovskaia does gleefully in her *Russian Ballet History*, but dismissiveness toward the unruly past can blind us to historical dynamics. Rather than disappear from the bill, *The Nutcracker* has become a Christmas fixture as familiar as the tree itself; in fact—to evoke Anton Chekhov's paradox immortalized by Viktor Shklovsky—too familiar to notice.[31] Today *The Nutcracker* is a historical monument; to rediscover it as a historical fact, we must peruse every early critical anathema on it. Present hindsight and bygone foresight must not quarrel; these vantage points are complementary.

Balletic values and failures are complementary affairs, meaning that, at one point or another, each is likely to flip into its opposite. This applies not only to critical reassessments of individual productions but also to elements of classical choreography and critics' criteria of judging a classical performance.

Consider virtuosity, the virtue of turning every step into a feat. Nowadays, virtuosity—the manifest mastery of movement—seems as integral a part of classical dance as are spindle-perfect spins, weight-defying jumps, or the string-strung straightness of pointes. Self-evident as such values may appear to a modern ballet-goer, none of them went unquestioned in old-time ballet lore. In epochs when what we call "classical" was referred to as "serious" or "noble"—such as eighteenth-century France and nineteenth-century Russia—virtuosity as such was a debatable property for a ballet dancer to display. Virtuosity ill squared with nobility; it seemed more fit for a fairground acrobat. I mentioned above Noverre's appreciation for–cum–apprehension of Fossano. Noverre was equally ambivalent about "the God of dance"

Auguste Vestris; of Vestris's younger rival, the virtuoso dancer Louis Duport, Noverre said, "He pirouettes out of sight, and with such velocity that the eye is dazzled.... [But] with less fire and petulance his dancing will mature."[32]

The complementary name for virtuosity was showiness. Vestris's mastery was too much on display for "people of sense and taste" (as Noverre categorized himself and those like him) to fully welcome it.[33] Noble dance is for the noble class, and the nobility, at least in their own eyes, are never showy. In the aesthetic vocabulary of the epoch, tours de force did not match such markings of nobility as grace and ease, simplicity (*facilité*) and elegance, lightness (*légèreté*) and naturalness—not in the sense of moving as nature had envisioned but in making the artifice of stem-straight torsos and turned-out limbs look like the most natural manner of moving in the world.

Through most of its history, ballet has been haunted by two complementary metaphors, one driven by ambitions, the other by premonitions. I have spoken briefly of the recurrent balletic dream of making the dancing body approximate a sculpted one. At the end of "Letter XXI," Noverre compares dance to a beautiful statue "whose pose is instinct with grace, and whose attitude is noble, but who lacks a soul."[34] A true art lover looks at statues just as Pygmalion did at his: wishing that his feelings might bring her to life, his reason might teach her to express herself. Likewise, Noverre concludes, too many ballets are still unendowed with intelligence (*peu de ballet raisonnés*), too many are mere divertissements waiting for an artist to give them a language and an intelligent story to tell.[35]

Predominantly doctrinal in Noverre, the sculpture analogy resurfaces in Carlo Blasis's 1830 *Manuel complet de la danse* as practical guidance for dance students, complete with illustrations of famous pieces: "This particular position, named *attitude*, is the most elegant, and at the same time most difficult pas in the [bacchanalian] dance; to me, it seems to imitate the much-admired [statue of] Mercury by J[ean de] Bologne."[36]

Leaping ahead another sixty years, we find the sculptural metaphor embodied in the dance classes taught in Petersburg by Petipa. Petipa's trainee Iosif Kshesinsky recalls, "[T]he right thing about concluding a pirouette was not to bring it to a graceful halt, but to freeze firmly and trenchantly—like a sculpture."[37] The myth of the ballet master endowed with the Pygmalion power of which Noverre dreamed is, on the floor of Petipa's ballet class, reversed: here, a living dancer is turned into a statue.

Complementary to the dream of turning ballet into sculptures-set-in-motion was the dread of its becoming a circus. Noverre's vision of ballet's

34 IMPOSSIBLE PROJECT

desired future was informed no less by the Fossano fear than by the Pygmalion power. The fear was widely shared. In his study on the spread of Vestris's technique, John V. Chapman quotes the French critic Julien-Louis Geoffroy, who in an 1804 review warned young dancers "seduced by [Vestris's] brilliant fame" against making their dance "more difficult than pleasing: they measure their distance from Vestris in numbers of pirouettes; and this emulation causes the students of Terpsichore to degenerate into circus acrobats."[38]

Chapman identifies two of the primary objections fueling such criticism. One was that the craze for tours de force led dance away from what it could achieve in terms of meaning. This line of argument is familiar to us from Noverre's *Letters*. The other objection pinpointed by Chapman had to do with style: tours de force, it was feared, were performed at the expense of grace, ease, and nobility.[39]

We have spoken of this objection in terms of class; indeed, the very verb "degenerate" used in Geoffroy's review is a clear indication of where ballet and circus stood on the social ladder of theatricals. But part of the concern had especially to do with aesthetics. (A category, however, hardly divorced from class, as will be discussed below.) Pivotal here is the word "difficult," which, in Geoffroy's argument just quoted, is contraposed to "pleasing" and, in multiple other contexts, to its direct antonyms such as "easy" or "simple." *Eh!* (C'mon!), exclaims Noverre, addressing the implied pen-friend of his *Letters*. "What could appeal to us better, Monsieur, than grace born from simplicity [*facilité*]? Difficulty only pleases when we do not sense it; when it conceals the effort beneath the cloak of ease and nobleness, letting us see legerity alone."[40]

Ballet *is* difficult. Even the slow and small-stepped minuet, the noblest of *danses nobles*, required from *danseurs nobles* a perfect command of chess-complex floor patterns. Yuri Slonimsky, writing in 1937, characterized some of the Blasis-codified pirouettes as perplexing (*golovolomnye*); for all that, Blasis, writing in 1820, discouraged dancers from executing them with acrobatic dexterity.[41] For the likes of Noverre and Blasis, as for a host of subsequent Russian Noverrians, the bright line between ballet and circus was drawn by the subtlety or, on the other hand, glaringness of the difficulty involved. The very term "tour de *force*" foregrounds the forcefulness, ergo difficulty, of tours so named. As Geoffroy quips in the above-quoted philippic, "The dancer who leaps into the air soon causes those who skim the ground to be forgotten; but the height to which the young Vestris has carried dance lowers the art in elevating the artist."[42] The choice is worded with a Newtonian clarity: the higher you jump, the lower down your feet push off the balletic stage—until it becomes a circus arena.

In the complementary universe of dance, all highs and lows eventually flip. In the wake of the 1789 Revolution, the image of nobility in France lost much of its onetime grandeur, and so did the grandest of dances, *danse noble*. By the second decade of the nineteenth century, as Chapman shows, the noble style called terre-à-terre had been upstaged by the once ignoble tours de force. Initially an occupation solely of men, "jumping out of sight" was soon taken up by female dancers, and in the epoch of Taglioni, aeriality was reinterpreted as inherently feminine.[43]

In Russia, the ideals of noble dance lingered—as a training and dancing tradition laid down in Petersburg by Noverre's follower Didelot, and as an enshrined value that orthodox balletomanes crusaded to perpetuate throughout the nineteenth century and beyond. In 1859—nearly thirty years after Didelot had been discharged as the head of the Petersburg company and the school—the critic Vasil'ko Petrov published an essay that, according to the ballet historian Alisa Sveshnikova,[44] gave voice to the consensus on the state of ballet in the interim year between two epoch-making Petersburg ballet masters: Jules-Joseph Perrot and Arthur Saint-Léon. Petrov's account sounds like both a lament and a litany—the lament for Didelot-imparted virtues, and a litany in which the said virtues are enumerated one by one, complete with their opposites—a convenient paradigm for us to comment on: "Pantomimic ballets are gone forever, the classical pas has deserted the stage; the minuet, once considered the alpha of dance as art, has vanished without a trace. The smoothness of movements has given way to velocity; pictorial groups, to kaleidoscopically changing patterns. Ballet has developed a character more in line with gymnastics. The more difficult the dance; the more strength and dexterity it requires of a dancer, the more pleasing it is [to the public]. Nowadays, no danseuse has time to think of grace because each is busy strengthening and developing her muscles, which requires daily gymnastic exercises."[45]

Danse noble, like ballet in general, was never seen as an isolated phenomenon. Noble dances, which our critic calls *klassicheskoe pa*, were expected to dovetail both with their close relatives, high-society ballroom dances, and, twice removed, with the rules of aristocratic comportment at large. When Petrov speaks of the disappeared minuet as "once considered the alpha of dance as art," he means of course balletic, that is, stage minuets. On the

36 IMPOSSIBLE PROJECT

other hand, as we learn from the 1856 memoirs of Didelot's disciple Adam Glushkovsky, in his time the minuet had been the basis of extraballetic dance classes, which children of the nobility were supposed to start taking at the age of eight or nine.[46] Why the minuet, and why so early? As we learn from Glushkovsky's memoirs, this dance was believed to accustom children to holding the spine erect and straight; the minuet seasoned boys for military service and girls for a proper gait and their corseted future. What this also meant, one may speculate, is that ballet spectators, most of whom, in the epoch of Didelot, belonged to the nobility, were spectators-in-the-know, people who knew the nuts and bolts of dancing. Much of the pleasure gained from watching *danses nobles* had to do with the joy of recognition.

Another feature that Petrov finds missing in contemporary ballets is the erstwhile *plavnost'* (smooth and slow quality) of movements, which, he regrets, has given way to swiftness. On the scale of old balletic values, *plavnost'* was as sure a token of nobility as was the straight, unbending physique. According to Glushkovsky, Didelot adhered to a system whereby the character of movement and the tempo of music had to match the genre of the ballet, the social status of the character this or that dancer impersonated, and even the professional rank of the dancer within the troupe. This is how Glushkovsky describes—top down, slow to swift—his teacher's hierarchy of dancing speeds:

> In Didelot's ballets . . . serious dances were performed to adagio music and a march. For the main danseur, Didelot would always compose smooth dances, with different attitudes, and very rarely admit an entrechat or a swift pirouette. The *demi-caractère* danseur danced to the *andante grazioso* and *allegro*; for him, [Didelot] composed gracious dances, which consisted of very different positions of the body and arms [than those of the first dancer] and included smaller and faster pas and pirouettes than those of the serious genre. As to the comic danseur, he danced to allegro music, and mainly performed different jumps, for instance, *tours en l'air*, and held the body and arms also in a different manner.[47]

All jumping is eccentric—literally and figuratively. Our social imagination puts the important, the serious, and the noble in the center—be it of a room or a country, to say nothing of the universe. Those in the center represent the center of gravity—and do not jump. Such is a social convention observed not only on the balletic stage but also on the social stage called life. In nineteenth-century ballet, as in the culture it inhabited, the sense of dignity squared ill with excessive physicality. "Slow movements are stately by their essence," reads, rather mockingly, Rule 4 in Balzac's tongue-in-cheek treatise "Theory of Walking" ("Théorie de la demarche"), written in 1833. "Ergo, we can, in general, contend that being economical in one's movements lends one's gait both nobility and grace."[48]

It may have been this cultural "default setting" of noble immobility that led Skalkovsky, a critic not overly sentimental about the epoch of Didelot, to suddenly critique Petipa's and Lev Ivanov's ballet *La Tulipe de Haarlem* for what he interpreted as a lack of choreographic decorum: "By the very nature of the pas de deux, a grand seigneur would hardly perform all the jumps and cabrioles staged for him here."[49] For the year 1887, this reprimand sounds a little anachronistic; perhaps our critic felt entitled to make it because, in his nonballetic hat as a high-ranking official and later the head of the Mining Department, Privy Councilor Kostantin Apollonovich Skalkovsky was quite a grand seigneur himself.

Next on the list of Petrov's grudges comes the decline of "pictorial groups" replaced by "kaleidoscopically changing patterns." "Groups" is a term no longer applied to corps de ballet, which nowadays we associate primarily with dance; the pictorial groups Petrov was nostalgic for in his 1859 essay were first and foremost associated with repose. In the language of nineteenth-century criticism, "groups and dances" was a set phrase; the staging of groups alongside dances constituted a separate clause of the pro forma contract between the Directorate of Imperial Theaters and a ballet master they hired. Groups and dances were understood as companion pieces—two complementary components of a ballet.

The kind of dynamics that old-school connoisseurs like Petrov valued in old-time ballets was not the *dynamic* dynamics of the classical ballet of today. It hinged not on the dynamism of movements per se but on a balanced alternation of movement and repose. The perfect ballet, it was thought, constituted a succession of dances interlaid with a set of restful groups. A pictorial group, hence the epithet, gravitated toward tableaux vivants, onstage realizations of known or imaginary paintings, which made the grouping meaningful and justified its stillness.

The balance between groups and dances could be tipped this way or that, but never too far. When, in lieu of forming a pictorial group, a corps de ballet would burst into a dance, the impression produced was as Petrov describes it, of "kaleidoscopically changing patterns." "Everyone is in a state of ceaseless motion," Théophile Gautier complained of the ballet *La Vivandiere*, which he found overloaded with dances. "This artificial exhilaration is tiring, the eye craves to rest on a quieter group."[50]

As a critical trope meant to convey eye-catching but empty-headed effects, the "kaleidoscope" metaphor was equally suited to ballets overburdened with groups at the expense of dances. "The music is so wretched and the story so poor," wrote Skalkovsky of the 1883 ballet *The Cyprian Statue, or Pygmalion*, staged by Petipa to the music of the amateur composer Prince Ivan Trubetskoi, "that the only thing left to the choreographer was to apply himself to groups. . . . But ballets that consist of groups alone look terribly cold and lifeless. They are no longer art, but rather a kaleidoscope."[51]

As already mentioned, the bright line was the display of effort, the issue Petrov presents as a binary choice between grace and force: "No danseuse has time to think of grace because each is busy strengthening and developing her muscles." All the more is Petrov surprised to discover that the Italian virtuoso Amalia Ferraris, who "combines strength, incredible resilience of muscles . . . amazing hardness of toes"—everything needed to overcome the "utmost gymnastic difficulties"—also dances gracefully. But then Petrov is quick to explain this anomaly away: "To be honest, [Ferraris's] grace loses to the nimbleness of feet; well, could this ever be otherwise?"[52]

Today we do not posit force and grace as mutually exclusive qualities of style; for us, these are complementary components of what we expect classical dancing to be like. In the mindset of a critic writing in 1859, grace could not co-occur with exercise, other than interlocked in a losing battle. Grace is natural, which, in Petrov's understanding, was tantamount to God-given. Grace should not reek of sweat. Grace does not strive to *wow* you; it *graces* the beholder with its presence.

To what extent can we rely on views like Petrov's as truly reflective of the ethos and pathos of post-1850 ballet lore? Here, too, we should beware a one-story narrative. Petrov's vantage point was from the auditorium, as was, of course, that of Skalkovsky, Pleshcheev, and every other critic. Complementary to it was, for instance, the view from the wings. In her memoirs, the Petersburg ballerina Ekaterina Vazem, active in the 1870s–1880s, tenderly recalls her consœur, Adèle Grantzow: "Her soft, pure, 'classical' *sensu stricto* dance was a true joy to behold for anyone who understood the art of choreography. Grantzow was unaware of any technical difficulties, her variations were as simple as a child's."[53]

Listening to Vazem, one is tempted to picture Grantzow as an exemplary *danseuse noble* straight from the Golden Age pined for by Petrov—the age in which innate grace, along with her companion virtues simplicity and ease, made technical aptitude and daily exercise unnecessary. In fact, nothing could be further from the truth. When, in late 1866, Arthur Saint-Léon introduced the German dancer Grantzow to the Russian public, the *Moscow News* (*Moskovskie vedomosti*) reviewer was "stunned" at how thorough a training her leg- and footwork revealed ("nogi ee porazhali svoei khoreograficheskoi vyrabotannost'iu").[54] And hers was not the filigree footwork of the terre-à-terre manner. On the contrary, "aeriality" or "ethereality" (*vozdushnost'*), the velocity of movements, the power of the pointe were, according to Pleshcheev's 1899 *Our Ballet*, among Grantzow's unsurpassable assets.[55] When Vazem said that Grantzow "knew no technical difficulties," this meant that her performance made onlookers oblivious thereof; she made it *look* easy. If for a critic like Petrov, dance could be *either* graceful or forceful, then for the likes of Vazem and Grantzow, no such alternative existed. From the view of a dancer, grace hinged on the dancer, not the dance.

Even so, the *fall of grace with the rise of technique* remained a powerful meme throughout the nineteenth century in Russia. It was precisely due to this overweening narrative that heavy-duty "classical" choreography would be rebelled against in the early twentieth century, first and foremost by young graduates of the Imperial Theater School, most vocally Michel Fokine.

Tracing this dispute between *force* and *grace* means examining it from two complementary views: from the vantage point of the broad balletic public ("broad" as distinct from "pure," namely, the balletomanes, regular reviewers, and the spectatorial elite nicknamed the "diamond row"), on the one hand, and, on the other, from the perspective of the Petersburg Ballet School. The public loved rollicking character dances and acrobatic jumps and was eager to count how many fouettés en pointes this or that ballerina would be able to pull off. What the purists looked down their noses at, the public endorsed wholesale by applause and attendance, and the Directorate of Imperial Theaters was no less sensitive to the income these fans brought than were the dancers to their applause. From the 1880s on, seasonally touring *virtuozki*, mainly from Italy, were booked at the Mariinsky Theater under the contractual obligation to be technically resplendent—for which, in turn, discriminating critics blamed the indiscriminating public. "The flung turn [*vertun*], or jeté en tournant, is, by the way, a concession to the depravity of our public's taste," Skalkovsky picked at Carlotta Zambelli, who, before her engagement

40   IMPOSSIBLE PROJECT

in Petersburg in 1901, had for several years been the *étoile* of the Paris Opera. "In Paris, the ballerina would not have permitted herself a jump like that."[56]

For all its reputation as a paragon of taste, every turn-of-the-century ballet lover knew that French ballet, once dominant in Europe, had seen its day. All the more powerful was yet another meme shared by Russian guardians of grace. In their eyes, the Petersburg troupe was the one and only keeper of the French classical tradition—as was the troupe's crucible, the ballet school, where the principles laid down by Didelot were kept alive by the Methuselah of dance pedagogy, Christian Johansson. Ballet schools, by the very way they used to be staffed, espoused a preservationist philosophy. As a rule, ballet teachers were recruited from among retired dancers, who tended to teach as they had been taught. Before taking charge of the Petersburg school in 1804, Didelot was involved in ballets staged in Paris and London by Noverre; thus it was quite natural that Noverre's lessons from the 1770s and 1780s should, via Didelot, take root in Russia in the first quarter of the nineteenth century. Before being hired as a dance teacher with the Petersburg Ballet School in 1860, Johansson had been a dancer trained by August Bournonville, who had been taught to dance by his father, Antoine Bournonville, who in turn learned to dance from Noverre.

A more complex but no less convincing genealogy could be drawn for Petipa as a dance instructor. When in 1886 Vazem, now a retired dancer, took over from Petipa the mid-level dance class for girls, she found that teaching in the Petersburg school had remained essentially unchanged since her own student years: "Here, one only taught 'classical' dances, i.e., how to perform a set of steps sanctified by the canons and traditions handed down by a succession of dancers and dance instructors of elder generations. This kind of 'classics' was considered the only foundation of choreographic pedagogy, and this was where the limit was set."[57] Within the walls of the school, "classical" dance came to mean the dance one learned in class—hence its other name, "danse d'école." It was owing to the school that, throughout the nineteenth century, St. Petersburg enjoyed the reputation of, as it were, a sanctuary city for the *danse noble* in the old French taste.

Taking guardianship of something, however, can be fraught. Along with inheriting the French tradition, Russian ballet culture had internalized the latter's distaste for its complementary other: the Italian ballet, with its eighteenth-century flair for acrobatic *grotteschi* and nineteenth-century craze for dancing on pointe. In Russia, the latter technique became a bone of contention.

The Case of the Toxic Toe

What technique could be more iconic of classical ballet than the pointes? A bow-taut instep of a woman's foot glimpsed on the cover of a book instantly tells us what the book is about. And yet the iconicity of pointe work is of more recent making than might be thought. Here, once again, old reference books can be of help. No entry for *puanty* is found in the first edition (1926–47) of the *Great Soviet Encyclopedia* (*Bol'shaia sovetskaia entsiklopediia*)—even if as a technical term "pointes" had been around for a century already. On the other hand, an entry under this title appears in the encyclopedia's second edition (1949–58), which means that, by the second half of the century, the step and its name had entered the area of general knowledge.

General knowledge is a dynamic system, which is why encyclopedias—repositories of general knowledge—come in consecutive editions. The inclusion of the pointes in the second edition of the *Great Soviet Encyclopedia* led to a revision of the entry "Marie Taglioni." The first edition, mapped out in the mid-1920s, characterizes Taglioni's art as "the purest and most accomplished epitome of ballet's classical school, whose core were the flight and the jump."[58] In the second, postwar edition, we find the reference to the flight and jump substituted by what sounds almost like a patent certificate: "T[aglioni] introduced the classical female dance *on pointes* to ballet." This statement is accompanied by a contemporary depiction of Taglioni as Sylphide frozen on pointe.

Neither of the two entries is factually false; rather, they complement each other. Knowledge, unlike law, allows ex post facto judgments. We readily project what we know—or, better, think—today upon what we know about the past, highlighting the seedlings we know would soon take root. All sources available to us attest that Taglioni did indeed win all hearts with her, as the first of the two quoted encyclopedic entries summarizes, "innate grace," "airy lightness," and "poetic performance." It is equally true, as the second entry asserts, that it was owing to Taglioni that the pointe technique gained a foothold in European ballet. To get to know a Taglioni in the round, one story, however encyclopedic, is not enough.

Pivotal to the Soviet school of ballet as shaped by Agrippina Vaganova and showcased by Galina Ulanova (whose sway over the public and powers that be was on a par with that of Taglioni, her predecessor of a century earlier) was the verticality doctrine: whether on the floor or in a jump, the dancer's spine must always be erect—as if a tree trunk were growing through it. In this

42 IMPOSSIBLE PROJECT

context, the pointe was but a natural extension of the dancer's body. Writing in the late 1930s, Liubov Blok, a keen interpreter of Vaganova's schooling practices, theorized the aesthetic purpose of the pointes thus: "Yes, [the pointe] is unnatural—it is fully a product of abstract thinking.... It is nothing more than an idea brought to its logical conclusion: try as you might stretch up on demi-pointes [*na polupal'tsakh*], the leg and foot will all the same subtend a broken line. For the legs and feet to form the same straight line as they do during the jump, [the danseuse] must stand on the tips of her toes."[59]

From the Soviet perspective in which pointe work was a sine qua non of classical ballet, its emergence in the early 1830s at the Paris Opéra seemed an unmissable milestone—to permit ourselves a pun, a historic turning point at which classical ballet came into its own. That Taglioni was thought to be the first to have signed, with her magic feet, an imprimatur for the pointe technique made her, in Soviet eyes, a precursor of Ulanova. (As the story of the canonization of pointe work deserves a separate inquiry, I return to it later in this book.)

All the more surprising, then, is that none of the many rapt pages devoted to Taglioni's triumphs in Pleshcheev's 1896 *Our Ballet* includes a single mention of her pointe technique. As with Pleshcheev, so Sergei Khudekov. The third volume (1915) of the latter's *History of Dances* includes two chapters on Taglioni; the fourth (1918) covers the Petersburg innings of her career in detail. Again, no mention of Taglioni's pointe work. And this despite the fact that most pictures reproduced in Khudekov's lavishly illustrated book depict Taglioni dancing sur les pointes.

Such omissions might at first seem like a historiographic passing-over of the most obvious, like a writer on Edison not bothering to mention the electric lightbulb. The historical picture, however, is often more complex than our hindsight. Were our nineteenth-century critics too impressionistic-minded to pay attention to technical detail or, perhaps, not versed enough in things balletic to know a pointe when they saw it? Hardly: Pleshcheev and Khudekov knew their history and theory of ballet—balletomanes prided themselves on being able to note and name the subtlest pas or attitude, to mark the slightest innovation this or that ballerina brought to this or that variation. Rather, the opposite is true: late nineteenth-century observers like Khudekov knew pointe work too well to trust it. In the fourth volume of his *History of Dances*, Khudekov is quite ambivalent about the pointe: he follows its evolution with a mix of appreciation and apprehension. And the more admirable he finds the technique, the more apprehensive he grows of its effect on what your typical balletomane found unique about "our ballet": the mission of the Petersburg-bred troupe to carry on the noble French tradition.

To the likes of Khudekov, the expansion of pointe technique was indicative of a perceived Italian invasion. In *History of Dances*, volume 4, Khudekov traces the latter back to the engagement in 1858 of Amalia Ferraris—the same Ferraris whom, we recall, Petrov in 1859 hailed as the preserver of grace amid the onslaught of tour-de-force-ism. "Triple pirouettes en pointes, something no one had seen before," Khudekov recalls, "and the smoothness of [Ferraris's] error-free pointework dazzled not only the public but also the entire Petrograd [Petersburg] balletic troupe."[60] The picture could hardly be any rosier, one might think, yet this is precisely where Khudekov senses a lion in the path: "Ferraris's sojourn in Petrograd had touched off the growth of undue virtuosity in the Petrograd ballet."[61]

The success of Zucchi in Petersburg in 1885, discussed at length in the introduction, precipitated a series of time-bound contracts with other Italian ballerinas, most of whom Khudekov was inclined to both admire and admonish. His remark that Zucchi, if needed, could have walked Nevsky Prospect end to end on pointes was, as a compliment, actually backhanded: in contrast to the exemplary (*obraztsovaia*) imperial stage, this proverbial Petersburg avenue epitomized the popular and thus, to Khudekov, questionable taste. Carlotta Brianza, who stepped on the Mariinsky stage in 1889, could, per Khudekov, "jump on pointes and perform double and even triple tours en pointes without visible effort. Her technical prowess amazed the public; from the aesthetic viewpoint, however, [Brianza] contributed nothing to fine choreography."[62] Antonietta Dell'Era (on contract with the Imperial Theater in 1892) turned out to be even more—and more perfidiously—perfect than Brianza: "No one doubted Dell'Era. She was nicknamed a 'Goliath' of technique. Her footwork astounded with the enormous power of her pointes. She would do three circles en pointes without a male dancer's support. Straight from kneeling, she would wind up standing on her toes. Hers were wonders of acrobatic choreography, the acme of perfection. No one prior to Dell'Era had ever demonstrated masterstrokes equal to hers."[63] But here comes the *but*: "Russian danseuses indeed bent over backward [*izoshchrialis'*] to imitate this star of acrobatic dance; but did her technical, soul- and meaning-lacking dances contribute anything to the development of art? This is the question.... Devotees of the French school, its elegant gestures and noble movements, answered this question in the resolute negative."[64]

44 IMPOSSIBLE PROJECT

The question, thus, was one of survival. The old-school members of the balletomane community had vested the Petersburg troupe with a mission: to keep *danse noble* alive. Every Italian arrival put that mission in peril. Pierina Legnani's stay in Petersburg (1893–1901) "turned Russian ballerinas into spinning tops."[65] To believe Khudekov, the moment Matilda Kschessinska, in an effort to out-Legnani Legnani, would send her body into a spin, "some of the first-row regulars [*pervoriadniki*] would start counting, almost aloud, the number of fouettés [*vertuntsy*]: one, two, three—ten, twenty . . . finally, thirty-two."[66]

The slippery status of pointe work is especially glaring in *Memoirs of a Ballerina of the St. Petersburg Bolshoi Theater*, which Vazem, the star of the 1870s, dictated to her son when well into her eighties. Vazem, whom Pleshcheev describes as an "assured, tireless, and hard-toed" danseuse who "thought nothing of double pirouettes, which, in her time, were considered life-threatening,"[67] sounds quite proud of her virtuoso reputation when, for instance, she recalls her pointe work in *Butterfly*, the ballet staged by Petipa in 1874. On one of her variations Vazem reminisces, "I did two pirouettes renversé on my toes, and froze, as the balletic jargon has it, 'à la seconde' (in the second position). This was a novelty. Before me, Henrietta D'Or did the same pirouettes, which everyone marveled at, in *Le Corsaire*, but she performed those on demi-pointes, which was much easier. I ended my variation with en-pointes jumps on one foot, something no ballerina had ever done before me. Balletomanes were quick to dub this pas the 'Vazem variation,' as there existed the Ferraris, D'Or, Grantzow, and so forth variations."[68]

Vazem sounds proud precisely in the terms that critics used to *censure* the "acrobatic" turn in choreography: for her, difficult equals good, priority counts, *that* variation was *mine*, and so on. In ballet lore, however, admiration and admonition are not mutually exclusive but complementary attitudes—just as admiration and admonition coalesce in your parents' peremptory "Climb down from that tree at once!" Two years after Vazem retired as a dancer, she accepted an offer to teach classical dance to the female middle class of the Petersburg Ballet School, a position she would hold from 1886 to 1896, the year in which Enrico Cecchetti, an Italian virtuoso-turned-pedagogue who was decidedly no stranger to pointe strength, tours de force, or other manifestations of choreographic virtuosity, was hired to teach senior female class.[69] In her role as instructor, Vazem's language noticeably changed. "Let me observe, by the way," she remarks in the last chapter of her memoir, "that in the late 1880s, when ballet had not yet been seduced

THE SHADOW OF NOVERRE   45

by the never-ending scurrying *sur les pointes* brought by a host of migrant Italian danseuses, pointe work was less of a priority than it is now. The pointe technique was deemed teachable in senior grades only. In junior and middle grades, pointe work was strictly off limits."[70]

Vazem here appears to blame the itinerant Italians, not for importing the pointe technique per se, but for making hard toes the common currency in Russia. Indeed, at the time of Vazem's stardom, dancing on pointes was not accessible to dancers ranking below soloists and ballerinas. By the rules of balletic hierarchy, coryphées, saying nothing of the corps de ballet, were neither shod nor prepared to go on pointes.[71] The en-pointe choreographic battalions we hold emblematic of classical ballet became so only in the twentieth century.

Vazem's memoir came out in the 1930s, which also happened to be the decade in which Blok worked on *her* history of classical dance, which harbors a complementary view on the "Italian" period in Petersburg's ballet and its favorite gimmick: dancing *sur les pointes*. "We are not yet fully conscious of the expressive potential of the pointe technique," Bolk writes, blaming ballet's past for having hindered that potential. "If ballet of the previous epochs can be reproached for something, it is not for having invented pointe work, but for not having understood it well enough, for having muffled its true voice."[72] Blok would have us lay "elegance" and "grace" to rest as "the mundane concepts [*bytovye poniatiia*] Skalkovsky and Pleshcheev have been pestering us with"; she credits Cecchetti the dance teacher with asserting the Italian power pas on the stage and in the classroom: "The professionalism of Italian danseuses inculcated in our ballet by Cecchetti was a life-giving breath, a window blown open, a jolt of fresh air. By way of imitating the Italians, by means of translating dance into dry and sharp lines of the Italian virtuoso technique, our danseuses managed to pull it out of its musty rotten swamp. This was but an ABC, a mere prelude, but also a needed run-up to the new standards that the new art would hold dance to. . . . The whirlwind raised by the 'thirty-two fouettés' was necessary to drain the marshes of formlessness."[73]

Rather than resting the case of the toxic toe, I'd like to table it for later. In the early twentieth century, the pointe technique was caught in a crossfire between backers of the "new ballet" like Michel Fokine and Vaslav Nijinsky and the ideologists of ballet for ballet's sake, Akim Volynsky and André Levinson, whose voice and argumentation pervade Blok's history of ballet. This and related controversies will be examined more closely later in the book. In the

46   IMPOSSIBLE PROJECT

meantime, here I would address some of the other complementary tensions that shaped the historical dynamics of the late nineteenth-century ballet that we now call "classical."

Head and Feet

As mentioned earlier, every development in ballet's history seems *in retrospect* a new leg on a continuous journey, but to those *on* the road, any such development was a crossroads—a choice to make, a problem to solve. To someone like Blok, writing in the 1930s, the story of the pointes sounds like a hundred-year odyssey across a rotten swamp, with Skalkovsky and Khudekov cast as her Cyclopes and Circes. On the other hand, it is not hard to imagine how, in the eyes of old-school balletomanes, the rise of the pointe technique represented a dilemma. What Blok calls "the marshes of formlessness" to be drained by the propeller of "thirty-two fouettés" was, after all, their preferred cultural habitat, whose ecology needed to be protected. In ballet's history, any new step could represent an existential threat.

Consider Noverre. Today we pay tribute to Noverre for a number of related innovations: having dancers remove allegorical character masks, banning speech and singing from the balletic stage, and redefining *ballet de cour* along dramatic lines. Not least, we also credit Noverre with launching the theory of ballet. Now a peculiar feature of Noverre's theoretical legacy was that, rather than develop incrementally, it snowballed around his 1760 *Letters on Dance,* which in his lifetime saw many revised and variously supplemented editions—in fact, so many that, to repeat Krasovskaia, a "comparative analysis [of them] could constitute a prized scholarly study."[74] New *Letters* would be added, some old ones supplemented, yet Noverre's main premises and contentions remained unchanged. The way Noverre must have conceived of theory was not as a succession of books but as one book that, like a tree, forks out and branches as time goes on.

As a side effect of this conception, some sections of the last antemortem edition of Noverre's *Letters* may appear to be out of step with his own reforms. In 1807, there was hardly a dancer left to remember, let alone put on, a musty mask of the kind that were de rigueur in pre-Noverre ballets. Shouldn't the author have cut or at least historicized, say, "Letter XXIII: On Facial Expression and the Inutility of Masks," in which the habit of masked dancing is vehemently attacked, and dancing with faces uncovered ardently defended?

That Noverre made no such abridgment may be explained by the consideration that any innovation in ballet is fraught with crisis. By eliminating the problem of the mask, Noverre had created a problem for the face. And he himself was the first to foresee this; in the *Letter* in question, he preemptively parries two principal objections, one having to with facial expressions, the other with facial features. Dancers, it is often said, are too preoccupied with footwork to think of their expressions; the pas they must perform are often so complex that the unmasked face would show a grimace. *Tant pis*, Noverre counters, let our dancers learn from great dramatic actors like David Garrick how to control their countenance whatever throws and throes their bodies may undergo on stage. In fact, he adds, our danseurs must learn this from our danseuses, for a woman knows how to look pleasant even in a most unpleasant situation.

The other problem had to do with nature. A masked dancer owes everything to their dancing skills. This does not necessarily apply to dancers without a mask. "You have told me more than once," Noverre responds to a worry voiced by his disciple-in-the-text, "that, before we abolish masks, we ought to make sure that every dancer has a face for theater [*physiognomie théâtrale*]."[75] Noverre's answer to this was that nature makes a natural casting director. Dancers born with proud and prominent features and a majestic gaze are natural-born danseurs nobles; a pleasant rather than prominent face, sensual and gentle, makes a perfect demi-character dancer; and comic dances of buoyant disposition require a dancer endowed with a jolly and animated face.[76] *Tout court*, there is always a place for every face.

The reality proved to be less comforting. Once stripped of a mask, a dancer was exposed to critical criteria unrelated to their dancing skills. A grid or, rather, a checklist of facial assessments would haunt dancers throughout the nineteenth century. Critics weighed your dancing skills against your looks. "M-me [Aleksandra] Vergina [is] a mediocre dancer," Skalkovsky opined in his 1875 review of *Tsar Kandavl* (*Le Roi Candaule*), "but she is pretty and cute, which is why the public loves her."[77] Or your dancing skills against your acting. "With incredible lightness and faultlessness did M-me Vazem handle the hardest bits of pointe work and most daring pirouettes in the charming *grand pas de Vénus*," wrote Skalkovsky of another part danced in the same ballet, with the following caveat: "Vazem's manner is somewhat cold, her facial work [*mimika*] insufficiently expressive."[78] Great as a dancer, poor as

48   IMPOSSIBLE PROJECT

a mime—Vazem's reputation of a lopsided genius stuck with her long after she'd retired, reemerging, for instance, in Pleshcheev's 1899 annals *Our Ballet*. Vazem's technique was "masterful"[79] and "impeccable,"[80] Pleshcheev asserts; "[h]owever, one cannot but point to Vazem's coldness—her face remained indifferent to what was happening on the stage."[81]

One of Noverre's most essential *Letters* is titled "Division de la Danse." The title is telling. The strength of Noverre's strategy was its divisiveness. For all their narrative trappings, allegorical or otherwise, ballets as conceived by the Sun King and his academicians were all about the art of dance. Noverre demoted the latter to the rank of craft (*profession*): "Dance as such [*proprement dite*] amounts to no more than the mechanics of steps and the methodical movements of arms."[82] Only when they combine dance with pantomimic action will a dancer legitimately merit "the title of *artiste*."[83] Noverre's term for this desired combination was *danse pantomime* or *danse en action*.

Here I would spotlight a nuance key to understanding the impact of Noverre's writings on ballet in nineteenth-century Russia. The notion of *danse en action* did not imply (as one might retrospectively assume) that *action* and *danse* were treated on an equal footing. The relationship within their sought-for union remained hierarchical; in the eighteenth-century mindset, any aesthetic category implied, by default, a value judgment. Action, throughout Noverre's *Letters*, is given preferential treatment: pantomime, in his language, is always linked and likened to *life* and *soul*; dance, to the body as to a machine. And like any unequal coupling, Noverre's idea of *danse en action* resulted, not in a union, but in a potential quarrel, ready to break out any time.

Indeed, Noverrian reforms, like time bombs, would explode into ballet's future, splitting it into complementary dichotomies. One of these became one of ballet's catchiest memes. Following Noverre's train of thought, from the "division of dance" one arrives at a division of the dancer: "Until the dancer's head takes control of their feet, the latter will always go astray."[84] In Noverre's synecdoche, "feet" stands for dance, and "head" for drama. Use your head, lest your feet spin out of control.

On the ground, however, curbing the feet was easier said than done. Instead of merging into a harmonious *danse pantomime*, dance and pantomime polarized, forming a complementary binary. Noverre's envisioned synthesis of drama and dance, like many a utopian aspiration, generated more bickering than harmony. The dosage of dance in a ballet was an intractable problem: a lot was always too much; a little, too little. Complaints about the excess of dancing became a permanent fixture in nineteenth-century critical discourse; on the other hand, the nineteenth-century public found pure miming boring. While Noverre and his followers dreamed of some perfectly synthetic *ballet d'action*, which would not just patch dance onto action but constitute a dance and a dramatic act all at the same time, a standard (if lean) compromise between the two, particularly favored by Petipa, was to section them by time slots reflected and numbered in the playbill. A mimic scene would be succeeded by a dance, followed by a mimic scene; typically, players would be dressed, made up, and brushed differently for each: in period costumes for mimic pieces, in tights plus hair waves plus rouge for classical dances.[85]

And yet throughout ballet's nineteenth century in Russia, the two modes of performance competed for time and room on stage. Every ballet was supposed to live up to the loftiness of painting or sculpture, but this rule remained somewhat of an aesthetic abstraction; flesh-and-blood danseuses, meanwhile, were prone to rebel with their feet. On the one hand, to quote an 1859 review by the music critic Mavrikii Rappaport, "everyone will agree that seeing dances alone, all evening long . . . spells boredom, and that, to dispel boredom, dancing must be combined with mime."[86] On the other, whenever one's pet danseuse appeared on the stage, the climate would warm and critics melt. In the ballet *Fiametta*, staged by Saint-Léon in 1864, Marfa Muravieva, who danced the lead, scarcely left the stage at all. Dancing prevailed, but the perfection of her dance was such that, as the critic Ivan Bocharov observed in the *Anchor* (*Iakor'*), even inveterate lovers of logically motivated action "completely forgot about characters and roles, naturalness and meaningfulness, and such nonsense."[87] In 1865 a ballet reviewer with *Fatherland's Son* (*Syn otechestva*) observed a similar attitude on the part of devotees of Maria Petipa, Muravieva'a lifetime rival: "M-me Petipa's plastic power carries the public away, so much so that no one cares any longer about content."[88]

What Noverre had envisaged as a road from *danse proprement dite* to *danse en action*, then, looks more like an endless wavering between the two. What "road" can one speak of if the entry "Ballet" that appeared in 1890 in Russia's prestigious *Brockhaus and Efron Encyclopedic Dictionary* reads as if ghostwritten by Noverre, as if Noverre still had to promulgate his precepts: "Ballets are increasingly required to incorporate serious miming in order to measure up to the dramatic arts. Evidently, ballet cannot rest on

50 IMPOSSIBLE PROJECT

dances alone, what it also needs is skillful acting."[89] One hundred thirty years later, we find Noverre's project back at square one.

In the language of Russian Noverrians, balletic variations unmotivated (or barely motivated) by narrative were "bare" or "naked dances" (*golye tantsy*), a term of course not free of innuendo. "Exemplary stages," a title officially conferred on the Imperial Theaters in the 1880s to demarcate them from private enterprises, were supposed to beware these. *"No room should be given in ballets to dances that are internally meaningless and not connected with the unfolding of action,"* the Moscow danseuse Lidiia Nelidova wrote in 1893 in her own *Letters on Ballet*, of which "Letter One: Ideals of Choreography and True Paths of Ballet" was the only to be published, or indeed written at all. "No exemplary stage should tolerate those spectacles, misnamed 'ballets,' that consist fully and solely of bare dances, to which a plot is merely pinned for decency's sake, in order to lend them a semblance of wholeness."[90]

Unlike Noverre's, Nelidova's *Letter* was less an outline than an outcry, one not untarnished by xenophobic jealousy of the success of migrant Italian danseuses. Indeed, from the perspective of 1893—when balletic tastes were largely defined by the likes of Brianza and Dell'Era—"the true path of ballet," as Nelidova calls Noverre's projections, may have seemed forever lost. Yet the power of Noverre's project was that, envisioned as a "path," it never actually worked as one. When Noverre juxtaposed "feet" to "head," he plotted, it turned out, not a course (as he intended) but an amplitude. Lost as Noverre's "head" may have looked in the 1890s, it would come back like the bob of a pendulum in the decade that followed—via the views held and ballets staged by Michel Fokine. But never, as I detail in the final chapter of this book, to stay for long.

Lost in Translation

The sad irony of Nelidova's idealism, critics loudly suspected, was that using a pen to affirm Noverre's ideals may have been the dancer's second choice. By all accounts, Nelidova was never a strong danseuse, and was twice denied, on professional grounds, a promotion to the rank of ballerina before she finally secured it.[91] Ballet is not about technique, Nelidova expostulates; ballet must open "a new page in the history of humankind . . . stirring empathy toward kindness and revulsion toward the unholy and the mean."[92] In his (well, mean) review of Nelidova's first appearance in Petersburg in 1897,

THE SHADOW OF NOVERRE   51

Skalkovsky quotes this and a handful of other platitudes from Nelidova's *Letter*, only to add, with an unholy delight, "What a formidable task! Now, be so good as to [*izvol'te*] express all this with your feet."[93]

With regard to Nelidova, Skalkovsky's remark was monstrously unfair. (If the right to comment on ballet is supposed to be licensed by dancing talent, then what to make of Skalkovsky and other critics?) On a more theoretical level, however, the remark hit yet another explosive problem preplanted by Noverre. Noverre's aesthetic program incorporated two contradictory instructions: one, to convert ballet into a dramatic vehicle; the other, to deprive ballet of words—the native medium of drama. *How to express this with your feet* became a maddening riddle endemic to post-Noverrian ballet.

Not that Noverre himself ever thought of this as a conundrum. In his philosophy, dramatic action hardly required spoken words; quite the opposite. Only when stripped of words does a language become *the* language, the tongue of tongues understood by all humanity. Tragedy is all about depicting passions, and, in the eye of a classicist like Noverre, human passions are best expressed in the universal language of gesture. That ballet is on a par with its sister arts, explains Noverre, is not despite but on the strength of being wordless: "Painting and dance have this advantage over other arts, that they belong to all lands and all nations; that their language is universally understandable."[94]

Ridding ballets of the spoken word opened a path toward a remapping of authorship. It stood to reason that libretti of comédie- and opéra-ballets had been authored by people skilled in rhetoric and rhymes. It takes a Molière or Philippe Quinault to produce a soliloquy or dialogue in verse as grandiloquent or witty as those recited or sung in Molière's 1665 *L'Amour médecin* or Quinault's 1681 *Le triomphe de l'amour*. By reducing ballet librettos to dance and gesture, Noverre reassigned authorship from literati to ballet masters like himself.

Noverre's own *livrets* were written with three goals in mind: to serve as a script for the player and a guide for the spectator and, no less important, to appear in print as a stand-alone book showcasing ballet as a full-fledged art form. With all due respect, monsieur, Noverre writes to Voltaire in 1763, in my ballet adaptation of a tragic love story from your epic poem *La Henriade*, I took the liberty of changing the sad ending to an apotheosis—a more appropriate finale for a ballet. To which Voltaire replied with all due humility, "You are turning into a living picture what on my part was but a flimsy sketch [*foible esquisse*]."[95]

52 IMPOSSIBLE PROJECT

It was not out of vanity alone that Noverre placed this and two other endorsing letters from Voltaire at the beginning of the second volume of the St. Petersburg edition (1803) of his own *Letters*, now titled *Lettres sur la danse, sur les ballets et les arts*. For Noverre, the nascent cultural reputation of ballet went hand in hand with the cultural prestige of the ballet master as an author. A 1776 collection of his libretti that included ones based on Aeschylus and Corneille flaunted the title *Recueil de Programmes de Ballets de M. Noverre, Maître de ballets de la Cour Imperiale et Royale*. Corneille is his source, but his program is *his* program.

It made Noverre proud to think of ballet as not only an equal to other *arts imitateurs* but also an art form that imitates *differently* from the way other arts do. Preempting a criticism of his *Horace*-based program anticipated from his nemesis Gasparo Angiolini, who "will say I have sinned against the Rules of Aristotle, and that my ballet does not contain the three unities," Noverre retorts in advance, "Aristotle's Rules were not written for the dance."[96]

A child of the Enlightenment, Noverre believed in the power of education to gentrify ballet from above. His advice to future ballet masters was to "devote all their spare time to studying history and mythology; read Homer, Virgil, Ariosto, Tasso in order to imbibe the beauty of poetry; learn the rules established by poetics."[97]

Noverre's faithful disciple Didelot shared his teacher's creed and, when in Russia, succeeded in replicating Noverre's cultural trajectory. Noverre, who thought of the genre of libretto as a sort of prose poem,[98] wrote one after the epic poem by Voltaire; Didelot staged a ballet after Pushkin's long poem *The Prisoner of the Caucasus* (*Kavkazskii plennik*). Voltaire found every work of Noverre's to be "full of poetry; painters and poets will quarrel to which of the groups you should belong";[99] Pushkin said something similar of Didelot.[100] No nineteenth-century ballet master working in Russia after him would match Didelot's recognition among the educated. By contrast, the last of the giants—the ballet master Petipa, a household name in our day—at the time of his tenure in Russia remained culturally invisible.

In the value system established by Noverre, it was on the wings of poetic libretti that the lowly craft of dancing would soar to the heights of art. As with all things Noverre, however, this ideal only set ballet in conflict with itself. Noverre's reform vested choreographers with the power of authorship, but it did not, in and of itself, raise the status of dancing. The axiological antithesis of *head versus foot* remained in force. Noverre's plan was to uplift ballet, not dance. True, the section in his *Letters* devoted to "qualities necessary for a

THE SHADOW OF NOVERRE   53

ballet master to have" begins with a discussion of footwork, but he is careful to distinguish between dancing and art: "At this time, sir, I am done speaking to you of your craft; from now on, our conversation will be about art, that is, about expression and that animated pantomime which is the soul and mind of dance."[101]

Historical fluctuations in the dynamics of balletic authorship may be conceived in terms of concurrent "texts"—narrative, musical, visual, and choreographic—each of which, at one point or another, claimed primacy. In the nineteenth-century perception, as Lynn Garafola points out, the master-text of ballet was the dramatic narrative it told; as a rule, it was librettists, not choreographers or composers, who would be billed as the authors of nineteenth-century ballets.[102] As if reflecting Noverre's plan in an inverted mirror, nineteenth-century libretto writing was by and large reassigned to professionals capable of a "well-made play" (*la pièce bien faite*)—playwrights for whom writing for the stage was precisely a craft. The practice was so taken for granted that Vazem remembers the ballet master Jules Perrot, who stood his ground, authoring libretti for his own ballets, as being a "balletic dramatist more than a mere choreographer."[103] In Vazem's telling phrasing, the title "dramatist" sounds more prestigious than "choreographer," even if, to recall Noverre's defiant *mot*, dramatists who wrote for ballet might typically know no more about the specifics of dance than did Aristotle.

The rift between the dramatic and choreographic nuclei of ballet grew all the wider as dramatic tastes changed, from Corneille's neoclassicism to Hugo's romantic theater and on to Eugène Scribe's "well-made" melodramas. Balletic narratives are generated in translation, from verbal librettos into nonverbal pantomimes. In the epoch of classicist ballets, most of the mime-enacted stories could be inferred from their titles, for example, Didelot's *Apollon et Daphné* or Noverre's *Jason et Médée*. In other words, in classicist ballets, narrative comprehension hinged on canonical foreknowledge, refreshed by a *livret* to be thumbed over shortly before the show.

As romantic and melodramatic plots replete with twists and turns came to upstage the déjà-vu aesthetics of classicist dramaturgy, foreknowledge devolved from an advantage to a spoiler. Thus Rappaport characterized Scribe's ballet-pantomime *La somnambule* as "a bit dull" (*skuchnovatyi*)—for the sole reason that its storyline was familiar from Vincenzo Bellini's opera *La sonnambula*.[104] Instead of being edifying and sublime, balletic plots were expected to be exciting and engaging.

A libretto, or *livret*—the very name used to refer to printed balletic programs nourished literary expectations. An indirect evidence of this comes from book-shelving practices. As we learn from an 1876 systematic inventory, in Glazunov's famed bookstore, ballet libretti used to be shelved not, as one might think, in the "Music, Singing, and Dance" section, where one would find Blasis's treatise on dance and the dance manual of Heinrich Cellarius, but rather in the "Theater" subsection of the section "Literature."[105] Yet it was precisely *literary* expectations that, in critics' opinion, the language of pantomime and dance failed to live up to. The vocabulary of mime was well suited to convey the limited set of classicist passions contained in the correspondingly limited repertoire of mythological, historical, and heroic plots; it was less capable of affording *intrigue*. As Théophile Gautier, the author of arguably the most perfect story ever enacted in ballet, described a run-of-the-mill libretto, "Nothing, but one situation after another."[106] That a story would dovetail with mime and dance as in Gautier's *Giselle* was rare. More typically, a nineteenth-century ballet libretto would be found either childishly thin or "purely anecdotal and decidedly impossible to comprehend without having read the program," Skalkovsky wrote in 1886 of Petipa and Alberto Vizentini's *King's Command* (*L'Ordre du Roi*).[107]

Changing along with dramatic fashions was the social and literary climate. As Russia approached the mid-nineteenth century, its erstwhile taste for lyric poetry gave way to the taste for socially charged journalism and sober prose. Imagine a reader raised on critical essays by Vissarion Belinsky and attuned to novels like Ivan Turgenev's *Fathers and Sons* (*Otsy i deti*) who, browsing the "Literature" shelf in Glazunov's Moscow bookstore chances on Saint-Léon's 1867 balletic reworking of Pushkin's "Tale of the Golden Fish" ("Skazka o zolotoi rybke"). In such a reader, ballet's question of questions—*How to express this with your feet?*—could elicit only one response: Why bother trying?

Indeed, the idea of a ballet telling a story without words generated the figure of the "candid," as opposed to the convention-savvy, spectator. Not unlike the eponymous hero of Voltaire's satire *Candide*, the candid observer is a literary mask used by authors and critics to de-normalize a social norm or un-conventionalize an artistic convention. When Saint-Léon set his balletic adaptation of Pushkin's "Golden Fish" in a Cossack village by the Dnipro River, he could hardly have concerned himself much with the question of how Petersburg ballet regulars might receive the spectacle of peasants dancing out their daily toils. Dancing, after all, is what draws ballet lovers to ballet. However, when Mikhail Saltykov-Shchedrin, a satirist and a critic of ballet (not to be confused with "a ballet critic") whose balletophobic philosophy I analyze in some detail in the next chapter of this book, wrote a tongue-in-cheek account of Saint-Léon's ballet, he began it precisely with the question "[W]hy are they dancing?" Ignoring the commonsense explanation ("because this is a ballet"), Shchedrin presents ballet's foundational convention as a form of social hypocrisy: "They are dancing because they are mending their nets, they are dancing because they are preparing the boat, they are dancing because they are villagers and, in this capacity, they *must* dance."[108]

Writing for ballet is always preaching to the choir, but a proper ballet libretto was expected, if only for decency's sake, to furnish a preemptive answer to the Why-all-this-dancing? question. The surest method was to spin your libretto around a character who is actually a dancer—a professional, as in *La Bayadère*, or an amateur, like Gautier's poor Giselle. Thus *Saltarello, or the Passion for Dance*, staged in Petersburg in 1859 by Saint-Léon after his own libretto, is about a ballet master (performed by Saint-Léon himself) enamored with no less than the Terpsichore of his dreams. Or take Petipa's 1865 libretto *Travelling Danseuse*, set in Spain. A gang of highwaymen stop a carriage, which turns out to belong to the famous danseuse Alma on her way to Seville. To cajole the robbers, she dances before them dressed as Sylphide. Meanwhile, Alma's valet Verra attempts to save *his* wallet by performing a maladroit character dance, which ends in what appears to be a travesty of *Giselle*'s tragic ending: like Giselle's lover, Albrecht, valet Verra drops dead of dancing fatigue. The next thing we see is Alma, having changed into a folk dress, perform a Spanish national dance. The robbers wind up disarmed by Alma's grace, and then (literally) by a posse of timely soldiers.[109] Not even Shchedrin could have called such dances unmotivated.

"Ballet masters spend months pondering the logical transitions between [i.e., rationales for] dances," Skalkovsky once said, in what sounds like an attempt to strengthen ballet's standing among dramatic arts.[110] It also sounds ("months") like an overstatement. Rather than lose time pondering, a librettist would normally resort to a stock motivation. When a ballet master like Petipa wanted to include a succession of sundry character and demi-character dances in a ballet like *Sleeping Beauty*, a stock solution would be to devote a whole act to a royal fête, with plenty of dancing on the menu to entertain the invitees (in reality, of course, the audience).

56 IMPOSSIBLE PROJECT

Notable among excuses to have a ballet character burst into dance was the setting of a dance class itself.[111] Take, for instance, "Danses de petits cygnes" from the last act of *Swan Lake* (not to be confused with the famous "Dance of the Little Swans" from Act 2). In twentieth-century versions of *Swan Lake*, the scene constitutes a stand-alone choreographic miniature, but according to the earlier, pantomime-heavy scenario, the cygnets dance because it happens to be time for their lakeside dance lesson, taught by their elder peers, the swan maidens who are thus amusing themselves while anxiously waiting for Odette to return to the lake.[112] The dance class setting was unique in its ability to serve both as narrative "cover" for a Terpsichorean display and as a way of laying bare ballet for ballet's sake—as in Bournonville's 1849 ballet *Le Conservatoire*.

When out of other options, a librettist would put a character to sleep— Petipa's signature device of importing unearthly characters into an earthly libretto. A proverbial dreamer, Petipa's Don Quixote falls asleep so that the public might enjoy variations featuring dryads and Cupid; Khudekov the librettist made the protagonist of *La Bayadère* an opium addict so that Petipa could stage the most beautiful pipe dream in the history of ballet: the *ballet blanc* in the Kingdom of the Shades.

To get a sense of ballet history's peculiar dynamics, we must keep in view its complementary manifestations: ballet as a project and a process. Ballet-the-project is how ballet emerges in contemporaneous ballet lore—now as a new-fledged *art imitateur*; now as a modernist experiment; now as an embodiment of music. Ballet-the-process, on the other hand, is how ballet functions on the ground. Again, the terms "project" and "process," as I use them, refer not to ballet's constituent parts but to its dynamically juxtaposed identities.

As follows from the evidence presented in this chapter, the project that defined ballet's dynamics in nineteenth-century Russia was Noverre's. As envisioned by Noverre, *ballet d'action* embodied a biunity of dance and drama authored and controlled by the enlightened ballet master, or, more precisely, the eighteenth-century idea thereof. The project prevailed but was transformed in the process. While Noverre's phraseology was holistic, its effect on the Russian world of ballet was polarizing. A rhetorical wedge was driven between the head and the feet. Instead of biunity, we witnessed a binary, an uneasy trade-off between narrative bits on the one hand and bursts of pure spectacle on the other, with narrative progress curbed by the evocation of another fête, another dream. Rather than support one another, dance and drama appeared to crowd each other out.

The crowding effect could be particularly frustrating when, from the mid-nineteenth century on, the Petersburg ballet stage tended to be monopolized by full-evening ballets. "Do not require your choreographers to stage three-hour-long ballets," Bournonville, the founder of Danish ballet, warned the Directorate when visiting the city in 1874, "or they'll be forced to [either] overstretch the mimic scenes, turning them into conversations between mutes, or over-satiate the public with entrées and ballabiles."[113] In other words, whether it was dancing or silent storytelling, three hours of one or the other was bound to be too much.

Petipa, the Man and the Machine

In Noverre's vision, enlightened ballet masters were to exercise authority over both dance and drama, stage and page. As we have seen, things did not work quite according to his plan. Dance as such, of course, remained the canonical province of choreographers, but even here their authority was not undivided. Noverre's disciple Didelot not only choreographed ballets but also, as we recall, preferred to school his dancers himself. While some of them (most famously Avdotia Istomina) evolved into balletic stars, classical ballet remained primarily an ensemble show. As, deeper into the nineteenth century, the success of a ballet grew increasingly dependent on individual ballerinas, so would the choice of pas and variations they performed. In Russia, the tipping point was Marie Taglioni's four-year tenure (1837–41) with the Imperial Theaters. Part of her triumph here, it was felt, was that she arrived in Russia armed with a set of ballets hand-tailored for her by her father, the renowned choreographer Filippo Taglioni. This changed the whole understanding of who was in charge on the balletic stage. As Pleshcheev would summarize these developments fifty years later, "Didelot was creating performers for his ballets, not ballets for his performers; Didelot's success was his own success, while the success of the undoubtedly talented Taglioni was, in essence, his daughter's success."[114]

In the wake of Taglioni's visit, family tandems of various kinds became a widespread practice in European ballet. Taglioni père became his daughter's choreographer, agent, and beneficiary; Petipa, at one point, relied on the success of his wife, ballerina Maria Petipa (née Surovshchikova) to boost his career as a choreographer. Just as important, in subsequent years Petipa would often retrofit his own choreographic ideas to the needs and abilities of a ballerina he happened to be working with (or, rather, for).

This development cast doubt on the choreographic text's stability, even its very existence. When, for simplicity's sake, we categorize choreography as a "text," we already overstate its consistency. "O body swayed to music, O brightening glance, / How can we know the dancer from the dance?" To put it in terms of Yeats's iconic lines, no dancer, unless she is a mechanical doll, ever goes through the same movements the same way. And how can we speak of choreographic stability or balletic texts when, to rephrase Pleshcheev's elegant chiasmus, it was ballets that were now adapted to their performer, not the other way around?

Indeed, during this reign of ballerinas, ballets were not just staged but often were written with a specific ballerina and her strengths in mind. A dancer who was a good mime would be given more drama; a good dance technician, more dances; and if elevation happened to be her forte, then the libretto would typically gain an extra fantasy scene (balletic fantasies being associated with leaps and flying). One reviewer, for instance, faulted Saint-Léon for not writing a ballet purpose-built to exploit the dramatic talents of the aging and plumping Carolina Rosati.[115] The pliability requirement could be applied to the music text as well. Skalkovsky wrote, "When writing music for solos, ballet composers are obligated to shape it according to [the particular features of the ballerina]."[116]

The stage life of any ballet is always a story of continuity and change, the latter driven predominantly by the needs and wishes of its next performer. Dance numbers, written anew or transposed from other ballets, would be inserted or removed together with their music; parts and variations simplified or complicated, depending on the ballerina's or even a soloist's technical prowess. In theory, ballets still justified themselves by having a dramatic unity; in practice, they looked more and more like a performance piece or variety show.

This was equally true of the lifespan of individual ballets and Russian ballet under Petipa as a whole. Well known for his flexibility both with the Directorate and with dancers, Petipa, Vazem recalls, would greet a ballerina by asking what kind of variation she "desired to dance."[117] Vazem's evidence is anecdotal, of course, but there does exist a corroborating document. In a letter from Petipa to Petr Tchaikovsky on the latter's score for *Sleeping Beauty*, the ballet master gives the composer a detailed set of desiderata, such as "No 8. *Pas de deux*. Aurora and Désiré. For their entrance, thirty-two b[ars] of brilliant music in 6/8. A rather large *adagio* with *fortes* and with pauses." On the same page, below the "variation for the male dancer," described at the same level of precision, we find the following telltale placeholder: "Variation for the *danseuse*. (For the present, don't compose it. I must speak with the *danseuse*.)"[118]

As a result, it sometimes happened that different ballerinas, dancing the same part in the same season, would be performing different variations. Compositionally, the true product of Petipa's choreography was not so much a specific ballet as the specific evening, with its specific performers and revenue. The module unit of choreography was thus not a ballet but rather a pas (a dance sequence of varying length, from a short variation to a grand pas) that would migrate from one performance to another, irrespective of the ballet performed. Ballet masters' authority over choreography further eroded as ballerinas and soloists did not hesitate to invent on their own or borrow from others a pas they found to their liking. A telling example of this is Petipa's restaging of *Paquita* for Zucchi, splendidly anatomized in a review by Skalkovsky:

> This old ballet, honorably present on the local stage for forty years now, under the influence of Zucchi has been rejuvenated and made all the more engaging. Apparently, Zucchi has been short of time or was perhaps unwilling to master the dances of *Paquita*. What she has mastered is only the mimics and the [character dance] Cachucha from Act Two. As to variations, Zucchi has replaced those from the first act with her old variation on the Feuilleton-Waltz by Strauss. In Act Three, she conferred the ballerina's grand finale pas to M-me Nikitina, leaving to herself the pas de deux performed with [Pavel] Gerdt, and a semblance of the mazurka.[119]

While never claiming authorship of pas or variations, dancers were serious about their ownership. Typically, a ballerina would be in charge of a number of choreographic variations, complete with corresponding musical scores, marked by her name as their proprietor. Thus many a music sheet in Evgenia Sokolova's archival papers at the Theater Museum in Petersburg bear the heading "Variation pour m-lle [So-and-So]," but not necessarily any indication as to which ballet this had been written for; some variations were prepared just in case.

60　IMPOSSIBLE PROJECT

It was customary among ballerinas (especially former ballerinas) to lend their variations to others. When, for instance, Olga Preobrajenska debuted in 1899 in *The Pharaoh's Daughter*, critics as a matter of fact noted that her performance as Ramzea included a variation from *Roxana, the Beauty of Montenegro* initially composed for Sokolova (her coach at the time).[120] It did happen, however, that ballerinas grew too possessive of their pas to readily share them with others. Matilda Kschessinska, for instance, is known to have instructed Riccardo Drigo and Petipa to excise all her personal variations from the music-cum-choreographic repertoire available to any other ballerina; both composer and choreographer complied, since she had paid them to produce these variations.[121]

At one point, the Directorate of Imperial Theaters had to issue a ban on ballerinas monopolizing a ballet. Regardless, the clout ballerinas like Kschessinska enjoyed at court often outshone that of court-appointed Directorate heads like Prince Sergei Volkonsky or Colonel Vladimir Teliakovsky. Upon retiring from the Mariinsky (and thus technically ceding her ballets to others), Kschessinska saw to it that a ballet courier removed every sheet with "her" variations from the orchestra's music stands before her successor could step on. As we learn from his diary, Teliakovsky was furious—not because the ballet's wholeness was so important to him but because the rights for the missing music belonged to the Directorate.[122]

Backstage anecdotes like this can provide a view on ballet that is usefully different from what we see from the front door. The phrase "classical ballet" conjures a clockwork-perfect gala text, carved in the ivory of flying tutus. And in a sense, this image is an accurate one—but only from one perspective. From another, classical ballet, when it wasn't yet *classical*, was always a makeshift affair, its parts and pas bound together and timed but loosely. Just *how* loosely, we learn from Fokine. His memoir, written in the 1930s, includes a vivid description of a choreographic composition of the kind Petipa would have him, a fresh-from-school danseur, and the then-young soloist Anna Pavlova, perform whenever the opportunity presented itself. "The choreography for these," recalls Fokine, "we mostly staged ourselves. In a sense they cannot be labeled as compositions at all. We did whatever we felt we could do best. I did high jumps and Pavlova pirouettes."[123]

These were one-size-fits-all kinds of pas de deux, uncommitted to a specific score or story. "There was no connection whatsoever between our 'number' and the ballet into which it was inserted. Neither was there any connection with the music." The "choreography" had to be coordinated on

THE SHADOW OF NOVERRE 61

the fly. "We began one adagio when the music began, and finished when the music came to an end," writes Fokine.

> The interval between the beginning and the end was spent in carefree floating, totally disregarding the musical phrasing. During such a *pas de deux*, Pavlova would say to me, "Take it easy, we still have a great deal of music left," or "Hurry, hurry!"—whichever the case might be. . . . Towards the end of such an adagio we would invariably walk downstage, always in the center, she on her toes with her eye fixed on the conductor and I following behind with my eyes focused on her waist, my arms and hands prepared for the 'catch.' At this moment she would often say: 'Don't forget to push.' To push meant—when a danseuse made one and a half spins on pointe, her partner had to propel her with one hand for her to complete the second spin.[124]

As this variation neared its finale, each participant's attention was on the conductor's baton—the musicians following it from the pit, Pavlova from the stage. For his part, the conductor would fix his eyes on the ballerina. "The orchestra, at this moment, usually provided the tremolo, which the conductor, Riccardo Drigo, held while Pavlova was finding her balance," recalls Fokine. "Now she would find it and spin. . . . I would give her the promised push. . . . Drigo would swing his baton. . . . The boom of a final drumbeat . . . and we would be very happy, frozen in a final pose."[125] So while it is often said that dancers dance to music, a ballet conductor might add "and vice versa."

Fokine's account, to be sure, is meant to deride the seat-of-the-pants nature of ballet-making under Petipa. In the chapter "Birth of a Choreographer," Fokine reminds the reader that, on *his* watch, whether he staged at the Mariinsky or for Diaghilev, every little movement would be decided by *him*, not a dancer: "I should like to emphasize the inadmissibility of improvisation in my ballets." No ballerina, not even Olga Preobrajenska, with all her mastery and standing, would be allowed to disrupt the ballet master's idea of the whole. "To me a ballet is a complete creation and not a series of numbers, and each part is connected with the others."[126]

Thirty years after the fact, Fokine still begrudged Preobrajenska an ad-lib exit in *Les Sylphides*. At the end of her variation, she was supposed to freeze on toes, "facing the audience as if imploring the orchestra to play still more softly." Instead, to Fokine's chagrin, she "left the stage on toes, in the same manner as Pavlova was to do immediately after her. Of course, her improvisation did not help Pavlova, or the ballet as a whole."[127]

62 IMPOSSIBLE PROJECT

No one disputes an author's authority over their text. Fokine, like Noverre and Didelot before him, understood the dance as a pre-embodied text—something a dancer could either perform or misperform. Few poets would leave it uncorrected if, during composition, a slip of their pen had yielded, say, a tautological rhyme instead of a true one. Preobrajenska's unplanned sur-les-pointes exit had likewise produced a tautological (hence unwanted) rhyme with Pavlova's preplanned one.

Ballet historians, however, are not obliged to follow Fokine, to prioritize *his* understanding of authorship over Petipa's willingness to "speak with the danseuse." The dancer is not a pen, nor is a dancer's exit a rhyming line in a poet's manuscript. Petipa, like Balanchine after him, would rather tailor a ballet to a danseuse than curtail her creative initiative and freedom. For them, the dance, and ballet at large, was a work to be co-authored and co-created in real time. Pavlova signals to Fokine to give her an extra spin; Drigo gestures to the orchestra to hold the tremolo till Pavlova finds her balance. Each variation is a real-time process of mutual matching—among the dancers, and between the dancers and the music. To those who dance, the dance is not *the* but *a* dance, each time spun anew.

No one understood this better than Petipa. When, with a straight face, he would have a ballet character yet again fall asleep, or would arrange yet another diegetic royal fête as pretext for the latest extranarrative assortment of dances; or when he'd simply have Fokine and Pavlova perform their adagios for no rhyme or reason—the excuse or lack thereof may have seemed nonsensical to a haughty Noverrian or an impatient democratic critic. But as far as Petipa was concerned, what really mattered was not how well the stitches looked but how well they held. The more barebones the plot, the better it covered bare dances.

Stitching and piecing together was also how Petipa shaped the company's repertoire and choreography. What variations would be included in a given ballet was a matter of negotiation, contention, and concessions on the part of the ballet master and the show's ballerina. What ballet to stage next was decided between Petipa and the current director of the Imperial Theaters, and what that next ballet should look like had to do with Petipa's current target audience: the critics and public (and via the latter, the Directorate). The ideal ballet master dreamed up by Noverre and Didelot was to be a well-read cultural giant, an *auteur* with a vision and full command of every aspect of the show. By contrast, Petipa fashioned for himself the image of ballet master not as a man of letters but a man of *process*. His mission, albeit never stated

THE SHADOW OF NOVERRE   63

so starkly, was to see ballet survive. And it did, even if barely, with Petipa at the helm.

Saving Ballet

In dance scholarship, we mostly rely on written evidence, found in critical reviews and memoirs penned by choreographers and dancers. As ballet historians, we must also be mindful of a third, more elusive but no less vital coordinate: the public. While ballet masters and critics campaigned for the elevation of dance's status to that of art and drama, the public voted with their feet—and *for* feet. "The majority among our public prefer dances to mimics," Mavrikii Rappaport complained in 1859; by the same token, upbeat character dances were deemed more popular than the classical pas, and acrobatic technique more than the classical style.[128] In other words, the popular and critical conceptions of ballet were inverted mirror images of one another.

This was a duality to reckon with, and ballet masters like Petipa struggled to navigate between the exigencies of balletic economy and the model imposed by the imperial stage. One day Petipa would thunder at the commercialism of the Moscow ballet ("You people are striving to squeeze into a ballet as many dances as you can without asking what fits and what does not, which results in a divertissement instead of an artistic whole"),[129] but every evening after every ballet performance in St. Petersburg, he would sit down and copy booking revenues into his diary. Not that any of that money went directly to him, but the Directorate of Imperial Theaters, albeit charged from the 1880s on primarily with ensuring its productions were "model" ones, was also keen to return some of the funds allotted to ballet. And revenues were not always convincing.

The image of the nineteenth-century Imperial Ballet as a bastion of prosperity was largely shaped in retrospect, at a time when many balletic careers, whether in Soviet Russia or emigration, were falling into disarray.[130] Unshakeable and monumental as it may have seemed from the twentieth-century perspective, ballet's institutional edifice in the epoch of Petipa was from time to time balancing on the verge of cultural and financial collapse. For all the efforts to dramatize and sanitize ballet, its cultural prestige could not match that of opera or legitimate stage; besides, in the opinion of liberal intellectuals, and for that matter of the very Directorate of Imperial

64   IMPOSSIBLE PROJECT

Theaters that had oversight of ballet, short-skirt classical dances bordered on licentiousness. Over the latter half of the century, ballet shows on the St. Petersburg imperial stage decreased from three to two a week (Sundays and Wednesdays) and, for some time, even to Sundays only.[131]

Ironically, the epoch remembered for *Swan Lake*, *Sleeping Beauty*, and other balletic triumphs was also when ballet's worthwhileness, and for that matter its very right to exist, would now and again be called into question. Is ballet economically viable and competitive enough to survive on the multigenre and multilingual imperial stage? Is ballet, as a medium, ideologically desirable? Such questions would be aired in the press, with discussants' criteria shifting from fiscal to pragmatic, and from liberal to nationalistic. Why pay to see ballets at all, a journalist wrote in the *News*, when balletic plots are mostly "tangled and vapid, unnatural, banal. The theater arts are nowadays striving for a healthy realism. Indeed, what kind of reform can there be in balletic dramaturgy? Imagine a ballet based on *Woe from Wit*." Then, in the same breath: "[T]he art of dance is not in keeping with the Russian national spirit and is out of tune with the Russian character."[132] And, art aside, ballet is a money-loser, creating a large deficit in the Imperial Theaters' budget.

On such occasions, balletomanes like Skalkovsky would object, "A government that pays for ballet from the Imperial Treasury should not be expecting ballet to bring a profit."[133] Moreover, "[t]he significance of ballet does not boil down to those ballet-only productions that are still shown on Sundays; dances are necessary for operas . . . [and] dances are met with in dramas, too." At this point, Skalkovsky's argument seems to echo the reasoning Louis XIV gave in his edict establishing the Académie Royale de Danse. "Ballet," pontificates Skalkovsky, "cultivates those dance teachers who, passing on their knowledge, teach Russia's respectable society how to walk, bow, and dance . . . for in the sphere of life, noble manners are no less significant than other virtues."[134] Notably, Skalkovsky's reference to ballets being "still" shown on Sundays indicates that he did not rule out the possibility that ballet-only evenings might not survive at all. Tellingly, his piece was titled "On the Issue of the Abolishment of Ballet."

No balletomane would have surrendered their art without a fight. What do we gain and lose if we let go of ballet as a self-sufficient unit? Even if stripped of financing and deserted by the public, Skalkovsky reasons, ballet would survive as a sideshow to opera. As a stand-alone spectacle, ballet had grown out of the early nineteenth-century opera and could easily grow back into it—as indeed was occurring elsewhere in Europe, in particular in tone-setting Paris. "Are they really planning to follow the Paris example and do away with ballet as a whole, leaving dance only as inserts into operas?"[135]

The balletic troupe would remain in full service (since operas ran more often than ballets, dancers tended to appear in opera productions more frequently anyway), but Skalkovsky warned, "[W]hat we are bound to lose is our [classical] choreographic school. Operas have little use for anything but groups and character dances, neither of which requires much training. In Paris, for instance, *les figurantes* for a group are recruited in the streets, the only requirement being that they have a shapely physique. And the moment our artists stop exercising in mimics and classical dance, you can say farewell to ballet. Our choreographic school is rightly considered Europe's best. . . . Along with the decline in dance teaching, [our] unique school will perish and the tradition will die."[136]

In the face of the doomsday scenario laid out here (at greater length than just this representative passage), Skalkovsky marshals an argument that in modern economics and psychology would fall under the "sunk cost fallacy." It has taken thirty years, that is, for Didelot's rod to beat our native *Mashkas* and *Matryoshkas* (lower-class girls) into the Zephyrs and Amours of the stage.[137] If the ballet is abolished, the decades of skills and labor invested in shaping classical dance are gone too, and our recruiters may as well just walk the streets, scouting for ladies with pretty legs.

Whatever the attention ultimately paid to Skalkovsky's argument, ballet was never banished from nineteenth-century Russian stages. The cost "sunk" into the classical school indeed loomed large. In the aftermath of October 1917, the existence of ballet (that "landowners' art," *pomeshchichie iskusstvo*, as Lenin once called it) would be at risk once more—but again, the sunk-cost argument won the day. Petipa's ballets, albeit refashioned, lived on at the Mariinsky (soon the Kirov) and Bolshoi theaters. As to the school, it was entrusted to Agrippina Vaganova, a disciplinarian worthy of Didelot.

The Old and the New

Skalkovsky had a point when he wrote that Zucchi's choreographic inserts and ad libs "rejuvenated [*Paquita*] and made [it] all the more engaging." The leeway that ballet masters gave dancers for private variations was a resource of novelty—a property the nineteenth-century public and critics expected

66 IMPOSSIBLE PROJECT

every ballet to possess. To the modern observer, oldness—vintage choreography, hoary stories—is the very thing that makes classical ballet classical. In the nineteenth century, by contrast, ballet was seen more as a spectacle than a museum piece.

Spectacles utterly *require* novelty, but this could be expensive. A truly *new* ballet would have to have a new story, clad in new choreography and performed by new dancers. In the real world, this seldom happened. A new story would have to be commissioned, a new set built, new costumes sewn; a rare director would endorse such production costs.

There was, however, a venerable workaround. Long-forgotten ballets, when staged anew, were known to do the trick. To be regarded as new, a ballet had, at minimum, to boast new pas or showcase new dancers (Skalkovsky: "The ballet passed for new because its performers were unfamiliar")[138] or feature modern-day visual effects and acoustic amenities (Skalkovsky again, writing in 1872: "Ballets have benefited greatly from developments in chemistry, physics, and music, from being more favorably lit, nicer colored and more felicitous as far as orchestration").[139]

Ironically, the pursuit of novelty at all costs made the balletic repertoire not diverse but monotonous. In financial terms, the main trade-off was production cost versus stage longevity. For a spectacle to pay off, it had to run fifty to a hundred times. Once it became clear that balletic "feasts for public eyes" had a longer stage-life expectancy than the traditional alternative, the Directorate began privileging lavish spectacles, staged to last—unlike the "economical" ballets endorsed in the 1870s under the administration of Karl Kister. As part of the new policy implemented in the 1880s, libretto authors would be offered a flat fee (up to 300 rubles) on the condition that the product would be fully owned by the Directorate; librettists would receive no per-performance bonus, as was customary for dramatic playwrights.[140] The plan was to invest in ballets that promised to become permanent repertoire fixtures.

As a result, ballets began gaining in size and shrinking in number. In the span of the 1891–92 season, for instance, only thirteen different ballets were shown on the Mariinsky stage, the sumptuous *Tsar Kandavl* (*Le Roi Candaule*) and *Sleeping Beauty* far ahead of the others in frequency of shows.[141] In the same season, titles in the repertoire of the Alexandrinsky Theater (the drama branch of the Imperial Theaters in St. Petersburg) numbered eighty-one—over six times more.[142] In other words, in terms of repertoire, by the end of the century the spoken drama and ballet were heading

THE SHADOW OF NOVERRE   67

in opposite directions: the former toward diversity, topicality, and turnover; the latter toward monumentality, stability, and, let's face it, stagnation.

The "new economic policy" had two notable corollaries: ballet's augmentation and segmentation. On the one hand, a grand ballet for the entire evening became standard. "They have taken to the habit nowadays of producing one grand ballet every year, all of them following the same hackneyed pattern," Skalkovsky complained. "What a difference . . . from the [eighteen-] twenties, the years when the Petersburg ballet used to be insanely popular. Aside from fantastic ballets, you'd be offered balletic operas and vaudevilles, mimic dramas, and sundry divertissements: patriotic, mythological, folksy."[143]

On the other hand, the growth of balletic form came at the cost of its internal integrity. Compare the two-act 1841 *Giselle*, following a simple story and the simple formula of all romantic ballets (first act earthly, second supernatural), with the full-length 1890 *Sleeping Beauty* (three acts and a prologue), with its handful of dramatic scenes sprinkled amid a great deal of loosely motivated dances—usually in some diegetic ball or festivity implanted in every act. The only balletic form to dovetail well with the grand-ballet format were so-called *benefisy*, benefit evenings, typically compiled by (or for) a dancer from their appearances in a number of different ballets. The public loved these and was not put off by the typically higher ticket prices. Whether a grand ballet or *benefis*, the full-evening format was, quintessentially, a balletic potpourri.

The notion of classical repertoire—every modern-day balletomane's Baedeker to the land of nineteenth-century ballet—did not in fact exist in that same nineteenth century. Today we value classical ballet *because* it's classical, a treasure of world culture, but the nineteenth-century balletomane would probably find our attitude toward the ballet of their time sentimental and overly preoccupied with cultural legacy. For them, ballet was all about spectacle, hence about novelty. The Directorate was typically keen to revive old ballets (a chance to reuse old sets and costumes), but in the eyes of the public and critics the only justification for a revival was to enjoy a new dancer or dances—even at the expense of losing the last vestiges of a plotline.

For example, to us, titles like *Esmeralda* and *Giselle* seem iconic; questioning their restaging sounds as strange as asking why one might care to revisit St. Petersburg or Venice. But as late as 1901, renewals of the old fueled Skalkovsky's fear for ballet's future: "It is unacceptable that in the twentieth century, we still treat the public to such ramshackle affair [*rukhliad'*] as

68   IMPOSSIBLE PROJECT

Giselle and *Esmeralda*, each of which is sixty years old. . . . [If this goes on], grand ballet will cease to exist."[144] For us, there is no ballet without *Giselle*; for the contemporary critic, another *Giselle*, and ballet is over.

Skalkovsky's worry was hardly his alone. In the moving mirror of contemporary opinion, the history of ballet in Russia looks like a perpetually imminent disaster, ever postponed by some last-minute rescue. All goes well under Didelot; after Didelot (was) retired, it was no longer ballets but rather ballerinas that saved ballet: Taglioni and Fanny Elsler in the 1840s; Maria Petipa and Marfa Muravieva in the 1860s; Zucchi in the 1880s, followed by a host of other Italian *virtuozki*. The triumph of foreign dancing stars, from whom homegrown dancers were supposed to learn, meant the burgeoning of dance and the thinning of plots—a tendency that, to those who would see ballet rise to the status of "serious" art, spelled yet another crisis. The Petersburg Ballet spent most of these years under Marius Petipa, whose cultural physiognomy, artistic strategies, and bureaucratic acumen were largely shaped by the purported shakiness of ballet as an institution in this period— and, not least, by his status as a contract foreigner at the imperial court (he became a Russian citizen only in 1894, at the age of 76).

Two points on the timeline seem to chart the fate of ballet in Russia. In 1760, Noverre spoke of serious and heroic dance that rises to the level of tragedy. In 1902, the essayist Dmitrii Filosofov—despite his closeness to Diaghilev, hardly an implacable devotee of ballet—wrote with a sense of surprise, "What could be more insignificant and even, from the standpoint of the progressive intelligentsia, more stupid than the story of some *Bluebeard* or *Raymonda*? . . . Yet in practice it turns out that all this cute nonsense [*milaia chepukha*] is . . . necessary, if Gerdt is to shine his art upon us."[145] In Noverre's plan, the dancer's feet would serve a noble plot; what Filosofov found a century and a half later was a joke of a plot in the service of a great performer. The "nonsense" being its only life support, even balletomanes were surprised ballet was still around.

Noverre's idea of serious pantomimic drama as central to ballet remained an all but official creed until the advent of modernism, but in practice, ballet people had effectively given up on it around the mid-nineteenth century. Step by step, balletic stories about heroic passions were replaced by dance after dance spun around a fairy tale or gallant stylizations. Overloaded with dances, ballets were bursting at their dramatic seams.

All the same, for the enlightened ballet-goer, having a strong dramatic plot remained ballet's raison d'être. Plots that would barely stitch dances together were, from the standpoint of intellectuals like Filosofov, a sign of ballet's

THE SHADOW OF NOVERRE   69

lapsing into its second childhood. Balletic stories became a byword for triviality, to the point of being parodied in vaudeville verses. Petipa's "epoch of masterpieces"—*Swan Lake, Sleeping Beauty, Raymonda*—was also that of ballet's identity crisis. To be a ballet master in times like this meant to be in the crossfire. In words, Petipa sounded as dismissive of "Italian trickery" as any high-minded balletomane; in deeds, his ballets proved tailor-made for the masterful footwork of Italian ballerinas, to whom he gave the freedom of inserting any variation they liked. It was under Petipa that the pointe gained the upper hand over plot.

Where others saw a clash between the foot and the head, Petipa was at a strange (for this period) peace. Amid the conflict, this choreographer-in-chief was likewise in charge of constantly sorting things out. The Imperial Ballet was a machine, meant to steadily produce a certain annual quota of ensembles and solos, dreams and festivities, and if the machine ran smoothly, Petipa's contract would be renewed at as steady a pace. (As a foreigner, his contract with the Directorate had to be periodically reviewed and confirmed.) The Directorate, the troupe, and critics alike valued Petipa as a diligent (even workaholic) professional who would never attempt to think outside the box of his canonical job description.

The enormous staff Petipa oversaw (dancers alone numbered over two hundred) made him a manager-cum-choreographer; a practitioner more than philosopher of dance, he knew all too well that choreography is a matter of manifold "moving parts."[146] And despite the ostensible precarity of his contract position, he succeeded in making himself indispensable. "In the theatre Petipa was a dictator in the literal sense," Aleksandr Shiriaev remembers almost admiringly. "The production of new ballets, the repertoire, the service of dancers, the distribution of roles between the principal dancers (I am not speaking here of the smaller parts)—all these questions were resolved exclusively by the first *maître de ballet* [Petipa]."[147] On the other hand, rumors of this enlightened despot's nepotism and role-mongering cast a shadow on his career and occasionally spilled over into the press.[148]

The Imperial Ballet was not an easy company to oversee, but Petipa had no interest in assistance. When at one point the then-director of Imperial Theaters, Ivan Vsevolozhsky, came up with the idea of instituting a "staging council," to bring together the librettist, composer, set designer, and choreographer of nascent productions, Petipa exploded in an (unsent) angry letter requesting for himself the status of "absolute overlord."[149] His conception of the ballet *master* was decidedly authoritarian.

70 IMPOSSIBLE PROJECT

This might lead us, when approaching Petipa's ballets retrospectively, to treat them as works of an *auteur*, as if an entire ballet fully emerged from his head, from libretto to last variation. But Petipa's ballets are more interesting than that. First of all, despite choreographer Petipa's status as a submechanism of sorts in the vast imperial machine, the final products that were his ballets were *man-made*. Second, Petipa would often retrofit his own choreographic inventions into the works of his choreographic contemporaries and predecessors. Third, as mentioned, Petipa would willingly open his ballets to any time-tested variation his newest ballerina brought in her wake.

Judged according to *auteur* logic, Petipa was an opportunist, but such logic may be too narrow a fit for the complex dynamics of nineteenth-century ballet, and Petipa's ballets specifically. The very notion of authorship, understood as the formation of a text per individual design, presupposes that text's immutability. But in Petipa's view, the balletic text is infinitely mutable and constantly in flux, and this is what keeps it alive.

Whether a ballet's road to longevity—even immortality—lay through textualizing its choreography has been debated throughout ballet's history to this day.[150] The question would often arise in discussions of dance notation projects. Recent revivals based on Nikolai Sergeev's transcripts of Petipa's ballets deservedly elicit our interest. But not all ballet masters of the past believed in the promise of notation. Noverre, for instance, had his reservations. And when the Directorate of Imperial Theaters requested Petipa's expert opinion of Stepanov's system of dance notation, the 1895 memo our ballet master wrote in response seems skeptical. Here Petipa defends the choreographer's right to interfere with choreographic tradition—or, for that matter, with ballet's musical text, the very score. If a ballet staged a century ago is still popular with dancers and the public, this attests not to its stability but to its susceptibility to change: "In their revivals of old ballets, ballet masters of talent will always shape dances according to their fancy, their aptitude, and the public taste peculiar to their epoch; never will any of them waste time and effort on copying what others did in the olden days. Note that Mr. Taglioni in his revival of [Jean Dauberval's] *La Fille mal gardée* (The Wayward Daughter) has replaced all the original dances with new ones, and added a new music score composed by Hertel. Each time I revive an old ballet, I, too, change it."[151]

Petipa had a point. The pastiche of catchy tunes that Dauberval used as a score when *La Fille mal gardée* was first shown in Bordeaux in 1789 would hardly suit Paul Taglioni's Berlin revival of it in 1864; a new score was commissioned from Peter Ludwig Hertel. Neither would a self-respecting ballet master like Taglioni or Petipa seriously consider restoring dances as performed in the eighteenth-century version of a ballet. In the nineteenth century, tastes in choreography were less attuned to vintage values than they have grown to be today.

Mal gardée indeed—to apply the eponymous phrase to Taglioni's "wayward" handling of Dauberval's ballet. Migrating from one revival to another (there were many) was but a skeleton of a story—a folksy farce about Lise and her secret beau, Colin, outsmarting Lise's prudish mother. The rest of it—more precisely, the balletic core of it—was each time restaged from scratch.

As described by Petipa, Paul Taglioni's revival of Dauberval's comic ballet emerges as an act of re-authoring. Which it no doubt was. But a question remains: which parts of this particular revival had to do with "asserting one's authorial vision" (our default understanding of authorship today) and which were perhaps dictated by circumstances or customary ways of problem-solving? Let's say, for argument's sake, that a "ballet master of talent," as Petipa categorizes Taglioni in his memo, would prefer to commission a new score for *La Fille* from a composer of equal talent, and let's say he had someone more prominent than Hertel in mind. But on the other hand, Hertel was a resident dance composer with the Berlin Court Opera, of which Taglioni was ballet master. To compose a score for a ballet, moreover, was not the sort of thing one requested of a composer with a big name. Not in 1864.

In Petipa's own revivals, too, it is not easy to tell where creativity ends and exigency begins. Reviving a ballet always entailed transposing it in time and space. The kind of troupe one had here and now (as opposed to *back there and then*), the available sets and costumes one would hope to repurpose, the set of stock choreographic variations begging to be performed—these and other resources at hand would claim authorship no less insistently than Petipa's creative genius.

To take another example: when in 1885, the Directorate of Imperial Theaters resolved to invite Zucchi to dance on its stage in St. Petersburg, the initial plan was to revive, for her debut, Taglioni's *La Fille mal gardée*, in which Zucchi had made her triumphant debut in Berlin nine years earlier. The revival was scheduled for December 1, 1885. It so happened, however, that Evgenia Sokolova, slated to appear in *The Pharaoh's Daughter* on November 20, fell ill, and Zucchi was asked to jump in. "Zucchi showed up, and pulled off a tour de force she alone is capable of," Skalkovsky reports.

72 IMPOSSIBLE PROJECT

"Within a fortnight, she managed to master a mammoth ballet in nine scenes, one of the largest and most difficult choreographic works ever composed."[152]

This also meant that less time was left to prepare the revival of *La Fille mal gardée*, now redefined as a benefit performance to honor Pavel Gerdt's twenty-fifth anniversary on stage. Gerdt was remembered as Colin from an earlier (1854) version of *La Fille* staged in Petersburg by Jules Perrot. Co-staged by Petipa and Lev Ivanov, the 1885 revival of *La Fille* to Hertel's score bore many a footprint—Zucchi's, from the Taglioni-staged Berlin version, plus Gerdt's from the Petersburg version staged by Perrot. The revival also included a number of new dances staged by Petipa to Ludwig Minkus's music. Crowning it all was a number from the Italian star's own performing portfolio. "To enhance the choreographic element," Skalkovsky says in his review, "Mme. Zucchi has interpolated a pas de deux she performs with Mr. Gerdt, truly a masterpiece of choreographic art,"[153] to a tune Pleshcheev identifies as Vincenzo Robaudi's love song "Alla stella confidente."[154] This is how Skalkovsky describes it: "With amazing purity and agility did the artiste perform the most difficult pas on pointe, namely pas fouetté; having completed two tours, she would end the third one tilting over the arms of the danseur, maintain balance in what would seem impossible attitudes, and conclude with an aerial flight alighting right into Mr. Gerdt's arms."[155]

So much for the question of authorship and the coveted longevity of ballet. In theory, Petipa understood authorship as the choreographer's freedom to innovate, hence the mixed feelings he had about capturing dance in notation. (Ironically, the twenty-first-century—that is, post-Soviet and post-Balanchine—rediscovery and canonization of Petipa as choreographic *auteur* is owed precisely to the discovery and staging of certain notations of *his* productions, including segments of *La Fille mal gardée*.) But in practice, as we just saw, considerations of innovation and originality never kept Petipa from resorting to various time-proven hits, whether from his own, Zucchi's, or Gerdt's portfolio of pas. In Petipa's revivals, the question of authorship was not a matter of what was new and what belonged to whom. Names loomed large on a poster or playbill, but on the ground, authoring a ballet meant coming to grips with ballet as a machine, which, every now and then, turned out another sausage.

Authorship was crucial, if understood differently, in the epochs before and after Petipa, that is, in the ages of neoclassicism and modernism. In the latter—the time of Nijinsky and Balanchine—authorship was mostly about otherness, about choreographic idiosyncrasies of style; in the former, the

THE SHADOW OF NOVERRE 73

time of Voltaire and Noverre, it was mainly about *books*, and it was hardly by chance that Nelidova, writing in 1894, portrayed the ballet master of yore as a "living book," a repository of all the knowledge needed for stage and school: "[H]e combined in himself a teacher, dancer, poet, artist, and musician; led the school and the ballet; his firm hand set the art [of ballet] on its destined path." Nowadays, Nelidova continued, the "living book" ballet master has become a legend of the past. "Today's ballet master (*maître de ballet*, meaning the manager or boss of ballets) is mostly a stage-producer of ballets, oftentimes a mere functionary, an administrative unit, or a *régisseur* of sorts. This is why ballet people can do so easily without a director, and even more so without a ballet master."[156]

Nelidova's description might seem unflattering, had this not been precisely how Petipa wished to be seen: with a low profile, and without pretensions to cultural status. Petipa was no Didelot, who would choreograph a Pushkin poem the moment it appeared, and would, in turn, be mentioned and footnoted by Pushkin as a genuine poet of ballet. Petipa, on the contrary, flaunted his poor Russian and his indifference to things nonballetic. But for all his low-keyness, Petipa had ways of getting things done, both on and off the stage.

One of Petipa's ways of getting the Directorate's ear was to use the press; confiding to a journalist that he never wasted time on copying dances and would always invent an old ballet anew would signal to higher-ups that his efforts could be better compensated, for instance, by paying royalties for choreography and librettos, and throwing in, perhaps, a bonus for every show.

Petipa's open ignorance of Russian culture mirrored Russian culture's own obliviousness to him, and its growing indifference to anything ballet-related. This attitude did not change even when, after the last of ballet's salaried composers had retired, the Directorate decided, from then on, to outsource its music to Russian (and preferably nonballetic) composers—a policy that resulted in Tchaikovsky and Glazunov writing for ballet. And yet, for all Tchaikovsky's reputation as a musician and the Mariinsky dancers' renown as the best-schooled ballet troupe in Europe, and for that matter amid still-impressive box-office receipts—for all of that, ballet's cultural reputation remained, at best, that of "an enchanting, fanciful relic of olden days, a delicate fragile thing to be cherished in a museum."[157]

Viewed from the inside, ballet's future looked more catastrophic than it eventually proved to be. By the dawn of the twentieth century, everyone, from Imperial Theaters head Vladimir Teliakovsky (who detested ballet and

74 IMPOSSIBLE PROJECT

repeatedly called for its elimination) to the last diehard balletomane, was convinced of ballet's moribundity. In 1908, Aleksandr Benois made a prediction to this effect that, however, history would be quick to refute: "You know how devoted I am to ballet, but I must confess that its present existence looks to me like a misunderstanding, or an outright *miracle*. How does this subtle, purely aristocratic toy [*zabava*] relate to all the 'serious' questions posed by our epoch? Has it anything to do with things democratic and social? Our ballet holds out only on the strength of tradition, as do [court-dress] liveries and all sorts of etiquette. Should a revolution or a mere crisis take place, ballet will vanish without a trace."[158] Two revolutions in fact took place in 1917; miraculously, even after the one in October, ballet didn't vanish. The legacy of Petipa—or, rather, of the Petipa machine—would see more than one reincarnation: on the Soviet (the Kirov and Bolshoi) stages; in Western productions; and in our present century, in notation-derived reconstructions.

Stage to Floor, or the Pragmatics of Ballet

But contemporaries had every reason to be worried. Not only did the late nineteenth-century vogue for virtuoso dancing upset the balance between pantomime and dance prescribed by Noverre's neoclassicist poetics; it also undercut ballet's foundational pragmatics: the link between how people move and dance onstage, and how they do (or should) in real life.

From day one—from King Louis XIV's first decreeing his Académie Royale de Danse into existence—ballet had been conceptualized in pragmatic terms, as an exercise good for your body, in times of both war and peace. Mutatis mutandis, balletic stance and locomotion retained the same pragmatics in nineteenth-century Russia. Not so in the centuries to follow. The main distinction between nineteenth-century ballet regulars and their later counterparts is that few of us moderns have ever taken dance classes.[159] For most of the nineteenth century, dance was an essential part of the liberal arts education, a skill any seeker of social acceptance had to learn. A ball or dance party was no mere entertainment but a site for communication. As a society person, you were expected to be reasonably good at the waltz, polka, mazurka, and, if you were of a venerable age, the minuet. These were also the dances you would typically see performed by professionals on balletic stages.

THE SHADOW OF NOVERRE   75

And not only there. Off duty, a ballet dancer was likely to moonlight as a dance tutor, teaching—in secondary schools or at family evenings or polite-society dance events—a light version of what they'd been taught the hard way in the Imperial Ballet School. Thus, in mid-nineteenth-century Petersburg, the success of the character dancer Felix Kshesinsky generated a craze for the mazurka, which he also taught personally, hands on, to high-society ladies. By the end of the century, the salon mazurka—the centerpiece of many balls—would be a mandatory subject in grade 5 in both men's and women's gymnasia, as well as in cadet schools. "The mazurka is very difficult to perform," admonishes A. D. Chistiakov in his 1893 *Methodological Manual for Teaching Dance in Secondary Educational Institutions*, for it requires that "the male dancer [*kavaler*] . . . lead his lady with delicacy and dexterity, giving her full freedom to display her grace; instead of getting ahead to show himself, he must lead the lady ahead of him."[160] Interpreted thus by one's instructor, a mazurka lesson was also a lesson in gender performance—witnessed, in particular, in the gallant implications of the standard balletic term used here for "male dancer," following the French *cavalier*.

From the epoch of Louis XIV through the latter half of the nineteenth century in Russia, the philosophy of dance and its social pragmatics changed little. Dance continued to be de rigueur for guardsmen, in effect a chapter in their overall training in deportment and posture; three types of curtseys ("normal, deep, and minuet-like"), and the subtle trade-off of dignity and respect when bowing ("respect is signaled not by the depth of the bow, but by its slowness"),[161] were taught in the first grade of the gymnasium. As in the time of the Sun King, one's social standing in Russia had to be manifested bodily, and it was the job of ballet people to show how.

Ball and ballet stood close on a continuum—not just etymologically but in terms of practical pragmatics. Alongside giving dance classes, ballet people were called on to help arrange now a masquerade, now a children's party, now a ball—much like the diegetic Masters of Ceremonies do in *Sleeping Beauty* and *The Nutcracker*. As if in mutually facing mirrors, the real-life society ball reflected balletic images of real-life society balls. And vice versa.

The give-and-take between the ballet stage and sundry amateur ballrooms was undercut in the last quarter of the nineteenth century, when being a ballet professional came to mean performing feats beyond the reach of mere mortals. The pointe technique was on the rise; Matilda Kschessinska's ability to repeat the incredible thirty-two fouettés scored earlier by Pierina Legnani could blow everyone's mind, from the *enfants* of the cheap-seats *paradis*

76 IMPOSSIBLE PROJECT

right up to the royal family, but this was precisely why balletic dancing was no longer as societally useful as her father Felix's mazurka once was. "Mere" gracefulness was in the public domain; being nicknamed "Steel Toe" was a badge of distinction.

But even had a late nineteenth-century ballet dancer been of a mind to relaunch the dance-floor mazurka fad formerly associated with Felix Kshesinsky, this could hardly have been possible. Ballroom dance fashions evolved at a pace far outstripping the ballet. By the end of the century, the mazurka was no longer *the* social dance; new ones sprung up that ballet was too slow to embrace. The pragmatics of ballet was wearing thin.

Still, even as "gymnastic" choreography was perceived as a fatal disconnect—of dance from art and life, and of technique from grace—the public did applaud the toe work. The coming revolt was brewing, rather, *within* ballet. As Fokine put it, by the end of the nineteenth century, ballet had come to disrespect itself.[162]

2

Modern Specters, or Body Politic to Body Balletic

This chapter reads ballet lore from a standpoint best described as existential. Over the course of the history of ballet, there have been moments when its very right to exist was questioned, tested, metaphysically theorized, or even, in the spirit of *credibile quia impossibile*, religiously asserted. From anger to anguish to fideistic fortitude—the gamut of rhetorical attitudes toward ballet in the latter half of the nineteenth century deserves a closer textual consideration, and broader contextualization, than ballet historians have so far provided.

Cultural images of ballet take shape at crossroads between arts. In the first half of the nineteenth century, whenever a ballet caught the eye of, say, Pushkin or Gogol, it was likely to spark an ecstatic literary miniature featuring Avdotia Istomina's jump or Marie Taglioni's elevation. But by the mid-1860s, the relationship had soured. Authors who posited social empathy and civic awareness as the main, if not sole, virtue of either poetry or prose eyed ballet, as André Levinson put it in 1910, with "hostile suspicion."[1] Indeed, decrying ballet, and denying it the status of true art, became something of a trend among democratically minded Russian writers. Once acclaimed as a medium of grace, ballet emerges, from the pages of Nikolai Nekrasov's 1866 satire-in-verse "Ballet," Mikhail Saltykov-Shchedrin's libretto parody "Project for a Modern Ballet" (1864/1868), or Tolstoy's *War and Peace*, as a medium of lies. In the democratic press, the very word "ballet" became a term of scorn.

What could have motivated such a change of heart? Soviet historiography tends to blame the victim. "Representatives of the democratic camp" in the 1860s, explains Vera Krasovskaia in her 1960s *Russian Ballet Theater*, harbored a "legitimate mistrust" (*zakonnoe nedoverie*) for ballet—a historical diagnosis poles apart from the "hostility" noted by Levinson.[2] While the rest of the arts—Russian literature, drama, painting, and even opera and music—are said to have successfully transitioned into the epoch of

Impossible Project. Daria Khitrova, Oxford University Press. © Oxford University Press 2025.
DOI: 10.1093/9780197653081.003.0003

78   IMPOSSIBLE PROJECT

revolutionary realism, ballet, per Krasovskaia, was "stuck" (*zastrial*) in the Romantic age.[3] If revolutionary-democratic writers like Saltykov-Shchedrin or Nekrasov had lost patience with ballet, Krasovskaia suggests, this naturally followed from the thematic shallowness characteristic of ballets staged in this period by ballet master Arthur Saint-Léon.[4]

As I will discuss in the first section of this chapter, we can gain a clearer sense of the anti-ballet lore of the 1860s by situating it in its native historical and literary context. What Nekrasov, Saltykov-Shchedrin, and Tolstoy wrote about ballet, it turns out, was least of all about ballets themselves: in their writings, ballet emerges, not so much as a reflection of things properly balletic, as a fact of literature and as a political act.

The late nineteenth-century culture wars around ballet, moreover, saw a peculiar meeting of extremes: in something of a contrapuntal polyphony, the voices berating ballet from without were joined by voices from within that bewailed its erstwhile grace and beauty. With some of these voices we are already familiar: the old-school partisan Vasil'ko Petrov, diehard Noverrian Sergei Khudekov, and danseuse and theorist Lidia Nelidova. Plus, as lamented by its friends and foes alike, ballet was a den of easy virtue. The later in the century, the further downward curved ballet's reputation, and the lower sank its chances of survival as a stand-alone spectacle. It hardly helped when, during Aleksandr Borkh's term (1862–67) as court-appointed director of Imperial Theaters, his name became a byword for all-around incompetence and when the fiscal belt-tightening introduced by Baron Karl Kister (director, 1875–81) proved nearly fatal. Between unofficial scorn and official mismanagement, ballet's crisis was turning existential.

In tracing ballet's path(s) to survival, it will be useful to distinguish between its conjoined yet separate identities—ballet as spectacle and ballet understood as classical dance—each with its own degree of openness to novelty and change. To stay in the game as a spectacle, ballet *needed* to change: new librettos and music had to be commissioned, new costumes tailored, and state-of-the-art light effects and equipment introduced, to say nothing of frequent scene changes rather than the sparse, "three-sets-per-production" diet Baron Kister sought to impose on librettists. It is these needs, and concomitant reforms from above, that I intend to detail in a case study of the administrative strategies and literary output of Kister's successor, Ivan Vsevolozhsky.

To persist as a spectacle, ballet relied on injections of newness and excess, but ballet's core identity, classical dance, was more resistant to change—recall the years of ostracism it took before *pointe* techniques could take their place in the accepted classical vocabulary of pas. Classical dance, that is, had a different logic of survival: for it to remain classical, it had to remain unchanged, which, in a changing world, required an ideology, of the kind a church might rely on to justify its existence, or a dynasty its continuing reign.

My aim in what follows is to juxtapose three images of late nineteenth-century ballet. I begin with its unflattering image in the mirror of democratic opinion; then examine the image of ballet as a luxury spectacle, as envisioned by its grandee reformer, Vsevolozhsky; and end with the cult of classical dance in the eye of classical dancers. These are, needless to add, three different yet, from a historian's standpoint, complementary perspectives.

The Emancipation of the Serfs, or the Sprite of the Valley

Historians of literature and of ballet have observed that, in their verbal assaults on it, Saltykov-Shchedrin and Nekrasov were not targeting ballet *per se* so much as weaponizing it against bigger targets: social ills, public mores, liberal (i.e., in their view, overly moderate) and conservative politics, and rival literary groups and ideological positions.[5] My aim here is to examine the literary techniques these two authors used to present ballet's conventions—its fanciful tales, airy-fairy characters, and pointless pointes—as symptomatic of the state of society at large. (I will treat Tolstoy's ballet phobia here but briefly: Tolstoy's views on dance and ballet will be discussed in the next chapter to clarify Michel Fokine's ambivalence about classical dance and its vocabulary.)

One such technique was what a modern-day observer might describe as manufacturing memes. Saltykov-Shchedrin's critical writings, no matter their topic—from Karolina Pavlova's latest book of poetry to contemporary currents in Russian political thought—feature a figure named the Sprite of the Valley, who derives from Saint-Léon's ballet *Orphan Theolinda, or the Sprite of the Valley*, which Saltykov-Shchedrin must have seen in St. Petersburg in December 1862. While Ekaterina Vazem (who danced Theolinda in a later Petipa revival) recalled its plot as tame (*skuchnovatyi*),[6] most Petersburg critics singled out Saint-Léon's *Theolinda* for exquisite choreography and astounding visual effects. Usually balletic lakes are painted on a backdrop, but in Saint-Léon's production the lake was made of a "real mirror ... which artfully doubled Ms. [Marfa] Muravieva's feet"; another technical marvel noted

80 IMPOSSIBLE PROJECT

by critics was the "small photographic image . . . that first appeared in a tree, looming, by means of a magic lantern, life-size in front of everyone's eyes, only to materialize as the living dancer Ms. [Liubov'] Radina."[7]

Appearing in this unearthly fashion (the effect, indeed, must have been achieved by the magic-lantern trick known as "phantasmagoria") was, of course, the eponymous Sprite of the Valley, whose narrative function was that of the "magic donor" or "helper" (*volshebnyi pomoshchnik*), to use a term from Vladimir Propp's 1928 *Morphology of the Folktale*. The person being helped is the other eponymous character, Theolinda. Abandoned by her heartless father, Count Wallenstein, young Theolinda has found temporary refuge in the home of the equally heartless farmer Storff. When the most eligible bachelor in the valley, Count Ulrich, pays more attention to Theolinda than to Storff's own daughter, Theresa, the farmer reaches for his stick to batter the ingrate.

Fortunately, Theolinda has no need to steer her own fate. As spectators are informed in the prologue, the Sprite of the Valley, having learned of Count Wallenstein's injustice toward his own daughter, has pledged to be her guardian spirit for the rest of her life. Each time we find Theolinda in trouble, her magic helper comes out of a tree, performs a lake-top pas-de-deux with her, and gets Ulrich to take note of her or knocks the beating stick from Storff's hands. Were it not for the Sprite of the Valley, it seems unlikely that Count Ulrich and his beloved Theolinda would have ended as husband and wife.

Deus ex machina is a time-honored dramatic device; likewise, no fairy-tale hero could possibly do without a magic helper. Saltykov-Shchedrin, however, treats the Sprite of the Valley, not as a narrative convention, but as one might a meme avant la lettre, a meme that had invaded Russia's whole mental makeup. "What kind of sprite is this? whence has it arrived? what paths did it use to steal into the ballet master's head?" asks Saltykov-Shchedrin in his 1863 political-philosophical essay "Modern Specters," in which an array of basic precepts—religious, legal, civic, and governmental—are called into question.[8] Are the keystone ideas of our society as strong and absolute as we are told, or is this a matter of mere mental specters, with tinselly stage-prop winglets sewn to their backs, cast as arbiters of our fate? "It dances and does righteous deeds [*blagodetel'stvuet*]; spins on one foot and, all at the same time, punishes villainy and rights misfortunes. Why does the stick, aimed at Theolinda, fall from the hand of perfidious Storff? Because Theolinda is patronized by the Sprite of the Valley, who snatches the aforementioned

MODERN SPECTERS   81

stick. How could it happen that Theolinda, whom the Sprite of the Valley hauls off to the bottom of the lake, not only does not choke and drown, but, on the contrary, dances thereon? Simply because that is how the Sprite of the Valley wills it."[9]

In real life, Saltykov-Shchedrin says in so many words, we are being danced by similar spirits. Say, for instance, that a man and woman are in love with each other, respect each other, think the same way, but before they can undertake to live together, the specter of family dances the couple to the altar—lest the specter of public opinion brand their union a "dog wedding" (*sobach'ia svad'ba*). The *choreography of living* clings to fantastic genres. Everything that exists does so, not because it has the right to but under the condition of serving some phantom purpose or other. In the era of serfdom (i.e., before its abolition in February 1861), it was taken for granted that a peasant's "lifetime achievement" (*zhiznennyi podvig*) was to pay the *obrok* (quitrent) and to toil the corvée (*barshchina*), as no one doubts that the lifetime achievement of a chicken is to be boiled in a soup. Both are sacrificed to the specter called duty.[10]

Saltykov-Shchedrin believed in the performative power of written words. One of his favorite techniques of specter-hunting was to pair the unlike, for instance, to choose a blatantly unballetic *something* and argue its similarity to ballet. What, it would seem, could be more unlike the wordless, · bodily medium of ballet than, say, philosophy, which is but words words and words? This is precisely why, in the course of polemics around "the Russian idea"—the "modern specter" nourished by Fedor Dostoevsky and his circle—Saltykov-Shchedrin coins the chimerical term "balletic-philosophical activities" (*zaniatiia baletno-filosoficheskie*).[11] In philosophy as in ballet, writes Saltykov-Shchedrin in his 1863 "Moscow Letters," we are faced with the same algebra of hollow reasoning. An unknown is taken for a known so as to "explain" the fates of dramatis personae: "The majority fails to realize that the notions complacently presented as [society's] keystones, foundations and strongholds do not, in essence, differ from the sprite of the valley—and yet, so it is. Let idealist philosophers descend into the sanctum of their hearts; let legal philosophers retest the principles they are poised to defend; and then, let both groups visit the first ballet that happens to be showing at the theater. They will discover and feel, with the color of shame on their faces, that their entire life had been devoted to nothing else than writing ballets."[12] Ballet, for Saltykov-Shchedrin, is nothing but fiction. So is the state ideology.

82 IMPOSSIBLE PROJECT

The Politics of Ballet, or the Ballet of Politics

We could note that the image of ballet that emerges in a piece like this is as spectral as its polemical targets. But this is only one aspect of the picture. The intellectual and cultural life of Russia in the 1860s–70s was largely bound up with the political, economic, and legal aftermath of the emancipation of serfs proclaimed by Alexander II in 1861. The grievances against ballet listed by a Saltykov-Shchedrin and Nekrasov were less about sprites and specters and more about the *terre à terre* problems of peasants' land.

The juridical mechanism and language of the emancipation was Byzantine; suffice it to say here that the reform split Russian public opinion into polarized factions. Loyalists hailed it as an act of outstanding, if overdue, beneficence and rushed to thank His Majesty on behalf of the peasants for news that touched the nation's heart. At the other end of the spectrum, revolutionary democrats, aka "nihilists," argued that a reform that condemned peasant families to decades of buying themselves out, working off land allotments from their local lords, was not an emancipation but another form of enslavement. And there were currents of thought that lay somewhere in between, some duly ridiculed in Saltykov-Shchedrin's 1864 parodic libretto titled "False Enemies, or Lie without Fear!" For instance, when the femme-fatale figure Annette Postepennaia (a telltale surname that could be rendered as "Graduella") jumps out of an inkwell, smiles enigmatically at the "domestic conservative" Davilov ("Crusher"), and cries "Understand me!" (*poimi*; possibly punning on *poimai*, "catch me!"), only to vanish back into the vessel she came from, this allegorizes those advocating the incremental emancipation of serfs, instead of the act's being decreed in one fell swoop.[13] Another movement, which Saltykov-Shchedrin defines as "native liberalism," is represented in his mock libretto by Gogol's famous liar, Khlestakov. The swifts roosting in pine trees in Act II, incessantly twittering folksy ballads, stand for the Dostoevsky brothers and their fellow ideologues of native exceptionality. And so on.

Each faction nursed its own image of the Russian peasantry, typically referred to by the male metonym *muzhik*. Odic poems and celebratory paintings dedicated to emancipation foregrounded the peasants' nascent hope. Typically in such works, a pregnant silence reigns in a peasant hut, as its inhabitants—a group of *muzhiki* sunk in thought; their wives (*baby*) attempting to hush their babies so as not to miss a word; the granddad, half deaf, leaning over the stove bench—listen as the emancipation edict is read

MODERN SPECTERS   83

out to them: in Apollon Maikov's 1861 poem "Picture (In the Wake of the Manifesto of February 18, 1861)," by a little girl, the extended family's sole literate member. An identical scene, with an almost identical caption, this time set in a communal haybarn with ten pensive peasants tightly grouped round a young reader (this time a boy), is represented in an 1873 oil painting by Grigorii Miasoedov. Whatever Saltykov-Shchedrin might have had to say of Miasoedov's scene, his verdict of Maikov's poem was loud and clear: "Who will be fooled by this balletic lie?"[14]

Ballet's own *muzhiki* belonged to a more buoyant and extrovert variety than Miasoedov's or Maikov's. In Saltykov-Shchedrin's parody, at the mere sight of their landlord, the *muzhik* corps de ballet bursts into an ecstatic "grand pas of bast shoes" (*bol'shoi tanets laptei*). "Why are they dancing?" asks Saltykov-Shchedrin, as he describes the villager dance from Perrot's 1851 *The Naiad and the Fisherman*. "They are dancing because they are mending nets; dancing because they are pulling nets from the sea; dancing because they are villagers, and, in this capacity, *must* dance."[15] Because, in a word, it is so comforting to see peasants as children of nature, happy by default. The name of Saltykov-Shchedrin's game is defamiliarization, that is, poking at the skin of ballet's all-too-familiar conventions to expose the skull of ideology lurking beneath.

In nineteenth-century culture, breaking into dance was seen as a spontaneous outpouring of emotions. Conversely, speaking—in private or socially, to say nothing of *public* speaking—was regarded as an acquired skill.[16] When it came to peasants' opinions being expressed at some official gathering, their speeches would typically be conveyed by a representative speaker (whether appointed by them or from above), which might explain why, in the eyes of the educated, peasants—children of nature—would rather dance than speak.

The very idea that peasants were entitled to an opinion, one that should be expressed and heard, emerged in the wake of the emancipation reform. After 1861, various rural festivities and pageants came into political fashion, where the estates low and lofty were to demonstrate mutual affection and rapprochement. One such fête comes down to us reflected in three different mirrors of press opinion. One of the three opinions was Saltykov-Shchedrin's, with "ballet" appearing in the attendant polemics, more than once, as a *political* label, so the event in question deserves a closer look.

In the autumn of 1863, a report on what became known as the "Kashin [District] Festivities," authored by Prince Shakhovskoi, came out in two installments in the *Tver' Province Bulletin* (*Tverskie gubernskie vedomosti*).

84 IMPOSSIBLE PROJECT

These festivities had been arranged by the Assembly of the Tver' Province's Kashin District Gentry to pay homage to one of their own, Petr Golovin, for his successful role as conciliator (*mirovoi posrednik*), an official arbiter whose job was to settle disputes between peasants and landowners. Shakhovskoi's report constitutes an ode to the love affair supposedly burgeoning at the time between peasantry and gentry, but it nevertheless credibly records a well-scripted spectacle, whose actors know their parts—now verbal, now silent, depending on the given participant's class affiliation. As Golovin, the retiring conciliator, is presented with a goblet, the noblemen indulge in toasts and speeches; the peasants, for their part, bow, wipe a tear when moved, and, time and again, treat their betters to bread-and-salt, an ancient offering to the household sprite (*domovoi*), reduced, in the imperial age, to a silent symbol of peasants' ever-preparedness to feed.

The essential—or, rather, conceptual—muteness of the peasantry would occasionally take verbal form. Alongside peasant pantomimes, the *Tver' Province Bulletin* showcased two peasant speakers, each voicing his lack of preparedness to speak. As if on a ballet stage, our Kashin peasants here delegate words on their behalf to what we might call the "librettists" of their lives: the landlords. Please say what we are unable to, as you are so good with words! The result is so "balletic" that, a few months after the event, this particular propaganda ploy incurred critical remarks from mutually opposed ideological camps. In October and November 1863, "The Kashin Festivities" report was reprinted by the Moscow Slavophile newspaper *Day* (*Den'*), now prefaced by its editor Ivan Aksakov; in December, a brief essay under the same title, authored by Saltykov-Shchedrin, appeared in the *Contemporary* (*Sovremennik*). In the latter piece, the toasts and speeches voiced at the Kashin festivities, and Aksakov's interpretation of them in his preface, are scrutinized with Saltykov-Shchedrin's signature wit.

One speech Saltykov-Shchedrin quotes with particular delight had been, or so the story goes, initially assigned to a group of peasant elders. "However," he explains, "these simple-hearted children of nature grew disconcerted by the formidable feat they were charged with, and so, instead of venturing to talk, they delegated this knotty task to the Kashin landowner Petr Nikolaevich Ladyzhensky, who thus became a nobiliary spokesman for peasants' feelings."[17]

As transpires from the transcript of Ladyzhensky's speech, the transfer of speaking privileges occurred during a meal Ladyzhensky was sharing at a long table with the peasant delegation—a display of democracy unheard of

MODERN SPECTERS 85

prior to 1861. "Between a dish and a glass of vodka," begins Ladyzhensky, "in the course of a simple and sincere conversation, the peasants have clearly and plainly communicated to me their feelings, which they now want me to share with you."[18] From this point on, Ladyzhensky speaks on behalf of the peasants, yet, as he does, his thoughts—now theirs—continue to pivot around the dining table. "The peasants are pleased to be sitting at the same table with us; they are flattered to have been admitted to our society, and for that reason, on their behalf and on behalf of all fourth-district peasants, they drink to your, gentlemen, health with greater sincerity than they used to in former times."[19] And so forth. "Simplicity embodied!" exclaims Saltykov-Shchedrin of Ladyzhensky's table talk. "Isn't this precisely the way, naïve Othello tells us, he had fallen in love with Desdemona?"[20]

In the mirror of opinion held by the editor of the *Day*, the Kashin festivities came out as politically correct yet stylistically crooked. True to his Slavophile views, Aksakov approves of the Tver' gentry's effort to spark a conversation between former serfs and their former owners; do not such conversations represent the germ of Russia's future pan-class unity, conditioned by grassroots values rather than borrowings from the West? "We are convinced that the peasants were sincerely thankful," concludes Aksakov in his preface to the Shakhovskoi report. "Which constitutes the main thing; as for the goblet, or speeches and toasts, these are mere aristocratic accessories, unrelated to the substance of the case; nor can they hurt the peasants' feelings."[21]

Aksakov does, however, express a concern in his preface. Reading the peasants' speeches, he says, he was struck by the makeover that authentic Russian peasants undergo as soon as they "enter the stage of officialdom."[22] Instead of authentic vernacular, what one hears is an artificially artless peasant-speak of the kind that professional litterateurs use to depict their folksy "little muzhik" (*muzhichok*), with their Russian "simple-heartedness" and "single-mindedness," their Russian *spasibo*. A believer in Russia's singular truth and path, Aksakov reproached his compatriots for a lack of interest in local, geographically specific mindsets and folkways; at one point, he even proposed to compile a scholarly volume based on local correspondences on the subject, to be sent to the *Day* from various Russian provinces—an ethno-Wikipedia of sorts.

Of all Russian writers, Saltykov-Shchedrin was least likely to let the Kashin festivities report in the *Day* go without comment. As a recent (1861–62) vice-governor of the Tver' province (quickly pushed into retirement for attempting to bend emancipation procedures to the benefit of local peasants

86   IMPOSSIBLE PROJECT

as opposed to landlords), Saltykov-Shchedrin (known in his vice-governor hat as Saltykov, his real name) must have been familiar with the terrain and personally acquainted with some of the gentlemen involved—if not Ladyzhensky, then Prince Shakhovskoi, whom Saltykov-Shchedrin in his essay nicknames *kashinskii letopisets* (the Kashin chronicler).

In his "Kashin Festivities" essay, Saltykov-Shchedrin shows as little patience for folksy peasants in folk costumes as Aksakov does in his preface to the Shakhovskoi report. Merrily thankful peasants; pious peasants holding the icon of the Savior; bread-and-salt peasants—writing elsewhere, Saltykov-Shchedrin likens all such discursive masks to "a corps de ballet dancing somewhere there, by the water."[23] On the other hand, neither does he buy into the Slavophile conception of peasants: peasants as menders of the national net, the peasantry as a link between the Russian soil and Russian soul. So far as Saltykov-Shchedrin is concerned, all such talk belongs to "balletic mythology" and "balletic ethnography."[24]

Indeed, as reflected in Saltykov-Shchedrin's essay, the expectations and frustrations voiced in Aksakov's preface loom as large as the grotesque glories of the Kashin festivities as such. Aksakov had been chagrined to find the peasant Aleksei Iakovlevich's speech seemingly ventriloquized. "Apparently, Aksakov is trying to tell us that what our Kashin chronicler depicts is a ballet," concludes Saltykov-Shchedrin, as if the rest of it, including Aksakov's grievances, were not.[25] Saltykov-Shchedrin had his own image (perhaps as literary as any other) of an authentic peasant finding himself cast as an extra at a fête like Tver's: a *muzhik* in a *sermiaga* (a smock of coarse, colorless cloth) asking himself, "What the hell! Why the hell are they distracting me from what matters [*ot dela otbivaiut*]?"[26] While Aksakov wonders how a peasant is supposed to act having entered the "stage of officialdom," Saltykov-Shchedrin's solution is simple: exit immediately.

Defamiliarization, or the Dance of the Frying Fish

On our mental map of ballet lore, outside observers like Saltykov-Shchedrin appear antipodal to balletomanes like Pleshcheev, Khudekov, or Skalkovsky, proud insiders to everything ballet. It should be kept in mind, however, that sounding like an outsider (or, for that matter, an insider) was, to a large extent, a cultural choice, signaled by using certain literary techniques. On the face of it, Saltykov-Shchedrin's attitude toward ballets was: if you've seen one, you've seen them all. At the same time, the number of informed references to actual ballet productions scattered among his writings leads one to conclude that his relationship with this art form was no "one-night stand." *The Naiad and the Fisherman*; *The Golden Fish*; *Météora, or the Valley of Stars*; *Orphan Theolinda, or the Sprite of the Valley*; *Beauty of Lebanon, or the Mountain Spirit*; *Fiametta, or the Triumph of Love*—whatever the subject of a conversation, Saltykov-Shchedrin was always ready to season it with an exotic-balletic toponym or name. Does this mean, perhaps, that for Saltykov-Shchedrin, ballet was not only a handy strawman but also a guilty pleasure? At one point in his review of *The Naiad and the Fisherman*, he chuckles at the torrents of sweat that wash the rouge from the face of the young lover Matteo to reveal the wrinkles on the face of the in-real-life old dancer Christian Johansson.[27] But how could he notice this detail, were he not watching Perrot's ballet using a pair of binoculars—the proverbial appurtenance of a ballet *regular*?

The mental map of ballet lore could use a bit of fine-tuning. Between a conscientious outsider like Saltykov-Shchedrin and a high priest of Terpsichore like Khudekov lay less a void than a certain intertextual terrain, which, albeit rugged, Saltykov-Shchedrin could negotiate with enviable skill. Not a balletomane by any stretch, when it comes to critiquing someone's ballet libretto, Saltykov-Shchedrin does not sound all that different from your typical balletomane or ballet critic. Even his most characteristically "anti-balletic" phrase—"Why are they dancing?"—was a not-infrequent rhetorical question by which a devout Noverrian might cuff a too free and easy librettist like Saint-Léon or Vsevolozhsky for neglecting Noverre's commandment to *put the story before the dance*. When Khudekov complains that, in Saint-Léon's ballets, "people dance not by virtue of necessity, but by a wave of the wand [*po shchuch'emu veleniiu*]; they dance whenever it pleases the ballet master to do so,"[28] or when the same Khudekov observes that, in Petipa and Vsevolozhsky's *Sleeping Beauty* "they dance till they fall asleep; dance while asleep; and dance as they wake up," he speaks from the standpoint of consummate expertise.[29] When Saltykov-Shchedrin, to requote the passage from his review of *The Naiad*, poses the same kind of question and answers that they are "dancing because they are mending nets; dancing because they are pulling nets from the sea," and so on, he is putting on the speech mask of the simpleton, or the ballet first-timer.

Saltykov-Shchedrin's favorite method of donning this mask was to "struggle" with ballet-specific vocabulary—to avoid identifying ballet pas by their ballet names or use a misnomer. Any self-respecting balletomane would

88   IMPOSSIBLE PROJECT

call a bourrée a bourrée or a pirouette a pirouette; Saltykov-Shchedrin would not, despite the fact that the meaning of "pirouette" (unlike most other ballet terms) was widely known in nineteenth-century Russia (this word even having found its way into Vladimir Dal's *Explanatory Dictionary*, launched in the 1860s). Instead, we read, "[Undine] rises on her toes, walks on her toes across the stage, and this means she 'loves Matteo.' All dance. In comes Matteo, spins on one leg, and waggles his head like an alabaster cat, which means that 'he is listening in ecstasy to the song of a nightingale.'"[30] (Quotes within Saltykov-Shchedrin's text are from the written program.)

There is a passage in Saltykov-Shchedrin's review of *The Naiad* that is suffused with defamiliarizing power, albeit lessened in our post-equine age:

> The scene is set nowhere in particular. Before the spectators' eyes is a seashore and a crowd of villagers of both genders. . . . In comes Gianina, performs a few curvets, thereby expressing that she is waiting for her fiancé Matteo, who finally appears. Matteo, for his part, spins on one leg, thereby expressing that today his betrothal to Gianina is going to take place. All leave. Matteo is alone; suddenly, something yawns upstage. It is a shell, out of which Undine comes out. She, too, performs multiple curvets, which must express that she is in love with Matteo. . . . Change of scene; the new set represents [the interior of] a fisherman's hut, in which Gianina, Matteo and his mother Theresa are shown flailing their arms and legs. Gianina makes several curvets, which means, "Honey, why are you deep in thought?" Matteo, too, makes several curvets, which means that he is sick at heart. Suddenly, a window is flung open, and into the hut flies Undine. Jumps and curvets start anew; Undine vanishes; Gianina and Matteo kneel.[31]

The word "curvet" (*kurbet*, from the French *courbette*) comes up quite a bit in this passage, but despite its "French" or "classical" sound, no such term exists in ballet's recognized vocabulary. Dal's *Explanatory Dictionary* gives its meaning as "rearing, making a horse lift and lower its forelegs." Correspondingly, *delat' kurbety* (to make curvets), the phrase Saltykov-Shchedrin uses here, is defined in Dal' as "to show off by way of making one's horse rear." Not that Saltykov-Shchedrin saw ballet as a horse opera per se. Rather, he meant to process the action and choreography of *The Naiad* through the eye of a ballet-illiterate observer, to expose ballet's inadequacy as

MODERN SPECTERS 89

a language. "Making curvets" was not a metaphor used to belittle dancers; it was part of a critical speech mask, a defamiliarizing device.

Saltykov-Shchedrin's view of ballet was histrionic and elusive, which may explain why its *complexity* would be lost on ballet historians. In the pages of Krasovskaia's *Russian Ballet Theater*, Saltykov-Shchedrin emerges as a sociopolitical sage, condemning ballet for its failure to outgrow its Romantic age and take up the social reality of Russia, the "vital . . . issues of modernity" (*zhiznennye . . . problemy sovremennosti*).[32] Nothing could be further from the truth. Saltykov-Shchedrin and Nekrasov (coeditors of the *Contemporary*) never expressed the desire that ballet address "vital issues of modernity"; on the contrary, if they had a "policy" on this question, it would be that the world of ballet and the empirical world be kept as separate as possible, lest ballet's disregard for facts prove infectious. A ballet scene set "nowhere in particular," as in the first act of Saint-Léon's *Naiad*, is, as ballets go, acceptable; what Saltykov-Shchedrin deems unacceptable is when Saint-Léon sets his balletic adaptation of Pushkin's "Tale of the Fisherman and the Fish" on a bank of the Dnipro River. "I hereby call all historical and geographical handbooks to witness," avows Saltykov-Shchedrin in his review of *The Golden Fish*, "that never has anyone caught a golden fish in the Dnipro river, especially not a golden fish in human form."[33] By the same token, the universe of ballet, with its meteors and planets obeying the will of a stage mechanic, ought to be kept at a sane distance from the celestial mechanics as explained by Galileo.[34]

In defending astronomy and geography from ballet's distortions, Saltykov-Shchedrin sounds jocular, but when it comes to social reality and cultural icons, his tone is earnest. His was a hands-off policy: hands off Russian peasants, hands off our Pushkin! To St. Petersburg's democratic press, the St. Petersburg ballet had nothing to do with things they would recognize as *theirs* or *Russian*.

It was in a similar spirit that Nekrasov produced what is widely considered the premier Russian verse denunciation of ballet: his 1866 satire "Ballet." A poem, a public accusation, and a critical document in one, Nekrasov's "Ballet" draws its power from three contexts. The first is mundane, in effect documenting a night at the theater. One frosty evening, the poet attends a ballet and is taken aback by a character dance performed by a leading danseuse of the Petersburg troupe—a dance that he, the poet, finds offensive. The dancer and the offensive dance are named in the poem: the dancer is

Maria Petipa; the dance, "Little Muzhik" ("Muzhichok"). Ballet historians had little difficulty determining when precisely Nekrasov's visit to the theater took place: on January 20, 1866, when, indeed, Petipa reprised her folk hit within the framework of *Florida*, her husband Marius Petipa's thinly threaded divertissement.[35]

The second context is the political outlook that Nekrasov largely shared with Saltykov-Shchedrin.[36] Both authors believed that the arts and artists must be kept honest. In the number in question, Maria Petipa entered cross-dressed as a dashing young peasant, wearing a red *rubakha* (a traditional tunic-like shirt), wide plush trousers, and a coachman's cap, topped with, of all things, a peacock feather (Figure 2.1).[37] While perfectly in line with nineteenth-century character-dance conventions (who asks whether performers of polkas or czárdás look like real-life Poles or Hungarians?), Petipa's outfit was at odds with that of the authentic Russian

Figure 2.1 Maria Petipa in her "Little Peasant Man [Muzhichok]" costume (1865?).

peasant as conceived by the ballet skeptics at the *Contemporary*. Saltykov-Shchedrin's authentic peasant, as we recall from his rebuke of the Kashin festivities report, is a male figure dressed in a *sermiaga*, a coarse, colorless linsey-woolsey caftan. Likewise, the authentic, non-danseuse peasant whom Nekrasov invokes in his poem wears a pair of "frozen little bast shoes" (*merzlye lapotki*) and a "plain fur coat" (*nagol'naya shuba*). Hence Nekrasov's sarcastic authentication of the costume Petipa sported as a little *muzhik*:

> Everything—including white gussets sewn into the shirt—
> Was genuine: on the hat, flowers,
> A Russian boldness in each sweeping gesture . . .
> You are not an artist, you are an enchantress!
> We never ever saw such a likeness;
> A real *muzhik*!"[38]

And hence the poetic pointe of Nekrasov's "Ballet":

> And you [my Muse] ponder, "O Paradise Houri!
> You are lovely, and airy, and light;
> Then, dance *The Maiden of the Danube*,
> But leave the *muzhik* in peace!"[39]

Leave the peasant, who is properly a topic for the "peasant question," and not ballets, alone—such could have been the summary of this quatrain, were Nekrasov's "Ballet" written in plain political prose. But it is not. Subtitled "Satire," "Ballet" is a satire in verse—a poem, and a complex one at that. Prose *posits* things, but poetry is an exercise in echoing: acoustic, semantic, intertextual. Consider the *muteness* motif that surfaces, time and again, in various peasant portrayals of the emancipation epoch. The peasant representatives who took part in the infamous Kashin pageant are depicted as being mute by choice. To believe the *Tver' Province Bulletin*, they delegated speaking to benevolent landowners—their *own* owners prior to 1861. No wonder Saltykov-Shchedrin dismissed Kashin-style spectacles of alleged comity between landowners and land-toilers as a mute "political ballet."

Nekrasov's "Ballet" ends on a tragic note. A frigid, snowy January. Having brought their sons to the borough conscription office, a host of peasant families, each driving their own family sleigh, return to the village. A sad,

92   IMPOSSIBLE PROJECT

silent procession across the snowy wastes. The muteness motif is back once more, this time to portray the "peasants' grief" (*krest'ianskoe gore*):

> The *muzhiks* sit still like mutes,
> Not even a song is heard,
> The women [*baby*] bury their faces in kerchiefs,
> Only a sigh sometimes bursts forth.

This heartbreaking tableau is meant to contrast and rhyme with the happy-go-lucky *muzhik* dance performed in Nekrasov's "Ballet" by Maria Petipa. Leave them alone, ordains the poet; dance some part from the antiquated bestiary of old romantic ballets instead. The irony of Nekrasov's second choice was that the naiad character featured in *Maiden of the Danube*, scripted and choreographed by Filippo Taglioni in 1836 for his daughter Marie, was a riverside foundling, mute from birth—as underwater creatures tend to be.[40]

Nekrasov's antipathy for ballet was itself an echo of having been in love with ballet for years. As it transpires from his poem, and as his contemporaries attest, Nekrasov was an unapologetic ballet habitué; he had his favorite seats, and indeed his own binoculars ever at hand. One of his younger friends recalled him advising that a writer starting out would be wise to become a ballet regular, for three reasons: ballet is beautiful; it pays to know it; and it is the right place to meet the right people.[41]

Nor was Nekrasov foreign to the typical balletomane routine of paying social visits to fledgling danseuses. "I was personally acquainted with Nekrasov," recalls Vazem. "On more than one occasion at the dawn of my artistic career, when I still lived in the building owned by the Theater Directorate next door to my classmate [Aleksandra] Vergina, [Nekrasov] showed up at my place. Each time he visited me, he would always ask me to invite Vergina as well, with whom he would conduct his husky-voice [*siplyi*] conversations. Nekrasov's infatuation went unrequited: soon [in 1873], Vergina married [Count Baranov], quit the stage, and left Petersburg."[42]

A more complicated picture of Nekrasov's poem vis-à-vis contemporary ballet emerges when, in addition to the factual ("a night at the theater") and political-ideological contexts, we place "Ballet" in the context of poetry per se—of established poetic conceptions of dance. Two such traditions proved seminal for Nekrasov's "Ballet": the extolling of dance as a vehicle of vigor and desire, as famously occurs in Pushkin's novel in verse *Eugene Onegin*, and the motif of the *danse macabre*, as evoked in Ivan Krylov's 1824 verse fable "Dance of Fishes" ("Ryb'ia pliaska"), whose story, in a nutshell, is as follows. In the course of inspecting his domain, a lion-tsar encounters a *muzhik* pan-frying a catch of fish over a fire.

> The poor [fishes] were jumping from the heat as high as each could;
> Each, seeing the end coming, was tossing about.
> ....
> "Tell me," asked the Lion, "What makes them
> Flap with their tails and heads?"
> "O wise tsar!" replied the *muzhik*, frightened. "Upon beholding you,
> they dance with joy."[43]

In "Ballet," Nekrasov taps into both traditions, playing one against the other. Leading into Nekrasov's poem is an epigraph from *Eugene Onegin*, Pushkin's tribute to "Terpsichore's little foot" (*nozhka Terpsikhory*), whose "conventional beauty" prophesies "invaluable rewards to the eye" and unleashes "a willful swarm of desires." Nekrasov did not adopt this epigraph with ironic intent; to the contrary, from the outset he declares himself to be in the same boat:

> Be aware, you people of taste,
> That I adore ballet myself.
> To those "hit by Cupid's arrow"
> Go my cordial cheers, not jeers!"[44]

Unlike Saltykov-Shchedrin, Nekrasov does not pretend to be an outside observer, unversed in the intricacies of pas. *His* speech mask is that of an insider, albeit one sheepish at the thought of what ballet reduces its devotees to ("Ballet makes us naïve, / This hour, we are silly"). This welcoming "we" made Nekrasov's poem easy to relate to—even if one did not share its political stance. Thus, in his 1896 *Our Ballet*, balletomane Aleksandr Pleshcheev cites "Ballet" several times, twice in connection with a corps de ballet making a felicitous exit in the face of encores: "Bis! . . . But the wind-like maidens / Flew off like a flowery garland."[45]

"Ballet" is an ambivalent poem—a critique of the eponymous art form, yes, but also a tribute to it, as witness its pivotal lines: "You are lovely, and airy, and light; / Then, dance *The Maiden of the Danube*, / But leave the

94 IMPOSSIBLE PROJECT

muzhik in peace!" Paying Terpsichore's little foot its due, Nekrasov would simply have it toe the line, as it were, between levity and gravity. You are lovely and airy and light; your choreographic *emploi* should be likewise: in a word, *unearthly*. But do stay away from the Russian peasants, who have their own, heavy and earthly dance to dance.

This is where Krylov's dance of the frying fish comes in. Counterpointing the description of Petipa's peppy *muzhichok* is a stanza set on a snowy waste with a lone peasant figure walking behind his cart instead of riding it, so as to lighten his horse's load. It is only this motion, or trudge, that, in Nekrasov's view, merits the name of "peasant dance." If heat is the reason that Krylov's fishes dance, Nekrasov's peasant dance is choreographed by bitter cold:

> In frozen little bast shoes and a plain fur coat,
> Hoarfrosted entirely [*ves' zaindevev*], [the *muzhik*]
>   performs his dance himself,
>
> . . . .
>
> Spurred on by biting frost,
> He dances behind his creaky cart;
> Dances as he carries on his day's march—
> And even sings songs![46]

In his mock review of *The Naiad and the Fisherman*, Saltykov-Shchedrin describes dancing as toil, senseless and tedious: "[Matteo] is shown picking flowers—picks one, shifts his foot aside, then presses his hand to his heart; picks another, shifts his foot, puts hand to heart. He is dripping with sweat, for ceaseless foot-shifting is exhausting."[47] In Nekrasov's "Ballet," it is a peasant's toil that is a dance. Inverse as they seem, the two metaphors have much the same defamiliarizing function.

Bor'ba s bor'boi bor'buetsia, "struggle struggles against struggle"—this pleonasm, a stock joke from the early 1950s, portrayed well the excesses of Soviet literary history.[48] In addressing the 1860s, Soviet ballet histories sound just as warlike. When Krasovskaia contends that, "in the epoch of its decline, ballet, in the eyes of [Saltykov-]Shchedrin and Nekrasov, was no longer an art, but merely an unsightly 'sign of the times,'"[49] she situates both authors *outside* ballet, as if the world of ballet were (to extend a metaphor from Joseph Brodsky's poem "To Mikhail Baryshnikov") some medieval "castle of Beauty"—moat, drawbridge, and all—assailed by the crusaders of realism and truth.

MODERN SPECTERS   95

But such images of ballet are, well, balletic. Nineteenth-century ballet was one branch in a ramified social infrastructure, which included various leisure-socializing activities and military or civic education. To borrow a term from anthropology and performance studies, the dance floor and dance class were liminal spaces that *linked*, rather than stood between, the stage and its complementary opposite, the street. There is no inside and outside to ballet, or, rather, its inside and outside segue into each other. This applies equally to writings like Saltykov-Shchedrin's "Project for a Modern Ballet" or Nekrasov's "Ballet." On the one hand, the latter was a satirical text, of the sort *Contemporary* subscribers expected to find on the pages of this cutting-edge progressive journal; on the other, it constituted a fact of ballet lore. And such lore was more than a mere echo or verbal reflection of what was going on in ballet. Lore often worked like feedback, and it is hardly by chance that, after a series of unsuccessful attempts to Russianize ballet's repertoire in Petersburg, the Directorate dropped the idea. Pushkin's *Golden Fish* frustrated more wishes than it granted. *The Little Humpbacked Horse* remained the box office's only "magic donor"—and this because the kids loved it, and the emperor too.[50]

Russian balletomanes were far from humorless. Krasovskaia called Khudekov's *Petersburg Newspaper* a den of balletomane wisecrackers; Skalkovsky's wit and vitriol were legend. Nor were Russian ballet dancers blind to the shaky truth value of their parts, or to the potential silliness thereof. In 1870, the Petersburg ballet dancer Aleksandr Chistiakov (the same Chistiakov whose 1893 *Methodological Manual for Teaching Dance in Secondary Educational Institutions* we looked into in the previous chapter) wrote a comic theater sketch titled "Balletomane" and subtitled "A Monologue with Couplets." This gained special prominence as performed by the heavyset comic Konstantin Varlamov (better known by the endearing nickname "Uncle Kostia"), famed for making theatrical use of his imposing weight, both when playing stout characters and mimicking balletic lightness. This is how Chistiakov-cum-Varlamov's balletomane tells the audience about a ballet he has just seen:

Morning... apparently, before four o'clock, as the entire village is asleep.... A young *paysan* is coming down the hill. A *paysan* means the same thing as our *muzhik* ... but look how different he is! Our *muzhik*, on the road, his *kaftan* on, his sack behind his back, walks pretty heavily, **like this** [*vot tak*]! And the *paysan*, dressed in silk stockings, wearing his booties, white

96 IMPOSSIBLE PROJECT

trousers, velvet cardigan [*banbetka*] similar to our waist jacket, a straw bonnet on his head, and a light bundle on a fine stick over his shoulder, walks—not *walks*, really, but hops from foot to foot, **like this!**[51]

"Balletomane" was written four years after "Ballet," so it is quite possible that Chistiakov's *muzhik* was walking in the footsteps of Nekrasov's.

Dance, War, and Peace

It was only to be expected that, in a story of ballet as partial and ideologically consistent as Krasovskaia's *Russian Ballet Theater*, what had been a war of words would become a war of *names*. Aside from being extraordinary writers and tireless advocates for the have-nots, in the wake of 1917 Saltykov-Shchedrin and Nekrasov, long since dead, turned out to have been on the right side of history. Hugely significant in their lifetime, the two names loomed even larger posthumously—unlike those of most of the people they polemicized against: commentators, philosophers, or ballet masters. But we might wonder whether the mid-nineteenth-century international celebrity Arthur Saint-Léon was even aware of the existence of a pestilent critic with the pen name Shchedrin, or if Maria Surovshchikova-Petipa had heard of Nekrasov's opinion of her "Muzhichok." (Her husband-choreographer most certainly had not.) Still, as restaged roughly a hundred years later in Krasovskaia's history book, a showdown between names like Saltykov-Shchedrin and Saint-Léon, or between Nekrasov and the Petipas, had a foregone outcome. A standing bronze monument to Nekrasov had been erected in the center of Leningrad, near Nekrasov Street, and a large monument to Saltykov-Shchedrin (seated) in Tver'. Maria Surovshchikova-Petipa died in Novocherkassk; her grave, along with the church she was buried behind, was leveled to make room for a city square.

Monuments do not smile. Missing in Krasovskaia's restaging are the hilarity and ambiguity of Nekrasov's and Saltykov-Shchedrin's forays into ballet. Both authors were *inside* outsiders, whose verbal caricatures of ballet were at once caustic *and* affectionate. Among prominent ballet skeptics, the only one who could be called a true outsider, and who was dead serious about his choreophobia, was Leo Tolstoy. In his "Ballet," Nekrasov, who used to frequent ballet and was not above dropping in on one young danseuse in the hope of wooing another, calls the corps de ballet a "flowery garland" of "wind-like maidens." Tolstoy, in his 1897 treatise "What Is Art?," resorts to the same trope to express a different stance: "And ballet, in which half-naked women make lascivious evolutions and intertwine in all kinds of sensual garlands, is simply an immoral performance."[52]

Tolstoy was well into his seventies when he wrote "What Is Art?" Anyone familiar with this late phase of his literary career will be quick to recognize, in the above verdict, a mixture of moralizing and misogyny endemic to the "Tolstoyan" doctrine. (Ironically, the energy of Tolstoy's rejection of ballet in "What Is Art?" would not discourage but rather invigorate a cohort of young ballet professionals—on which more in the next chapter.) But in his younger years, too, Tolstoy had little patience for ballet, as seen, if vicariously, in *War and Peace*, written in the 1860s—the decade in which, we recall, Saltykov-Shchedrin and Nekrasov unfolded *their* critical campaign against ballet.

In some ways, Tolstoy's critique of ballet echoes those of Saltykov-Shchedrin and Nekrasov; in others, it is uniquely his own. This alone makes *War and Peace*, on top of being a historical reflection on Russia's Napoleonic war and a piece of historical fiction, a useful lens on the cultural history of dance. In three consecutive parts of book 2, Tolstoy presents the reader with a paradigm of dances, each tinged by an emotional attitude on the part of young Countess Natalia Rostova. Part 3, chapter 15 sees Natasha at a grand ball given in St. Petersburg on the eve of 1810; the crème de la crème of Russian nobility gathered is even graced by the presence of the emperor. Here, Natasha feels self-conscious and confident all at once. Self-conscious, because this is her first appearance in so lofty a venue; confident, because, having been raised in a family of aristocrats, with tutors and all, she is thoroughly prepared for a successful debut, well-versed in how to move and converse and, above all, in the abstruse art of ballroom dancing. "She stood with her slender arms hanging down, her scarcely defined bosom rising and falling regularly, and with bated breath and glittering, frightened eyes gazed straight before her, evidently prepared for the height of joy and misery."[53]

As described by Tolstoy, the ball represents a paradigm of dances—but also a syntagm, in the sense that the *order* of dances constituted the backbone of every ball. First comes the slow, ceremonious Polonaise, headed by the smiling emperor, who leads the lady of the house, albeit failing to keep time to the music (*ne v takt*) in doing so. A young lady without a male escort, Natasha finds herself cut off: "She had but one thought: 'Is it possible no one will ask me, that I shall not be among the first to dance? Is it possible that not one of all these men will notice me? They do not even seem to see me, or if they do they look as if they were saying, "Ah, she's not the one I'm after, so it's not worth looking at her!" No, it's impossible,' she thought. 'They must know how I long to dance, how splendidly I dance, and how they would enjoy dancing with me.'"[54]

Natasha's chance to show herself comes with the second dance, the waltz. Her future fiancé, Prince Andrei Bolkonsky, is said to be "one of the best dancers of his day and Natasha danced exquisitely. Her little feet in their white satin dancing shoes did their work swiftly, lightly, and independently of herself, while her face beamed with ecstatic happiness."[55] There is more dancing, with Natasha much sought after as a partner; a merry cotillion, announced, per custom, shortly before dinner, serves as a vehicle for the first romantic conversation between Natasha and Andrei.

To mingle in high society, one had to know the rules and master the skills, with the skill of dancing, in particular, de rigueur for all, except perhaps the emperor. Nowadays the phrase "one of the best dancers of his day" would conjure a Nijinsky or Baryshnikov; Tolstoy, writing in the 1860s of people fifty years earlier, says this of Prince Bolkonsky, an army officer whose main ambition is to reform the Russian military charter. Likewise, the way Tolstoy describes Natasha's footwork betrays a connoisseur of choreographic lightness and elegance. When it comes to the Baryshnikovs and Nijinskys of Natasha's time, like the famous French ballet star Louis-Antoine Duport, Tolstoy's, and by extension Natasha's, connoisseurship disappears.

We learn about this later in the story, when Natasha visits Moscow to meet her fiancé's family; in the interim, the Rostov family spends summer and autumn on their ancestral estate in the countryside. One September evening, after a day-long ride with hounds, Natasha and her brothers Petr and Nikolai spend an evening in a neighboring village as guests of a distant relative whom everyone (including the author) calls "little Uncle" (*diadiushka*). "A fresh-looking, handsome old man with a large gray mustache,"[56] as Tolstoy portrays him, Uncle is on good terms with his domestic serfs, one of whom, a portly woman of forty named Anisya Fedorovna, acts as Uncle's cook, housekeeper, and unwedded wife—something the reader is quick to infer by the obvious pride the two take in each other as the evening unfolds: "[Anisya Fedorovna] stepped aside and stopped at the door with a smile on her face. 'Here I am. I am she! Now do you understand "Uncle"?' her expression said to Rostov. How could one help understanding? Not only Nicholas, but even Natasha understood the meaning of his puckered brow and the happy complacent smile that slightly puckered his lips when Anisya Fedorovna entered."[57]

MODERN SPECTERS 99

Notably, the family harmony that Tolstoy wants us, along with Natasha and Nikolai, to read from the faces of the unwedded couple, remains asymmetrical, not only in terms of class but also of Tolstoy's literary mise-en-scène. A peasant by birth, if a housewife in fact, Anisya Fedorovna remains standing by the doorway while her lord regales his relatives at the table. After an abundant succession of dishes and drinks (Tolstoy lists over a dozen), Uncle's coachman Mit'ka plays the balalaika to entertain the guests, then Uncle himself asks Anisya Fedorovna to bring his guitar and sings. Singing segues into dancing: Natasha picks up a headscarf and, famously, iconically, bursts into a peasant dance.

The above description could apply to a genre scene from an eighteenth-century family novel or early nineteenth-century society tale (*svetskaia povest'*). On the one hand, this lineage is quite natural: as Boris Eikhenbaum has shown, *War and Peace*, with its enhanced attention to bygone ways of both "polite" society and peasant life, represented a revival of these then-outdated literary genres.[58] On the other hand, there is a specifically Tolstoyan logic to the characters' actions and feelings during the merriment at Uncle's place. To understand what lesson Tolstoy sought to convey with this scene, we need, once again, to evoke the political and ideological battles of the 1860s.

In the 1850s, Tolstoy had been ideologically close to Saltykov-Shchedrin and Nekrasov, and indeed his earliest prose appeared in the *Contemporary*, but in the wake of the emancipation manifesto, views on "the peasant question" resulted in a divergence. After a brief and rather frustrating tenure as a conciliator (which ended when the local gentry realized every case would be reconciled in the peasants' favor), Tolstoy opted to "conciliate" on paper rather than on the ground. The picture of the cross-class mirth that reigns under Uncle's roof, that is, seems almost an unwitting companion piece to that report of the Kashin festivities held in 1863 to honor a conciliator of Tver' province—a saccharine hymn to the friendship of peasants and their would-be liberators that Saltykov-Shchedrin labeled mere "ballet." Except that said festivities were held *after* the emancipation reform, whereas the scene in question, albeit written also in the 1860s, is set some fifty years prior.

In the Kashin report as in *War and Peace*, the axis of cross-class unity is Russianness, colored as religious and officious in Kashin, and presented as elemental, spontaneous, and intuitive in Tolstoy. In keeping with his usual writerly tendency, Tolstoy writes against the grain of the reader's expectations. The repository of folklore, one would think, would be the "simple folk,"

100   IMPOSSIBLE PROJECT

but when Anisya Fedorovna hands Uncle his guitar, it is he, a former army or guards officer (as the reader infers from a drole byword Uncle's sentences are peppered with), who turns out to be a spigot of folklore, pouring forth one folk song after another: "'Uncle' sang as peasants sing, with full and naïve conviction that the whole meaning of a song lies in the words and that the tune comes of itself. . . . As a result of this the unconsidered tune, like the song of a bird, was extraordinarily good."[59]

Unconsidered, unlearned, natural, birdlike—all this, in Tolstoy's scheme of things, signals a sudden burst of Russianness that culminates in Natasha's Russian dance. Preceding the dance is a telltale mise-en-scène, in which the spirit of Russianness, like a relay baton, is passed from a peasant woman to a young countess.

The only two women in the room, Natasha Rostova and Anisya Fedorovna, remain central to Tolstoy's mise-en-scène throughout the evening. Anisya Fedorovna's first entrance, as Tolstoy stages it, is nothing short of regal. The door is pushed open by an invisible barefoot girl, and in comes Anisya Fedorovna carrying a large loaded tray, "[w]ith hospitable dignity and cordiality in her glance and in every motion."[60] She reigns over the dinner ("[t]he smell and taste of [which] had a smack of Anisya Fedorovna herself: a savor of juiciness, cleanliness, whiteness, and pleasant smiles")[61] yet knows her place when it comes to savoring music: "Anisya Fedorovna came in and leaned her portly person against the doorpost."[62] Paradoxically, Anisya Fedorovna combines portliness and lightness; twice in the space of the chapter does Tolstoy's narrator direct the reader's attention to her "light step": "[T]his woman . . . trod very lightly."[63]

Which, of course, makes her a natural-born dancer. When, coaxed by Uncle, Natasha comes to the fore, sets her arms akimbo, and strikes a posture of readiness to dance, she does so "with such precision, such complete precision, that Anisya Fedorovna, who had at once handed her the handkerchief she needed for the dance, had tears in her eyes, though she laughed as she watched this slim, graceful countess, reared in silks and velvets and so different from herself, who yet was able to understand all that was in Anisya and in Anisya's father and mother and aunt, and in every Russian man and woman."[64]

Natasha's, then, is not just a peasant dance, but also, as it were, a *relay*-dance, as the kerchief handed her by Anysia Fedorovna, a peasant woman *and* probably a good dancer herself, serves as the equivalent of a baton. The coda of the above quote sounds almost biblical in its widening enumeration of tribes. The bottom line is: the kerchief—a sine qua non for a woman in a Russian folk dance—which the young countess receives from a genuine peasant woman, epitomizes Russianness across class borders.

Which is precisely why Tolstoy hastens to distinguish it from a *shawl*, an item used analogously in French character dances: "Where, how, and when had this young countess, educated by an *émigrée* French governess, imbibed from the Russian air she breathed that spirit and obtained that manner which the *pas de châle* would, one would have supposed, long ago have effaced?"[65] In other words, Frenchness can be learned; Russianness can only be "imbibed" from "Russian air." Recall Natasha's first ball in St. Petersburg, where she shone precisely on the strength of her preparedness for that particular entrance. It took the likes of Countess Rostova years of being taught by professionals how to dance well. At Uncle's, she triumphs for all the opposite reasons: "[T]he spirit and the movements were those inimitable and unteachable Russian ones that 'Uncle' had expected of her."[66]

Transfiguration through dance: what occurs with Natasha this evening is meant to seem miraculous. "She's ridden all day like a man," comments Uncle, looking at Natasha, "and is as fresh as ever!"[67] Tolstoy would have us see Natasha's peasant dance as an impulsive, spontaneous eruption of joy, endemic to people close to the land. Yet, viewed from a more sober perspective, Tolstoy's fictional miracle at Uncle's is utterly "balletic" in the worst sense, up to the fact that, around the time he conjured it in *War and Peace*, a "peasant dance" set to the same folk song ("Po ulitse mostovoi") was featured in Saint-Léon's folktale-sourced ballet *Little Humpbacked Horse*, which would soon become a byword for cheesy pseudo-Russian stylization.

Un paysan from Chistiakov's sketch "Balletomane," as conveyed by portly Varlamov, is trotting *en dansante*; Perrot's fishermen, as we recall from Saltykov-Shchedrin's parody-review, "are dancing because they are pulling nets from the sea; dancing because they are villagers, and, in this capacity, *must* dance."[68] This is how Valerian Svetlov, writing in 1915, summarized "old-school balletic logic": "We are very tired, say the villagers, and, therefore, let's dance!"[69] Nor did peasant dances require rural settings filled with "Russian air" (which Saltykov-Shchedrin would, in any case, have identified as another "modern specter"). In Tolstoy's time, as in the time of *War and Peace*, the *russkaia*—the Russian dance—was a set piece of salon entertainment. Were such *urban* peasant dances truly peasant? On Tolstoy's scale of values, hardly. On the other hand, by Nekrasov's standards, or

102   IMPOSSIBLE PROJECT

Saltykov-Shchedrin's, *any* image of a happy peasant was but another literary specter; neither would accept fatigue as an incentive to dance.

Natasha's next encounter with dance occurs in Moscow, to which Tolstoy takes her after this sojourn in an Edenic rural Russia. Her reintegration into the life of the urban aristocracy is presented as a fall. In the wake of that waltz and that unforgettable cotillion at the ball in St. Petersburg, her maiden heart has been promised to Prince Andrei. In Moscow, it is preyed upon by an experienced seducer, town rake Anatole Kuragin—an affair in which Anatole's sister, the beautiful and cynical Hélène, acts as a co-conspirator.

The setting for the fall of Natasha's poor heart is the Bolshoi Theater, on a night when Moscow's beau monde is gathered to see the famous French danseur Duport (a real figure from the time of Didelot inserted into the fictional framework of *War and Peace*) dance in an entrée de ballet in the midst of an unnamed opera.[70]

In reading Tolstoy's account of what goes on in Natasha's mind as she watches the performance, we should recall that, as a girl brought up in a family of the Rostovs' standing, she knows very well what opera is (her singing teacher had been Italian), and has taken dance lessons; why, at the age of fourteen, she had even expressed the aspiration (albeit clearly jocularly) of a balletic career. A dialogue with her brother, four years before the fateful visit to the Bolshoi:

> "[W]hat are you up to now?"
>
> "Now?" repeated Natasha, and a happy smile lit up her face. "Have you seen Duport?"
>
> "No."
>
> "Not seen Duport—the famous dancer? Well then, you won't understand. That's what I'm up to."
>
> Curving her arms, Natasha held out her skirts as dancers do, ran back a few steps, turned, cut a caper, brought her little feet sharply together, and made some steps on the very tips of her toes.
>
> "See, I'm standing! See!" she said, but could not maintain herself on her toes any longer. "So that's what I'm up to! I'll never marry anyone, but will be a dancer. Only don't tell anyone."[71]

Thus Natasha the youngster (this chapter is set in 1806) has not only seen Duport but also sports a few balletic steps herself. Yet four years later, as Natasha sits in a box at the Bolshoi, she finds herself incapable of either following the action of the opera or comprehending the vocabulary of ballet. When, at the outset of a choreographic entrée, a corps de ballet is brought to the stage, Natasha seems ignorant of the very concept; what she perceives before her are just "men and women with bare legs [coming] in from both sides and . . . dancing all together."[72] And when a soloist enters to perform a sequence of cabrioles, what Natasha sees is this: "Then the violins played very shrilly and merrily and one of the women with thick bare legs and thin arms, separating from the others, went behind the wings, adjusted her bodice, returned to the middle of the stage, and began jumping and striking one foot rapidly against the other."[73] Neither does she recognize the idol of her childhood: "Then one of the men went into a corner of the stage. The cymbals and horns in the orchestra struck up more loudly, and this man with bare legs jumped very high and waved his feet about [*stal semenit' nogami*] very rapidly." Apparently, the pas Natasha perceives this way is an entrechat; we know who performs it only because Tolstoy adds a bracketed aside: "(He was Duport, who received sixty thousand rubles a year for this art.)"[74]

Salient in Natasha's inner account of all three dances is Tolstoy's attention to anatomy: Duport's bare legs; the bare legs of men and women of the corps de ballet; and the female soloist's thin arms and thick legs, also bare. As Natasha's absent gaze wanders from the stage to the audience, we are to connect the nakedness of the dancers' lower limbs (in reality, they would be in tights)[75] with the exposed upper torsos of the ladies in attendance, whose nudity Tolstoy consistently overstates: "all the women with gems on their bare flesh"; "seminude [*ogolennye*] women in the boxes"; Hélène, "quite unclothed" and "scantily clad" (literally: nude, *golaia*); the same Hélène, "her whole bosom completely exposed."[76] The theater is a machine of seduction: "[L]ooking into [Anatole's] eyes [Natasha] was frightened, realizing that there was not that barrier of modesty she had always felt between herself and men."[77]

What occurs in Natasha's mind as she watches the opera is, as Tolstoy wants us to read it, a regrettable rite of passage from the rural to the urban, and from the real to the artful. "After her life in the country, and in her present serious mood," explains Tolstoy, "all this seemed grotesque and amazing [*diko i udivitel'no*] to Natasha. She could not follow the opera nor even listen [literally: hear, *slyshat'*] the music; she saw only the painted cardboard and the queerly dressed men and women who moved, spoke, and sang so strangely in that brilliant light."[78] Gradually, however, this insistent sense of strangeness subsides—not least owing to the enthusiasm with which everyone else

104   IMPOSSIBLE PROJECT

applauds and cheers. In the beginning, Natasha sees the opera and ballet as would her "inner peasant." But under the influence of what would nowadays be called peer pressure, Natasha, as Tolstoy makes us witness, slips back into the skin of a young countess, educated by an émigrée French governess—the skin she had shed, if temporarily, at Uncle's place.

> [W]ith rapturous faces everyone began shouting: "Duport! Duport! Duport!" Natasha no longer thought this strange. She looked about with pleasure, smiling joyfully.
>   "N'est ce pas qu'il est admirable—Duport?" Hélène asked her.
>   "Oh, oui," replied Natasha.[79]

Owing to Viktor Shklovsky's 1917 essay "Art as Device," Tolstoy's aloof depiction of the opera in *War and Peace* has become a master example of what, in the early days of Russian formalist theory, became known as *ostrannenie*—in Russian, an easily graspable neologism, rendered in English either as "enstrangement" (whose strangeness and transparency match Shklovsky's original coinage) or as the more familiar "defamiliarization." Perhaps the most straightforward way of "enstranging" a thing like an opera is to keep calling its fundamental conventions "strange," "grotesque," or "bizarre," as we just saw Tolstoy's Natasha do several times in the space of a paragraph. Another is the strategy of renaming or, rather, unnaming the thing you are describing. "Tolstoy's method of enstrangement," says Shklovsky, "consists in not calling a thing or event by its name but describing it as if seen for the first time, as if happening for the first time."[80]

This strategy becomes more obvious when we consider the textual history of *War and Peace*. Tolstoy is known for the layers upon layers of revisions he would subject his manuscripts to before publishing or republishing them. If, for instance, we review some of the changes he made to the segment in which Natasha describes, in her head, the second and third acts of the opera in question, we are struck by how consistently he crosses out words that betray certainty and knowledge and replaces them with various lexical obliquities. In an earlier version, we are told that "behind the scenes, a saucepan was struck three times and everyone knelt down and sang a prayer"; in the final version, the "saucepan" is replaced by "something metallic"—a textbook example of Shklovsky's enstrangement by unnaming.[81]

The same logic, mutatis mutandis, applies to narrative modality. Frequent in the earlier version of the theater scene is the word "bad" or "badly" (*durnoi*, *durno*); used six times in a single paragraph, "bad" colors Natasha's inner narrative with a *knowledgeable* disaffection. The scenery of the third act includes pictures of knights with short beards, "painted particularly badly, so badly as can only be done for a theater stage."[82] This appraisal, included as it is in Natasha's train of thought, would cast her as a skeptical theater *regular* and a *connoisseur* of the fine arts, so it is not surprising that Tolstoy omitted it, along with both "badly's," in the final version. Clad in "bad costumes," the "tsar and tsarina" of the show sing "very badly"; here, too, both "bad" and "badly" are gone. The only "bad" of his initial six that Tolstoy ultimately keeps pertains to a solo that the "tsar" performs before sinking into a "crimson throne," perhaps with an eye to contrasting the "tsar's" aria with Uncle's singing while playing his guitar, which Natasha, one book before, had found incredibly *good*.[83]

As these reproof words are excised, the modality of Natasha's account shifts from critical involvement to enstrangement. For example, her perception of a pas performed by the dancer who turns out to be Duport originally read, "[T]his man with bare legs jumped very high and very badly";[84] upon revising the passage, Tolstoy replaced the phrase "and very badly" with "and waved his feet about very rapidly."[85] Both statements convey Natasha's distaste, but while the former is still evaluating the dancer's skill (negatively), the latter questions the point of dancing per se—questions its very sanity.

Unnaming is, so to speak, a cultural punishment. Stripping an entrechat of its balletic name is tantamount to demoting it.[86] The same is true of gestures, particularly when these are codified, as are many in opera and nearly all in ballet. Gestures *mean*; a meaningless gesture is, strictly speaking, a contradiction in terms. Tolstoy, much like Saltykov-Shchedrin in his parodic review of *The Naiad and the Fisherman*, robs gestures of meaning. Here as there, people on stage merely "wave" or "flap" (*razmakhivaiut*) their arms and hands. It is as if we were watching a movie version of an opera, and, all of a sudden, the soundtrack were turned off. Operagoers come to an opera to *listen*; Natasha *stares*, seeing nudity on the stage and in proscenium boxes. Guiding her stare, Tolstoy turns a night at the opera into a display of dubious delights.

Tolstoy's technique of enstrangement becomes clearer if, following Johan Huizinga and Yuri Lotman, we posit art and culture as a game that is only valued by, only *real* to those who accept its rules. Lotman's textbook example of the relational reality of games is, fittingly enough, the "Games" chapter of Tolstoy's first novel, *Childhood*, published in 1852 in Nekrasov's

Contemporary.[87] It is summer. Disheartened by his elder brother Volodya's reluctance to join him, their young sister Liubochka, and her tutor's daughter Katen'ka, the novel's protagonist and first-person narrator Nikolen'ka, just over ten, recalls long winter evenings the four of them used to spend riding a make-believe carriage: "[W]e used to cover an armchair with a cloth, and make a carriage of it; one took the coachman's seat, another the lackey's, the girls were in the middle, three stools were the three horses, and we started off on the road. And what different kinds of accidents used to happen on that road, and how merrily and swiftly those winter evenings passed away!"[88]

That summer, Volodya's attitude toward games has changed: "[H]e may have had too much common sense and too little imagination to take complete enjoyment in the game of Robinson."[89] The younger children eventually convince Volodya to play with them, but he does so half-heartedly, and the game is spoiled: "Volodya's condescension gave us very little pleasure; on the contrary, his lazy and weary look destroyed all the charm of the game. When we seated ourselves on the ground, and, imagining that we were rowing out to catch fish, began to row with all our might, Volodya sat down with crossed arms, and in a pose which had nothing in common with the attitude of a fisherman. I told him so; but he answered that we should gain nothing by swinging our arms [*makhat' rukami*], and that we should not get far away anyhow."[90] According to Volodya's (rational) logic—ponders his little brother—three stools for horses would not get you very far, either. But "to judge by what was going on now, there would be no game. And if there were to be no game, what, then, would be left?"[91]

Natasha Rostova's role in the opera chapter of *War and Peace* is akin to that of Volodya in the "Games" chapter of *Childhood*; to borrow a term from the English translation of Huizinga's 1938 treatise *Homo Ludens: A Study of the Play-Element in Culture*, both are being the "spoilsport." Children play that they are rowing—Volodya calls it "swinging one's arms" (literally, "flapping"); whether opera singers are shown fencing, issuing a command, or expressing desperation, Natasha uses the same verb, "to wave" or "to flap" (*makhat'*). So does Saltykov-Shchedrin for every *pas d'action* in either Perrot's *Naiad* or Saint-Léon's *Golden Fish*, which begins with "Galia (m-me [Guglielmina] Salvioni) running onto the stage, arms flapping to signal that her old husband is always asleep, leaving her, Galia, ungratified."[92]

The more Tolstoy's prose develops into the moral preachment of his later years, the bolder becomes his experiment in enstrangement. His 1886 "Strider" ("Kholstomer"), narrated by an embittered old horse, is

MODERN SPECTERS 107

enstrangement incarnate. Much of it is about games that Strider refuses to comprehend. Human behavior is defined not by actions but by words; this much the horse understands. Strider has also observed how important for people is the game of "mine": "They agree that only one person may say 'mine' about any particular thing. And the one who says 'mine' about the greatest number of things, in this game whose rules they've made up among themselves, is considered the happiest."[93] One thing the poor horse finds hard to fathom, however, is why those who call it "theirs" never ride or feed it; why is this left to others?

In *Resurrection* (1899), his last novel, Tolstoy himself takes up the role of spoilsport earlier delegated to Volodya, Natasha, and the horse. In a pas-sage that even the weathered iconoclast Victor Shklovsky calls "monstrous," Tolstoy defamiliarizes something quintessentially familiar to anyone born in the Orthodox faith in nineteenth-century Russia, regardless of class, age, or gender. The scene is set in a prison church; the narrator's voice is strictly authorial:

> The essence of the service consisted in the presumption that the small pieces of bread cut by the priest and dipped in the wine, accompanied by certain manipulations and prayers, became the body and blood of God. These manipulations consisted in the priest's raising his arms at stated intervals and, encumbered as he was with his gold cloth sack, keeping them in this attitude, kneeling from time to time and kissing the table and all objects upon it. But the principal act was when the priest, having taken the napkin in both hands, evenly and methodically waved it over the saucer and the golden cup. This was supposed to be the moment when the bread and wine are transformed into the body and blood, and therefore this part of the service was performed with special solemnity.[94]

Tolstoy's, of course, is an ABC of enstrangement. To begin with, he institutes a taboo on calling things by their names: the Eucharist remains unnamed; the sleeveless phelonion (*felon*) worn by priests during liturgies is reduced to a "sack," not so much a garment as a nuisance each time the priest raises his arms. The religious rite is referred to as a "manipulation," as if the activity of a trickster or conjurer. The whole cannibalistic ballet culminates in the priest "waving his hands" with a prop, which Tolstoy enstranges as a "napkin," over what he calls a "saucer." A man of letters, Tolstoy believed in the Gospel and mistrusted clerical pantomimes. As far as he was concerned,

108   IMPOSSIBLE PROJECT

the liturgy had no more to do with the Holy Scriptures than Saint-Léon's *Golden Fish* had with Pushkin's "Tale of the Fisherman and the Fish."

Young Nikolen'ka, Tolstoy's alter ego from his first novel, worries, "And if there are no games, what is left?" In the span of some fifty years from *Childhood*, Tolstoy evolved into a semblance of Nikolen'ka's elder brother Volodya, a disbeliever in games. Arguably the greatest spoilsport in history, the post-fiction Tolstoy enstranges fiction, from Shakespeare's to his own. Coleridge famously observed that fiction requires a "willing suspension of disbelief"; it could be added that this suspension is *itself* suspended, willfully, in enstrangement.

The Artiste-Director

Nomina sunt odiosa. That every instance of ballet-bashing considered so far—fictional or factual, candid or pretended—would be marked by an avoidance of naming names was more than a rhetorical device, a matter of enstrangement; it was a *political* stance. To name means to acknowledge. Stripped of names—as in Saltykov-Shchedrin's writings or Natasha's perception—ballet becomes a bland and faceless institution, an establishment plain and simple. True, Nekrasov names Maria Petipa, but only to admonish her for balletizing the *muzhik*; and while Tolstoy mentions Duport, this is just to inform the reader how much he earned for his "mincing feet"; and when Saltykov-Shchedrin, for once, lets fall the name of the illustrious ballerina Marfa Muravieva, the epithet he chooses sounds like a backhanded compliment: "M-me Muravieva was quite pretty [*ochen' mila*]."[95]

"Quite pretty" is an intentional misnomer, of the kind we encounter time and again in Saltykov-Shchedrin's wry writings on ballet. Ballet lore (not unlike folklore) is prone to aggrandizing. Whichever side a balletomane might take in the epic rivalry between Petipa's wife Maria and Saint-Léon's star Muravieva, neither of the two were to be described as anything short of magical, incomparable, or peerless—or else gone was the epic scale of the (somewhat comic) struggle between "petipists" and "murav'ists," two self-proclaimed factions of the balletomane community that enjoyed sparring over whose dame was the chosen one. As to "quite pretty," the epithet was reserved for corps de ballet.

Being in a corps de ballet bordered on namelessness—as one infers from the title of Petr Boborykin's "Second-from-the-Water," a moving

MODERN SPECTERS 109

piece of fiction, examined in the next chapter, about a dancer reduced to performing in the rear row of the imperial corps de ballet. Not every member of the corps de ballet, however, faced relegation to the status of "et-cetera danseuse." Unlike Boborykin's heroine, front-row danseuses—most of them coryphées—could hope to see their names in the morning papers.

But to merit this, one had to dance well or to be, well, pretty. "A number of Moscow danseuses have successfully transferred [to Petersburg]," reports Skalkovsky in the *New Time* (*Novoe vremia*), "owing either to their dancing skills (M-mes Roslavleva and Geltser), or outward appearance (M-me Bakerkina)."[96] It also helped to know how to "sell" a look: "M-mes Borchardt, Bakerkina, Vasilieva and other comely coryphées [*khoroshen'kie korifeiki*] looked pleasing in graceful 'paysanne' costumes [in Petipa's 1896 *Bluebeard*]."[97] And how to engage an eager onlooker in a game of glances: "[In Saint-Léon's *Graziella*], [o]ur corps de ballet, still graced by M-mes Chumakova, Borchardt, Bakerkina, Berestovskaia and others, worked heartily with their feet and eyes [*i nozhkami, i glazkami*]."[98]

Also helpful were connections. Skalkovsky's constant name-dropping of the "*khoroshen'kaia* M-me Bakerkina"[99] had less to do with the newsworthiness of our comely coryphée than with her attendant clout. At the time, a name in a review worked like a "like" button in social media today. It helped maintain a rapport between the reviewer and the reviewed and, in the case of Nadezhda Bakerkina, between Skalkovsky and a fellow balletomane, Bakerkina's powerful patron General Petr Durnovo.

Ballet reviews used to buzz with names. Add here the names of the composer and conductor, the librettist and ballet master, the costume designer and backdrop painter, not to forget the effects wizards: the stage machinist Andreas Roller and his Moscow counterpart Karl Valts. Until the 1880s, the least likely name to encounter in the onomasticon of ballet criticism was the name of the current director of Imperial Theaters—unless, like Stepan Gedeonov (in office 1867–75), he tried his hand at a libretto, or, like Baron Karl Kister, proved a spectacular disaster.

Being *in* ballet presupposed some know-how: how to dance, decorate, or make music. But being *in charge of* ballet required none. None of the five directors serving from 1833 (the year the office was instituted) to 1881—aside from Gedeonov, who divided his time (alas, unequally) between running the Imperial Theaters and the Hermitage Museum—had come to this position from the arts.

110   IMPOSSIBLE PROJECT

The very mechanism of appointing a director of Imperial Theaters seemed almost calculated to avert any eventuality of competence. Because the next-in-turn director used to be named by the current minister of the Imperial Court, in consultation with the emperor (and not, for instance, with Perrot or Marius Petipa), the deciding factor was not artistic promise but some unrelated—military, diplomatic, or bureaucratic—renown. Appointed director of the Imperial Theaters at the age of sixty-two, Andrei Saburov (1858–62) was a former Cavalry Guards colonel; his successor, Count Aleksandr Borkh (1862–67), appointed at the age of fifty-eight, had served as a chargé d'affaires at the Russian embassy in Florence, later becoming a big shot at the Ministry of Foreign Affairs; Baron Kister (1875–81), as a former head of the Court Exchequer (*kassa Dvora*), may have been more informed about ballet, but mainly about its cash losses—which Kister undertook to stanch with fiscal tightwaddery that defeated the purpose.

Director Borkh died of a stroke in August 1867; the same month, in the wake of Borkh's death, Nekrasov wrote yet another ballet-related satire in verse, titled "The Parable of Kissel." Set, befitting a parable, in a nowhere kingdom, the ballad features a generic director of the Imperial Theaters, named after *kisel'* (berry juice thickened with starch), and thus conjuring associations with this dish's uncertain taste and gelatinous texture. A composite portrayal of two prototypes, Borkh and Saburov, Nekrasov's Kissel, a tired old man, is placed in charge of ballet by his sovereign the tsar, in recognition of Kissel's erstwhile military triumphs—*brutish* triumphs, Nekrasov specifies—over enemies foreign and domestic.[100]

But then comes a plot twist. Instead of perceiving his new post for what it is—a sinecure—our hero rushes to reform the Imperial Theaters according to his idea of propriety and order: he bans cross-gender casting, for instance, and institutes a uniform haircut and daily parade-ground drills. The result, to the tsar's displeasure, is empty houses.

> The moral: while it may be hard
> To tear down a fortress wall,
> The temple of Melpomene
> Is even harder to run without the know-how."[101]

Nekrasov's parable is not a cautionary tale; he knew the system too well to expect things to change. Rather, it sounds like a lament—for ballet, of course, not for its recently departed figurehead. Would ballet survive another director like Borkh?

The democrat Nekrasov had good reason to look askance at top-down appointments. Given the lackluster backstories epitomized in Nekrasov's parable, it was almost unthinkable that a director of Imperial Theaters might one day turn out to be, for instance, a gifted stage performer or an all right playwright or, say, an accomplished draughtsman and costume designer or an admirer of classical music who envisioned, to boot, that serious composers should write for the ballet—until, one day in 1881, precisely that happened. Handpicked by the just-enthroned Emperor Alexander III and the just-appointed minister of the Imperial Court, Count Illarion Vorontsov-Dashkov, the new director of the Imperial Theaters Ivan Vsevolozhsky was all of that, and would prove more: a patient and provident theater reformer, a strategic spender, and, to the extent possible for a high-ranking courtier, a man able to keep his political and cultural agendas separate.[102]

Vsevolozhsky, whose directorship would last eighteen years, died in October 1909. Later that month, an essay subtitled "From Personal Recollections" by Vsevolozhsky's old acquaintance Petr Boborykin appeared in Moscow's *Russian Word* (*Russkoe slovo*). Had the piece, which opens with the elegiac "Yet another fresh grave,"[103] been a proper obituary, it might have been titled, as on a headstone, "Ivan Aleksandrovich Vsevolozhsky, 1835–1909." But Boborykin chose a title that would make a point: "The Artiste-Director" ("Direktor-artist").[104]

The coinage harbors a homily. Instrumental to Vsevolozhsky's appointment as director of the Imperial Theaters and his many successes in this capacity had been, in Boborykin's view, not Vsevolozhsky's prior professional achievements in the realm of foreign affairs but his younger-days hobby: playing comic characters in French comedies—in French.

Memoirists, obituarists, and biographers agree: from the 1860s to the mid-1870s, Vsevolozhsky did enjoy acclaim in Petersburg as a topnotch comic actor.[105] Not that he was a darling of the broad public like, for instance, Konstantin Varlamov on the Alexandrinsky stage; that particular walk of life was off-limits to the nobility. Vsevolozhsky played before his peers, on the home stage found in any self-respecting patrician household, from mansions to palaces. His was the world of aristocratic theatricals, a two-centuries-long, largely invisible, and yet-to-be-written chapter of theater history made by, as they were then called, "noble amateurs" (*blagorodnye liubiteli*).

112   IMPOSSIBLE PROJECT

What does it mean to be an "amateur actor"? The notion has changed considerably from Vsevolozhsky's time to our own. One variance is that of prestige. Today, amateur stages are seen as poor relations of professional ones, but in eighteenth- and nineteenth-century Russia, the word "amateur" carried an *elitist* connotation. In the Age of Enlightenment, performing on an amateur stage meant the enlightened addressing the enlightened, frequently in a play that was supposed to be enlightening. If, for example, as an amateur, you appeared in a tragedy by Voltaire, your audience could reasonably expect that your part was hardly the only Voltaire you'd read (which, then as now, might be the case with a professional actor) and that, after the show (followed, as a rule, by a dinner for everyone), you might be inclined to some pleasant philosophical conversation.

Then there is the variance in backgrounds. The modern amateur actor is unlikely to have received any training at an acting school. This, of course, is true of the eighteenth and nineteenth centuries as well, perhaps even more true; the Imperial Theater School, or any such kind of school, was no place for the well-born. But this is just half the story. We should keep in mind that instruction in the arts, in noble homes and high-estate schools, was largely about *making* and *doing* art. Earlier in the book, I had occasion to stress how important it was, if you wanted to be a society person in nineteenth-century Russia, to be something of a dancer. The same, to varying degrees, was true of other skills. For a society lady, for instance, it was de rigueur to be able to play music and sing; to be a true gentleman meant wielding the pen, at least enough to inscribe a madrigal or an *ésprit* in a lady's album.[106]

To be something of an actor paid as well. "Playing in French, I grew accustomed to its style and idiom, and taught myself to articulate correctly and clearly," explains Ivan Dolgorukov, recalling in his memoir his youthful amateur performances at his uncle's home theater in Moscow in 1781.[107] "[N]o language schooling can give you what [stage] practice will, to say nothing of how it enriches the memory with many a verse—a resource that later helped win my way into society."[108]

Amateur theatricals and professional productions may be thought of as complementary, and intertwining, opposites. Socially, noble amateurs on the one hand, and actors who played for a living on the other, formed two separate communities; culturally, these were two facets of the same whole. A stage remains a stage, whether it is the vast one at the Alexandrinsky or more like a platform at your uncle's place. Likewise, a drama is a drama, whether enacted by amateurs or professionals. The same applies to criteria of quality. To excel

MODERN SPECTERS   113

in a Molière or Corneille, an amateur was expected to hew to the rules of elocution and expressive movement long in place on legitimate stages like the Comédie Française in Paris. Acting as an *occupation* may have been dubious, but when it came to acting techniques, the noblest of amateurs would look to those who played for a living. In his (non)obituary of Vsevolozhsky, Boborykin recalls a conversation he had back in the 1860s with Adolphe Dupuis, then a leading actor with the French troupe at the Mikhailovsky Theater. "Had I been a theater entrepreneur," confided Dupuis to Boborykin, "and had a comic actor of [Vsevolozhsky's] talent applied, I would have offered him twenty thousand francs a year on the spot."[109] Dupuis's tribute is doubly counterfactual: he was not an entrepreneur, and Vsevolozhsky would never have agreed to become a professional actor, even had he needed the money. But Boborykin knew that, for a true amateur, the approval of a true professional meant more than your uncle's invariable *très jolie*.

Being an amateur, of course, was an expense, or an investment, as emerges from Dolgorukov's comments. One thing it could earn you was *visibility*— among one's peers and, with luck, before the sovereign. This was how, explains Filipp Vigel' in a bilious memoir written some time before 1856, Vasilii Pushkin (Aleksandr's uncle, b. 1766) launched his society career. At eighteen, as Vigel' has it, Pushkin "used to recite, at soirees, lengthy tirades from Voltaire and Racine, acquainting the public with names as yet little known in Russia; at twenty, he played Orosmane in [Voltaire's] *Zaïre* in domestic theaters, and composed couplets in French. How little it took to become famous back then!"[110]

Domestic stages varied in size and significance, depending on the size and significance of the domicile that housed them. The one on which young Prince Dolgorukov used to tower must have occupied the larger part of a living room, with the smaller part allotted to the audience. Vsevolozhsky's path as a comic actor, bookended by two lengthy assignments abroad—in the Hague until 1863 and in Paris after 1876—took him all the way up the amateur "career" ladder to the roomy stages of the Grand Dukes' Court (*velikokniazheskii dvor*) at the Anichkov Palace, where children of the royal family, including the crown prince, used to reside. Instrumental in this ascent, as can be inferred from various French and Russian sources, was Vsevolozhsky's admirer, the professional actor Dupuis.

Busy as he may have been at the Mikhailovsky Theater, Dupuis did not shun (or could not afford to refuse) two side jobs, both at the Grand Dukes' Court in the Anichkov Palace. In 1872, his biographer Francisque

114   IMPOSSIBLE PROJECT

Sarcey informs us, Empress Maria Alexandrovna offered Dupuis the position of *chtets*, a tutor responsible for reading and explaining "masterpieces of [French] classical literature to the royal offspring."[111]

Dupuis's other sideline, which, we learn from Russian sources, goes back to the 1860s,[112] was directing—and this is where Vsevolozhsky, that stately star of princely stages, comes back in. That noble amateurs and trained professionals did not mix on stage does not mean they did not team up behind the scenes. "[Dupuis] was in charge of most spectacles staged at court and the Grand Dukes' palaces," informs Sarcey. "He directed [*dirigeait*] amateur companies that enjoyed the luxury of presenting their comedies on stages of such stature."[113]

A noble amateur, inspired and guided by a professional actor of the Petersburg French troupe, wins acceptance at the court of the crown prince, his siblings, and their retinue. Cut to ten years later, as the prince-turned-monarch puts our amateur actor in charge of a host of professional theaters (including the French troupe, by then sans Dupuis). In the nineteenth century, an appointment like this made sense, and not only because of the hierarchy of social estates or the catching of a rising ruler's eye. An amateur artiste was particularly suited to become Boborykin's "artiste-director." A professional actor just needs to be good at acting; to stand out as an amateur meant being an actor *and* a showman who thinks of everything, from music to costumes and props.

Crucially, it also meant being accustomed to the fact that showmanship is about spending money, not saving it. (To say nothing of *making* it.) What made Vsevolozhsky a savvy theatrical administrator—and not an *administrator*-administrator, like his predecessor Kister—was a conviction that squandering can actually pay. Formerly in charge of the Court Exchequer, Kister was strictly a bottom-line man. He well understood that ventures like the Imperial Ballet or the French troupe of the Imperial Mikhailovsky Theater would never be profitable; the logical conclusion was that the only way to improve the court's finances was to cut spending.

As a result, the French company in Petersburg was practically "killed off" (*ubit navsegda*), as Skalkovsky put it.[114] Kister failed (or did not try) to retain the expensive Dupuis; other prominent players were likewise lost. Earlier, Petersburg headhunters would poach from major Paris stages, targeting no lesser game than Conservatoire graduates, but under Kister, as the *Prompter* (*Sufler*) newspaper reported in 1882, vacancies in the French troupe would be filled with "mediocrities recruited not even from second-rate theaters in Paris, but from provincial theaters in France, or, worse, in Belgium."[115]

Figure 2.2 Ivan Vsevolozhsky, "The Preparatory Class for the Theater Administration, according to the Syllabus of Professor Skalkovsky," a sarcastic reaction by Vsevolozhsky to Skalkovsky's reproaching of the Directorate for not having professional dance skills.

116   IMPOSSIBLE PROJECT

In ballet, Kister ordered economizing on what is nowadays called production values (the period term *montirovochnaia chast'*, the "mounting department," is no longer in use); sets, stage effects, and costumes were to be repurposed or retailored rather than made and sewn each time anew. Kister ordained a limit of no more than three sets per show; as to effects, ballet old-timers who had seen Taglioni's *Maiden of the Danube* in 1842 are said to have been left wondering where the final-act fountains had gone in its 1880 revival (with Vazem in the title role), and why the young Rudolph (Pavel Gerdt) is made to find himself among river nymphs simply by trotting out from behind the wings instead of leaping (as would befit his madness) into the underwater world. "In general, our ballet's machinery is in a terrible state," Skalkovsky observes.[116]

Indeed, in the space of six years of Kister's directorship, the *spectacle* of ballet in Russia shrank considerably. What Saltykov-Shchedrin refused to embrace, and Kister fell short of understanding, was how native to the medium of ballet was the *extraordinary*: river naiads, sprites of valleys, and suchlike *genii loci* in love with local mortals; mad leaps instead of trotting; in short, feasting one's eyes, as opposed to the fast Kister imposed. "A ballet bereft of luxurious staging ... makes decisively no sense," fulminated Skalkovsky. Not even in economic terms: "Treat us to a genuinely spectacular ballet, and it will stay in the repertoire for as long as half a hundred shows."[117] In the long run, higher production values will pay off, argued Skalkovsky again in 1883 (i.e., two-plus years into Vsevolozhsky's directorship), drawing on recent historical lessons: "Ballet is a spectacle for the eye, and, as such, calls for sumptuous staging. ... Old luxurious ballets from the 1850s feed our repertoire to this day, while the cheapo, moneysaving ballets [*desheven'kie ekonomnye balety*] from Baron Kister's time failed to last more than three or four seasons."[118]

That even Skalkovsky, a diehard Noverrian, would call ballet a "spectacle for the eye" heralded a new, post-Noverrian thinking, which, as often occurs with such shifts, seemed to result in the return of some fairly *pre*-Noverrian phenomena. Richly costumed and vaguely allegorical, the *ballets de cour* that had been in vogue in grand palaces in Renaissance Italy and sixteenth- and seventeenth-century France were, indeed, sumptuous spectacles, designed primarily to delight the eye; what Noverre undertook by way of wedding it to drama was to redefine ballet as an art for hearts *and* minds. Vsevolozhsky took an opposite tack. Encouraged by the new emperor, and with new infusions of cash from the new minister of the court, the new director of the

MODERN SPECTERS 117

Imperial Theaters set out to restore ballet to its original opulence and grandeur, lost in the lean years of Kister's rule.

There are reasons to assume that Vsevolozhsky's penchant for profligate, unapologetically unserious, and downright childish ballets (as the likes of *The Nutcracker* and *Sleeping Beauty* were deemed by many a critic at the time) was his answer not only to Kister but also to Noverre. Noverre had frowned on the ballets staged by the Paris Opéra in the mid-eighteenth century as *ces extravagantes mascarades*;[119] Vsevolozhsky reveled in sartorial splendor: under his rule, ballets, to quote Vadim Gaevsky, "could be called costume symphonies and costume orgies, or, if you will, costume empires."[120] Noverre wanted his ballets to *mean*; Vsevolozhsky did as well, up to a point, but especially wanted them to *shine*.

In more than one way, Boborykin's "artiste-director" was also an *auteur*-director. That a director of the Imperial Theaters would write librettos was not unprecedented (Stepan Gedeonov, for instance, authored *Mlada*); what *was* unheard of was Vsevolozhsky's additional hat of costume designer. As subscribers to *The Yearbook of the Imperial Theaters* learned from a firsthand account by Mariinsky staff artist Evgenii Ponomarev in 1900 (one year after Vsevolozhsky's retirement), in the eighteen years of his directorship, Vsevolozhsky designed 1,087 costumes for a total of twenty-five productions (mostly ballets, plus a handful of operas and balletic inserts therein).[121] His masterpiece in this regard was *Sleeping Beauty*, whose apotheosis, Ponomarev reminds us, has the Sun God wearing a replica of the costume worn by the Roi Soleil Louis XIV in 1653's *Ballet Royal de la Nuit*—a costumer's homage to ballet's days of Eden, before Noverre had come to shame dancers for appearing, actually, dressed.[122]

On the other hand, much like Noverre before him, Vsevolozhsky insisted on the historical accuracy of costuming. A connoisseur of the history of material culture, he could be quite particular about what was worn when. So much so that, at one point, his historicism became the talk of the troupe. In a newspaper vignette, Skalkovsky conveyed tidbits from the banquet Virginia Zucchi gave for her co-dancers and select balletomanes to celebrate her 1886 *benefis* appearance in *The King's Command* (*Prikaz korolia*), a ballet set in sixteenth-century Spain:

"Have you noticed a novel feature about ballet?" "What feature?" "About costumes and sets." "What about them?" "Every costume sports crosses,

118 IMPOSSIBLE PROJECT

whether on mantles, breasts or sleeves! Even on the frescos, everyone wears a cross." "Checked against history! ... Indeed, nowadays every production is staged with archeological precision." "Yes—an entire act takes place in a nunnery, with maiden dancers wearing crosses around their necks! ... In any case, this is a novelty—no such rigor had been practiced in choreographic arts before! ... Do you approve of this?" "[Do I *what*]?!—such things are up to those in the know, not simple folk like you and me."[123]

Vsevolozhsky's "archeology" was more a matter of arts connoisseurship. A collector of sixteenth- to eighteenth-century figurines, miniature paintings, and sundry decorative items, Vsevolozhsky was keen to put fine arts at the service of the stage and assert ballet as a spectacle for the eye. Like Carlo Blasis before him, or Michel Fokine, Aleksandr Benois, and Sergei Diaghilev later, our artiste-director wanted ballet to make the most of its *Gesamtkunstwerk* potential—to engage painting and sculpture no less than movement and music. The Directorate knows nothing about dance, fulminated balletomanes. Should I and my assistants perhaps take a crash course in ballet, asks Vsevolozhsky's caricature in response (Figure 2.2).

Arguably, Vsevolozhsky's pluckiest venture in this regard was the one-act *Les Ruses d'Amour, or The Trial of Damis*, one of the last ballets he masterminded, and a feat of his dress design to boot.[124] Set in France in the age of rococo, *The Trial of Damis* is a sartorial story, quintessentially, a masquerade. Could Damis, engaged to marry Isabella without having met her, love her were she not Countess Lucinda's daughter and heiress? To test this, Isabella swaps clothes with her maid Marinette; fooled, Damis indeed falls in love with the putative soubrette, asking "Marinette" to elope. Isabella, re-dressed as herself, rewards Damis with her hand.

The premiere of this petite ballet was timed to a major change in Vsevolozhsky's career. In 1899, he was asked to retire from his post as director of the Imperial Theaters and take up that of director of the Hermitage Museum, which put him in charge not only of paintings and sculptures but also of the Hermitage Theater.

Designed for a coterie of eminences, first among them the royal family, the Hermitage Theater counted under three hundred seats facing, arch-wise, an accordingly minuscule stage. It was on this tiny stage that *The Trial of Damis* opened in mid-January 1900, the first month of Vsevolozhsky's new (and final) office. As if to celebrate the change of hats, Vsevolozhsky arranged *The Trial of Damis* to seem now like a ballet, now like a painting. The backdrop against which a series of period—terre-à-terre—dances unfolded featured the rococo essentials: shrubbery, a stone balustrade, and a tree swing. Encasing the backdrop was a painted picture frame, whose brushwork mimicked the whimsical woodwork of rococo *boiseries*. Was this an undersized stage or an oversized canvas? The instability of scale added to the artful ambivalence of two art forms.

So did the costumes and gestures depicted in thirty-seven sketches Vsevolozhsky made for *The Trial of Damis*. What he wanted the ballet to achieve, informs Ponomarev in the above-mentioned 1900 survey, "was to revive the epoch of Watteau."[125] This entailed more than mere stylization. *D'après Watteau*, reads one of Vsevolozhsky's sketches for *Damis*. *D'après* is not the same as *à la* Watteau, not just "in a Watteau-esque manner." As Yulia Belova has shown in a recent study, Vsevolozhsky makes use of scores of identifiable iconographic sources, known to him *de visu* or via prints.[126] And not from Jean-Antoine Watteau alone: the gorgeous, flower-trimmed dress— the dress de résistance of the show—worn by Pierina Legnani, who played Isabella, mirrors one from a 1730 painting by Nicolas Lancret (Figure 2.3),

Figure 2.3 Nicolas Lancret, *La Camargo Dancing* (1730–32). The State Hermitage Museum. Alamy.

120   IMPOSSIBLE PROJECT

an artist as responsible as Watteau for the debonair image of French life in the age of rococo.

Tableaux vivants, also known as onstage "realizations" of familiar paintings, were not foreign to nineteenth-century theater aesthetics.[127] At the Bolshoi in the 1860s, for instance, narrative paintings like Konstantin Flavitsky's *Princess Tarakanova*, brought to life by Moscow's ballerina Anna Sobeshchanskaia under the guidance of the machinist Karl Valts, constituted a whole separate subgenre.[128] That said, Vsevolozhsky's plan for *Damis* went well beyond such straightforward déjà-vus. His was a complex, transmedial trick. First of all, the model for Lancret's painting was herself a ballerina, Marie Camargo (hence the painting's title, *Camargo*), whose attitude and attire ballerina Legnani revived on the stage of the Hermitage Theater in 1900. Second, aside from her other choreographic innovations, Camargo was (and remains) remembered for a radical, at the time even scandalous costume reform: to provide her footwork more leeway, she shortened her dancing skirts to calf length. It was in one of her succès-de-scandale dresses—feet bravely exposed (with the foot-level view the painter grants onlookers on the painting)—that Lancret had depicted his Camargo, and thus did Vsevolozhsky dress Legnani (and later Preobrajenska). Choreographed by the clever Vsevolozhsky, two ballet dancers and their ballet dresses spoke to one another across two countries and epochs (Figure 2.4).

Third, Lancret's portrait of Camargo was part of the Hermitage Museum collection, which made the dialogue between epochs, countries, and art forms also a dialogue between adjacent rooms: the Hermitage Gallery this way, the Hermitage Theater over there. Here, Vsevolozhsky's past as an amateur actor returned with a vengeance. Any home-theater artiste worth his salt knew to make use of whatever was at hand—a collection of plays in your uncle's library, for instance, or a period portrait hanging next door. In this respect, every amateur actor was also an amateur *Gesamtkünstler*. Vsevolozhsky remained so throughout his life.

Such, in a nutshell, was Vsevolozhsky's creative career as an *artiste*—a costume designer and, while uncredited, a mastermind of set design. No less important for the history of ballet was Vsevolozhsky the director—a showman and policymaker, a participant in court policies at large, and, as I am going to show, the author of a politically ambivalent libretto.

Figure 2.4 Olga Preobrajenska and Pavel Gerdt in *The Trial of Damis* (1900).

Vsevolozhsky the Reformer

First, let me reiterate the main methodological premise of this study, namely, that when it comes to ballet, there is no direct access to the historical truth. The principal vestige of ballet's past is ballet lore. To understand ballet historically means to explore what it looked like from various, often contrary period perspectives. Is dancing *sur les pointes* an asset or a nuisance? Do not Zucchi's irresistible histrionics present too much of a temptation for Russian—ergo, classically schooled—ballet dancers? Or take the question of politics. To the likes of Saltykov-Shchedrin and Nekrasov, as we recall, the world of ballet, peopled by Maidens of the Danube and Sprites of the Valley, looked socially irrelevant. (Which, to such democratic critics, itself evinced a political, i.e., conservative, outlook.) Whereas, seen from Vsevolozhsky's perspective, ballet was itself all about politics. For one thing, ballet's precarious existence hinged on the whim of this or that potentate; for another, a ballet was de rigueur at court events of political prominence: royal birthdays and marriages and, most important, coronations, where danseurs and danseuses were expected to enact the national narrative, with a heavy focus, of course, on the present monarch. For that matter, as I plan to show, the most outwardly frivolous of balletic fairy tales could be deployed to promote the current ruler's geopolitical maneuvering and, at the same time, to caricature the reigning ideology.

The story of ballet's survival (and the story of *which stories* were to be enacted on balletic stages) would be incomplete without consideration of ballet's many points of contact with policy, foreign and domestic. Could ballet be saved by some reform from above? Toward the end of the directorship of Karl Kister (whom balletomanes invariably referred to as *Baron* Kister, to stereotype him as a German dryasdust), it seemed increasingly unviable as a stand-alone event. "Once a significant art form," deems the *Comprehensive Yearbook* [*Vseobshchii Kalendar'*] *for 1879*, "these days ballet has lost its allure: because the public no longer attends it, ballet in our Northern Palmyra [St. Petersburg] has become a luxury instead of necessity. . . . [It] has seen its day. The time has come for ballet to take its bow, and henceforth only reappear on stage as *un grand spectacle* embedded in opera shows."[129] Russian ballet lore of the latter half of the nineteenth century, beginning with Petipa himself, was aghast as full-evening ballet-only shows vanished from the capitals of Europe.[130] Would Petersburg be next?

MODERN SPECTERS   123

The Ministry of Alexander II's Imperial Court was hardly unaware of the crisis within the Imperial Theaters but could at best muster, in true bureaucratic fashion, an ad hoc committee. Appointed by Kister's superior, ministry head Aleksandr Adlerberg, the committee was "to base [the prospective reform] on a preliminary systematic review of legislative decisions on corresponding issues."[131] Normally, such phrasing might signal a kicking of the can well down the road, perhaps to never. But in this case, history acted fast. We know the precipitous events that led, among other things, to the theatrical reforms of 1881. Alexander II was assassinated; his successor Alexander III asked *his* minister of *his* Imperial Court to reach out to Paris and offer Kister's position to that amusing part-actor, part-diplomat Ivan Vsevolozhsky, coached to act by that remarkable actor from Paris, Adolphe Dupuis, the new tsar's erstwhile elocution tutor. This, to be sure, was a usual who-knows-whom kind of appointment, but it was also something else. That a stage-struck Francophile like Vsevolozhsky came to replace a notorious *baron* was a political move, and part of a trend—the weakening of the pro-German lobby in the high echelon of Russia's governmental apparatus—that would culminate, ten years later, in Alexander III signing the Franco-Russian Alliance (on which more below).

Reform became a key word during Vsevolozhsky's directorship. As Vladimir Pogozhev relates in detail in a memoir, his appointment as Vsevolozhsky's chief of staff began with a nine-month-long hands-on inspection of every aspect—administrative, financial, technical—of the way Petersburg's Imperial Theaters had been run. Pogozhev's findings were summed up in a memo Vsevolozhsky addressed to new court minister Vorontsov-Dashkov. This official, in turn, transformed Vsevolozhsky's memo into *his* report to Alexander III, who read it and penned the following resolution: "So this is where Kister's famous economy has gotten us. It can't be helped [*delat' nechego*], everything must little by little be put into a decent and proper shape [*v dolzhnyi i prilichnyi vid*]."[132] A sum of 180,000 rubles was allocated to right the wrongs of Kister's rule.[133]

The most anticipated reform was the lifting of the metropolitan monopoly, by which public performances on Petersburg and Moscow stages had been made the exclusive right of the Imperial Theaters. Originally a measure of ideological oversight of the repertoire, under Kister the monopoly had been extended to every sort of staged entertainment (including music concerts) and monetized; even if its prospective performance was approved as

124   IMPOSSIBLE PROJECT

morally/politically acceptable, a given private enterprise still had to pay the Directorate a permit fee. "Nowadays . . . it is hard to fathom what a stronghold [*tverdynia*] [the monopoly] was back then," recalls Boborykin in his 1909 tribute to Vsevolozhsky. "Back in 1880, when Anton Rubinstein came to Moscow to conduct his *Demon*, he and I had breakfast together, and he exclaimed: 'A parliament will be declared in this country before the monopoly of Court stages is lifted.' . . . [But Vsevolozhsky] was appointed in 1881, and, just one year later, private theaters were allowed."[134] Here, too, history acted faster than predicted.

The end of the Imperial Theaters' market monopoly on March 24, 1882, did not put court and private stages on an equal footing. An underperforming private enterprise could go bankrupt—an outcome not permitted the Imperial Theaters. To fulfill the emperor's brief that they be put in "decent and proper shape," Vsevolozhsky in a sense replaced the government's literal monopoly with a new one, on theater *status*. Per his reform project, the Imperial Theaters were to constitute "a *model* [*obraztsovyi*] governmental institution that sets an example for other Russian theater enterprises" (in other words, to be treated as preeminent by definition—on the very strength of being named "Imperial"); "a *brilliant* institution [*uchrezhdeniem blestiashchim*] that measures up to the dignity of the Imperial Court" (i.e., serves as a showcase for the Court, itself a showcase for the empire); and finally, they were to be "*economical* when spending, and generous when producing."[135]

This latter, rather gnomic point of Vsevolozhsky's manifesto echoed specific measures taken to safeguard the Imperial Theaters from failing. Wherever the 1881 subsidy of 180,000 rubles came from, from this time on the Directorate was supported primarily by an annual subsidy (2 million rubles) from the State Treasury, plus funds from the Imperial Cabinet (i.e., the tsar's own funds).[136] Materially, this step led to more lavish spectacles and fewer worries about returns; symbolically, to entertainment venues being rebranded as sites of edification.

Unprofitability was now to be redeemed, as it were, as an expected attribute of an "educational" institution. Pleshcheev, writing in 1896, defined the gist of the new statute: "The Imperial Theaters are non-commercial institutions that pursue the goal of ethical education."[137] As Vsevolozhsky's right hand Pogozhev never tired of emphasizing, the "model" status of the Imperial Theaters went hand in hand with the gravity of classical plays in their dramatic repertoire, of which the Directorate's annual quota was no fewer than ten.[138]

MODERN SPECTERS   125

But where did ballet figure in all this? Despite Noverre's efforts (now largely forgotten, in any case), ballet's standing repertoire included no equivalent to a classical play. A seasoned balletomane, Pleshcheev knew how far removed from "ethical education" ballet's actual reputation was. Silent from birth and staffed mainly by younger females and frequented mainly by older males, ballet could hardly stand the test of respectability Vsevolozhsky and Pogozhev seemed to be imposing. Ballet's days seemed as numbered as ever—unless, miraculously, it would prove financially viable. (Which, miraculously, ballet under Vsevolozhsky came closer to being—once he and Petipa resolved to hire the touring Italian ballerina Zucchi away from the private enterprise *Abandon Sorrow* [*Kin' grust'*].)

As the historian Murray Frame has shown, the *model* status bestowed on the Imperial Theaters followed the (initially Austrian) idea of the *national* theater, whose mission was to establish and promote the domestic cultural canon—which, in nineteenth-century Russia, included promoting Russian as a language.[139] You could put up a play by Schiller, but for your production to rank as *model*, it had to be in Russian. Small wonder that the Petersburg German Theater was dismantled. In 1886, the same fate befell, for all its commercial success, the Italian Opera Theater in Petersburg (which felt like "amputating a healthy limb," recalled Pogozhev):[140] the Imperial Russian Opera Company, it was held, had to be more prominent.[141] Russian opera was "Russian" primarily on the strength of the language used for its arias and librettos, many of which were (often doctored) translations from Italian or German. The Imperial Theaters were faced with a choice: speak Russian or be history.

Naturally, the nonverbal art of ballet was harder to Russianize. No translation was needed for a Russian speaker to understand the gamut of emotions which the Italian star Zucchi imparted to the medieval Paris maiden Esmeralda. In this sense, the language of ballet remained (then as now) the tongue of tongues. Indirectly, however, ballet, too, was affected by the new linguistic policy. Ever jealous of extra-ecclesiastic spectacles, the Church authorities barred stage performances during Russian Orthodox Lent. At one point, foreign-language shows were exempted from the ban, but ballet, despite being top-heavy with foreign masters, composers, conductors, machinists, and invited stars, found itself under this regulation alongside Russian opera and drama—for the simple reason that its rank and file were predominantly of the Russian Orthodox faith.[142] Besides, in 1886, in the wake of the termination of the Italian Opera, the ballet troupe was relocated

126 IMPOSSIBLE PROJECT

to the Mariinsky Theater, where ballets alternated with Russian-language operas.[143] Ballet was, in a sense, Russified by proximity.

When it came to ballet productions, the Russification effort boiled down to Russifying the music or, rather, the cohort of music writers. Gone were the days when the position of staff ballet composer was traditionally filled by a foreigner, like the Italian Cesare Pugni or his Austrian successor Ludwig Minkus, whose employment in Petersburg was terminated in 1886. For that matter, the very concept of ballet-specific music was on its way out. Ballet scores would now be outsourced to Russian composers, whether those with established reputations, like Glazunov or Tchaikovsky, or more obscure ones; what mattered was their citizenship.

Vsevolozhsky faithfully executed the Russian "national theater" policy handed down to him and could even, at least in the case of engaging Tchaikovsky, do so enthusiastically, but in general it was not what *he* would have preferred. An admirer of the French playwriting tradition (no one ever considered shutting down the French dramatic troupe in cosmopolitan Petersburg), Vsevolozhsky was rather dismissive of Aleksandr Ostrovsky, in private referring to his grassroots Russian, juicy-dialect plays as *la kapusta* ("la sauerkraut," to venture a nearly English equivalent).[144] But now, to assess where this Russian Geist was blowing from and driving to, we need to step back and take in the bigger picture.

A Sleeping Kingdom

The history of theater and literature in Russia never lacked for influence, or interference, from above. But no art form saw its fate so hinge on the moods and habits of the sitting monarch as ballet. When, by the late 1870s, the number of ballet-only evenings per week dwindled from two to one, everyone kept asking when the last shoe would drop. Was ballet fated to be relegated, from a stand-alone, every-Sunday spectacle, to a mere dance supplement to *grand opéras*, as *The Comprehensive Yearbook for 1879* projected? This did not occur. As seen in published fragments of Alexander III's personal diaries, on Sunday evenings, having attended church and inspected the military parade, the then crown prince would pay a visit to the ballet—a habit he might not have been willing to drop.[145] Twice a week may have been once too many, but do we perhaps owe it to the accustomed routine of one man that the phoenix of Petersburg ballet kept regenerating every Sunday?

MODERN SPECTERS 127

In considering Alexander III's personality and style of rule, it is important to keep in mind that he was born and raised as what British royal genealogists call a "spare." Unlike his elder brother, Crown Prince Nicholas, who died of marrow disease, Grand Duke Alexander had not been groomed in the arts of reigning; as a second son of the ruling monarch, he had been primed for the military walk of life. Nicholas died in 1865, so the royal family had ample time to re-tutor Alexander as befit a crown prince. But this meant more than additional lessons in history and law. The old-school empresses and emperors of Russia had positioned themselves as worldly individuals, well versed in European thought and culture. Catherine II read Montesquieu and corresponded with Voltaire; Alexander's grandfather Nicholas prided himself on his (alas, literal) command of literature. Sullen and sluggish, Alexander seemed decisively unfit for the role of enlightened autocrat. His recourse was to replace the expected attribute of "enlightened" with something better suited to his disposition and physique. How about "authentic"?

Key to Alexander's self-fashioning, as Richard Wortman has shown, was a spade-like peasant beard, the likes of which no Russian ruler had ever worn.[146] The beard marked the stocky, unrefined tsar as naturally *Russian* and went well with his reluctance to speak. The new tsar distrusted talk and wanted his subjects to follow suit. This was a political position. Alexander's mentor, the reactionary par excellence Konstantin Pobedonostsev, used the pejorative *govoril'nia* ("all talk") to refer to various sorts of democratic institutions: parliaments, local self-government, independent courts, the free press.[147] Talk meant trouble; Alexander III would prefer to sanitize its usual nesting sites, from living rooms to stages.

Coming to his assistance in this, it turned out, was dance. Once a hotbed of free thought, under Alexander III high-society salons gracefully segued into dance floors. Talk is a token of discontent; dance, of prosperity. Following Alexander's enthronement, observes Wortman, "gracious socializing replaced the discord of politics. Oppositional salons closed. Society 'danced more and criticized less,'" as Princess Radziwill put it in her memoirs.[148]

Ballet was part of this bulwark against inherently subversive talk. How well-versed Alexander was in ballet's history is hard to say, but one thing he must have known for sure: ballet was the offspring of the French monarchy, a vestige of the ancien régime, and, if for this reason alone, had to be preserved. Philosophically, this attitude matched the overall conservative doctrine that gained prominence under Alexander III. The mission of Russian civilization was to preserve the values squandered in the West. Had Moscow

128 IMPOSSIBLE PROJECT

not enshrined the true faith that had been trampled in ancient Byzantium and Rome? Was Russia not the last bastion of absolutism, the sole form of rule approved by God? Alexander III would hardly be aware of it, but ballet in Russia entertained a similar—messianic—self-conception, believing itself called to right what had gone wrong elsewhere. True, this credo was just one part of ballet's internal lore, but it proved powerful enough to keep things rolling.

Inborn reticence and self-styled curtness (his favorite term of approval was *del'no*, "practical" or "to the point") cast Alexander III as a man of action, which, thankfully, he was not;[149] despite his training until he became crown prince, as a warrior, Alexander's was the only reign in Russia's history that did not see a single war. His rule is primarily remembered for its domestic agenda, masterminded by the professed obscurantist Pobedonostsev, and for a foreign policy that resulted in shifting the diplomatic alignment of Europe. At home, Alexander III exercised what Wortman defines as a patriarchal scenario of power, positioning himself as a strict but loving father of the nation. The beard and the nine fanciful onion domes atop the Church of the Savior on Spilled Blood, designed as if to polemicize against the otherwise rectilinear geometry of Petersburg, contributed to this scenario as well. Central to Alexander's national mythology was imaginary Muscovy—the pristine, pre-Petrine, unenlightened, godly Russia of the past—and its imaginary enemy, soulless Western bureaucracy, which Alexander associated primarily with Germany, including, internally, German nationals within Russia's ruling elite.

Geopolitically, indeed, Russia under Alexander III was headed toward an alliance with Germany's adversary France. The process involved an exchange of diplomatic visits (during one of which, surreally, the Russian autocrat agreed to stand to attention as the French sang "La Marseillaise")[150] and climaxed in an architectural "exchange," with Russia building a bridge on the Seine, and France on the Neva, that endure to this day. Not every historian, perhaps, would endorse the idea, but the fact that the Francophile Vsevolozhsky, while still in Paris, had been offered Kister's position could be taken as an early sign of the bigger political changes to come.

Ironically, as Vazem recalls Vsevolozhsky saying, before he became director of the Imperial Theaters, he had never seen a ballet "in the proper sense of the word."[151] But this should not be taken literally; by "proper sense," Vsevolozhsky meant *grand ballets*, which, indeed, were not available to audiences in Paris during his residence there. Ballet in Paris flourished in

MODERN SPECTERS   129

other, more fashionable forms, with which, so far as we know, Vsevolozhsky would have been familiar. Under his directorship, ballets in Petersburg would acquire a certain fashionable Frenchness, which not everyone there found it easy to abide. Along with many in the City of Lights, Vsevolozhsky must have been swept up in the craze for *féeries*, fantasy ballets in which spectacular visuals took the upper hand over *pas d'action* and dramatic conflict. Hence *The Magic Pills* and *Sleeping Beauty*, *ballets-féeries* whose inclusion in the repertoire Vsevolozhsky pushed for, despite Petipa's initial reluctance.[152] (Ever the dandy, Vsevolozhsky would shrug off Petipa as an old-timer, *vieux genre*.)[153] Also, Vsevolozhsky's pairing *The Nutcracker*—yet another *ballet-féerie*—as a double bill with the one-act opera *Iolanta*, was a *Paris* thing to do. The latter was set in fifteenth-century France; its companion piece was based on a Francophone literary source.[154] The doublet premiered in 1892, a few months after a military convention was signed between the Russian and French general staffs.

In an empire like Russia, ballet had an additional reason to survive, one that no longer obtained in republican France. Unlike democratic *govoril'nias*, the silent medium of ballet could, on occasion, be employed to celebrate the monarchy, as many a court ballet had in seventeenth-century France. In May 1883, Petipa staged *Night and Day*, a full-evening ballet conceived to echo, in imagery and message, the *Ballet Royale de la Nuit* performed in Paris 230 years earlier, a *ballet de cour* that celebrated and starred the fourteen-year-old Louis XIV. Masterminded (and apparently ghostwritten) by Vsevolozhsky, *Night and Day* was timed to the long-awaited coronation of Tsar Alexander III and his spouse, Tsarina Maria, formerly the Danish Princess Dagmar. (Once a spare, always a spare: Alexander married his late brother's fiancée.)[155]

Under Alexander III as under the Sun King, time-proven topoi of dawns and sunsets were invoked to allegorize historical epochs, past and coming. A moonlit stage (by machinist Karl Valts); nature is asleep. Naiads, dryads, wilis, and other nocturnal creatures circle around the Queen of the Night (Evgenia Sokolova) and the Night Star (Maria Gorshenkova). But lo! the Genii of the Day (led by the Daytime Queen Vazem) awaken to triumph over the Genii of the Night. The Sun rises; "nature is resurrected," as the libretto has it.[156] In the apotheosis, the nations of the empire enter one by one to perform their folk dances, from "Siberian shamans" to "Crimean Tatars" and from Finns to Ukrainians, Georgians, and Poles. Finally, the Genius of

130   IMPOSSIBLE PROJECT

Russia (a woman in a folk costume) is carried in by an eagle, surrounded by allegories of legislation, the military, fine arts, sciences, and four more, the last of them commerce. All ends with onion domes looming on the horizon; the libretto refers to them as "luminous church-heads [*glavy tserkvei*] of Russia's cities,"[157] but another allusion should not be ruled out: it was in the same coronation year, 1883, that Alexander III enjoined a nine-headed church to be built on the Peterburg site where his father's blood had been spilled.[158]

Presiding over the clash between day and night was the (alleged) proto-Slavic god Chislobog (literally, "the god of numbers"; one reviewer describes him as Chronos, another as Time itself),[159] enacted by Aleksandr Chistiakov hung high above the battle. The "Sun-Tsar" (Tsar'-solntse), described as a character in the libretto, was probably deemed too lofty a part to entrust to a dancer; his appearance, after Chislobog awards victory to the forces of light, is signaled solely by what Pleshcheev disappointedly describes as an "allegoric glow."[160]

This glow, like the rest of the ballet's allegorical images, was easy to see through. The triumph of the dark forces that had extinguished the sun of yesterday, Alexander II, was but a temporary thing, and could not have been otherwise. By laws as irrevocable as time itself, the monarchy always regenerates. To drive the idea home, the allegoric dawn was followed by figures of nature's awakening: birds, butterflies, and bees. Likewise meaningfully, the Genii of the Day, shown shackled by sleep in the first part and routing the perfidious nocturnals in the second, were performed by girls— young pupils of the Petersburg and Moscow ballet schools. There is something of a metaphorical pileup here—the girls awakening from darkness to light; their nubility reflecting the seasonal awakening, and suggestive of life's endless cycle—but it all goes to serve the coronation message: dynastic succession is in the nature of things.

As has been observed, *Night and Day* was a dual, Janus-faced affair.[161] Archaic as it appeared as a ceremonial spectacle, as a ballet it was downright trendy. On the one hand, its story reached back to that foundational, seventeenth-century *Ballet of the Night* (except that, unlike the Roi Soleil who played his own royal, celestial self, *our* less lively Sun-Tsar, even if allowed to climb the stage, would hardly have managed a pirouette); on the other hand, what it enacted was unlike your conventional balletic story. Whereas, among Russian balletomanes, the pas d'action remained a matter of faith, public taste across the rest of Europe was shifting from dramatic ballets to *ballets-féeries*, which were considered at once greatly entertaining and silly.

A new trend emerged in the 1880s that wedded the choreographed figures and light effects peculiar to *féeries* to more edifying stories. The trendsetter was Luigi Manzotti's 1881 *Excelsior*, a Milan ballet that made a splash in Paris in early 1883. A philosophical extravaganza purporting to summarize nothing less than the progress of Western civilization, Manzotti's megaspectacle was about the battle of enlightenment against obscurantism, emblematized, unsurprisingly, by light and darkness, respectively. Unlike Russian rhapsodes of the Romanovs, however, Manzotti—a Garibaldian and progressive—saw this elemental battle not as a cycle (day replacing night, one Alexander replaced by another Alexander) but as a vector leading humankind from the dark ages toward the age of eternal electricity; while the finale in *Night and Day* was crowned with distant onion domes of churches, looming on the horizon of *Excelsior* was a steam locomotive crossing the Brooklyn Bridge.

Night and Day proved Janus-faced also with regard to domestic and foreign policy. In it, Vsevolozhsky contrived to combine the conservative ideology of Alexander III's Russia with the latest Paris chic. The courtier in Vsevolozhsky strove to please his increasingly nativist sovereign, but being also a man of the world, he wanted to reassure that world (in particular, the diplomatic corps and other foreign nationals accredited to the coronation) that on *his* watch, ballet remained cosmopolitan and up to date. That *Night and Day* succeeded on both fronts was owed to the kind of value reversal seen, time and again, in cultural history: whatever may, at one point, be condemned, banished, or ridiculed as preposterous and obsolete is bound to come back with a vengeance at another time.[162] It took a century or so for Noverre and Noverrians to affirm the supremacy of *ballets d'action* over *ballets de cour*, and another century for the action-poor, entrée-after-entrée principle of the timeworn *Ballet Royal de la Nuit* to resurface in *Excelsior*, dressed as the latest trend. Distinct from the *ballet d'action* conceptualized by Noverre and canonized by Noverrians, ballets like *Excelsior* and *Ballet de la Nuit* were not about people but about ideas, or rather, emblems and allegories.

Reminiscent of the festive joys of *ballets de cour*, the light-minded genre of *ballet-féerie* felt free to loosen the Noverrian taboo on the use of words on the balletic stage. (*Magic Pills*, for instance, a *féerie* that bordered on vaudeville, included singing and dialogue.)[163] The same was true of the genre's

132   IMPOSSIBLE PROJECT

more serious—political, ideological—outgrowths like *Night and Day*. As the happy insects of the Day scene give way to ecstatic "tribes of Russia" (*plemena Rossii*) gathered to "hail the rising luminary," their singing is heard—most likely performed off stage, and definitely in Russian.[164] That a *féerie* like *Magic Pills* could include songs was because such was the fashion in the West, but songs in a *coronation* ballet, singing the praises of the tsar— this was clearly a political phenomenon.[165] In its own eyes, the empire was a choir—a unison of "peoples of Russia," who sang Russia in Russian and not in their "tribal" tongues.

The presence of ethnically costumed magi arriving in Moscow from Russia's outskirts was de rigueur for coronation festivities generally. In the ballet, the empire's diversity was symbolized, unsurprisingly, by the divertissement of folk dances. This harked back to the tradition of late seventeenth-century *ballets de cour*, with their catalogues of exotic ethnicities; to the dancing "savages" and "Chinese" of the eighteenth-century opera *The Amorous Indies* (*Les Indes Galantes*); and—to leap over countless character dances in Romantic ballets—to nineteenth-century Russia's balletic best-seller *Konek-Gorbunok*, or *The Little Humpbacked Horse* (1865), in whose apotheosis the many ethnicities (*narodnosti*) of Russia, each owing their liberty to the liberator-tsar Alexander II, performed their particular dances, choreographed for them (or, rather, for him) by Arthur Saint-Léon.

The imperial idea of diversity always implies a "first among equals." In Russia, ethnonational balletic divertissements followed a protocol: they would open with "every nationality join[ing] the Russian *khorovod* [roundelay, or circle dance]" and end with pupils of the ballet schools performing "the Great-Russian *trepak*."[166] ("Great-Russian" was an ethnonym used to distinguish Russian persons or things from their Ukrainian ["Little-Russian"] counterparts; of course, the terms are now—and forever—obsolete.)

Gory Stories, Infant Spectators, and Other Memes of Ballet Lore

Night and day; the kingdom asleep, the kingdom awake. Awakening would take center stage once more in Vsevolozhsky's libretto for *The Sleeping Beauty* (1890). Today we place Petipa and Tchaikovsky's masterpiece where it indeed belongs: above period politics, whether foreign, domestic, or court-internal. "The time is unimportant, as is the place," say George Balanchine

MODERN SPECTERS 133

and Francis Mason of this balletic fairy tale in their canon-setting *101 Stories of the Great Ballets*,[167] referring, of course, to the time and place of action. When their compendium was published (1954) and updated (1968, 1975, 1989), this could be said of the ballet itself; so many times and in so many places was *The Sleeping Beauty* restaged and redanced. But when Vsevolozhsky wrote it, did the story of *The Sleeping Beauty* seem as "timeless" as it does nowadays? In what follows, I plan to revisit Vsevolozhsky's libretto to pose precisely this question. But first, a quick overview of ballet lore and political palaver of the 1880s that preceded and, in a way, prefigured the miraculous decade of the Petersburg ballet.

For all the official success of *Night and Day*, ballet's existence remained no less precarious than before. *Night and Day* was not included in the repertoire; monetizing a show custom-staged for the coronation would have been like trying to auction off the crown. (True, Alexander III did ordain a total-show encore, but this was to be performed for the royal family alone.)[168] The other new ballet of 1883, *The Cyprian Statue, or Pygmalion* written and composed by Prince Ivan Trubetskoi, an amateur composer living in Paris, flopped commercially and critically, with attempts to renew it in 1885 and 1887 coming to naught. The unfortunate *Pygmalion* remained Petipa's only attempt to refresh the repertoire from 1882 to 1885. All other premieres featured in this period were renewals of Perrot's and Saint-Léon's ballets.

Unlike the emperor, Vsevolozhsky's right hand, the perceptive and persevering chief of staff Vladimir Pogozhev, was not a ballet lover; as he confessed, he would be asleep in his seat as soon as the curtain went up.[169] His attitude, echoed by Vsevolozhsky, was wait-and-see. Revivals were enough to keep Sunday evenings busy; whereas new ballets, even if successful, meant losses. The ballet company was the biggest spender and smallest earner in the Imperial Theaters. True, the new "model stage" doctrine seemed to brush aside such nonlofty considerations as profitability, but all such doctrines were enforced higher up, in particular by Court Comptroller Nikolai Petrov, whose exacting abacus Vsevolozhsky's office had to reckon with (Figure 2.5).[170]

In 1892, Pogozhev—cagey, but a committed reformer—assessed ballet's status and prospects thus: "The old criteria of quality by which classical ballets were judged, and which still prioritize, unlike in Western Europe, choreographic training in our ballet school, have receded into the background. Public interest in ballet productions can only be sustained owing to: an exceptional star; a luxurious staging; the quality of music."[171] The way forward is not to cling to what we have, but to do what has been done

Figure 2.5 Ivan Vsevolozhsky, "Kontrol'naia kletka" (The Comptroller's Cage), a caricature featuring Vsevolozhsky locked up by Nikolai Petrov, the court comptroller.

MODERN SPECTERS   135

elsewhere. "Presently in the West," continues Pogozhev, "ballet has merged [*assimilirovalsia*] with the *féerie*. The Imperial Theaters must face this fact and take steps to embrace it."[172] What is to be done with the troupe? "As ten years of experience have shown, the significance of classical ballet and demand for it have faded, which means that the ballet troupe must be treated mainly as a necessary accessory to opera, and utilized primarily in spectacle-style shows [*priurochivaia spektakli ee po preimushchestvu k zrelishcham*]."[173] And vice versa: the genre of *féerie* opened the door into ballet for "dramatic and even operatic personnel."[174] Pogozhev's was thus a verdict of death for stand-alone ballet.

A cavalry officer in his previous service, Pogozhev was a straightforward strategist who assumed that today's trend would continue, or intensify, tomorrow. But as we have seen, ballet history is hardly marked by linearity. For that matter, Pogozhev was perspicacious enough to keep his would-be relegation of ballet on paper. His boss Vsevolozhsky had a penchant for writing ballet librettos, designing costumes, and staging lavishly; the prevailing ideological winds in Russia were not favorable for the modernization and Westernization of anything; as regards music, imposters like Prince Trubetskoi did occur, but there was also Tchaikovsky; and Pogozhev's cure-all "exceptional star" appeared in the form of Virginia Zucchi (Figure 2.6). Music, lavishness, stars—these, per Pogozhev, were ballet's best bets. And so, despite having, as late as 1892, an extreme reform up his sleeve, Pogozhev never pushed it. Ballet could remain afloat by tacking.

Zucchi's arrival in Russia, which segued into a tenure on the imperial stage (1885–88), would have a considerable impact on ballet lore.[175] Her first appearance on the tiny private stage of an amusement park in a Petersburg suburb occurred on June 6; on June 8, in a review by the noted balletomane Nikolai Bezobrazov, Zucchi was singled out for her "lovely telling eyes" and her "pointes that look as if they are made of steel."[176] About four months later, reviewing her star performance in Petipa's version of *La Fille mal gardée*, Bezobrazov decided that this simile was insufficient: "To call Zucchi's pointes steely would be an understatement [*malo nazvat' stal'nymi*]."[177] And his mention of Zucchi's "telling eyes" would soon by joined by a chorus of attestations to this dancer's mesmerizing dramatic force. Whether the Italian ballerina starred in *La Fille mal gardée*, *Brahma*, or *Esmeralda*, she, to quote a review signed "A Most Aged Balletomane," reduced to tears "not only the boxes but even the stalls."[178] (Why "even the stalls," wondered Pleshcheev; were they presumed to be occupied by "cold and heartless folk"?)[179]

Figure 2.6 Ivan Vsevolozhsky, a caricature featuring Virginia Zucchi on a pedestal and Aleksandr Frolov, manager of the Petersburg ballet, worshiping her as a deity.

MODERN SPECTERS 137

Zucchi's effect on Russian ballet lore was twofold. On the one hand, her undeniable dancing and acting skills united the stalls, galleries, and boxes (including the august ones) in one resounding, week-in, week-out encore. On the other, Zucchi polarized public opinion: some (albeit in the minority) were dissatisfied, not with the quality of her performance, but with her very presence on the local scene. Inveterate nativists like Sergei Khudekov— the same Khudekov who wrote that Zucchi, if needed, could have walked Nevsky Prospect end to end on pointes—feared that standing ovations in the gallery could corrupt Russian-school danseuses into adopting such Italian tricks.[180] Others found other reasons—related to music or culture at large— to look at the Zucchi phenomenon askance. The Zucchi years brought a temporary triumph to Russian Noverrians. Her toe technique may have bordered on virtuosity, but her power as an actress, as emerges from contemporary writings, was in making her characters relatable and easily legible; Skalkovsky and Pleshcheev were moved to call her performance "silent poetry,"[181] and Aleksandr Benois, who became a Zucchi fan in his teen years, would in his memoir extoll her "amazing gift for clarifying without the help of words, whether in a dramatic scene, or in a dance."[182]

To claim a mime's movements are expressive enough to compete with words would seem like unequivocal praise, but ballet lore was of two minds on this point. "Zucchi's weakness," wrote Herman Laroche, a Petersburg music critic and close friend of Tchaikovsky, "lay in the fact that the contemporary direction of ballet strives for the certainty of verbal speech."[183] The clarity of Zucchi's mime made ballet music sound like program music, which Laroche disparaged; Tchaikovsky, too, according to Laroche, disapproved of Zucchi for the same reason.

In the cultural landscape of the day, the Zucchi phenomenon aligned with the aesthetics of veracity. According to Benois, Zucchi's impact on him as a young man was comparable only to that of the lifelike acting and staging of the Meiningen Ensemble, which happened to tour Russia around the same time as Zucchi.[184] The balletomane Bezobrazov linked Zucchi to naturalist literature "in the spirit of Émile Zola";[185] Laroche, to the *verismo* movement in Italian opera.[186] Common to Zola and Zucchi was the aesthetics of suffering—which was not uppermost in Laroche's and Tchaikovsky's, or Petipa's and Vsevolozhsky's, conception of the art of ballet.

In 1888, having discontinued Zucchi's annual engagements, the Directorate, to the dismay of hardcore balletomanes, plotted a different course: away from what was now branded "bloody dramas" and toward

138   IMPOSSIBLE PROJECT

Tchaikovsky and fairy-tale *ballets-féeries*. To shore up the new policy, its champion, Laroche, cited Tchaikovsky's suitably naïve defense of ballet against those who condemned it as a "salacious and seductive" spectacle: "Ballet is the most innocent, the most moral of all arts. Why else would they bring children to ballets?"[187] The wishful image of innocent ballet, with a child (rather than a *roué*) as its model audience, heralded a new turn that Khudekov, in his 1913–18 *History of Dances*, complains might be called the infantilization of ballet.[188] On the Mariinsky stage, *The Sleeping Beauty* proved to be the first step in this direction.

Laroche's was a passionate attempt to defend Tchaikovsky's ballets from their no less passionate detractors. Both camps took recourse in the rhetoric of *fall*. Seasoned balletomanes viewed *The Sleeping Beauty* and *The Nutcracker* as signs of ballet falling into its second childhood—and this following Noverre's enlightened sophistication and Zucchi's mature, humane, and tragic art! But as Laroche saw it, it was precisely Zucchi who had precipitated ballet's fall from its Romantic Eden into the squalor of modernity. "Perhaps you hope to save [ballet] by introducing elements of a bloody drama," railed Laroche, addressing Zucchi's partisans. "Zucchi, in *Esmeralda*, doesn't let you sleep, and the masterful representation of the young woman, mutilated by torture, strikes you as the last word of choreographic progress."[189] A history-versed balletomane might have retorted that *Esmeralda*, tortures and all, was actually first staged in 1844, the heyday of Romantic ballets, and that *Esmeralda*'s enthusiasts were hardly holding it up as suitable for children. But then, what was at stake here was rather ballet's *future*.

Laroche's ideas for reforming ballet harbored, just below the surface, certain political and ideological considerations. "In recent years, bloody drama has widened its rule in this country. It has occupied small private theaters and summer amusement venues. Where an operetta songstress used to sing her silly songs and show her denuded form, now villains are shown scheming their schemes [*zlodei kuiut svoi kovy*], and revolvers and daggers are rampant."[190] Laroche's readers were expected to associate these signs of the time with the bombs and daggers used by revolutionary terrorists against the powers that be, first and foremost the bombs that killed Alexander II in 1881. As in the streets, so in the imperial ballet, which, alleged Laroche, was becoming no place for "the dreams, the joy, the faith of a child [*detskaia greza, detskaia radost', detskaia vera*]."[191]

This triad of childlike virtues, supposedly being lost amid the onslaught of ballet's gore-lovers, represented a strong political hint. (Which Laroche's readers were primed to take; this essay originally appeared in Mikhail Katkov's *Moscow News* [*Moskovskie vedomosti*], a mouthpiece of the ideological doctrine of arch-reactionary Konstantin Pobedonostsev.) Notions like "the dreams" or "joy" of a child did, if vaguely, pertain to the aesthetics of ballet, but what Laroche describes as childlike faith resonated specifically with Pobedonostsev's paternalistic view of power, the idea that, as summed up approvingly by Dostoevsky, "the people is the tsar's son; the tsar, its father [*Narod—syn tsarev, a tsar'—otets ego*]."[192] An educator by vocation and obscurantist by conviction, the ober-procurator of the Most Holy Synod would have preferred a return to prelapsarian ignorance, before that fatal encounter with the tree of knowledge; he is remembered to have said, "A view exists that, as far as enlightenment and knowledge, the people of Russia are an infant. So be it: what could be more adorable, more enviable than an innocent, unspoiled infant!"[193] It was this infant, the baby born in Pobedonostsev's head, that Laroche and Tchaikovsky ushered into the auditorium of the Mariinsky.

As observed from the far left by a Nekrasov or Saltykov-Shchedrin, the agendas of Pobedonostsev and Vsevolozhsky seemed deplorably similar. But viewed from closer by, the picture was more varied and dynamic and featured feuds, patronages, and court intrigues. One such feud took place in 1883 between Pobedonostsev and Court Minister Vorontsov-Dashkov regarding the latter's proposal to unban music performances during Lent;[194] another in 1886 when, without first asking Pobedonostsev's approval (which would not have been forthcoming), Vorontsov-Dashkov arranged a reading of Leo Tolstoy's *The Power of Darkness* in the presence of Alexander III. Pobedonostsev was enraged: the everyday brutishness of peasant life (Tolstoy's play was based on a real-life court trial) undercut the ober-procurator's childlike conception of the Russian peasantry. He was also displeased with Tolstoy's aesthetics. "Not even Zola would debase himself to Tolstoy's level of realist brutality," he wrote in a letter to the emperor.[195] (Whether the topic was Tolstoy or Zucchi, Zola was the bogeyman at hand.)

That in his 1909 tribute to Vsevolozhsky, Boborykin could dub him the "artiste- director" was also because, alongside designing costumes for ballet, Vsevolozhsky loved salon cartooning. Several collections of his caricatures survive; some, like that of Boborykin himself, were amicable, others less so. One undated cartoon casts Pobedonostsev as Flaubert's St. Anthony;[196] a halo hovering above his balding head, the ober-procurator is shown praying away a Zucchi-like, scantily clad danseuse (Figure 2.7). Pallid, skeletally thin, and broad-eared, Pobedonostsev seemed custom-made to stand for

Figure 2.7 Ivan Vsevolozhsky, "La Tentation de Saint Antoine" (The Temptation of St. Anthony), a caricature satirizing Konstantin Pobedonostsev's opposition to allowing music performances, including ballets, during Great Lent.

reactionary Russian officialdom, as he did in works by Tolstoy, Andrei Bely, and Aleksandr Blok.

The Russian verb *sharzhirovat'* seems somehow more friendly than its ostensible English equivalent, "to caricature." In general, Vsevolozhsky's caricatures belong to the genre known as "friendly sketch" (*druzheskii sharzh*), although as mentioned, the degree of friendliness could vary. A worldly man, and a man of wit, Vsevolozhsky could not but scorn a mirthless dogmatist like Pobedonostsev. As Vsevolozhsky knew, Pobedonostsev patronized Tchaikovsky, who with age was growing increasingly patriotic and monarchist, to the point that, in 1883, he was entrusted with composing a coronation cantata. But whether or not he bought into the childlike-spectator notion of Tchaikovsky's friend and spokesman Laroche, Vsevolozhsky *was* all for *féeries* and for reengaging Tchaikovsky to write for ballet. Scorn though he might, as an artiste, everything Pobedonostsev stood for, Vsevolozhsky the director needed him as a companion in this campaign.

That the battles waged at court by factions jockeying for policy clout should find their way into Vsevolozhsky's cartoons is hardly surprising, but these skirmishes would also be reflected in his ballet libretto, which *is* surprising, given ballet's reputation in Russia (as shaped by, among others, Nekrasov and Saltykov-Shchedrin) as the least politically relevant of all arts.

Enter Aurora

Not unlike its co-creator Vsevolozhsky, *The Sleeping Beauty* (1890) was many things at once: an exercise in sartorial excess (its production costs ate up a whole fourth of the Imperial Theaters' annual budget); a bone of contention between Noverrians and (to coin a term) "féerians"; and a masterpiece of political double entendre: a celebratory spectacle and a cautionary cartoon. *The Sleeping Beauty* worked like a crystal ball, reflecting back to you what you wished to see when gazing into it: the joy of eternal awakening or the torpor of a hundred years' sleep.

The narrative kernel of *The Sleeping Beauty* replays the allegorical arc Vsevolozhsky had previously tested in the coronation ballet *Night and Day*. In both, darkness gives way to light, sleep to awakening, desolation to jubilation, and the eternality and naturality of natural cycles—circadian or seasonal—is projected on the (all too) human laws of dynastic succession. There is, however, a significant difference: *Night and Day* was an allegory,

142 IMPOSSIBLE PROJECT

pure and simple, but *The Sleeping Beauty* is also a story about *characters* and is borrowed from a specific source and set in a specific country.

As mentioned earlier, the choice of country and source was far from random. King Florestan's kingdom is a fictional France, and his dynastic denominator, the fourteenth, points to Louis XIV, the dancer-king, who appears in the *Sleeping Beauty* apotheosis titled "Helios en costume de Louis XIV." Why France? A proud Francophile who had served diplomatically in Paris, Vsevolozhsky knew that the "Russo-French rapprochement" of 1891–94 was in the works, so the time was politically ripe for a ballet not only set in France but also based on a Francophone literary source.[197] His choice was Charles Perrault's fairy tale *La Belle au bois dormant*, written, appropriately, in what was seen as the golden age of absolute monarchy, as well as the century when Louis XIV created his Académie Royale de Danse.

How adaptations deviate from their sources can be historically telling. Vsevolozhsky tampered liberally with Perrault, to adjust his tale to the demands of ballet as a medium, to pad the plot with allegorical connotations, and to make it more relatable to ballet audiences—not least, the royal couple. Vsevolozhsky cut and pasted. Thus he cut the entire second part of Perrault's story, beginning with these words: "Two whole years passed since the marriage of the prince and princess, and during that time they had two children. The first, a daughter, was called 'Dawn' [*Aurore*], while the second, a boy, was named 'Day' [*Jour*] because he seemed even more beautiful than his sister."[198]

This abridgement was no doubt motivated by the need to fit the accepted ballet format. Vsevolozhsky did, however, borrow the daughter's name, Aurore, only to reassign it to her mother: in lieu of Perrault's Princess Primrose, the sleeping beauty of the ballet version is referred to as "Aurora." Vsevolozhsky did this for two reasons: one allegorical, the other odic. The former is obvious: princes and princesses, like dawns, always return, as we have seen them do in *Night and Day*. As for the latter, the current empress Maria Feodorovna's maiden name, Dagmar, Danish for "daughter of the day," included the concept of "dawn"—an opportunity promptly made use of by many an odic writer in Russia.[199] It is for this reason that Aurora's tutu depicted in Vsevolozhsky's costume sketch is painted in dawn-pink colors (Figure 2.8). In this sense, Vsevolozhsky's choice was strategically, if vicariously, odic.

Another politically prudent step on Vsevolozhsky's part as librettist was to select a fairy tale, the genre cherished by kids and kings alike. However much

Figure 2.8 Ivan Vsevolozhsky, Princess Aurora, a costume design for the first production of *The Sleeping Beauty* (1890). Courtesy of Saint-Petersburg State Theatre Library.

144 IMPOSSIBLE PROJECT

The Sleeping Beauty increased the representation of children in the audience, there were quite a few to be seen onstage. The peasant waltz in the first act matched Pobedonostsev's wished-for world to a T: a crowd of balletic peasants, including many a ballet-school pupil, blissfully hail King Florestan as their beloved tsar-father (*tsar'-batiushka*). Children's dances were favored "in the highest quarters," according to Khudekov,[200] and, judging by what Iosif Kshesinsky recalls, prior to the 1880s involving young pupils in ballets had been more of an exception than a rule.[201] People of taste disdained the costumes as gaudy, but this made them childlike and kid-friendly; Vsevolozhsky styled them after *images d'Épinal*, or their Russian equivalents, known as *lubok*, sharply colored narrative prints aimed at the less literate. Benois recalls having seen, as a child, a series of magic-lantern slides on the subject of Perrault's sleeping princess;[202] this is how Vsevolozhsky's spectacle must have appeared to contemporaries. Magic lanterns were popular with children, children were popular with the emperor—it all fit the peaceable scenario of power under Alexander III described by Wortman.[203]

To a conservative like Pobedonostsev, every dawn, spring, and childbirth signaled the same good news: an eternal return strongly bound up with the concept of *stability*. This was why Pobedonostsev iconized "innocent infants" (whose pure minds were to be kept clear of the "squalor of the natural sciences")[204] and why he could produce a programmatic poem (yes, the ober-procurator wrote poetry) like "Old Leaves." Despite this title, his poem is about spring. In it, we find a vegetative parable illustrating the central tenet of native conservatism: nothing but what has always existed shall be allowed to exist. Refrain from plucking autumnal leaves, it implores, lest you harm the vernal ones to come: "For no new thought is able to convey / A meaning deeper than of olden day."[205] It has often been said: "came a new dawn" or "came the spring." But as Pobedonostsev would have emphasized, these things rather *return*.

Vsevolozhsky the librettist was not averse to political symbols of this kind. In Perrault's original, the fairies are nameless; they are numbered and differ in age and by where each sits on the scale from good to bad. After one old and wicked fairy has cursed the princess to die, a young one commutes the penalty to years of sleep. As if to reward the good fairy, Vsevolozhsky gave her a vernal name lifted from *Donkeyskin*, that other tale by Perrault: the Lilac Fairy. The lilac, a harbinger of spring, prefigures the princess's awakening after one hundred springs.[206]

MODERN SPECTERS 145

As the cartoonist in Vsevolozhsky must have known, allegories can sometimes cut both ways. At the risk of treating poetic tropes pedantically, we could note that spring follows winter, not autumn, as dawn succeeds night rather than evening. Seasonal imagery was bound to backfire on Pobedonostsev, whom Russian political lore consistently identified with Russia's *winter*. "Freeze Russia," the counterreformist slogan of the religious philosopher Konstantin Leontiev, was likewise associated with the ober-procurator, who is often said to have first devised it.[207] No less proverbial was an assessment of Pobedonostsev by Leontiev: "He is like frost; he prevents further decomposition; but nothing will grow while he is here."[208] Until, that is, the Lilac Fairy disposes otherwise.

What further consolidated Pobedonostsev's image as a political necro-mancer was his campaign for prioritizing the study of classical languages over natural sciences in gymnasium curricula. "I cannot help citing one of his marvelous sophisms used to eulogize [dead languages]," wrote the émigré journalist Aleksandr Amfiteatrov. The sophism in question is this: "Ancient Greek and Latin, deemed dead because no longer used in living speech, shall thereby give new life to living speech, breathe the spirit of youth into it." Comments Amfiteatrov, "Again, his usual propensity for rot, carrion, de-composition.... Not to mention the logical incongruity of this *alive because dead* and *dead because alive*."[209] There was, one must mention, a method to Pobedonostsev's incongruity: the dead languages, like old leaves from his eponymous poem, lend their former force to sprouting speech. Sophistry, indeed.

A forest kingdom bewitched to endure a century of sleep; Russia, "frozen" through the effort of a hoary reactionary—the former was bound to be read as an allegory of the latter. That Vsevolozhsky was not only aware of this sub-versive reading but also counted on it as he worked on *The Sleeping Beauty* ballet became obvious in 2016, after the art historian Arkadii Ippolitov made public a set of Vsevolozhsky's cartoons collected and preserved by his right hand Pogozhev. Two of these, in tandem with Ippolitov's expert comments, cast light on political innuendos inscribed in Vsevolozhsky's courtly canvas. One, captioned "La table de nuit de la Belle au Bois Dormant" (Sleeping Beauty's Nightstand), is a still life depicting a sort of sleeper's toolset: a book, a candle, sleep medicine, and a bell to call the maid if needed (Figure 2.9). The sleeper is off frame; as Ippolitov suggests, the sleeping beauty in ques-tion must be Russia herself.[210] Each object on this nightstand bears a face

Figure 2.9 Ivan Vsevolozhsky, "La Table de Nuit de La Belle au Bois Dormant" (Sleeping Beauty's Nightstand).

Ippolitov identifies as belonging to Russia's conservative elite. The bottle-man filled with the sedative "Morphine" is Interior Minister Dmitrii Tolstoy; the bell-man is Katkov, editor of the reactionary *Moscow News*; and the candle-face belongs to Education Minister Delianov. Instead of a candlewick, a brass candle extinguisher is shown crowning the Delianov-faced candle; as Ippolitov reminds us, current in the political vocabulary of the time was the phrase "the extinguisher [*gasitel'*] of enlightenment."[211] (The joke hinges on the fact that, in Russian, the Ministry of Education, Ministerstvo narodnogo prosveshchenia, was literally that of "the people's enlightenment.") In the foreground, we find the bible of liberal thought, *The Spirit of Law* by Montesquieu; the book is closed; creeping between its pages is bookmark-flat Pobedonostsev.

When Vsevolozhsky was at work on his ballet version of Perrault's tale, suggests Ippolitov, "somewhere latent in his consciousness [*podspudno gde-to v soznanii*] was the parallel between [Alexander's] empire and the dead kingdom entangled in thorns."[212] But this seems too cautious. The other cartoon Ippolitov adduces to support his supposition makes it clear that Vsevolozhsky was quite mindful of the parallel. Its caption, "The Bells of Corneville," invokes the title of a French comic opera set in an abandoned abbey whose bells, once sonorous and mirthful, hang motionless and silent. Each bell—ten in all—features the face of a reactionary figure in the government of Alexander III, including, of course, Pobedonostsev (Figure 2.10).

Figure 2.10 Ivan Vsevolozhsky, "Les cloches de Corneville" (The Bells of Corneville).

148 IMPOSSIBLE PROJECT

The picture looks almost eerie—a gallows in the dusky sky above the lifeless cityscape of Petersburg.[213]

In Vsevolozhsky's libretto, the very concept of an entire sleeping *kingdom*, soon to become proverbial of Russia, was a piece of balletic license, as it were. In the source fairy tale, only the princess and her attendants are put to sleep. Her parents return to the capital: they have a country to run. In the libretto, the king and queen fall asleep along with their daughter. In Perrault, the temporary time-freeze is an unfortunate family affair, but Vsevolozhsky opted to freeze history itself. No bells will chime here for one hundred years. The same old kingdom, with the same monarch at its helm, comes back to life upon the expiry of the curse.

Deriving thus from a fairy tale, the allegory of Russia as a maiden immobilized by Pobedonostsev's necromancy would itself prove mythogenic. From the imperial stage, the image migrated into satirical magazines of 1905–7, to prose and poetry of the 1910s, and to Soviet cinema of the 1920s, generating new parallels and extensions as it changed hands and media. Pobedonostsev's protruding ears inspired caricaturists to cast him as a vampire bat menacing a bare-necked sleeping beauty, as, for instance, in a cartoon from 1905 captioned "The Evil Genius of Russia" (Figure 2.11).

Alternatively, Pobedonostsev's pale eyes, framed by his black-rimmed glasses, could lend his face an owl-like look, hence these famous lines from Blok's 1910–21 long poem *Retribution* (*Vozmezdie*):

> In those distant, deafened years
> Sleep and darkness reigned in hearts:
> Pobedonostsev over Russia
> Spread his enormous owlish wings.

Four lines below, Pobedonostsev's poetic identity shifts to that of a magus who transfixes Russia the way Svengali does his Trilby: "By peering into her eyes / With the glassy gaze of a sorcerer." Blok's Russia does not seem to resist the sorcerer's spell. Instead, we see her lulled into sleep, as though listening to a teller of bedside tales, perhaps Perrault's.

> The clever talk of the magic tale
> Makes it is easy for the beauty to doze off;

Figure 2.11 "Evil Genius of Russia," a caricature featuring Pobedosnostsev as a vampire bat and Russia as a sleeping maiden. Cover of the first issue of the weekly *Strely*, October 30, 1905, edited by I. M. Knorozovsky.

150 IMPOSSIBLE PROJECT

> Her mind grows misty; hopes, and thoughts, and passions
> Become a dream. . . .
> Yet even when darkly charmed, suntanned remain her cheeks;
> And even in the grip of the necromancer
> She looks so full of strength.[214]

Indeed. It was only to be expected that, in the wake of the 1917 Revolution in Russia, the emphasis in the sleeping beauty meme would shift from falling asleep to waking up. Consider, for instance, Sergei and Georgii Vasiliev's film *The Sleeping Beauty* (1930), set in a sleepy provincial town whose sole theater serves to entertain only the local elite. One of the film's characters, a ballet dancer (played by Tatiana Vecheslova), is shown performing, week in, week out, the part of Aurora in Vsevolozhsky's *Sleeping Beauty*. until one day her naval namesake, the cruiser *Aurora*, turns her cannon in the direction of the Winter Palace and fires a salvo said to shake the world and herald a new historic dawn. Gone in smoke were the wicked fairy Carabosse and her historical doppelgänger Pobedonostsev; as readers of Saltykov-Shchedrin in particular must have felt, the time had come to snap out of the balletic slumber, for what had the art of ballet been till now, if not a national vial of morphine?

Kings would seem to have good reason to take fairy tales personally, as kings and kingdoms figure so prominently in them. Vsevolozhsky both won and lost the hinting game embedded in *The Sleeping Beauty*. Won, because the ballet would prove not only the most popular to come out of his directorship—from 1900 to 1911 only *The Little Humpbacked Horse* would be performed more frequently on the Mariinsky stage[215]—but also, as noted, a veritable manufactory of memes. Lost, because Alexander III was not among *The Sleeping Beauty*'s fans. The emperor could hardly have disliked Tchaikovsky's music or Petipa's choreography. But the story was so bizarre, and King Florestan's kingdom so vulnerable to the magic whims of a contentious old witch.[216] And this at a time when the country needed stability, hence a firm hand. Why would Florestan pardon a group of *tricoteuses* caught carrying spindles in full view, in violation of his royal ban on the possession of spindles, on pain of death? Had Alexander's late father been more strict, his assassination might have been prevented. Then there was that liberal campaign, petitioning mercy for the perpetrators. Pobedonostsev was right to call pardoning regicides a "grave sin."[217] Still, King Florestan, swayed by his softhearted wife, lets the offenders off. And why call them *tricoteuses*

MODERN SPECTERS 151

instead of "spinners"—doesn't this word smack of the French Revolution, of infamous Parisiennes knitting away among the spectators at guillotinings? Alexander III's muted response to *The Sleeping Beauty*, the curt verdict of *très jolie* (*ochen' milo*), could have been motivated by any of these unsavory associations.[218]

No revolutionary by any stretch, Vsevolozhsky did believe in monarchy with a human (as opposed to ghoulish or owlish) face. One key measure of this quality was the monarch's capacity for clemency—to those suspected or found guilty of plotting against them. Clemency was the best scenario of power, Corneille signaled to young Louis XIV in his play *Cinna, ou la Clémence d'Auguste*, staged in 1641 to mark the Sun King's upcoming marriage; conveying the same message was *Cinna*'s Italian descendant *La clemenza di Tito* by Pietro Metastasio (1734), which elicited a host of operatic adaptations, some to become favorites at coronation celebrations—of Elizabeth in Moscow and of Leopold II in Prague. The clemency message was especially germane when the given ruler had come to power under other than cloudless skies, as was the case (albeit under disparate circumstances) with both Elizabeth and Alexander III of Russia. Elizabeth heeded the clemency call; Alexander did not, and must have found it annoying to be reminded of the fact, especially on a Sunday, at the ballet.

Florestan XIV's pardon of a group of *tricoteuses* guilty of the illegal possession of prickly spindles, which comes in the privileged position of the very first scene of Act I, signals Vsevolozhsky's belief that mercy from above could halt the cycle of violence—a belief shared by Leo Tolstoy, who in a letter to Alexander III urged him not to hang those implicated in the assassination of his father. Both Tolstoy and Vsevolozhsky bet on clemency as the true road to social healing. In the program Petipa wrote as an aid to Tchaikovsky, after the *tricoteuses* are forgiven, a stage direction says, "General jubilation"—the same words signaling the closure of the coronation ballet *Night and Day*—followed by a merry peasant waltz symbolizing, in Vsevolozhsky's wishful vision, an accord between the monarch and his subjects.[219] There was, however, another idea about what the populace wanted; as Pobedonostsev wrote the tsar, the people "were starving for retribution."[220]

A press meme that gained currency in Russia during the First World War posited that when two political forces are clenched in mortal combat, a "third force" (*tret'ia sila*), hitherto less conspicuous, is likely to emerge. Like many a political phantom of its kind, the third force was a complementary image. A member of the Socialist Revolutionary Party like Viktor Chernov

152   IMPOSSIBLE PROJECT

could envision it as the revolutionary liberation hovering over the two belligerent camps.[221] On the other hand, the political physiognomy of the third force could be seen as uglier than the two it was to supersede. In the wake of the assassination of Alexander II on March 1, 1881, this dynamic seemed to explain Pobedonostsev's clout at court: the monarchy lost a monarch, the terrorists lost their top guns—and, in the midst of it, the figure of the ober-procurator loomed large.

Among those holding this view may very well have been Aleksandr Blok and Ivan Vsevolozhsky. As the ballet master Fedor Lopukhov recalls, the prologue to *The Sleeping Beauty*, prior to 1905, contained a scene in the throne room, in which Carabosse materializes from flame and smoke; startled, King Florestan jumps aside, whereupon the wicked fairy installs herself on the throne.[222] Compare this to the aftermath of the regicide as described in Blok's outline to *Retribution*: "March 1. Everything hazes up. Soundless like an owl, Pobedonostsev lands on the throne."[223]

A throne left empty, if only for a moment, presents a danger to the dynasty that holds it. When kings die, how to protect what, in the language of democracy, would become known as the "peaceful transfer of power"? European history saw this problem arise each time a monarch died. One solution, invented by theologians and jurists in the Middle Ages, was that, physically or otherwise, the throne would never be left empty. When the ruler's *physical* body, that is, was no longer available to fill the throne, a *symbolic* body was to be used as a stopgap. In the final section of this chapter, I will take a closer look at this medieval theory of *crown survival*, whose metaphysics of equilibrium left an imprint on the survival of ballet.

The Third Perspective

What ballet was at this or that point of its history depended on the different perceptual perspectives involved. In this chapter, I have tried to re-create three perspectives on ballet: from afar, from above, and from the inside, as it were. To conclude it, I would like to focus on this third ideological perspective, that of the insider. What was ballet in the mind's eye of ballet professionals: ballet masters, ballet dancers, ballet school teachers, and their students?

The question presumes, of course, that such a general perspective can be said to exist. In terms of the ranks and professional profiles involved, the

Petersburg ballet troupe was a motley tribe. It included character and demi-character dancers, mimes and comics, and a veritable bouquet of ballerinas to fill any bill—comedic, dramatic, or romantic. Not to mention Nekrasov's "flowery garlands of wind-like maidens," the corps de ballet—a notoriously underpaid crowd, compared to any other rank. *The ballet* encompassed so many dancers' lives, each different from the other; could members of so diverse a crew have had anything in common, so far as their perception of ballet was concerned?

And yet, for all the discrepancy in salaries and profiles, "ballet people" (*baletnye*, as nineteenth-century opera artistes and dramatic actors called ballet professionals) were believed to have something in common: an acute sense of occupational piety. At least this is what we learn from the memoir *Backstage Chronicles* (1896) by Aleksandr Nil'sky, an Alexandrinsky dramatic lead remembered for his Hamlet, Khlestakov, and Ivan the Terrible. "Ballet artistes, as I have grown to know them, are heart-and-hand devoted to their métier; they take their dancing and miming more seriously than we dramatic actors take any of the characters we play, however complex," Nil'sky confides, alluding to what he sees as the paradox of the ballet dancer. "Many times in my life have I observed a dancer or ballerina offer prayers and cross themselves repeatedly while waiting for their bravura exit—only to dart onstage, all smiles, in order to display yet another ingenious trick of their trade."[224]

Nil'sky's point is a thought-provoking one. There were, indeed, two selves—two faces, two bodies—to ballet. The offstage—unsmiling—self included precisely those prayerful moments in the wings, hours spent weekly at the barre, and years at the ballet school, where the sense of vocational devotion Nil'sky notes in his memoir was inculcated from young adolescence. At the ballet school, learning how to dance was tantamount to instruction in a faith.

To get a sense of how ballet looked from the third perspective, that of the *baletnye*, these offstage moments, hours, and years are worth exploring. Central in this regard was the notion of *classical dance*, which was not just a set of choreographic movements and postures for you to practice but also a system of choreographic values to identify with and, as important, a hieratic narrative for you to make your own.

Unsurprisingly, the practical canon of classical dance is amply covered in the literature. Comparatively less has been said about the rise and fall of classical *values* in the course of the seventeenth through twentieth centuries, one

154 IMPOSSIBLE PROJECT

of the most turbulent epochs in European history; in this respect, my plan is to draw on as much ballet lore material as needed to make the picture, if not comprehensive, then coherent. Finally, so far as I am aware, no attempt has yet been made to approach the notion of *classical ballet* as a *mythos*, a self-narrative with ramified implications of survival and salvation. This is what I intend to undertake, piecing together tales and legends culled from ballet lore of different provenances and periods.

The whole concept of what is, to this day, called "classical dance" hinges on the idea that dance has two lives: one given it by the body of a dancer, the other, extracorporeal, existing in the abstract. A dance can be performed or else transcribed, that is, can exist while unperformed.[225] Ever since the Académie Royale de Danse, we have been taking the *body versus form* dichotomy for granted, so much so that, when, around a century ago, William Butler Yeats concluded a poem with the question "How can we know the dancer from the dance?," cognoscenti were quick to enshrine this as a poetic revolt against the tyranny of the commonplace—that is, against the conviction that unembodied choreography was quintessentially superior to any act of its embodiment, however masterful; that a live dancer, skillful as they may be, could but approximate the Platonic perfection of the classical.

This conviction was, as I intend to show, the underlying creed of what in Russia became known as *classical dance*. The very term "classical"—redolent of antiquity, of the neo-incarnations thereof, and, all at the same time, of your everyday dance *class*—seemed to raise dance to the level of arts otherwise taken as loftier than it. Of these, sculpture was held to be the loftiest. In the previous chapter, we touched on what a psychologist might term *sculpture envy*, the Pygmalion-like vision that runs through the teachings and teaching practices pursued at different times by Noverre, Didelot, Petipa, and, most explicitly, by Carlo Blasis in his 1830 *Manuel complet de la danse*. If only the humanly imperfect body of a dancer could morph into a perfect semblance of a sculpted body, of the kind that mesmerizes us in (neo)classical marble. Did not Hegel himself define the art of sculpture as not just another imitative art but the art that transcends bodily fallibility and frailties? Sculpture, per Hegel, strips the human body of what is organic, individual, physiological in it; the sculptor essentializes the body by ridding it of the inessential.[226] As will be discussed in the next chapter, Akim Volynsky applied the sculptural analogy to the silk tights ballet dancers wore on the stage: initially introduced for considerations of modesty, these wound up contributing to the overall aesthetics of the show. By smoothing skin, tights sculpturized ballet.[227]

MODERN SPECTERS   155

Ballet found its sculptor—and its Hegel—in Blasis. If the sculptural body manifests in rational geometric proportions, so must the dynamic body of dance. Not, of course, that Blasis saw the geometries of dance and sculpture as isomorphic; a virtuoso dancer himself, Blasis knew only too well how little the relaxed grace of, say, *contrapposto* had in common with the anything but natural, outturned physicality of ballet (e.g., 180 degrees in the first position, not less and not more). Rather, he modeled ballet according to the terms and apparatus of geometry. No body is geometrically perfect? All the better: the geometry of dance will persist as an impossible perfection.

Things *classical*—classical statuary, classical narratives—had been haunting balletic diegeses all along, but it was only relatively recently, around the latter half of the nineteenth century, that the modifier "classical" came to be regularly applied to dance itself. It is an open secret, to be sure, that the alphabet of choreographic figures still referred to as "classical dance" long predates this; a credible historiographic tradition tracks it back to at least the 1660s, the decade marked by Louis XIV's founding of the Académie Royale de Danse. Whether we foreground continuity or change depends largely on our perspective as historians, but we can agree that the choreographic alphabet rooted in the late seventeenth century remains the foundation of ballet technique. What did change over time were its names: now *l'Art de la Danse*, now *danse noble*, now *the French school of dance*, now *the old French school*, now (and up to now) *classical dance*. Some of these names deserve a closer look, insofar as one such name or other may be evocative of choreography's role in the ever-changing history of aesthetic and political values.

Consider "Letters Patent of the King to Establish the Académie Royale de Danse in the City of Paris Decreed March, 1661." Strange in an inaugural document of this kind (although hardly uncommon in later ballet lore) is the note of disquiet running through it, as if establishing an academy of dance were some sort of emergency measure. "Although the Art of Dance has always been recognized as one of the most honorable and necessary methods to train the body," reads the opening paragraph of "Letters Patent,"

> during the disorders and confusion of the late wars, there were introduced into said Art, as in all the other arts, such a great number of abuses with the potential to ruin many irreparably; so many ignorant and clumsy persons have permitted these errors to creep into public exhibitions that there are astonishingly few left who are even capable of teaching; by dint of long years of study and practice they have managed to withstand falling into

156   IMPOSSIBLE PROJECT

those severe faults whereby an infinite number of ignorant persons have disfigured and corrupted the Dance as it is performed by the great majority of persons of quality [*les gens de qualité*].[228]

The royal complaint, in a word, was that the civil wars in France (whom else to blame if not unruly Frondistes?) had somehow managed to pollure—*défigurer & corrompre*—the once pristine choreography of court ballets. The Académie's job, or call it a rescue mission, was to sort the wheat from the chaff, in other words, to establish a canon. There must be some overarching trajectory from the Louis XIV who was a dancer known to excel in one ballet after another to the Louis XIV who supposedly proclaimed, or at least inspired, *L'État, c'est moi*. Either correct or else corrupt—this was how Louis XIV, a rhapsode of absolute monarchy, preferred to treat any alternative, whether political or balletic. (And what good are academies without administrative power? Louis's could grant or deny teaching licenses to freelance dance masters and could fine any contraveners of the canon.)

As a state institution, the Académie Royale de Danse faded away during the French Revolution. But it was well before the 1790s—in fact, around the late 1670s—that it became clear to everyone that the Académie had defeated its own (Louis-declared) purpose. As it turned out, instead of stepping up their balletic exercise, *les gens de qualité*—those nobly born, the principal recruits of court ballets—would rather ensconce themselves in theater *boxes*, gladly ceding the stage to professionals. Nobles, it was felt, should dance solely at noble balls. Such were the winds of cultural (and class) history, against which even the Sun King was powerless.

More lasting than Louis's Académie as an establishment, and more productive than its on-the-ground politics, proved to be the very idea of dance as in need of institutional guardianship. Skeptics might liken it to Andersen's tale of the emperor's new clothes, but the fact remains: it is to institutions like the Académie that we owe the notion of what I referred to earlier as "unembodied" dance: dance as a mental concept or as a pictogram on paper—in a word, dance as an abstraction. A kind of dance that could endure without dancers.

How can we know the dancer from the dance? Louis XIV could, and those who could not, in his view—the hordes of dancers branded in the Letters Patent as *le nombre infiny* (*sic!*), *des ignorans* (*sic!*)—were a menace from which *dance* had to be protected.[229] Embedded in Louis's philosophy of dance was a conviction that dance was a patrimony to be passed on—and on and on—unchanged.

The same thought, itself unchanged, is to this day nested in the concept of *classical dance*. When executing a pas, a classical dance student is not supposed to do it *beautifully*. You do your pas correctly, or bust. "I was at times carried away," confesses Fokine, recalling the years when he, a recent graduate, was entrusted with teaching at the Imperial Theater School, "[and] lectured in my classes about beauty and aesthetics. This was a daring, unheard-of innovation: to talk about beauty during a dance class—what impudence! Everything was expected to be 'correct,' and nothing more."[230] Characteristically, if somewhat inconsistently, Fokine, on the same page, swears allegiance to his teacher, the apostle of classical correctness: "All [my teaching was] in complete accordance with the marvelous schooling transferred to me by Christian Johansson."[231]

Anecdotal evidence, it seems, can be trustworthy when firsthand. Stories abound of the apostolic ethos predominant at the Theather School in Petersburg, all centering on Johansson, whom his pupil and acolyte Nicolas (Nikolai) Legat, writing in 1932, called "the Grand Old Man of the dance," adding, as if this title were not enough, the following description: "a giant in his art, who elevated the technique of the ballet to superhuman levels, and imbued it with the dignity of a religion."[232]

In Legat's apotheosis of his beloved dance professor, the presumed Russian term rendered as "grand old man" (the original is lost), *starets*, is itself of religious origin. In Russia, *startsy* were the monastic "elders," visiting whom in their hermitages—call it spiritual tourism—was a trend among late nineteenth-century religious philosophers and religious-minded literati, including Dostoevsky and Tolstoy. (The former immortalized this figure in Father Zosima; the latter lived long enough to himself earn the unofficial but universal title of *velikii starets*, the Great Old Man, of literature and, by extension, of Russian life at large.)

Johansson was only in his forties when he began teaching classical dance, but ballet lore's predominant image of him is from his later life, when he stood (frailly) as a sort of Master Yoda of Petersburg choreography. "Christian Petrovich Johansson was in his eighties when I began taking lessons with him," recalls Fokine:

Tall, hunched with age, hardly able to move himself, he taught us how to dance. ... When Johansson arrived for lessons he was assisted up the three flights of stairs by the Legat brothers, each holding him by an arm. This was their special privilege as senior pupils. With their assistance he would reach the huge dance hall and would sit down, violin in hand, with his back to the mirror which ran the width of the wall. . . . He would hardly speak. With barely perceptible hand movements he would communicate to us the steps he wished us to do. It would seem that he was no longer able to see or understand what was going on about him. But actually he saw everything and would notice the minutest mistake. It was not an easy task to follow him. A moment of dead silence would follow every order for a combination of steps. Everyone would be thinking, trying to figure out the combination. Then one of us would attempt to dance it out. Usually it was not completely correct and Johansson would almost imperceptibly shake his white head. We would all gather in front of the maestro, bending over him, and with great concentration try to learn what details had been omitted or incorrectly executed. The concentration added a special value to each lesson.[233]

Sentimental though they may be—understandably so, as both Fokine's and Legat's memoirs were written in exile in the 1930s—testimonials like theirs do properly convey the climate of elder-worship peculiar to ballet schooling. It was as if Johansson's venerable age stood, part for the whole, for *the age of classical dance*; it was only Fokine's and his classmates' herculean parsing of the ancient master's meaning that kept classical dance from going extinct. Far from dance training as a mere honing of skills—the most trivial interpretation we could place on what occurs in dance classes nowadays—it was as if classical dance were an abstract idea, an invisible something to be passed on, so long as your teacher's body could yet move.

The third perspective on ballet—from the standpoint of the *baletnye*, distinct from that of critics like Nekrasov and Saltykov-Shchedrin, or bosses like Vsevolozhsky and his monarch—is a historical reality to reckon with. For one thing, it is quite different from the situation of a modern-day parent selecting an activity for their young adolescent. Nowadays, the choice between the barre and a ball is, let's face it, a trivial one: if your child is bored by ballet, they can always try out for soccer. But in the epoch when Fokine and the Legat brothers were making *their* career choices, choosing the barre—boarding school and all—was tantamount to choosing a destiny. Today we tend to associate ballet with training; from the nineteenth-century perspective, ballet was, above all things, a *teaching*.

Two Historical Mythoi: Apostolic Succession and Movable Dance

The inside view of ballet history entails taking seriously what at first might seem frivolous. "[O]nly if we deem ballet trivial can we ignore background and masters, upon which, by apostolic succession, it has been built." Thus did Lincoln Kirstein, the tireless promoter of ballet, who both chronicled its past and was key to its twentieth-century prospects, open his 1970 treatise *Movement and Metaphor: Four Centuries of Ballet.*[234] The phrase "apostolic succession" recurs across Kirstein's ballet writings. His premise was that, from day one, ballet, besides its obvious existence as an art form, had also been a full-fledged institution—not unlike a state religion, or a state itself. (It was within the fold of a state, let us recall, that the first ballets emerged.) Ballet's history is thus both a story and a political program, which Kirstein calls "apostolic succession" by analogy with the ecclesiastic doctrine that traces Church history all the way back to the disciples of Jesus.

Kirstein's phrase "has been built upon," that is, is quite pointed, recalling as it does the image of *Peter* as the *rock* on which the Church is founded. Kirstein was a ballet builder and may have believed that alongside retrospective history—what happened yesterday or four centuries ago—there is also a *projective story*, a narrative to sell. His metaphor of apostolic succession, that is, seems a blueprint for his own ongoing bridging of classical ballet from the Russian to the American school. In its canonical—ecclesiastic—iteration, the idea of apostolic succession exists in two planes: as a metaphysical doctrine that posits the perpetual continuity of Christ's teaching as an invisible essence, and in the earthly implementation of this continuity, whereby Christ's teaching is believed to be passed from person to person as an uninterrupted sequence of clerical ordinations, accompanied by impositions of hands. Apostles die, as do bishops, but before they do each transfers the immortal authority believed to be in their temporary possession to the next mortal in line.

This kind of person-to-person transfer of spiritual power, observed in most Christian denominations, was what moved Kirstein to compare his conception of the unique foundations of ballet history to apostolic succession. "Unique" because, while Pushkin did not need to meet Byron or Southey personally to glean what literary historians say he did from English romantic poetry, and while in fine arts and drama, too, historical trajectories were not dependent on interpersonal apprenticeship, the transfer of *dance*

160   IMPOSSIBLE PROJECT

as a skill and a teaching, or doctrine, was not a matter of artwork to artwork or mind to mind, but foot to foot. Just as, traditionally, the papacy goes back to Peter, so would an exemplary ballet student—like, in their respective memoirs, Legat and Fokine—trace classical dance at least to Auguste Vestris (called in his time the *dieu de la danse*).[235] To quote Fokine, their mutual teacher Johansson "was himself the pupil of the Danish ballet master August Bournonville, son of Antoine Bournonville, who in turn was a pupil of Jean Georges Noverre and Auguste Vestris. That is how the direct line or artistic succession from the first sources of the classic ballet art of Noverre, Vestris, Maximilien Gardel and Bournonville was handed down from master to master and was safeguarded and preserved by Petipa and Johansson, who were my contemporaries despite the great differences in our ages."[236]

Apprenticeship in this view becomes a form of kinship. "Abraham begat Isaac; and Isaac begat Jacob; and Jacob begat Judas and his brethren,"[237] and so on down to the present generation. Historical explanations of ballet, not unlike biblical genealogies, may sound quite monotonous and uneventful, until we ask how their steady reproductive pace dovetails with the tumultuous timeline of European politics and culture.

Addressing this conundrum, one could fulminate against ballet's irresponsiveness to historical change, as Fokine did in 1918, echoing Saltykov-Shchedrin's earlier jeremiads: "World events follow one another; arts undergo an evolution from romanticism to realism to impressionism to expressionism; are shattered by cubism and futurism. . . . Only ballet goes on stereotypically smiling and drawing its arms apart obligingly as, in pink tights and satin slippers, it performs before the public its centuries-old pas."[238] Alternatively, one could interpret ballet's purported indifference to history more positively, in the philosophical spirit of *ars longa, vita brevis*. Thus does Kirstein, having proudly surveyed, with Olympian hindsight, the past four centuries of this art form, declare, "[T]he ballet, which has been quite unaffected by social eruptions—political, religious, or technological—and has survived the French Revolution of 1789, European revolts of 1848, and the Russian Revolutions of 1905 and 1917 as a court style, is, in essence, untouched."[239] Kirstein makes it seem as though, owing to a kind of apostolic immunity, classical dance remained forever *classical*: unblemished, impeccable, unchanged.

Such, in a nutshell, is the *hindsight* history of classical dance. But viewed from within, this history appears, not as a story of ballet's imperviousness, but of its multiple intersections with history at large. The lens of contemporary ballet lore, including various sagas of ballet's genesis and past, reveals a history of ballet that seems far less serene than Kirstein's summation would have it. With each European cataclysm of the kind mentioned by Kirstein (who curiously omits the French Revolution of 1830), ballet quickly found itself in peril. As told from the inside, the history of ballet is a tale of ballet's near-miraculous rescues, some of which crystallized into mythogenic narratives that themselves helped secure its ultimate survival.

In Russia, the *baletnye* and balletomanes alike embraced an amalgamated historical mythos that foregrounded both succession and salvation. Take the "elder" Johansson, a Swedish dancer schooled in Denmark in the French *danse noble* tradition, who spent most of his professional life in Petersburg, some twenty years dancing, some forty teaching. In the classroom, he was revered as a maestro and a sage. As Legat recalled, "Christian Johansson always used to say to me: 'The Russian school is the French school, only the French have forgotten it.'"[240] Legat would most likely have heard this from his elderly dance master in the mid-1880s. This was a time when novelty and dissent, rather than fidelity to a tradition, were being held up especially by the young as a prime value of art. In those days in Paris, the name Société des Artistes Indépendents sounded cool, more so than Académie Royale de Peinture, an institution that had been in charge of arts training and exhibitions since even before Louis XIV founded his Académie Royale de Danse.

True, by the late nineteenth century ballet's own age of dissent was just around the corner. (Thus would the memoir of one of ballet's first *indépendants*, Fokine, be subtitled *Against the Tide*.) But to give Kirstein, Johansson, and Legat their due, classical dance proved less susceptible than its sister arts to the climate of change. Having eventually adopted certain elements that ballet masters like Johansson and ballet critics like Khudekov had struggled against for years—especially the virtuoso-style dancing *sur les pointes*—the classical idiom seldom diverged from its age-old fundamentals, and when it did, it did so without admitting it. On the contrary, twentieth-century theorists like Akim Volynsky and André Levinson would retrofit the classical vocabulary's somatic conventions to meet sensibilities nurtured on modernism.

A modern fancier of classical art is likely to frequent a museum; to experience classical dance we, as in days of yore, will book a theater ticket. The difference, Legat emphasizes, is that the only thing standing between classical dance and oblivion is the dancer's performing it till death and passing it on

162 IMPOSSIBLE PROJECT

before then. *Saving* in this view is not unlike its meaning in our own computer age, a synonym for *storage*—for which, back then, no medium existed. Per Legat, dancers are creators, no less than Tolstoy, Repin, or Tchaikovsky, the difference being that "between composers, writers and painters on the one hand, and dancers on the other ... the art of the latter cannot be recorded on canvas or on paper; it lives in our bodies and in our hearts; and paying homage to all from whom we derived our art, it is for us of that great generation to hold the torch aloft, and with it light coming generations on their way."[241]

Different faith cultures meet the challenge of change differently. Religious groups like Old Order Amish and Hasidic communities impose time-resistant dress codes and daily habits. Particularly productive for the Russian conception of ballet's history was the medieval doctrine of the movable empire, *translatio imperii*, according to which, to avoid profanation by this or that worldly circumstance, the genuine—metaphysical—kingdom must now and then be moved from one worldly abode to another. This idea resonates in the Russian religious concept of Moscow as the third (and final) Rome: after Orthodox Christianity fell twice—first in Rome (now Catholic), then in Byzantium (now Muslim)—it was in Russia that the true teaching had finally settled, forever.[242] The "Moscow, the third Rome" idea was born in the mind of a sixteenth-century monk, but in the reigns of Alexander II and Alexander III, it gained notable *political* currency in the Russian Empire.

"The wind breathes where it wills;"[243] attributed by John the Evangelist to Jesus, this might sum up the mythos of the "movable empire" of dance, as promoted by the likes of Johansson, Legat, and a host of balletomanes in late nineteenth-century Russia. In outline, this is how the story goes.[244] Officially introduced in Paris in the 1660s, in the wake of the French Revolution of 1789 and in the course of its nineteenth-century aftershocks, the culture of *belle danse*, or *danse noble*, lost much of its veneer, as did noblesse as such and other old virtues associated with the royal court.

It was now that the apostolic idea of salvation came to the fore. Having no language barriers, dance is an inherently movable medium. Court-to-court migration had been routine in the universe of ballet from the beginning of time; the whole concept of ballet as a spectacle, in effect, not to mention the word "ballet" itself, arrived in seventeenth-century France from sixteenth-century Florence.[245] As the political plot thickened in France and across Europe, however, ballet lovers grew ever more inclined to read this or that balletic relocation not as some commonplace career move but as a

MODERN SPECTERS 163

significant, *political* one, or, as Russian ballet lorists tended to understand it, as a sacrosanct mission.

Consider the tribe of Bournonvilles, from which, per Legat and Fokine, stems the exodus of noble dance from France. Summoned by the ballet-loving Swedish monarch Gustav III, a Lyon-born, Noverre-trained French dancer named Antoine Bournonville moved to Stockholm in 1782, where he lived and danced till 1792, the year his crowned patron happened to be shot in a coup during a masked ball at the Stockholm Opera. At that time, Bournonville was already in Copenhagen, which seemed a haven for him to settle in—together with Mariane Jensen, his newfound Danish wife and dancing partner—for the rest of their lives.

(The plan did not go without a hitch. "Bournonville's promising career in Denmark almost came to an end before it began, thanks to his republican sympathies," informs the historian Patricia McAndrew. Reportedly, when staging an in-house ball for the French legation to Denmark in January 1793—the heyday of the Reign of Terror in Paris—Bournonville had the nerve to choreograph the cotillion, set to the tune of *Ça ira,* such that it evoked the mechanics of beheading.[246] The jest went as flatly with local lords as Vsevolozhsky's adorning of *The Sleeping Beauty* with a dance of spindle-armed *tricoteuses* later would with Alexander III.)

In Denmark, Antoine begat August, who would become known as the sire of the so-called Bournonville method, owing to which—as with the Amish or Hasidic suspension of change via uniform—the *belle danse*, its primal elegance intact, remains to this day enshrined at the Royal Danish Ballet in Copenhagen. Such, in short, was the Scandinavian path of the expatriate *danse d'école.*

Its path in Russia appears less straightforward, at least as conveyed by the principal pilgrims and commemorators. Enter, again, Christian Johansson, a Swedish dance prodigy deemed so promising that, cosponsored by the French-born Swedish crown prince Oscar, young Johansson was given the opportunity to spend two years in Copenhagen studying the *belle danse.* Which he did, but instead of bringing the French tradition back to Stockholm, Johanssen smuggled it to Russia, where he married a Russian woman and raised a daughter, Anna Johansson, who would star as a soloist in the Petersburg Ballet and would succeed Legat in teaching what had been her father's class at the Mariinsky.

As Legat genealogizes the spread of the French influence to Russia, he pays particular attention to cross-ethnic marriages and the mixed issue thereof,

164   IMPOSSIBLE PROJECT

an earthly factor without which heavenly ballet would hardly have been so movable: "Johansson was a pupil of the Bournonvilles (father and son), who in turn were pupils of Vestris. The French succession was also handed down to my father, Gustav Legat, who was professor at the Imperial School in Moscow. . . . My mother was Russian, but my father, like Johansson, was a Swede, though he and Johansson always spoke French together. But my father's mother, my grandmother, was Constance Lede, a Frenchwoman, and a brilliant dancer at her time."[247]

Legat's narrative of the French *belle danse*'s survival abroad is less about natural grace—the staple of Bournonville's teaching method—and more about *grace* in a metaphysical sense. In Legat's telling, in Russia the French style, no longer in demand at home, seemed to be not just reembodied but reensouled. This was where ideological constructs like "Moscow, the third Rome" and *translatio imperii* came in handy. As posited by a range of nineteenth-century Russian cultural theories (and correspondingly ridiculed by mockers like Saltykov-Shchedrin), there exists such a thing as the Russian soul, the innermost receptacle of divine grace and human virtue. It is from this—mystical, spiritual, nationalist—perspective that Legat's 1932 memoir presents the classroom wisdom he imbibed from Johansson in the late 1880s: as a tradition fortuitously preserved in soulful Russia.

"How true this was," recounts Legat, "I discovered when I came to make my debut at the Paris Grand Opera" in 1908. As Legat and Matilda Kschessinska rehearsed a scene, the Paris Opera folk gathered around to observe. "[W]e were very nervous, for Russians were still regarded as semi-barbarians at the beginning of this century," Legat confesses. Next, the tables turn: "Mme Mory, then chief ballet mistress at the Grand Opera, fell on our necks and exclaimed: '*Voila des vrais danseurs, jamais je n'ai vu pareils!*' And the then assistant ballet-master, Leo Staats, asked me: 'Tell me please, what school is yours?' If any question could have astonished me, it was surely this! But I answered the simple truth. 'Yours,' I said, 'your school, the French school, which you had lost, but which we Russians have not only preserved but have poured into it our Russian soul.'"[248]

The story sounds suspiciously neat, but it does accurately convey ballet lore as it stood at the turn of the century. Pretentious as Legat's "soul" talk may seem, we as ballet historians must recognize that lurking beneath such twaddle lay the contemporary conviction that the dance survives only on account of *succession*. Reviving the French *danse d'école* by pouring a measure of "Russian soul" into it is like a magic plot twist from a Russian fairy tale. But to call the life-giving ingredient "soul" was but another way of asserting a doctrine considered as incontrovertible in ballet as the *extra Ecclesiam nulla salus* was to the Church. To live immortally, the body of body movements called *danse* must stay in constant contact with the mortal bodies of living dancers. It was as if Terpsichore had two mutually indispensable physiques: one physical, the other metaphysical.

Surviving by Splitting

In France itself, ballet history could be peaceful or turbulent, depending on currents of thought in the country's politics and art. That the French citizen in Denmark Antoine Bournonville could stage a salon dance to the tune of *Ça ira*—the battle hymn of tumbril-happy sans-culottes—was because, among other things, as the dancer heard from his confreres in France, the symbolic Goddess of Reason inaugurated in 1793 in the cathedral of Notre Dame was (reportedly) played by a ballet dancer of the Paris Opera.[249] On the other hand, as everyone understood, it was the streetwise *Carmagnole* rather than the salon minuet that was *the* dance of the First Republic. Under Napoleon, the picture changed, and so it did, again, in the age of romanticism.

In certain historical epochs, the artistic and political currents of taste would pull ballet in opposite directions. The 1830s in France is a case in point. "From time immemorial," wrote Hippolyte Auger in his 1840 treatise *Physiologie du théâtre*, "the French school of dance retains the reputation of being the greatest, truly classical."[250] How could this be? Per the logic of political history, in the wake of the July Revolution of 1830, the repute of *danse noble* appeared to be beyond retrieval. The art of dance fell from grace in every sense. In 1831, King Louis Philippe, who tried his best to dissociate the newly founded July Monarchy from the lifestyle once enjoyed by the House of Bourbon, franchised the Opera, its ballet company included, to a private entrepreneur. (The deal, just in case, involved a state subsidy.) "People [here] no longer strive to indicate by their appearance that they belong to the noble estate," Karl Ludwig Börne observes in his 1831–33 *Letters from Paris*.[251] The political reputation of dancing (social dancing included) declined along with the French school of dance's raison d'être, teaching how to move with *noble* grace.

But from the standpoint of art, Auger's enthusiasm had a stronger basis than the political situation would imply. It was precisely in the 1830s that

166 IMPOSSIBLE PROJECT

French ballet joined the orbit of the romantic movement in arts, following poetry and drama. In the wake of Marie Taglioni's (romantically sepulchral) turn in the opera *Robert le Diable* in November 1831 and her subsequent ethereality in the ballet-pantomime *La Sylphide* in March 1832, ballet was once again the rage. The (to be sure, romanticism-fueled) revival of dance may have worked in counterpoint with the fashionable distaste for anything that smacked of the ancien régime, but then, art history has never insisted that sociopolitical and artistic preferences work in tandem. If, indeed, a back and forth between art and politics exists, its dynamics is often complementary rather than concurrent.

Ballet's romantic turn, peaking roughly in the mid-nineteenth century, redefined it as radically as had Noverre's reform in the 1760s and after. As discussed in the first chapter of this study, the innovative power of Noverre's project was to drive a wedge into what had been considered an indivisible whole. Noverre *split* ballet in two senses. First of all, choreography: the dance. Previously conceived as an integral art of *belle danse*, this now proved, as explained by Noverre, an uneasy balance of the drama-driven *pas d'action* on the one hand, and frivolous dancing for dancing's sake, on the other, the latter slighted by Noverre as a relic of Louis XIV's Académie Royale de Danse aesthetics. Second, Noverre's artistic ideology split the dancer's very body, pitting their "head" against their "feet." In this plane too, we recall, Noverre preferred the head. (Even if, as a ballet master, he knew full well how indispensable these purported opposites are to one another.) In a word, in order to galvanize ballet, Noverre polarized its basic toolkit: the dancer and the dance.

At the core of the romantic revolution in ballet was a fission as potent as that of Noverre, only this time the affected area was first and foremost ballet's diegetic world. The split ran, as Bénédicte Jarrasse puts it in her study of ballet's romantic lore in France, between *imaginaires* and *représentations*.[252] Wherever you used to look—at the allegorical universes (planets and luminaries) of court ballets of yore, the anacreontic pastures of classical ballets, the Noverrian narratives bursting with passion and action—ballet's had been a more or less homogeneous domain. Not so when it came to romanticist dieseges, whose sine qua non was the very duality—heterogeneity, bipolarity—of what was performed before one's eyes. It was no longer a choice between mimetic *or* imaginary; a truly romantic ballet was all about the back and forth between the two. Key for the romantic storyteller is what occurs between the worldly and the otherworldly.

Specifics vary, but as a rule, the more familiar of the two worlds, the one we humans inhabit, was mapped on empirical geography. *Giselle, or The Wilis*, albeit made in France, is set in medieval Germany; *La Sylphide*, also made in France, in old-days Scotland. Aside from the playbill, the fact is signaled by character dances. This was another romantic novelty: if previously character dances signaled social status (don't all peasants dance as peasants do?), in romantic ballets they became ethnically marked: Scottish peasants dance in heavy boots, Germans dance waltzes.

Antipodal to well-lit human civilization, meanwhile, were strange nocturnal worlds dominated by ethereal and ephemeral creatures, pulled, along with ethnic dances, from the folklore so treasured by national romanticism. Locations and elements varied—woods, waters, dreamscapes—as did their immaterial inhabitants, from passionate sylphs to vengeful wilis to the naiad of the Danube and on to Saltykov-Shchedrin's "beloved" Sprite of the Valley. But whatever their name or provenance, these nonhumans shared a certain *Familienähnlichkeit*, to borrow a term of Wittgenstein. First, in contrast to colorfully costumed earthlings, our *genii loci* would typically enter clad in white (hence the term used to evoke the second act in most romantic ballets, *ballet blanc*, introduced, I would conjecture, by Levinson). Second, with regard to choreography, a Marie Taglioni seemed to defy gravity. If preromantic *belle danse* was conceived as an art of noble locomotion among humans, dancing in a romantic ballet was increasingly conceived as flying. "To your feet—your wings," Victor Hugo inscribed on a book he sent to Taglioni as a gift after seeing her dance in *La Sylphide*.[253] Next to Taglioni's aerial techniques, even the wildest of Fossano's peasant jumps seemed pedestrian.

From the pedantic perspective of Ober-Procurator of the Holy Synod Pobedonostsev, the likes of wilis and sylphs were pagan deities best kept at bay, especially during Lent. But the spiritual outlook of the romantic stage was not so *either/or*. There are pagans and there are pagans, Hugo argues in his manifesto-like "Preface to *Cromwell*" (1827); some are akin to the spirit of Christianity, some not. "[Classical] paganism, which molded all creations from the same clay, minimizes divinity and magnifies man," explains Hugo, who, it turns out, is no great partisan of the pantheon of Greek and Latin antiquity. Their gods are too material, too humanlike to be proper gods. "Far from proposing, as Christianity does, to separate the spirit from the body, [the ancient theogony] ascribes form and features to everything, even to impalpable essences, even to the intelligence. In it everything is visible, tangible, fleshly," *Cromwell*'s author complains. "They eat, drink, and sleep."[254]

168   IMPOSSIBLE PROJECT

Perhaps counterintuitively, Hugo contrasts these too-human classical gods with the deities of tribes that civilized antiquity used to disdain as "barbarian," deities whom he lovingly describes as immaterial. "Have the fleshly naiads, the muscular Tritons, the wanton Zephyrs, the diaphanous transparency of our water-sprites [*undines*] and sylphs [*sylphides*]?"[255] Hugo calls the latter creatures *our*, not to account himself some pre-Roman Gaul but because, as a romantic author, he believed that those wonderous minds of yore responsible for conjuring these evanescent sprites of nature were already part and parcel of what he calls *l'imagination moderne*, which alone "can give to its fairies that incorporeal shape, that purity of essence, of which the [classical] heathen nymphs fall so far short."[256]

Amazingly, Hugo's preface to romanticism combines three trains of thought hardly thinkable together: a critique of the classical pantheon; an apologia for local pagan (*payenne*, literally, *of the land*) sprites; and—the worst blasphemy of all—an encomium to Christianity (of all things) as a source of true poetry and drama. It was Christian thought that, per Hugo, drove a splitting wedge into what the ancients, including Homer, had conceived as one indivisible world, where "Ajax defies Jupiter, Achilles is the peer of Mars"; where hell is a geographically specific precipice, and "heaven is a mountain."[257]

"Christianity on the contrary," Hugo goes on, "draws a broad line of division between spirit and matter. It places an abyss between the soul and the body, an abyss between man and God."[258] The first thing God did to create the universe was to separate light from darkness. In the same manner, by way of splitting, there emerged the art of drama:

> On the day when Christianity said to man: "Thou art twofold, thou art made up of two beings, one perishable, the other immortal, one carnal, the other ethereal, one enslaved by appetites, cravings and passions, the other borne aloft on the wings of enthusiasm and reverie—in a word, the one always stooping toward the earth, its mother, the other always darting up toward heaven, its fatherland"—on that day the drama was created. Is it, in truth, anything other than that contrast of every day, that struggle of every moment, between two opposing principles which are ever face to face in life, and which dispute possession of man from the cradle to the tomb?[259]

Hugo's "Thou art twofold" alludes succinctly to the Neoplatonic current in Christianity, but it also represents an artistic challenge that would lead, a few years later, to the emergence of the romantic ballet. Can you, through your dance, embody a flighty pagan fairy, who, at the same time, is also a saintly Christian creature ready to sacrifice her life—and flight—in the name of love? Taglioni showed she could and, after years of performing Sylphide and other modern specters on Petersburg and Paris stages, earned herself a saintly, not to say Christlike, renown. (Gautier famously called her "a Christian dancer.")[260] *Imitatio Christi*, the behavior prescribed to believers by Church fathers from the apostle Paul onward, became the backbone of the Taglioni mythos in ballet lore. Among the *baletnye*, Taglioni's offstage persona hinged, as much as anything, on the (likely accurate) biographical legend according to which her ascent to glory came at the price of being sacrificed, by her own father, on the altar of daily six-hour exercises, some ending with her falling in a faint.[261]

With the example set by Taglioni, conduct imitative of Christ became a staple of romantic ballets. In the "white act" of *Giselle*, the audience received mixed signals. On the one hand, wilis were killer ghosts, and poor postmortem Giselle becomes, if reluctantly, one of them. On the other, of the gestures we know to have been performed by wilis in the second act, two stemmed from Christian iconography. The stock gesture of all wilis—arms crossed on the chest—signaled humility: it is with her arms likewise crossed that St. Mary received the good news from the archangel Gabriel in many an Annunciation painting, and Catholic tradition prescribed this pose for the interring of the bodies of the deceased. The other gesture, performed by Giselle alone, alluded powerfully to the "life in Christ" doctrine. Standing by her own grave with a massive cross over it, Giselle spreads her arms wide, both to protect her exhausted Albert and to imitate the crucifixion.[262]

It is this twofold, dichotomous but complementary body of the romantic ballet that Jarrasse explores in her 2017 cultural history of French romantic ballet titled, appropriately, *Les Deux Corps de la danse*, the two bodies of dance. As she demonstrates, romantic ballet used to draw its audience into a guessing game of shifting identities: now representational, now imaginary; now sublime, now grotesque.[263] The list of romantic ambiguities will hardly ever be exhausted.

Complementary Bodies

Ballet is *two-bodied* also in another, less obvious and scarcely addressed (except perhaps in ballet lore) way. This has nothing to do with specific balletic productions or periods like romanticism, but rather with ballet's institutional or, more precisely, *corporate* ideology. In Western European cultures,

170   IMPOSSIBLE PROJECT

the phrase *les deux corps*, the two bodies, is venerable, deriving from medieval political theology. When, in the above-cited passage from "Preface to *Cromwell*," Hugo describes the human being as actually "two beings, one perishable, the other immortal, one carnal, the other ethereal," he not only evokes the Christian dogma of the mortal body versus the immortal soul; he also echoes the time-honored justification of corporate continuity (or perpetuity), be the corporation in question Virgil's *imperium sine fine*, an incorporated city like Bologna or Boston, the Catholic or Russian Orthodox Churches, or the school of dance called *danse d'école*.

An autocracy's primal concern is its own permanence. Earlier in this chapter, I mentioned the telltale scene that, according to Fedor Lopukhov, had been part of the prologue to *The Sleeping Beauty* until expunged by Nikolai Sergeev after the 1905 Revolution. Per Lopukhov (who played Tom Thumb as a student), King Florestan, startled when Carabosse bursts into the throne room from thin air, jumps from his throne, whereupon the wicked fairy installs herself on it.

It was to spare their kings such surprises that medieval theologians and crown lawyers devised the metaphysical theory thoroughly researched and richly commented on in Ernst H. Kantorowicz's 1957 historical treatise *The King's Two Bodies: A Study in Medieval Political Theology*. As the author shows at some length, while the theory had diverse religious roots and broad philosophical and literary repercussions in the works of Dante, Shakespeare, and others, its core idea is easily graspable, even as formulated in Elizabethan legalese:

[T]he King has in him two Bodies, *viz.*, a Body natural, and a Body politic. His Body natural (if it be considered in itself) is a Body mortal, subject to all Infirmities that come by Nature or Accident, to the Imbecility of Infancy or old Age, and to the like Defects that happen to the natural Bodies of other People. But his Body politic is a Body that cannot be seen or handled, consisting of Policy and Government, and constituted for the Direction of the People, and the Management of the public weal, and this Body is utterly void of Infancy, and old Age, and other natural Defects and Imbecilities, which the Body natural is subject to.[264]

In other words, even when *naturally* vacated, *politically* no royal seat is ever up for grabs. The invisible body politic is there, guarding the gap between *The king is dead* and *Long live the king*.

MODERN SPECTERS   171

As ubiquitous, if less intuitive, was the concomitant idea that the king's body politic was more than a mere figure of speech, but was conceived as a scaled-up replica of the natural body—a social mechanism whose operations and anatomy were analogous to human biomechanics. In today's mind, stale idioms like "head of state" and "diplomatic hands" hardly conjure the images of corresponding body parts; nor do we necessarily discern the outline of the human body in notions like "corporation" or "corps de ballet." But such associations were clear when these terms were coined: "[T]he Members [of the King's Body politic] are his Subjects, and he and his Subjects together compose the corporation . . . and he is incorporated with them, and they with him, and he is the Head, and they are the Members, and he has sole Government of them."[265]

These days, the term "corporation" pertains more to the world of business than to institutions called upon to shore up loftier matters like religion or ballet. But as Kantorowicz shows, the two-body concept goes back to the apostle Paul's metaphysical metaphor of the Church as "Christ's body" and Jesus as its head. In the Middle Ages, Paul's initial metaphor was conceptualized as *corpus ecclesiae mysticum* (the "mystical body of the Church"); with time, it was adopted by the ideologues of other institutions that, like the Church, claimed continuity beyond a lifespan. "[H]e is incorporated with them, and they with him" was a meme that vouchsafed a putative unity of monarch and kingdom, pope and laity, bishop and diocese, and so on—for once we agree that we are parts of the same body, how could the body politic survive without its head? (A question that, of course, would have to be answered repeatedly in political history.)

As the idea of corporate immortality gained momentum, it came to be applied, aside from pope or king, to all manner of abstract universalities. Thus the corporation of medieval lawyers both served and embodied the mystical body of the timeless *universitas* called *Justitia*. Any community, if its members wished and could afford a scholiast to write it up, could declare itself incorporated. Thus, at one point, Bologna's lawyers pronounced their city an eternal corporation, whose mortal inhabitants and crumbling walls belied an immortal, indestructible body called (from the city's Latin name, Bononia) *Bononitas*, that is, Bolognity.[266] (If it is true that the Americanism "baloney" derives from "Bologna sausage," then *Bononitas* may as well be seen as philosophical baloney avant la lettre.)

Anything but medieval, ballet, nonetheless, formed a sui generis corporation. The *universitas* of this corporation was "classical dance," as the

172   IMPOSSIBLE PROJECT

old-school French style of noble choreography became known in nineteenth-century Russia—a new name signaling a new development in this art form. As mentioned above, ballet's romantic age saw a notable transformation in the sphere of character dancing. In Noverre's times, the term "character dance" referred to the grotesque gestures and eccentric jumping peculiar, Noverre believed, to low-class merriments of the kind depicted in the genre paintings of David Teniers. In romantic ballets, under the sway of national romanticism, the previous meaning of "character dances" was replaced by stylized national dances, whether folksy or gallant.

The romantic drift toward vernacular choreography redefined, by contrast, the old-school French *belle danse* as universal, for what is the art of moving across the floor with effortless grace and innate restraint, if not a transnational token of nobility? Per this logic, "French belle danse" was a misnomer; the phrase "classical dance," as in "classical Latin"—the noble tongue no longer spoken by simple folk but only studied in class—sounded more appropriate. It was this formerly "French," now "classical" language of ballet that became the *universitas*—the *Bononitas*—of the corporation called the imperial ballet. As I intend to show in the next chapter, under the pen of early twentieth-century theorists like Levinson and Volynsky, what had emerged in late nineteenth-century ballet lore as "classical dance" was honed into a vision of a philosophical body language, a newfangled *universitas* to be enshrined by the Soviet balletic corporation as well as, outside Russia, by the likes of Kirstein and Balanchine.

Kantorowicz's historical study is least of all about ballet. It is about what the author dubs "fictitious immortalities," wished into existence by the powers that be and certified by pundits in the employ thereof. The king's better body—the body politic—is, as a *fictitious* immortality, akin to the emperor's new clothes. But the medieval meme described so insightfully by Kantorowicz lived a far longer life than did the sartorial fraud in Andersen's tale. Why?

In their odd ways, fictitious immortalities are real—at least real enough to fight over. To a social critic like Saltykov-Shchedrin, classical dance was but the art of raising your leg instead of telling the truth. But to a youngster raised at a ballet boarding-school, in whose curriculum *zakon Bozhii* ("God's Law," the class where you were instructed in the Russian Orthodox faith) came *second* to the dance-class barre, classical dance, with its prophet Johansson, was the closest thing to religion.[267] Here, classical dance became your second body: the immortal body balletic.

And, like some religions, this cult came complete with a salvation narrative. Let us recall Leo Staats, the Paris Opera assistant ballet-master who had the nerve to compliment Matilda Kschessinska and Nikolai Legat for their impeccably executed *pas de deux*. We do not know what Staats expected in reply (other than perhaps a *merci, monsieur*), but he could hardly have been prepared for a hieratic pronouncement on how the kind of dance the French had allowed to slip from their grasp found a new soil and soul in distant Russia. On the other hand, it is hard to fault Legat for this faux pas: stories of how the Russian ballet school saved *danse d'école, and* of how the Russian Orthodox Church had picked up and run with the teaching of Christ fumbled in Constantinople and Rome, were fed to ballet pupils by their dance instructors and catechists daily.[268]

Daily, and, so to speak, in adjoining rooms. Surprisingly, especially as compared to ecclesiastic policies enforced in pre-1830 France, Russian Orthodox clergy were supposed to take part in, rather than dissociate from, institutions responsible for theatrical education. The Imperial Theater School had its own chapel, equipped with everything that Russian Orthodox, Catholic, or Lutheran faculty and students would need to pray, confess, marry, or baptize their babies. (Members of other religious groups were not admitted to the school.) By and large, ballet students, upon graduation, preferred to stick to this accustomed, if modest, venue of worship rather than shift parishes as they moved house. Pavel Gerdt, of the Lutheran faith, married there, as did Karsavina, a Russian Orthodox,[269] and so did Balanchine in 1922, that is, at a time when a church wedding was seen as an embarrassing atavism.[270] Pavlova once embroidered a carpet for the chapel, crosses and all; Fokine painted an icon for it, which, after a moment of hesitation (Fokine had the reputation of being a Tolstoyan) was consecrated and duly installed.[271] For the *baletnye*, the house chapel and the dance class next to it were part of their natural habitat, much as the local church becomes a second home in a closely knit community. No wonder your belief in Jesus Christ and your trust in the Lord called dance would occasionally blur.

And then there were the balletomanes like Skalkovsky, who routinely bestowed on Russian dancers the title of "keepers" or "guardians" (*khraniteli*) of classical dance.[272] Empty as they may sound, such epithets pointed to a fracture in the presumed oneness of the dancer and the dance. In the light-hearted epoch of Vestris, choreographic perfection was seen as humanly attainable; like his father before him, Auguste Vestris was hailed by admiring throngs as *le dieu de la danse*. In the new epoch, its ethos defined by dance

174 IMPOSSIBLE PROJECT

pedagogues like Johansson and propagandists like Skalkovsky, no dancer could claim the status of perfection: this belonged exclusively to classical dance as an abstraction. It was as if an invisible wedge had been driven between the dance and those who embodied it. The act of dancing was now experienced as an uneasy give and take between two complementary bodies: your body natural and *the* balletic body. You cannot own classical dance; you can only preserve it as is, and pass it on.

Doing classical dance was understood as *serving* it, like being a servant of God. The founding father of American ballet lore, Lincoln Kirstein, did not mince words and called the classical idiom a "catholic absolute dogma of the dance."[273] As Susan Sontag lamented in her 1987 essay "Dancer and the Dance," whenever you attempt to congratulate a ballet dancer—and this includes Baryshnikov—on a splendid performance, what you get in response instead of a thank you is "a disconsolate litany of mistakes that were made: a beat was missed, a foot not pointed in the right way, there was a near-slippage in some intricate partnering maneuver. Never mind that perhaps not only I but everyone else failed to observe these mistakes. They were made. The dancer knew. Therefore the performance was not *really* good. Not good enough."[274]

This kind of "cruelly self-punishing objectivity about oneself," suggests Sontag, is rare to come by in an actor or pianist or singer and must be a side effect of how classical dancers are brought up: their *formation professionelle*. Ballet dancers are trained to see themselves not from the viewpoint of the actual audience they perform for but "as viewed from the perspective of an ideal observer, one more exacting than any real spectator could ever be: the god Dance."[275] As ballet dancers perform, they *serve* their art—an action experienced not just aesthetically but ethically. A misstep, even if unnoticed by ballet lovers in the auditorium, remains a sin against classical dance, whose scriptures are not yours to mess with. To this day, ballet professionals term a well-turned movement "clean," as opposed to anything less than this, which is "dirty," a complementary dichotomy harking back to scriptural, if not proto-scriptural axiology.[276]

* * *

How many ballet histories does it take to capture ballet's protean selves? The more the merrier, but at least three. Earlier in this chapter I quoted the nineteenth-century drama actor Aleksandr Nil'sky who, in his 1896

Backstage Chronicles, speaks of the two opposite faces he recalls seeing on his ballet colleagues: the smiling, carefree face put on for onstage appearances, and the backstage one, when, waiting in the wings, a dancer could be overheard praying to God (the god Dance?) that no slippage occur in this or that partnering maneuver and that no injury consign her to dancing evermore "by the water"—in the rear line of the corps de ballet, next to a lake or other body of water typically painted on the backdrop. Or take Saltykov-Shchedrin's merciless 1864 review of *The Naiad and the Fisherman*, in which the ever-caustic critic detects torrents of sweat on the face of the young and carefree Matteo performed by a tired, aging danseur. *Onstage* and *Backstage* should be the titles of the first two histories we need to consult if we seek a sense of ballet's evolution in the round. (With the onstage history itself needing to attend to its downstage and upstage tiers.) We need to know, as much as the story of smiling, the story of sweating; not just the triumphs, but also the despair. One is the history of ballet as art; the other, its history as a corporation.

The third ballet history we ought to always keep at hand is the history of lore, for how else can we account for the complex back and forth between ballet's contrasting faces? These were not Janus-like faces, looking in two opposite directions; rather, they were complementary, looking at and speaking with one another; at times, the two faces reciprocally morphed. This interaction between ballet's everyday and its Sundays, as it were, was documented vicariously or personally, contemporaneously or in retrospect: in letters, diaries, memoirs, and fictions. While wordless onstage, once offstage the world of ballet grows quite verbose. Susan Sontag and Leo Staats, beware! Ballet lore can be a bulwark of corporate wisdom and a spreader of corporate memes. That we Russians are serious about dancing, *cher Monsieur*, is because, dance-wise, Petersburg has become what Moscow once became, when the rest of the world had squandered the true faith: the new Holy Capital—in this case, the new Paris. No matter that, as it changed countries of residence on the route from Gaetano Vestris to Nikolai Legat, classical dance changed names, from *French belle danse* to *danse d'école* to *klassicheskii tanets*, or that it espoused romantic elevation at one point and surrendered to pointework at another. Corporate ideology prefers stability, not change.

Needless to say, the world of twentieth-century art had little room or patience for things called classical. Nor were modernist art lovers likely to buy into a story of old spiritual values lost and found. The model image of the modern artist was more that of a rebel than a guardian. Against all odds, however, the cult of the classical dance survived, revamped and rethought along lines befitting modernist sensibilities, like the geometric philosophy conjured by such pioneers of abstract art as Kandinsky and Mondrian or Lissitsky and Malevich. None of this reconceptualization, as I intend to show in the chapter that follows, would have been possible were it not for ballet-lore gurus like Levinson and Volynsky and the influence they wielded on the *baletnye* as well as the general public. For, as Noverre never tired of reminding the reader of his *Letters*, no foot is ever complete without the head.

3

Ballet as a Verbal Art

Apostasy and Theodicy

The career of Vaslav Nijinsky, arguably the most legendary among twentieth-century male dancers, was cut short by insanity. No fewer than ten doctors—among them, Alfred Adler, Sigmund Freud, Sándor Ferenczi, and Carl Jung, to mention the names whose cultural standing matched Nijinsky's—were summoned to help at different times. That psychological analyses failed to bring results, explains Adler in the only extant medical statement about Nijinsky's case, is because the process "hinges on the establishment of a creative contact between doctor and patient," and Nijinsky, from the time of his hospitalization in 1919 till his death in 1950, "did not speak and only occasionally broke into a friendly laugh. The attending physician informed me that this patient was always quiet and could not be forced to speak. At the time, even his wife was unable to draw him into conversation."[1]

It is to Nijinsky's wife, Romola, that we owe Adler's written testimony regarding the former dancer's medical condition. In 1936, in the wake of Adler's visit to the sanatorium at which Nijinsky stayed, Romola asked Adler to write a preface to her ill husband's *Diary*, which she was preparing for publication. Proceeding from the diary, Adler identifies Nijinsky's condition as schizophrenia, caused, in the doctor's view, by the "inferiority complex"—a concept (and term) introduced to psychoanalytic theory by Adler himself. The inferiority complex, Adler explains, is the downside of a complementary antinomy. In his prospective but ultimately unused preface to Nijinsky's diary, Adler posits that persons endowed with extraordinary abilities, especially those accompanied by early successes, tend to develop self-expectations that border on delusions of grandeur: "[H]ad he not been an outstanding figure of the stage? Had he not been admired on two continents? Had not his name been in the mouths of all persons who worshipped his incomparable art?" The sky's the limit, but beware of shooting beyond it. "The person strives for godlikeness," concludes Dr. Adler, "and, in extenuation of his failure to attain it, complains that other persons and circumstances have blocked his way to

Impossible Project. Daria Khitrova, Oxford University Press. © Oxford University Press 2025.
DOI: 10.1093/9780197653081.003.0004

178 IMPOSSIBLE PROJECT

the heights."[2] In classical mythology, the gods punish mortals for trying to equal them; psychological mythoi tell us it is we who punish ourselves.

Whatever the medical worth of Adler's analysis, it can be of use as a piece of ballet lore. Indeed, if a diagnosis were needed, or possible, of the psychology and pedagogy of classical ballet, the back and forth between "godlikeness" (as Adler defines Nijinsky's "meaning of life") and inferiority complex might be as good as any. And come to think of it: Nijinsky's inability or refusal to speak to either his doctors or his wife—wasn't this a psychiatric by-product of ballet's ban on words? And was not the whole idea of serving life in mental isolation a form of protest against dancers' life as service to ballet, with its compulsory communality, first at the boarding school, then upon the boards? Like any overcommitment, the commitment of the *baletnye* to ballet was pregnant with rebellion—choreographic, political, and human.

The View from the Water

From the front, nineteenth-century ballet looked like a giant miniature carved in the ivory of flying tutus. Each of the young ladies wearing those tutus had her own place, her own point of view, her own story of ballet. If you were in the rank of ballerina, Petipa would ask you what you'd prefer to dance. You knew he did not ask this entirely out of solicitousness. New productions—with new music, original libretto, and sets built afresh—were rare; it was cheaper and faster to stage a revival of a *Giselle*, *Esmeralda*, or *Paquita* with a couple of new variations commissioned perhaps from Minkus or Drigo and choreographed by Petipa himself, or maybe Lev Ivanov. Or to ask the ballerina, in the best-case scenario a new arrival, to use whatever variations she may have in her portfolio in order to defamiliarize an all too familiar ballet. Bringing a new dance, or better, a new dancer with a new dance in her wake, added novelty to old ballets.

Now, if you were a budding soloist like young Pavlova, with young soloist Fokine as your supporting partner, you were, as we heard from Fokine earlier in the book, left more or less to your own devices. Just dance whatever you do best. But what about the rest of the dancers?

In the usual spatial axiology, up is better than down. But in ballet, if your rank is lower than soloist or ballerina, your place to dance is higher upstage. Here, you ceased being a figure in a game and became a piece in a set. Petipa was known to rehearse with individual dancers. As to the corps de ballet,

BALLET AS A VERBAL ART 179

he preferred to deal with them at home, moving around a set of cardboard cutouts till all of them formed a satisfying composition.[3]

Being a set piece, you possessed no name. To a ballet master, you were what your place was within the space of the stage. If you were a rank-and-file corps de ballet dancer, the way you would be addressed was "You there, by the water." Or "Second from the water," at best.

Two explanations exist as to the origin of this balletic term, one derived from a metaphor, the other a metonym, both time-honored. The first one comes down to us via Noverre but is probably of earlier creation. There is nothing a dancer of talent, diligence, and taste will not achieve, sermonizes Noverre in one of his *Letters*; the half-talented ones will always trail behind. "There are, among dancers, also those who have no talent whatsoever, have no taste, intelligence or a pleasant face; they linger in obscurity; we put them in the rearguard of ballets; and, since some rocks and sea are often depicted on the backdrop, we call them 'coastguards' [*garde-côtes*]."[4] A nineteenth-century Russian manuscript gives a different explanation: "Bad danseuses, the coryphées, are named 'the first one from the water, the second one from the water.' This meant their place to dance is upstage, in front of the hind curtain, behind which a water tank is kept in case of fire."[5]

Viewed from the backdrop, in reverse perspective, your life in ballet looked rather bleak—professionally, contractually, and fiscally. Professionally, corps de ballet dancers were consigned to dancing in large groups, with coryphées dancing in groups of six to eight. Typically, after you graduated you joined the ballet company's corps de ballet, occasionally in the rank of a coryphée, rarely of a soloist. The young and ambitious, like Fokine or Pavlova, would take extra classes and be promoted quickly; early prodigies like Spessivtseva would be groomed to grow into a ballerina as promptly as ballet's sluggish system of seniority allowed; for Preobrajenska, it took years. Not everyone made it, of course, otherwise there would be no corps de ballet to make the Petersburg ballet proud and famous. As in sports, a balletic career hinged on one's genetic suitability for classical dance, but also on chance and effort. Dancers with injuries or those (and there were many) with zero devotion to the profession would be relegated to the water ranks for life.

Contractually, the moment you, as a child, were accepted into the ballet school, you walked into a trap. After the first—trial—year, training, education, and boarding came free of charge for most, yet with a form of debt bondage attached. Seven years of schooling, you were told, constituted your debt to the crown, which you repaid in the course of your mandatory years

180 IMPOSSIBLE PROJECT

on the stage, which, during the nineteenth century, dwindled from twenty to ten. Your retirement pension (more than modest) was to be understood not as something you'd earned but as a bonus, for which you, dear dancer, ought to be thankful—and, out of thankfulness, to serve two extra years.[6]

Fiscally, life by the water was penurious. In 1870 Sergei Khudekov, the belletrist and balletomane with backstage knowledge of dancers' real-life conditions, published a roman à clef titled *The Small World of Ballet: Living Pictures* (*Baletnyi mirok: Zhivye kartinki*), in which the salary of a corps de ballet dancer is said to be fourteen and a half rubles a month. "This kind of salary is barely enough to pay for [your ballet] shoes," a fictional mother from Khudekov's novel warns her stagestruck daughter, Katia.[7]

While it is true that toward the end of the century, corps de ballet salaries more than tripled, they still fell short of the cost of living of someone relying on her salary alone. If we set 300 rubles a year—the average annual income of a factory worker in Imperial Russia—as a standard of urban poverty, the annual income of a corps de ballet dancer, 600 rubles, can at best be defined as semi-poverty. "Customarily, everyone entering the [Petersburg Ballet] company received the same compensation, regardless of talent," recalls Fokine. As a result of their successful graduation performance in *Paquita*, suggests Fokine, his class of 1897 became an exception. "For many years the starting salary had been fifty rubles a month. . . . I was now drawing the sum of sixty-six rubles and sixty-six kopeks per month."[8] To which Fokine's son and translator, Vitale Fokine, writing in the 1960s, added the following footnote: "Thirty-three dollars and thirty-three cents."[9] Dividing by two sounds like too simple an operation for cross-epochal currency conversion, but then, Vitale Fokine was not a comparative economist. Neither am I, but in any case, even accounting for inflation since the time of this calculation, a dollar a day does not sound like much.

In short, as a corps de ballet danseuse, you were in need of financial support. Some were married, but when a savvier consœur dares the novice coryphée Katia—the unrealistically idealistic heroine of Khudekov's *Small World of Ballet*—to count how many married corps de ballet dancers (*kordebaletnye*) she knows, Katia struggles to name more than six.[10] "Well, let me now tell you how many of us, while unmarried, have entered in what they nowadays call civil matrimony," Katia's interlocutor retorts. "Don't look so disconcerted, Katia! . . . Many, deary, many; such is the path lying ahead for most of us."[11]

BALLET AS A VERBAL ART   181

The small world of ballet and the big one beyond it—everyone, except apparently Khudekov's Katia prior to this exchange—was acutely aware of said path. Responses differed. The Directorate, knowing full well how many men came to the ballet for the dancer, not the dance, took it philosophically—reasoning, perhaps, that a modicum of vice was in the nature of the beast. Righteous ballet lovers like Khudekov blamed wealthy patrons; in a vitriolic digression from the novel's plot, Khudekov rebukes such men in no uncertain terms: "They eye a ballet artiste as one might a piece of purchasable meat, a tidbit that, after a hearty meal, could stir their flaccid organisms [*rasshevelit' ikh driablyi organizm*]. . . . Years and years will pass before people notice a human being in an artiste—this will not happen until this type of a ballet *habitué* becomes extinct."[12]

"Polite" society, from which such patrons typically came, would rather blame the victim. Whether it was a matter of the corps de ballet or ballerinas, ballet always enjoyed (without enjoying it) the reputation of a demimonde. Far from entertaining the idea of "civil marriage," a respectable person would imagine a ballet dancer as a *soderzhanka*, a "kept" (read: "fallen") woman. Even Marie Taglioni, the dancer who, in her stage image and public persona, was held to be a paragon of spirituality and chastity, was persona non grata at gatherings of the Petersburg beau monde—unlike women musicians and singers.[13]

A gentleman by birth and upbringing falls in love with a ballet dancer; a story like this has been rehearsed across ballet lore more than once. Typically, such a turn of events confronts both parties with the thorniest dilemma: *he* must choose between his love and family honor; *she,* between his love and the stage. Khudekov's heroine Katia, who by midnovel grows from a coryphée into a soloist, somehow contrives to keep her balletic career a maiden voyage. "Luxurious attire, which the small world of ballet is so keen on, was out of her reach. Being a soloist, Katia was always neatly dressed, but, short of silk and velvet to put on, she kept aloof from all the parties, banquets, and picnics arranged by various balletic voyeurs."[14]

Early in the novel, Katia is told of one Prince Petr Tobolsky, someone who never misses a ballet in which she has a variation. A sterling gentleman, Tobolsky does not even think of stretching his admiration beyond the auditorium, yet Katia keeps misconstruing her admirer's intentions, for hasn't she been told that, if a ballet *habitué* confesses his love to you, it can mean only one thing?

182 IMPOSSIBLE PROJECT

At last the words "hand in marriage" are uttered, but this is where the prince's mother becomes a hindrance, threatening to curse and disinherit the wayward scion of the Tobolsky clan. The wedding takes place despite her, and a year later there is still no reconciliation. The only way out, it transpires, is for Katia to quit the ballet (which, in society's eyes, or so Khudekov implies, would remove her from the zone of ill-repute). The last sentence of the novel ends with an ellipsis, in which the attentive reader will hear not only relief, but also regret: "Of course, this was immediately done, and Katia's surname never since appeared on posters..."[15]

A balletomane and ghost-librettist for Petipa, Khudekov gave his novel an ending worthy of a ballet libretto, or a Disney version thereof. A more sober picture of the small world of Russian ballet may be glimpsed from the short story "The Second from the Water" ("Vtoraia ot vody," 1897) by Petr Boborykin. Its heroine is a dancer whose balletic career has been thwarted by injury, such that her function on the imperial stage has been demoted to that of penultimate line of the corps de ballet, her salary reduced to kopeks, and her rank to a numeral: the "second one" from where the backdrop starts. She has had a balletomane for a lover, whom she eventually married but who is shown to be scornful of her. Unlike Khudekov's heroine, Boborykin's finds a way out, not through marriage but through a separation from her unloved and unloving husband. The Second-from-the-Water is now resolved to open a school of dance to start training "people on the outside" (*liudi s voli*), that is, people outside the "prison" of professional dance training, to revitalize the balletic art.[16]

Unlike in Khudekov's novel, whose world of ballet is confined to the imperial stage, in the Boborykin-imagined world (with the state theater monopoly recently lifted) ballet can be either imperial or private, either a field in which you serve or one in which you are allowed to create. The Second-from-the-Water loathes being in *any* service, whether of the imperial administration or of her husband. She begins to disdain ballet as a dancing machine of which she is only a cog. The moment the idea of opening a private dance school crosses her mind, she falls in love with ballet again—now as an art. Art is freedom of choice; in Boborykin's view, service and art are mutually exclusive.

Boborykin's short story is the world of ballet shown in reverse perspective, from the point of view of a woman at the backdrop. Seen this way, it is a world without choice. Your place in the universe depends on the choices of *others*, not just the Directorate and choreographer but your viewer. Endemic

BALLET AS A VERBAL ART   183

to any performance, the performer's dependence on the audience was especially hard to bear in ballet, given that there was always a predator spectator in pursuit of the dancer, not the dance.

The system did not change overnight; what did change by the end of the century, and what would trigger future systemic changes, was that ballet people began to perceive such dependencies as shameful and humiliating. And not only the dancers by the water. "Women of the new balletic generation," Elizaveta Time writes of her friends Tamara Karsavina and Lidia Kiaksht (known as Lydia Kyasht after her move to Britain), "loathed the mores of the Petersburg [Mariinsky] Theater, with its wealthy patrons, its claque, its air of servility. Both wanted to have a family."[17]

This wish hardly seems extravagant, but amid the strictures imposed on a dancer it sounded like a dream of rebellion. For ambitious soloists like Karsavina and Kiaksht, having a family was not a pretext for abandoning the stage but a pledge of independence from the audience—the domineering beast that you, a beauty, were hitherto expected to enchant.

Employment versus Service

"I'd be glad to serve, / I loathe being subservient." Michel Fokine cites these famous lines from Aleksandr Griboedov's play *Woe from Wit* as the epigraph to the chapter in his memoir *Against the Tide* devoted to his experience as a young dancer at the Mariinsky.[18] In that chapter, titled "The Beginning of Service and Disenchantment in Ballet," Fokine includes his interpretation of Griboedov's lines: "Actors cater to the public demand. Instead of serving art, they are *subservient* to the public."[19] Like the outsider Boborykin, the insider Fokine finds balletic plots embarrassingly silly. "Sometimes, while waiting for a part, I would say to myself: 'The joy of being a painter! You do not depend on anyone, choose your own task, and do what your heart tells [you]. Whereas in ballet, you either stay behind the scenes, or get such a stupid part in such a stupid ballet that you feel ashamed to step upon the stage.'"[20]

The "shame" Fokine mentions here clearly nods to the beloved notion of Leo Tolstoy—a famous novelist famously ashamed of being one, a Christian ashamed for his Church, a human being shaming the human race through the mouth of a tired horse. Months before Fokine graduated from the Imperial Theater School (1898), he, like most readers, must have been thunderstruck by Tolstoy's essay "What Is Art?," which could as well have been

184 IMPOSSIBLE PROJECT

titled "What Is Wrong with Art?" A denunciation of everything about art—art theory, artistic institutions, and art's idols old or new, from Beethoven to Mallarmé—"What Is Art?" is particularly merciless toward opera and ballet. Himself a ballet doubter, Fokine found a spokesman for his views: "With what disapproval, what disdain does Tolstoy, my favorite, my beloved writer, speak of ballet!"[21]

Likely inspired by Tolstoy's title, the young Fokine emerges in the memoir as an incessant questioner. "What is ___?" is an essentialist question, philosophy's greatest challenge. But so eager was young Fokine to take it up that at one point he compiled a questionnaire and mailed it to fellow dancers, to this effect: What is ballet, what is its use, is it an art form for all, or just an "empty amusement" (*pustaia zabava*) for the few?[22]

As Fokine recalls, some respondents answered earnestly, but most resorted to humorous metaphors or witticisms. Particularly striking was Mariinsky first danseur Georgii Kiaksht's answer, which, cynical as it sounded, came naked as truth herself: "Ballet is pornography."[23] This definition, provided by a ballet professional, converged in the mind of the young graduate Fokine with that given by ballet's archnemesis Tolstoy: "And ballet, in which half-naked women make lascivious evolutions and intertwine in all kinds of sensual garlands, is simply an immoral performance."[24] If so, then where do we go from here?

Several other points made in "What Is Art?" resonated with Fokine's misgivings about ballet. Take the fad for elaborate pointe work. Popular with the public, the trend was frowned upon by critics and by the less conventional among choreographers, a category soon to include Fokine himself. Ballet seemed to be about nothing more than toes; ballerinas were reduced to spindles. For this lamentable reduction, Tolstoy had an explanation. What we might call ballet's foot fetish is as inevitable a corollary of specialization as the finger fetish in music, the tongue fetish in poetry—all flow inevitably from the professionalization of art:

[H]undreds of thousands of men devote all their lives from their earliest youth, in order to learn how to twirl their feet very rapidly (dancers); others (the musicians)—to learn how to run rapidly over the keys or over the strings; others again (painters)—to learn how to paint with colours everything they see; and others—to know how to twist every phrase in every way imaginable, and to find a rhyme for every word. And such people, who frequently are very good, clever men, capable of any useful work, grow wild in these exclusive, stupefying occupations and become dulled to all serious phenomena of life, and one-sided and completely self-satisfied specialists, who know only how to twirl their legs, their tongues, or their fingers.[25]

Not only is art detrimental to one's individual development; it is also a punishing and cruel institution—another point in Tolstoy's "What Is Art?" that seemed all too applicable to the small world of grand ballet: "For every ballet, circus, opera, operetta, exhibition, painting, concert, printing of a book, we need the strained labour of thousands and thousands of men, who under pressure perform what frequently is destructive and debasing work."[26]

Indeed, the Imperial Ballet was first and foremost an officialdom; its school, in effect a barracks. Of all walks of life, ballet was the closest to military duty. Ballet students were obligated to wear uniforms and, in addition to their balletic drills, boys also had marching exercises.[27] A ballet career was strictly regimented, with a closed pipeline from school to theater: nearly all school alumni continued at the theater; nearly all theater personnel were school alumni. Often your future rank (and thus your place on the ballet stage) was assigned by "far-seeing professors" in the course of your schooling, whose word could be final.[28] (It was not until 1904 that the Directorate would allow a danseuse of a rank lower than ballerina to petition for a debut in a leading part.)[29] Then came years of mandatory service, then mandatory retirement—aside from solitary instances when a retired dancer might become a choreographer or coach or assigned a walking part as an evil fairy or kindly king.

"In which we serve"—in the nineteenth century, such a clause could be added not only to a naval vessel or an infantry regiment but also to ballet. In his 1973 study "Theater and Theatricality in the Structure of Early Nineteenth-Century Culture," Yuri Lotman speaks of an internal affinity between balletic spectacles and military parades in the reign of the balletomane Nicholas I. Both are predicated on a sense of order: tidy lines, iterative movements, predictable unfoldings. Unlike in war or in a romantic drama, "the question 'what happens next' is of no importance for a parade or a ballet."[30] In the eyes of Nicholas I and his brother and predecessor Alexander I, the uniformity of parades and ballets "was an aestheticized model of perfect organization—not only of the army, but also of the state at large."[31] Unattainable in real life, obeisance and orderliness could be enforced in the drill square and enacted on stage.

186 IMPOSSIBLE PROJECT

As ballet in Russia evolved into *grand ballet*, there seemed to be a convergence between the corps de ballet and the military corps. Under Alexander I, a fencing teacher in the Imperial Theater School was contractually obliged also to "compose [stage] battles" (*sochiniat' srazheniia*);[32] male-performed military-themed dances were included in a variety of ballets throughout the century.[33] Nicholas I had famously detailed guardsmen to teach female dancers how to hold arms in the militarily titled ballet *La révolte des femmes*.[34] And as mentioned in chapter 2, as a young man Nicholas's grandson Alexander III followed a rigid Sunday route, from mass to parade-ground review to the royal box of the Mariinsky Theater for a ballet. All three institutions—Church, military, ballet—had one thing in common: the notion of *service*.

The dichotomy of service versus employment is crucial to the innovative dynamics of Russian ballet. According to nineteenth-century legislation, Russian subjects had the duty and privilege of *serving* their sovereign, whereas foreigners could only be *employed*. Consequently, the demography of nineteenth-century ballet fell into two parts: on the one hand, domestically trained dancers, Russian subjects in the service of the Directorate; on the other, a foreign constituency, visiting ballerinas and the *premier maîtres de ballet* from Didelot to Petipa, all of them hired hands. Being *hired* entailed initiative and creativity; *serving* was all about fulfilling your duty. (What the concept of service entailed for ballet dancers may be gleaned from the cynical witticism of Konstantin Skalkovsky: "Some say that [in the old days], our corps de ballet used to be better than it is now. [This is because] back then, they were fed less and beaten more.")[35]

Observers like Skalkovsky saw this workforce asymmetry as productive and in the early 1900s fretted that there seemed to be no replacement for the lingeringly retiring *creative* Petipa. "Russian ballet masters are utter hacks [*polnye bezdarnosti*]," wrote Skalkovsky in 1904; the remark may have been aimed at the prospective candidate Aleksandr Gorsky (for a time, backed by the Directorate), then a ballet master at the Bolshoi in Moscow. "Russian [dancers] have always been excellent performers, keepers [*khraniteli*] of the old French school of dancing. None of them was ever capable of creating something individual."[36] Little did Skalkovsky know that Fokine, then serving as a danseur at the Mariinsky Theater, was already reading his Tolstoy.

Indeed, Skalkovsky was too quick to consign the "keepers" of classical dance to the drudgework of keeping. The innovative spirit breathes where it wills. Aleksandr Benois relates an overnight transformation that occurred in the Mariinsky troupe, specifically in Pavel Gerdt—one of the pillars of the classical school—as a result of Virginia Zucchi's sojourn in Russia: "Gone was the academically erect carriage considered to be the main merit of the Russian school of ballet. . . . All of a sudden, Gerdt lost all the soldierly deportment that had been inculcated in him at the ballet school."[37] So much for Skalkovsky's "keepers": schooling and drilling, military or balletic, are sometimes not so difficult to slough off. Among the ranks, a mutiny was brewing.

Mutiny of the Mute

To borrow Shklovsky's favorite analogy, asking why ballet dancers never speak on stage is like asking why the knight in chess always moves in an L-shaped manner. Like any art form, ballet has its strictures, but they are not necessarily "endemic" to it, like rules when you sit down to a game of chess. The ban on onstage speaking, for instance, is the result of a protracted seesaw battle. Thus Noverre, who led a tireless campaign against the practice of twinning dancing with singing, did so with an eye to strengthening ballet's autonomy from opera. He waged his war on words cagily, step by step. His was less of a ban than a friendly suggestion: "A well-staged ballet can therefore do without the aid of words."[38] What might work better than onstage singing, Noverre would add, would be for the dance master to hide a singing choir behind the scenes[39]—a device to the likes of which Diaghilev resorted to more than once—for instance, in Fokine's 1914 *Coq d'Or* (Golden Cockerel) or in Bronislava Nijinska's 1923 *Les Noces*.

One way or another, in the nineteenth-century ballet "no words on stage" was eventually written into law. In France, the ban was instituted at some point in the first third of the nineteenth century; in the sixth edition (1835) of the *Dictionnaire de l'Académie*, ballet is defined as a "dramatic story told in dance . . . a theater piece in which action is represented *solely* [*n'est . . . que*] by dancers' gestures and attitudes."[40] There were a few verbal loopholes, like a tune from a known operatic aria slipped into a ballet score, so as to provide ballet spectators with a mnemonic cue; and bravado exceptions; at a climactic point of her *travesti* routine as a corsair, Maria Surovshchikova-Petipa would, to everyone's delight, shout out in Russian, "Fall aboard!" (*Na abordazh!*).[41] But the default setting of ballet was the convention of muteness.

188   IMPOSSIBLE PROJECT

Under her breath, Pavlova could instruct Fokine to give her a spin, but if she said something for the public to hear, she would be fined.

Artistic restrictions—the flatness of a canvas or silence of ballet—are taken for granted by everyone involved: by the artist, dancer, or beholder. Unless, that is, the restriction in question is over-enforced, or, as happens in empires like Russia, becomes too evocative of other, more irksome restrictions of a sociopolitical or disciplinary nature. Théophile Gautier, a connoisseur of ballet and the author of the libretto for *Giselle*, would hardly seem to have cause to remark on balletic muteness. But in a visit to the Russian capital, where he admired the "choreographic battalions" of the Petersburg corps de ballet (they "never make a mistake in their maneuvers"), we find him additionally enthralled by the fact that, much like troops on parade, these girls kept their eyes down and mouths shut. "Here, no chat or chuckle is exchanged; no one winks downstage or toward the front rows. This is a true world of pantomime, where the word is absent, and the action does not go beyond the established bounds."[42] Gautier's panegyric dates from the late 1850s; we can infer that, in his view, the girls in Parisian corps de ballet had become too chatty and unsoldierly.

But if Gautier longed for good old onstage discipline, the Russian dancers he admired for maintaining it may themselves have been of quite a different attitude. In Russia, the ban on onstage words was all too redolent of real-world suppression of speech. A good peasant is a mute peasant—such was the upshot of Saltykov-Shchedrin's scathing account of the conciliatory spectacle in Kashin, a show of loyalty dismissed as "balletic" by progressives and Slavophiles alike. Nor were Russian balletic battalions at peace with their vaunted muteness. At one point in *Our Ballet*, Pleshcheev remarks, with a touch of surprise, on the unconventional manner of miming adopted by the cast of the ballet *The Talisman* (1889), in which "some of the [artistes] used a totally new mimic device, which contradicts any notion of facial gesture: repeatedly, they recurred to lip movements, as if speaking inaudibly."[43] Where will the *baletnye* wind up next, Pleshcheev wonders sarcastically. "For that matter, why not follow the example of the late N. O. Gol'ts, who, having performed a Russian dance, exclaimed loudly: 'That's how we do it [in Russia] [*vot kak u nas*]!' Whereupon the veteran artiste was, naturally, fined."[44]

Gol'ts, who died in 1880 (that is, sixteen years before Pleshcheev's history came out), was long remembered for, among other things, his recurrent attempts, as we might phrase it today, to *unmute* the medium of ballet.

BALLET AS A VERBAL ART   189

Khudekov recalls Gol'ts's escapade from 1864 when, all of a sudden, as though to encourage his diegetic sons in *The Little Humpbacked Horse* to break into the *trepak*, Gol'ts shouted at the top of his voice, "'Hey guys, don't be shy! Look alive! Let's go! [*Chto zhe, rebiata, ne robei! Zhivo! Valiai!*].' And he started dancing. The audience, unaccustomed to the spoken word, was absolutely delighted."[45] But Khudekov was not and sided with the Directorate: "[Gol'ts] was made to understand that it is inappropriate for a ballet artiste to 'wag his tongue'—this is what his feet and legs are for."[46]

"Don't be shy, lassie!" exclaimed Gol'ts on another occasion—in 1878, while performing a Russian folk dance with Matil'da Madaeva. Another round of applause, and another comeuppance—this time, an explanatory memo tendered to Karl Kister, in which Gol'ts assured the then-director of Imperial Theaters that the transgression was "inadvertent, resulting from an excess of sentiment."[47]

Antics like Gol'ts's were not entirely out of the ordinary; an internal *Bulletin of Writs* (*Zhurnal rasporiazhenii*) existed to file and register infractions of all kinds, including that of speech. Gol'ts was, of course, an inveterate trickster, and a showman who tended to think that if you got fined for something that earned applause, that was money well spent. But there may also have been more to this; why else would Gol'ts's famous *That's how we do it here* reemerge in a diary entry of Nikita Okunev as late as 1918, more than fifty years after the fact? Not every case of theatrical hooliganism calls for a historical explanation, but Gol'ts's very much seemed to. First, we should recall that Gol'ts was born in 1800, one year after Pushkin, and as a new-made (1822) *premier danseur* of the Petersburg troupe, starred in the Pushkin-based *Prisoner of the Caucasus* (1823). Here was a King Nestor of a dancer, as one critic dubbed Gol'ts in 1874,[48] who remembered ballet from its glory days—when ballet, steered by Gol'ts's mentor Didelot, lived face to face with Russian cultural material, eager to grab and stage a literary hit only a year after its first appearance in print. The remarkably long-lived Gol'ts, who danced into his eighties, might have seen the Petersburg ballet as sadly transformed over time into a cultural antihero, a Russia-based non-Russian species of spectacle, which, aside from one little humpbacked horse, steered clear of native sources and, as Saltykov-Shchedrin observed, of local problems. And to top it off, barred its Russian-speaking troupe from talking, lest anyone hear what they might have to say. Justly does Okunev recall Gol'ts as someone who addressed his fellow Russians in the audience, not only on stage: *That's how we do it* [*in Russia*].[49] We do, in fact, speak, and not just caper.

190   IMPOSSIBLE PROJECT

Exit Strategy

That's not to say that the Petersburg ballet school was all about footwork and drills. While it is true that, under Didelot, its curriculum was narrowly choreographic (plus the catechism), in the latter half of the nineteenth century things began to change. In the 1880s, professional training was supplemented with general education courses matching the fifth grade of gymnasia and with certain liberal arts subjects: drawing, music, recitation, and, at one point, aesthetics.

In terms of vocational self-esteem, this educational reform had two different, if equally logical, consequences. On the one hand, a dancer's mind was no longer seen as solely an appendage to their feet; on the other, the school of ballet remained nothing more than a feeder school for the imperial balletic stages on which they served. With their feet.

Having partaken of the tree of classroom knowledge, some ballet students began looking around for an escape. Given the growing size of the ballet troupe and the shrinking number of ballet nights per week, it was not hard to combine dancing with something more exciting—especially for men, whose stage load was less than that of women, and especially if the man in question did not take his dancing duties *too* close to heart. "I was lucky," recalls Iosif Kshesinsky (class of 1886), "that my class was small, and my classmates were not the shallow sort [*vertoprakhi*] who could think of nothing but dance." He goes on to recount various cases of what we might call balletic brain drain: "Having graduated from the Theater school, Vladimir Stepanov took a course in physiology at the University. . . . Aleksandr Fridman joined the Conservatory and wound up as a Kapellmeister of the Preobrazhensky Regiment orchestra (one of our finest). Apollinarii Voskresensky enrolled in the Academy of Arts. . . . Nikolai Petrov audited courses at the Technological Institute. . . . Finally, as to myself, having graduated from the Theater school, I enrolled as an auditor of forestry courses, and only a combination of circumstances prevented me from devoting myself fully to studying forests and the architecture of nature."[50]

While the ambitions of this particular class ranged from physiology to forestry, dancers' extraballetic activities typically remained within the arts, ranging from music to sculpture. Judging by an extensive list preserved among Fedor Lopukhov's papers at an archive in St. Petersburg, virtually every male dancer of the imperial stage had their private *violon d'Ingres*.[51] For ballet folks, to dance was to serve; to create meant to do *something else*.

BALLET AS A VERBAL ART   191

There was another way out, available mainly to troublemakers: to be forced into early retirement. This was precisely what happened to Kshesinsky himself in 1905 when, inspired by the first Russian Revolution, he and a handful of other dancers confronted the Directorate with labor claims, one having to do with raises, another with rights. The dancers demanded a share in decision-making, which in the context of the Imperial Ballet was tantamount to reaching for the crown.[52]

The sense of being confined for life to the balletic stage was somewhat eased by certain freedoms chiming from the world outside. In the 1880s, as discussed in chapter 2, the state monopoly on theaters was lifted. Ballet's path from imperial isolation to the larger world of art went through the burgeoning realm of private, sometimes amateur enterprises. When a private theater entrepreneur, sponsor of a charity evening, or children's party planner wished to include a ballet number in their show, they would seek out a ballet professional to choreograph and stage it. Vaslav Nijinsky's first steps as a choreographer came as he staged correspondingly fledgling ballets performed by attendees of various children's celebrations;[53] young Kasian Goleizovsky, later a great influence on young Balanchine, was in charge of balletic numbers at a "theater of miniatures," one of those variety-format venues that mushroomed in Petersburg and Moscow in the 1910s.[54] For ballet professionals like Goleizovsky or Fokine, working for amateur sideshows was a form of freedom—mixing with people "on the outside," artists and high society, be it poets, actors, or, last but not least, impresarios and patrons of modern arts like Sergei Diaghilev.

The possibility of doing ballet, moreover, no longer necessarily meant seven years in training from the age of twelve or younger. Now (albeit still rarely) a privately trained amateur could launch a professional career on private stages, as did Ida Rubinstein under the tutelage of Fokine; Nikolai Legat's disciple and future wife, Nadezhda Nikolaeva; and Natalia Trukhanova, whose name outshone that of her tutor Ivan Khliustin (Clustine).

As noted in the previous chapter in connection with Ivan Vsevolozhsky's actorly exploits, amateurship (*liubitel'stvo*) in turn-of-the-century Russia had a better name than professionalism. The latter was associated with cynicism and craft, not art; amateurship, with spirituality and unselfish devotion. In part, we owe this attitude to Tolstoy's "What Is Art?," which preached that the folksy Russian epithalamium sung by braided peasant women in celebration of Tolstoy's daughter's wedding was closer to art than a concerto by Beethoven, a composer so professionally committed to composing music

192 IMPOSSIBLE PROJECT

that not even losing the ability to hear it would deter him.[55] Even more influential, perhaps, was the example of the enlightened amateur Konstantin Stanislavsky, who, like Fokine, admired Tolstoy's philosophy of art and despised all things *theatrical* about theater, no less than did Fokine the *institution* of ballet.

The cultural prestige of dance amateurship rose dramatically in the course of Isadora Duncan's guest performances in Russia in late 1904. Both Stanislavsky, an unapologetic amateur in charge of the most successful and prestigious drama theater in Russia, and Fokine, a professional by training and an amateur in spirit, had their hearts won. Unschooled in dancing *sur les pointes* and heedless of the intricacies of the turned-out stance, Duncan was the embodiment of amateurship. Oblivious of cultural hierarchies, she used any music she liked, from Beethoven to Chopin, compositions hitherto considered too serious to be hopped and capered to. What's more, she was taking dance back to antiquity—not to the zephyrs and cupids of Didelot but to "real" antiquity, antiquity as captured in the raw.

Lastly and most important for the future of ballet, Duncan was willing to *speak*; in multiple interviews and a lecture enticingly titled "The Dance of the Future," she spoke to ballet people and intellectuals at large about the meaning of her and their art. Speech begets speech: in Russia as elsewhere in Europe, Duncan was on everyone's lips. This proved a turning point in the twentieth-century evolution of ballet: proverbially silent, ballet was now *talking*.

Prior to Duncan's first visit to Russia, dance had not been a subject of cultural reflection, perhaps because there it was primarily associated with the Imperial Ballet. Writings devoted to ballet were parochial and scarce. Essays by balletomanes like Skalkovsky were mainly read by balletomanes like Skalkovsky.[56] And despite coming out under a pseudonym ("Balletomane"), Skalkovsky's *Ballet, Its History and Place among Fine Arts* (1882) may have hindered his career in the Mining Department of the Ministry of State Properties.[57] (Devotion to such an unserious subject could damage one's reputation.) "Very little has been written on ballet, and most of the existing writings are old enough to have become bibliographic rarities," laments Lidia Nelidova in her 1894 *Letters on Ballet*. "In Russian, there is only one book, Mr. S[kal'kovsky]'s, in which ballet is addressed."[58]

Nelidova's *Letters* (in fact, "Letter One," the only one she published) represented a cri de cœur regarding the intelligentsia's indifference toward ballet. "Undoubtedly," she writes, "the absence of popular choreographic

BALLET AS A VERBAL ART   193

literature has played a decisive role in society's estrangement from ballet and choreography."[59] Of course, the reverse could also be argued; but Nelidova's point about the give-and-take between the written and the danced seems a cogent one. Ballet, arguably the most evanescent of all performing arts, endures (prior to the age of motion pictures, that is) only in the mirror of the mind—in writings like Blasis's and Noverre's. What is not talked about does not exist.

Duncan's arrival in Russia reignited the cultural curiosity about dance that Russian intellectuals had lost since the time of Taglioni.[60] Despite the steady supply of ballet reviews in the press, ballet seemed too abstruse, and at the same time too trivial, to constitute a matter for general discussion. It took a balletomane or a dance professional to get a sense of every complexity of classical choreography; on the other hand, no words were needed to appreciate the magnificence of the thirty-two fouettés performed by Legnani and Kschessinska. The discursive potential of Duncan's dances lay precisely in their uncodified appearance. Suddenly, everyone—not only balletomanes, choreographers, and dancers, but also poets, artists, and thinkers—had something to say about Duncan. Her bare legs and light attire, to some, evoked Hellenic innocence; to others they suggested promiscuity. Likewise, Duncan's lack of a turned-out physique bespoke either her dilettantism or else the artless dance to come—artless like the dance of nymphs in nature. Here was the dance as imagined by Nietzsche (or the dance of Nietzsche as imagined by Duncan): dance as the beginning of everything, a self-sufficient entity in which all other arts were embryonically present. Duncan's was a dance and a statement on dance at the same time—not only in the sense of being talked about but also because, with Duncan, dance itself became a form of speech. As the young poet and *Rus'* newspaper contributor Maximilian Voloshin, writing from Paris, informed his Petersburg readers in May 1904, a few months before Duncan's advent in person, "Isadora Duncan expresses through dance what other people say, sing, play, write, and draw."[61]

Her arrival could bridge the gap between dance and discourse because the "Duncan phenomenon" had somatic and discursive sides to it. "The Dance of the Future," the lecture she brought with her and was always ready to deliver at sundry gatherings and venues, meshed and married opposites like "the language of the soul" and "the movement of the body"; dances of ancient Greece and of the imagined future; dance as religion and dance as liberation. Duncan's liberated "She" was what she projected as the "dancer of the future": "She will realize the mission of woman's body and the holiness of all

194   IMPOSSIBLE PROJECT

its parts.... She will dance the changing life of nature, showing how each part is transformed into the other.... She shall dance the freedom of women."[62]

This kind of talk resonated with turn-of-the-century Russian intellectuals, whose discourse likewise combined democratic sensibilities with a stilted style and arcane vocabulary. No less important, like most of the Russian intelligentsia Duncan was publicly dismissive of ballet. Glaringly absent from her dancing was the somatic dichotomy pivotal to Noverre-inspired choreography. Noverre, we recall, had little faith in dance as such, claiming that only via the balletic pantomime—the language of hands and faces—could footwork connect to the pinnacles of *art*. But Duncan featured no such vertical; she was all mime and dance at the same time. "The piano player began Chopin's mazurka, and Isadora Duncan began singing and talking—with her feet [and legs], with her hands [and arms], eyes, mouth," the journalist Aleksandr Filippov wrote in 1904, patently stunned by the absence of the usual mazurka choreography. "There was no dance, no pas."[63]

When Fokine, who as we recall was a questioner, graduated from the ballet school and joined the Mariinsky in 1898, he was surprised to discover that ballet dancers never talked about ballet. "I raised various questions, but they just waved me away. The mood was: if you can jump high and spin fine, your work is to jump and spin."[64] But about ten years later, the "mood" changed dramatically. Not only did ballerinas like Anna Pavlova, Matilda Kschessinska, and Vera Karalli willingly share their thoughts on Duncan; philologists like André (then still Andrei) Levinson, philosophers like Vasilii Rozanov and Akim Volynsky, writers and poets like Maximilian Voloshin and Andrei Bely, and other "people on the outside" joined the polyphony of dance talk. A 1909 interview conducted with Fokine by a correspondent of the *Stock Market News* (*Birzhevye vedomosti*; one of many interviews that Fokine gave to the press) begins with this epochal assessment: "Ballet is at the center of attention nowadays; people speak of ballet; people quarrel about ballet."[65] Early in the new century, ballet was in again—as it had been early in the previous one.

No wonder young Fokine began theorizing about ballet even before trying his hand at choreography, and never stopped. The culmination of his theory was, perhaps, a 1914 letter to the *Times of London* in which he offered five principles of the "new ballet." The figure five, no doubt, echoed the five feet positions of classical dance: Fokine was bold enough to suggest replacing the quintessential alphabet of ballet with something of his own invention. But for a "new ballet," his choreographic doctrine was remarkably conservative.

BALLET AS A VERBAL ART   195

That dances ought to be wedded to action; that action needs to be rich in content; that virtuosity is a sin—all these credos replicate nineteenth-century critical clichés, which, in turn, replicated Noverre's precepts. "Ballet is a genre of dramatic art in which actions, passions, feelings and moods are expressed by means of mime and dance," writes Fokine in his 1928 opinion on American ballet—a later variation of what he insisted on in his 1914 letter to the *Times*: "[D]ancing and mimetic gesture have no meaning in a ballet unless they serve as an expression of its dramatic action, and they must not be used as a mere divertissement or entertainment having no connection with the scheme of the whole ballet."[66]

Fokine's conception of dance in classical Greece was, true enough, inspired by Duncan's style, but even his ancient-themed ballets—*Daphnis and Chloe, Eunice,* and *Narcissus and Echo*—followed Noverre's time-proven recipes. In Fokine's antiquity, as in Noverre's and unlike in Duncan's, myth and drama came before dance. In his insistence on the unity of action, Fokine always remained a classicist. In his view, dance per se—antique, classical, or character—had no intrinsic value. What Fokine aspired to was the high status, if only in one's own eyes, of the ballet master as a *creator*—a status not seen in Russia since Didelot. Always credited in the playbill as a ballet's "choreographer," Fokine craved more: to be billed as the ballet's *author.*

In a letter to dance critic John Martin of the *New York Times,* Fokine rerouted talk of the sources of his balletic endeavors, from the world of dance (Diaghilev, Duncan) to that of art (Michelangelo, Rodin) and music (Wagner, Gluck), and to Stanislavsky and Tolstoy.[67] As mentioned, Tolstoy's supreme moral-literary concept of *shame* had a firm grip on the young Fokine, and the same could be said of Stanislavsky. Paradoxically, Tolstoy's "What Is Art?" licensed both Fokine and Stanislavsky to be *ashamed* of their arts—Fokine, of virtuosity and pornography; Stanislavsky, of thespian make-believe. Other influential concepts of Tolstoy's ethos included truth (*pravda*) and *vera*, the Russian word that can mean "faith," "trust," or "belief": trust in truth, faith in God, belief in togetherness, whether the togetherness of peasant women's singing as extolled in "What Is Art?" or that of (men's) communal farming celebrated in *Anna Karenina.*

It was this—Tolstoyan—configuration of values that had primed Fokine's and Stanislavsky's visions of their otherwise so dissimilar métiers. When Stanislavsky would interrupt the rehearsal of a contemporary drama with his legendary *Ne veriu!* (I don't believe it!), the phrase seemed to match the truth-or-bust program of the Moscow Art Theater, but to apply the credibility

196 IMPOSSIBLE PROJECT

criterion to what must be, by anyone's standards but Fokine's, an utterly fantastical narrative—a myth from Ovid rendered in the hieroglyphics of dance—this was more perplexing. And yet time and again we encounter Stanislavskian watchwords—"trust," "emotional experiencing," "believability"—in Fokine's writings on ballet.[68]

But Fokine would hardly have seen any contradiction here. What we are used to categorizing as "realist" is contingent not on similarity but on belief. To be believable, Fokine maintained, a ballet did not need to be lifelike; all it needed was for people to be willing to believe in the unbelievable. This was also what Stanislavsky required from actors, and in Fokine's view, as for that matter in Noverre's, a ballet dancer was first of all an actor. The moment this actor succeeds in believing themselves to be in ancient Greece or at a fairground in St. Petersburg of the 1830s, *their* sense of truth is passed on to the audience. Fokine and Stanislavsky believed in belief, which transfigures a piece of stagecraft into a miracle of art.

In the case of ballet, it is only logical that this kind of transfiguration should have occurred not at home but abroad. In Paris, the patrons that Russian ballet dancers saw from the stage were not the ones they saw at home. The latter were so *much* at home at the Mariinsky that they bequeathed their seats like heirlooms and were on a first-name basis with many a dancer. As Valerian Svetlov wrote in 1911, "In no theater in the world is the interaction between audience and artists as close as in our ballet. This is why it is not the ballerina Preobrajenska who dances today, but rather our dear friend Ol'ga Osipovna."[69] Technically professional, when it came to modus vivendi, the Russian ballet felt decidedly amateur.

But as ballet went westward, it estranged itself in its own eyes, as befit (per Shklovsky) true art. Gone was the tiresome symbiosis between balletomanes and the *baletnye*. Parisians who came to see touring Russians did so with an eye not to the dancer but the dance. Had ballerina Olga Preobrajenska joined Ballets Russes, she would have ceased being "our dear friend Ol'ga Osipovna," and become "ballerina Preobrajenska." The effect worked both ways: not seeing yourself through the eyes of all the usual Khudekovs meant seeing yourself as an artist. The transformation was such that the one-time artistic director of Ballets Russes Benois confessed he found it difficult to recognize Russian dancers of their own troupe on a Paris stage.[70] *Belief*— the artistic quintessence sought by Fokine and Stanislavsky—was, strangely enough, born of strangeness, of cultural and geographic distancing. By the same token, Parisian audiences were fascinated most of all by things that

BALLET AS A VERBAL ART   197

seemed remote—twice removed, as it were—from ballet "proper," from the classical ballet they used to know. The Orientalized "Polovetsian Dances"—not, strictly speaking, a ballet but rather an act from the opera *Prince Igor*, complete with singing in the Russian language—proved more popular than the refined pantomime-ballet *Le Pavillon d'Armide*, set in France of the ancien régime. It was a grassroots Gesamtkunstwerk like "Polovetsian Dances" that Parisians applauded and recognized as Ballets Russes.

The Languages of Dance and the Languages We Speak

"Nonsense pauses to ask herself: why am I actually doing this? In response to her own question, Nonsense raises her leg high in the air. Thus begins the 'Dance of Four Raised Legs,' interrupted by the 'Extraordinary Flight of Essayists.'"[71] When the progressive *Contemporary* (*Sovremennik*) ran Saltykov-Shchedrin's sarcastic libretto "Project for a Modern Ballet" in 1868, readers could scarcely have imagined that someday something of the kind might be staged in the form of a ballet, let alone performed by a professional ballet troupe. Saltykov-Shchedrin's was, after all, a verbal critique of ballet's inability to speak. According to the progressive press, which was verbal (even verbose), ballet was mute and meek—too much so to count as real art.

But while ballet, unlike its sisters opera and drama, is indeed no verbal medium, it is nevertheless, like them, a verbal art. Ballet is verbal, first, on the strength of its incessant lore and second, because of its uncanny ability to convey *messages*, albeit by nonverbal means. This latter consideration applies, most glaringly, to verbal utterances encoded by mimic means. To say "I am the queen of swans," all a nineteenth-century ballerina needed to know is how to refer to "I," "crown," and "swans" by drawing outlines in the air. Less literally but as unequivocally, a librettist like Benois and choreographer like Fokine could make ideas known not only by committing them to paper (both, as we have seen, were adept with pen and print) but also by using the medium of dance itself. You could mount a pulpit to anathemize, Savonarola-style, classical dance, or you could use three dancers and their arms and feet to achieve the same.

Indeed, why not discuss the future of ballet using the very language of ballet? To do so, all you needed was to arrange a diegetic show-within-your-show, playing its fictional players against each other so that the perceptive ballet-goer might read your ballet not just as a piece of entertainment but

198   IMPOSSIBLE PROJECT

also as a silent manifesto on ballet. This was precisely what Fokine tried his hand at in Paris in 1911. One of his most powerful choreographic statements against the "old ballet" remains *Petrushka*, a balletic production that takes the image of the ballerina in ballet to the point of parodic absurdity.[72]

Fokine's *Petrushka* is set in a snowy St. Petersburg square of the 1830s, amid Shrovetide (Butter Week) fairground attractions. It has four protagonists: the Magician (a puppeteer, also referred to as the Charlatan) who runs a puppet show and the three live puppets under his power: a Pierrot-like male, Petrushka; Petrushka's longed-for Ballerina (she has no other name), flirtatious and silly; and her own hypermasculine love interest, the Moor. That in *Petrushka* we encounter a live ballerina that plays the role of a puppet Ballerina is not so much an in-joke as a paraphrase of Fokine's theoretical reasoning, as seen, for instance, in his later memoir, where we find him lamenting ballet's lack of dramatic effect: "Everything [in ballet]— the costumes of the ballerina, the appeal to the audience, the continuous interruption of action—led me to conclude that the ballet lacked its most essential element: presentation to the spectator of an artistically created image."[73] From there, Fokine proceeds to formulate the paradox that became the germ of *Petrushka*'s plot as well as of its choreography. To begin with, he critiques the figure of the ballerina, not in the general sense of "any female ballet dancer" (as the term is understood nowadays) but specifically that of dancer of the highest rank within the company:

> [In "old ballet,"] the ballerina interpreted a role on the stage—[that of] the ballerina, because the ballerina was the most important person in the ballet, and because a dancer who achieved this title is very proud of her position. She wished it to be clear to everyone, immediately upon her entrance on the stage, that she was not just a dancer but the ballerina. In the pursuit of acquiring the ballerina look, there evolved a special proud stance: a unique habit of holding the head almost immobile, the stretching of the neck, and a peculiar gait. To sum up, there evolved a standard pattern by which one could readily distinguish a ballerina from plain mortals—but from which, of course, it was impossible to guess what role the ballerina was supposed to be interpreting.[74]

The Russian original of the first sentence above is more direct: *Baleriny izobrazhali na stsene ... balerin.* "On stage, ballerinas played ... ballerinas."[75] (As opposed to the character they were cast as, that is.) As Lynn Garafola puts it, "The Ballerina, in fact, stood for everything [Fokine] most despised."[76] The absurdly exaggerated turnout of the Ballerina's feet and legs points to Kschessinska as a probable prototype; even Volynsky, a critic who on the whole admired Kschessinska, couldn't help reproving her excessive turnout, especially the overuse of the second position.[77] After attending a performance of *The Talisman* in November 1910, Imperial Theaters director Vladimir Teliakovsky, who was less fluent in ballet grammar, expressed the same sentiment in his diary: "I have seldom seen such a triumph of vulgarity, banality, and tastelessness [*poshlost'*] as I have today. Starting with Kschessinska herself, with her short skirt, chubby *outspread legs*, and bare arms, expressing utter smugness, a call for the audience to enter her embrace [*prizyv publiki v ob'iat'ia*]."[78]

Like Teliakovsky, Fokine detested the second position. In his eyes, it was the original sin of ballet, a humiliating orientation of one's body toward the audience:

The so-called second position (with feet and legs apart) is so anti-aesthetic and yet, unfortunately, the most ubiquitous in ballet dancing. Moving feet and legs to the sides is so vulgar. What could be less beautiful than outspread legs? What kind of natural movement could originate from it? And yet, it is the second position that most pas are based on: *glissade, assemblé, echappé,* all kinds of *entrechat,* etc.; why did ballet technique have to come down to this ugliest, flat position of the body? The reason is that ballet is performed mostly "facing the audience." The orientation of a dancer's face and body flatly toward the public, which the dancer respects and expects approval from, is the most basic gesture of "classical" ballet, its main meaning, which turned-out dance is called to express.[79]

Notably, the "turnout" Fokine takes to task is not just one particular trait but the very foundation of ballet dancing; every dancer begins every class from the first position of the feet, the alpha and omega of the balletic turnout. Fokine emphasizes his campaign against ballet by building the Ballerina's movement on the idea of flatness: the complete turnout of her feet and legs coupled with a completely stiff torso, head, and neck, all arranged frontally (Figures 3.1 and 3.2). It is as if the Ballerina were frozen in the second position, facing the audience and unable to turn, as we do in life, toward another. His Ballerina does not, indeed, play anyone but herself, *the* Ballerina, whose only interlocutor is the public.

Figure 3.1 Aleksandr Benois, "Ballerina," a costume design for Tamara Karsavina in *Petrushka* (1911).

To compound matters, and sharpen the polemical edge of *Petrushka*'s metaballetic message, the story features two other female dancers. Both are diegetically human (that is, not puppet) dancing girls engaged in the Shrovetide fairground festivities. One of these street performers is an acrobat, the other a ballet danseuse—the only characters, besides the puppet Ballerina, whom Fokine allows to dance *sur les pointes* (Figures 3.3 and 3.4). That the two are shown locked in a shameless competition for public acclaim, plus tips from the fairground crowd, puts ballet dancing on the same footing with circus shows. In Benois' costume design for the Barrel

BALLET AS A VERBAL ART 201

Figure 3.2 Tamara Karsavina as Ballerina in *Petrushka* (1911).

Organ-Grinder their competition is shown parroted by a pair of minuscule puppet ballerinas trying to outdance one another on the top of the grinder's barrel organ (Figure 3.5). This, and other such tricks Fokine resorts to in *Petrushka*, all constitute choreographic paraphrases of his theoretical tenets. Levinson interprets the metaballetic message of Fokine's polemical choreography thus: "The vernacular 'classicism' [*ploshchadnaia 'klassika'*] of the street dancer who sloppily throws her legs around ... as well as the mechanical dance of the 'Ballerina' in the first scene are funny as an over-the-top distortion of high forms of dance."[80]

Figure 3.3 Aleksandr Benois, "The First Street Dancer," a costume design for *Petrushka* (1911).

This onstage duel is also a clever parody of ballet's backstage warring—the rivalry that could occur between two ballerinas, which Fokine observed when, as a young man, he joined the Mariinsky amid the epic competition between Kschessinska and Preobrajenska. To the amusement of those in the know, the backstage battles spilled over onstage. For most of the second half of the nineteenth century, at any given moment there were two ballerinas in the company; the rivalry between the two, each supported by her own cheering section of balletomanes, used to be a fun part of the balletic game, expected and thoroughly enjoyed by audiences—a custom inherited,

Figure 3.4 Aleksandr Benois, "The Second Street Dancer" (also known as The Acrobat), a costume design for *Petrushka* (1911).

perhaps, from Roman *circenses* and revived in twentieth- and twenty-first-century sports.

A specific target of Fokine's spoof here is the tradition of breaking with tradition. In the carnivalesque spirit theorized by Mikhail Bakhtin in the 1930s, the time-honored tradition, sacredly upheld at the Mariinsky Theater, of building a whole ballet around a single ballerina, was allowed—nay, prescribed—to be broken once a year, during Shrovetide, an all-Russian equivalent of carnivals in Catholic countries.[81] At the last ballet evening of Maslenitsa (the Butter Week), *both* ballerinas would appear on the Mariinsky

Figure 3.5 Aleksandr Benois, "The Barrel Organ-Grinder," a costume design for *Petrushka* (1911).

stage, turning it into a semblance of a wrestling ring for their fan factions to compete in applause and tributes.[82] Crucially, *Petrushka* is set specifically during the Shrovetide festivities.

A remarkable piece of historical evidence from the time of the ballet's making has been brought to our attention by Garafola. In her memoir, Bronislava Nijinska, who played one of the street dancers, recalls a telltale consultation with Fokine. What acrobatic trick might she have up her sleeve, inquired the choreographer. "I started to imitate Mathilda Kschessinska, her *cabrioles* and her *relevés* on toe from the last act of *Le Talisman*, the *coda* that

Figure 3.6 Enrico Cechetti as Magician in *Petrushka* (1911).

was always accompanied by thunderous applause in the Mariinsky. 'This is perfect, it is exactly what is needed,' Fokine laughed."[83] Who wouldn't? The critical prejudice against virtuosity as circus-like acrobatics went back to Noverre himself and was certainly harbored by Fokine, and so here a perfect

Figure 3.7 Enrico Cechetti in class with Anna Pavlova.

choreographic paraphrase was finally found for it. In speech or written form, it would have seemed a boring cliché to encounter yet another purist holding forth on Kschessinska's too acrobatic choreography; but it must have been hilarious to watch Nijinska as a fairground acrobat imitating Kschessinska.

BALLET AS A VERBAL ART   207

Particularly since Nijinska's parody had an immediacy and freshness about it. Petipa's *Talisman* had been renewed just a year prior, in late 1909, with new dances composed by Nikolai Legat. After its premiere at the farewell benefit for Preobrajenska, *Le Talisman* was considered to "belong" to Kschessinska from 1910 on. Thus the precise target of Fokine's parody was both relevant and obvious to those in the know. There was a personal enmity between Fokine and Kschessinska (and Legat), but the parody here targets not only individuals but, more important, the methods of the "old ballet."

The most eloquent example of this in *Petrushka* is the role of the Magician, the mysterious owner of the Theater of Living Figures, bossing his puppets around with a commanding stick, which serves him now as a flute, now as a magic wand (Figure 3.6). The role was created for Enrico Cecchetti, a legendary teacher hired by Diaghilev to lead daily class for the Ballets Russes. It was to Cecchetti's lessons that leading ballerinas like Kschessinska and Preobrajenska owed the virtuoso technique that Russian dancers of the 1890s credited as "Italian." The staff that the Magician uses to control and threaten his puppets onstage would have reminded the performers of the very real cane Cecchetti used in class to beat out the rhythm, often on the very heels of his hapless pupils (Figure 3.7).[84] Consequently, Nijinsky-Petrushka's onstage revolt against Magician-Cecchetti was not only a plot twist but also a metaballetic in-joke. Reminiscent of degrading technicity was the very concept of the in-story puppet show, ironically titled, on the Magician's marquee, "Living Figures"; the fact that, unlike the puppet-Ballerina, who intentionally overdoes the outturned second position, Petrushka dances with feet turned in (anticipating Nijinsky's against-the-tide choreography in *The Rite of Spring*) was but another kick at the biomechanical canon held sacred by Johansson, Cecchetti, and their ilk.

The dance writer André Levinson was an opponent of Fokine's philosophy of dance, but despite or perhaps because of this, in reviewing the 1920 Petrograd version of *Petrushka* he seemed to discern the choreographer's intent more clearly than any other reviewer. "The way each of the puppets moves is inscribed into the narrow and angular mobility range prescribed by its soulless mechanism," observes Levinson. "The drama arises from the vain attempts on the part of these captive souls to transcend the constraint of their mechanical gestures and break out into the world of free expressive movement."[85] Here we find Levinson—a staunch supporter of, to put it bluntly, rather mechanical conventions of classical dance—deploying, intentionally or otherwise, a lexicon rather befitting Duncan and her eloquent fans. "Free"

208   IMPOSSIBLE PROJECT

and "expressive movement," that is, were slogans of the "modern dance" culture, while "mechanical constraint" and "captive souls" were just the sort of phrases a Duncan or Fokine would use in disdaining the strictness and discipline of ballet class. Levinson had clearly "gotten" the "moral" of Fokine's fable—but was it a *ballet* fable? Judging by his two reviews of *Petrushka*, Levinson was impressed but not convinced; one review concludes with this caveat: "Of course, Benois's work [*Petrushka*] is not a ballet."[86] As a culinary traditionalist I happen to know once complimented his wife's cooking, "Your borscht is truly delicious, but it is *not* borscht."

Levinson was not alone in this view. At the time, few categorized *Petrushka* as a ballet. Even in its own program, *Petrushka* was described as "amusing Russian scenes" (*russkie poteshnye stseny*). Notably, this Russian setting was not the fairy-tale Russia of, for instance, 1910's *Firebird* but rather a clearly defined time and place: Petersburg in the 1830s. Just as Gol'ts had done with his Russian dance in *The Little Humpbacked Horse*, Fokine rebelled in his native tongue, going beyond the boundaries of ballet as an idiom that, in Russia, still felt enforced from above and from abroad. In school it had been drilled into his head that Russian dancers were "keepers" of the classical flame, and so he associated classical dance with the French *belle danse*. As he exclaimed in ironic disbelief regarding a ballet set in antiquity, "The Greeks dance in French."[87]

To Fokine, the language *mattered*. As befits a ballet, *Petrushka* is mute, but it is not entirely wordless. First, there is that signboard inviting us to come view the "living figures"; then there is Stravinsky's score, which includes a number of recognizable melodies from Russian folk songs, likely to bring to mind the underlying lyrics. One of these songs is that very "Po ulitse mostovoi" (Along the Paved Street) to which Tolstoy's Natasha famously dances at her uncle's place. Which is quite natural; after all, *War and Peace* was every Russian reader's nightstand Bible.

We thus come back to the issue of "Russianness" in ballet. As mentioned earlier, in Russia it was a stretch to think of ballet (whether the institution at large or particular productions) as "Russian." From the 1860s until after the revolutions of 1917, only two ballets performed on the Mariinsky stage were set in Russia. One of them, as already noted, was Saint-Léon's 1864 *Little Humpbacked Horse*, which became a byword for silliness and whose choreography was, like that of all grand ballets, a patchwork of styles, from strictly classical to a variety of folk dances showcasing the breadth of the empire.

Figure 3.8 Léon Bakst, "The French Doll," a costume design for *The Fairy Doll* (1903).

210   IMPOSSIBLE PROJECT

The other ballet set in Russia, titled *The Fairy Doll* (*Feia kukol*), is a more interesting case. Staged by the Legat brothers in 1903, *The Fairy Doll* was a localization of the then-famous Austrian hit *Die Puppenfee*, first staged in Vienna in 1888. As in the original, the action unfolds in a toy shop, but the remake's designer, Léon Bakst, opted to move this establishment from Vienna to mid-nineteenth-century Petersburg—the city where, eight years later, Fokine's carnivalesque *Petrushka* would also be set.

As in *Petrushka*, *The Fairy Doll*'s cast of characters was mixed. It combined humans—the proprietor, a doll duster, two shopping families, a team of salesclerks, a comic postman—and playthings, from dolls and puppets (one of the latter, a Pierrot, was performed by young Fokine) to wooden soldiers, drumming hares, a chimneysweep, and, of course, the eponymous fairy (Figures 3.8, 3.9, and 3.10). And, like *Petrushka*, *The Fairy Doll* featured a love triangle, with a female doll, "incapable of serious feelings," and two male puppets, one playful and carefree, the other inconsolably sad.[88]

Aside from the expensive one-off dolls, there were corps-de-ballet dolls, impersonated by ballet school pupils, among them Bronislava Nijinska, then thirteen. According to Nijinska's book of memoirs, she played a doll whose persona, not unlike in the recent *Barbie* movie, was defined by the dominant color of her attire: "I was a pink doll, and I remember what a delight it was for me as a child as I put on each detail: the pink openwork socks over white tights, ruffled pantalettes showing beneath the short, full, ruffled, white muslin skirt of the dress. I had a wide pink ribbon over one shoulder tied to a bow below the waist, and tiny pink bows tied on each wrist just above the short white gloves. Over my golden curly locks I wore a light, lacy bonnet tied with a ribbon under my chin."[89] Light, funny, Biedermeier-cozy, consciously kitschy—the critical acclaim for *The Fairy Doll* would have been unanimous, were it not for Sergei Khudekov, that Carabosse of Russian ballet lore. He found no few faults, presumably pre-irritated by the setting—a corner boutique on Nevsky Prospect, instead of an Indian temple, royal palace, or Egyptian pyramid. Here, "living, talented dancers and danseuses are compelled to mug and pull antics [*krivliat'sia i lomat'sia*] in their attempts to ape mechanical dolls."[90] Khudekov's objection had less to do with the dancers than with the dolls they were to ape—their domestic provenance and rustic looks. None could hold a candle to Saint-Léon's exquisite *Coppélia*; these dolls "are not even French-manufactured dolls, but gilded-Russian handicrafts [*russko-susal'nogo kustarnogo proizvodstva*]."[91]

BALLET AS A VERBAL ART   211

Saint-Léon's Dr. Coppélius makes his lifesize dolls as humanlike and pretty as he can—so much so that young Franz mistakes one for a real girl and falls in love. By contrast, the makers of *The Fairy Doll* sought to play up their dolls' *doll*-ness. Bakst modeled them on examples from his (then) friend Benois's collection of Russian handcrafted toys, many of which, as Benois lovingly phrased it, "combined gaudy coloring with canny ingenuity."[92] The 1900s being the epoch in which the arts looked up to crafts, Bakst wanted his dancing dolls to epitomize the simplicity and resourcefulness of his homeland's homemade merchandise for kids; fittingly enough, the proprietor of Bakst's doll shop is himself a toymaker who can, if need be, repair a broken doll.[93] Was it the affinity with the familiar toybox that made playing in *The Fairy Doll* an enchanting experience for child dancers? "Bakst was not only meticulous about each costume, he also designed our makeup and applied it himself. I had two bright red round spots on my cheeks and long eyelashes that Bakst had drawn on my face," recalls Nijinska, adding, "I cannot remember feeling happier or more proud in any costume in the theater."[94]

Among the terms that make up Khudekov's critical vocabulary, there is one in particular that highlights ballet's path from something generically "French" to something perceived—especially in France—as peculiarly *Russian*. This would be *balagan*, which denotes the makeshift fairground booth wherein sundry harlequinades of questionable taste used to be put on during Shrovetide. In the mid-nineteenth century, the timeframe in which *The Fairy Doll* and *Petrushka* are set, *balagans* boasted plebeian repertoires centering the adventures (amorous or otherwise) of commedia-dell'arte-derived characters.[95] Small wonder if, in critical parlance, the word *balagan* became a derogatory metaphor. A stage show described thus would constitute, in the speaker's opinion, unworthy tomfoolery; as applied to a public or political event, *balagan* amounts to a "farce" or "circus."

Given the *balagan* origins of puppet Petrushkas and pantomime Pierrots, ballet critics like Khudekov feared aesthetic contagion. Writing of Petipa's 1900 *Harlequinade*, Khudekov advised Vasilii Stukolkin to dance the part of Pierrot "with somewhat more restraint," because "the Pierrot of the Mariinsky stage must have nothing to do with the Pierrot of the era of [Wilhelm] Berg's and [Abram] Leifert's *balagans*."[96]

Khudekov's concern was not unfounded. Artistic values are prone to flip, and it was only to be expected that, as the new twentieth century unfolded, the *balagan* would be reassessed, both as a show and as an aesthetic concept.

Figure 3.9 Léon Bakst, "The Postman," a costume design for *The Fairy Doll* (1903).

Figure 3.10 Léon Bakst, "The Officer's Servant," a costume design for *The Fairy Doll* (1903).

Figure 3.11 Léon Bakst, set design for the first scene of *The Fairy Doll*, with Nevsky Prospect in the background (1903).

Aleksandr Blok and Vsevolod Meyerhold did the former with their powerful 1906 production *Balaganchik* (*The Fairground Booth*), while Benois offered a striking conceptual reassessment of the *balagan* in his essay "Shrovetide," printed in the newspaper *Rech'* (Speech) in 1917 (two or so weeks before the February revolution rid Russia of its last emperor).

It so happened that Benois's first encounter with theater occurred during the Shrovetide festivities in Petersburg. In 1874, when he was only four, recalls Benois, his elder brothers took him to the "main *balagan* street" that Admiralty Boulevard turned into in this season: "This [*balagan*] is owned by [Vasilii] Malafeev, there is [Vasilii] Egarev's, the two farther off are Berg's and Leifert's."[97]

> It was through *these* doors that I entered the kingdom of Melpomene and Thalia, and it is undoubtedly owing to having first met them [in a *balagan*] that, throughout my life, I remain on intimate terms with the two muses. Here I saw them act in total freedom, act in front of a genuine crowd goggling at them, hurling at them gale upon gale of genuinely mirthful laughter. Here I came to know the meaning of "theatrical exaltation [*teatral'noe vozbuzhdenie*]." I walked out of the *balagan* befuddled,

Figure 3.12 Aleksandr Benois, set design for *Petrushka* on the Field of Mars in St. Petersburg (1911).

intoxicated, beside myself. . . . To this day, when tempted to question the virtues of theater, all I have to do to restore my absolute faith in the mystical power and profound humanity of stage as such is to conjure up that primal ecstasy I found myself in [watching that *balagan* show].[98]

In light of this, Benois's motivation to set his and Stravinsky's *Petrushka* in the Petersburg "*balagan* boulevard" during Shrovetide becomes entirely clear. In doing so, moreover, Benois not only followed his personal passion for street theater but drew inspiration from Bakst's audacious setting of *The Fairy Doll*, not in ballet's generic "parts unknown" but in the middle of hyperfamiliar Nevsky Prospect (Figures 3.11 and 3.12). As for Fokine, *Petrushka*'s choreographer had his own reasons for seizing the opportunity. Whether the lowbrow amusements of street crowds in Russia's Petrine capital qualify as "Russian folk art" remains an open question, but Paris balletgoers of 1911 could scarcely have cared less, and Fokine went along. For him as a choreographer, Petersburg was, first and foremost, a city, and setting a ballet in a city (and not against yet another lake backdrop) enabled Fokine to arrange crowd scenes at odds with the parade-like symmetry and synchronicity of traditional corps de ballet. In this, Fokine's *Petrushka* followed in the footsteps of Aleksandr Gorsky's scandalous 1902 version of *Don Quixote*, in which the throng's individual members moved not in unison, but rather in

216   IMPOSSIBLE PROJECT

carefully calculated diversity. Small wonder if the old guards like Petipa and Johansson condemned Gorsky's experiment as the end of ballet as they knew and loved it.[99]

"Bis!... But the wind-like maidens / Flew off like a flowery garland," wrote Nekrasov, perhaps with a touch of nostalgia, in his poignant 1866 satire on ballet. The end of ballet—in this case, corps de ballet—as we know and love it was precisely the effect new choreographers like Gorsky and Fokine were after. Setting your ballet not in a valley or on a lakeshore but in a tavern of Cervantine Barcelona or, better yet, in a Petersburg *balagan*—how better to replace a too orderly garland with the orchestrated disorder of the street? Fokine's *Petrushka* was Khudekov's worst nightmare brought to life: a show in which ballet and *balagan* converged.

Indeed, marrying Russian balagan to classical ballet made a preposterous mésalliance. It was one thing to call the *balagan* the true home of Melpomene; Meyerhold, Konstantin Miklashevsky, and Nikolai Evreinov, to mention but three of this period's theater reformists, had been saying this for years. But the abode of Terpsichore, too? Khudekov never wrote about *Petrushka*, but had he, his opinion could hardly have differed from what he said about *The Fairy Doll*: "[T]otal excessive apery, having too little to do with the art of choreography."[100] In other words, as Levinson had it, Benois's ballet was not a ballet.

If *balagan* and ballet were hard for Khudekov et al. to pronounce in the same breath, likewise *Ballets Russes* rolled off the French tongue but not the Russian. As late as 1910, reflecting on the premiere of *The Firebird* in Paris, Benois still struggled to put these two words—"Russian" and "ballet"—together: "[I]t was decided to perform this genuinely Russian ballet (oh, what an awkward combination—the problem is in the very word 'ballet' [*vse gore v etom slove 'balet'*], which inevitably suggests something affected and rococolike [*rokokoshnyi*])."[101] In the word "ballet" itself, that is, Benois heard, first and foremost, an indication of a particular *style*, with the time and place peculiar to it. ("Rococo-like" cannot but conjure eighteenth-century France.) Fokine shared this view; in classical dance—the choreographic acme of the "old ballet"—he saw only a particular style, which he did not object to in itself but rather to its hegemony.

What had grown in Russia into the cult of classical dance, Fokine maintained, had to be returned to the time and place of its origin. *Klassicheskii tanets* must become, once again, what it had been: *belle danse*, pure and simple. *Les Sylphides*, he recalls in his memoir, was his answer to critics who accused him of "rejecting dancing on pointes and destroying old traditional ballet." Fokine's thought ran deeper: unlike Duncan and other proponents of modern dance, he did not *reject* classical dance as such, but rather its claim to universality, the insistent use of it for ballets set in different cultures (from India in *La Bayadère*, to Spain in *Don Quixote*, to Russia in *The Little Humpbacked Horse*). For Fokine, classical dance was what it was: the old French school of dance, a particular style suitable for productions set in a corresponding time and place.

In effect, Fokine's was a call for stylization. He and Benois shared a penchant for the past. (Which, though they would hardly have acknowledged it, must have been owed at least in part to Vsevolozhsky.) Stylization, as understood by the artists grouped around the magazine *World of Art*, was all about period motivation. Romanticism justified dancing *sur les pointes* in *Les Sylphides* and *Carnaval*; *danse noble* was good for *Le Pavillon d'Armide*, the Fokine-Benois ballet set in France in the seventeenth and eighteenth centuries. Classical dance, in Fokine's view, had colonized local cultures; like a trapping of empire, it had grown into an unquestioned standard, a Latin hammered into students in any country's gymnasia. St. Petersburg ballet remained, to Fokine's eye, too *imperial* to be Russian.

This explains why Fokine never tired of emphasizing the ethnic authenticity of his productions, of touting the trips he made to discover "real" folk dances. And indeed, however stereotypical and exoticizing his findings may now seem, many of his ballets can be described as exercises in choreographic ethnography—of "the Orient" in *Scheherazade*, of Spain in *Jota Aragonese*, of India in *Le Dieu bleu*. Fokine's interest in folk (or "character") dances was both political and ballet-internal.[102] It irked him that, except for one short-lived attempt at the turn of the century, character dancing was not taught in the Imperial Theater School. Classical dance—anatomically unnatural and no longer relevant for social dancing—was prioritized in the ballet school curriculum, just as Latin instruction was in secondary education. Character dancing, by contrast, was considered something you just came by naturally, like a native language. Indeed, the Imperial Ballet had a number of well-known dancers employed as extracurricular "native speakers" of their home dance cultures, such as Felix Kshesinsky, responsible for mazurkas, and Alfred Bekefi for czárdáses. In the imperial hierarchy, once typecast as a "character dancer," no one, however skillful, could become a ballerina or *premier danseur*. Fokine's forays into ethnography were part of his effort to flip the values, to foreground character dances, make them central to the

218　IMPOSSIBLE PROJECT

choreographic axiology. Diversity—ethnic, religious, linguistic—resists hierarchy.

Resisting, or indeed reversing hierarchies was the stubborn core of Fokine's choreographic theory and his revolution in ballet. To Fokine, a ballet based on classical dance constituted an orthodoxy, an oppressive monotheistic religion. From the perspective of the "keepers," to favor the diversity of character over classical dances looked like an apostasy. And Fokine indeed conceived it as one—as a creative relapse to the unruly vigor of balletic paganism. Fokine's was the rebellion of character dances against classical dance, of living languages against Pobedonostsev's deadly Latin, of the upstage populace against the downstage patricians. If Kirstein describes the history of ballet in terms of "apostolic succession," then, looking at Fokine, one is tempted to call this succession "apostatic." Perhaps the most useful way of parsing the history of ballet is to bear both complementary continuities in view.

Fokine the Apostate

Fokine's memoir, or creative autobiography, is subtitled *Against the Tide*. Which currents the memoirist sees himself swimming against is quickly apparent to the reader: as discussed above, the Imperial Ballet's hegemony, the classroom cult of classical dance, and so on. But aside from that, we learn that Fokine's defiance of the tide came in the wake of another apostate, Tolstoy, officially excommunicated from the Russian Orthodox Church for his attempts to construe Christianity *extra ecclesia*. And there is still more to the tidal map of turn-of-the-century Russian culture worth mentioning in connection with Fokine's creative evolution.

Fokine's career as a choreographer began in 1904, when he composed a libretto based on Dmitrii Merezhkovsky's 1896 translation of the second-century AD Greek novel *Daphnis and Chloe*.[103] Merezhkovsky was a symbolist poet and novelist with a particular interest in the history of religion, especially apostasies; in the latter half of his creative career, Merezhkovsky devoted himself to devising a teaching he called the Third Testament, a hoped-for synthesis of Christianity and paganism.

Fokine's choice of a literary source for his debut as a librettist, and also the Russian translator of this source, are noteworthy. Around the time Fokine graduated from the ballet school, Merezhkovsky earned international

BALLET AS A VERBAL ART   219

acclaim for his trilogy of novels titled *Christ and Antichrist*. The first of these books, *The Death of the Gods: Julian the Apostate* (1895), told of the fourth-century Roman emperor who tried to restore a reformed paganism as the official religion instead of the recently adopted Christianity. Fokine may likewise have been struck by Merezhkovsky's preface to his translation of *Daphnis and Chloe*, in which the translator expresses a longing for Greek paganism and extolls the novel's author (traditionally known as Longus) for this endeavor to return from culture to nature.

The second novel in Merezhkovsky's trilogy, *Resurrected Gods: Leonardo da Vinci* (1901), focused on the influence of pagan cults, especially that of Dionysus, on Renaissance art. As becomes clear from this choice of subject, Merezhkovsky, along with Russian modernists in general, was inspired by Nietzsche's *Birth of Tragedy*. Long associated with the classroom drilling of "dead languages," after Nietzsche antiquity (especially Greek antiquity) seemed appealing and fresh, and the revived myth of the "golden age" of civilization was now presented in a fin-de-siècle style, that is, with erotic and religious overtones.

As mentioned earlier, the belatedness of Russia's modernist renaissance had especially to do with politics. Russian conservatives, led by Pobedonostsev, made every effort to intensify the study of ancient languages in gymnasia—at the expense of natural sciences, believed to hinder the pursuit of the spiritual. The reformed curriculum was conceived as an antidote to political-mindedness—a remedy that, not unpredictably, led to opposite results. "For a quarter of a century," writes Levinson, "the government had tried to curb turbulent youth by means of the classical ferule ['flogging rod of antiquity,' *antichnaia rozga*]. Greek was loathed as much as was the royal blue of the gendarme uniform."[104] Against this backdrop, the newly liberated, natural, "out-of-school" antiquity lent a hand to intellectual opposition. Wasn't the dawn of humanity a model for its renewal in the future?

This widespread hope clarifies the unprecedented enthusiasm with which the Russian intelligentsia hailed the arrival of Duncan in late December 1904. Duncan had contracted Grecophilia from Nietzsche, just as Russian intellectuals had, and like them she conceived of ancient Greece primarily as *staged*. Her warm reception in Petersburg and Moscow was primed in particular by two recent productions of classical dramas: Euripides's *Hippolytus* (in Merezhkovsky's translation), staged in 1902 at the Imperial Alexandrinsky Theater by Yuri Ozarovsky and designed by the future stage designer for the Ballets Russes Lev Bakst, and Sophocles's *Oedipus at Colonus*, also in

220 IMPOSSIBLE PROJECT

Merezhkovsky's translation, staged at the same theater in the fall of 1904. *Hippolytus*, instantly the talk of the town, was one of the first attempts at symbolist drama in Russia. What made it innovative was that, instead of focusing on the tragic plot, its stagers sought to reconstruct the way the play might have been staged in ancient Greece.[105] Anticipating Fokine's programmatic foregrounding of corps de ballet, for instance, was the important place allotted to the chorus. The result, as Vasilii Rozanov describes it, was "Greece in the nude, in and by itself, unvarnished by books and printing houses, by school and the labors of learning, [a Greece that was] free, light, accessible to all."[106]

This was not the image of antiquity endorsed by the imperial school curriculum. Foregrounding libraries and museums, the official conception of antiquity presupposed not its eventual revival but rather its trustworthiness as something deceased and inert. Nor did it seem like a good idea to resurrect the ancients onstage. As it was, the Orthodox authorities barely tolerated theaters; imagine turning the imperial Alexandrinsky into a venue of paganist revival?

Stoking the fire, Merezhkovsky wrote a programmatic essay on the religious roots of the ancient theater, in which he provocatively conflated Christianity and paganism. No wonder his preface to *Hippolytus* was censored. As Teliakovsky, the last director of the Imperial Theaters, put it in his diary, "The conviction that the theater is an infernal place [or 'foul place,' *poganoe mesto*; more on the word *poganyi*, a cognate of the English word 'pagan,' below] is so strong that they do not even allow [Merezhkovsky] to keep the phrase 'the religious significance of theater.'"[107]

That Christianity came to succeed, and therefore supersede, the pagan worlds is a theological or even political observation. When mapped on the timeline of political history, at a certain point the Christian faith did succeed paganism, as, for instance, in the late tenth century in Kyiv. But from the standpoint of cultural history, our perception of turning points like this can change. As we have seen in the case of ballet, art and culture evolve by splitting rather than succeeding. What seemed to be two successive ideological formations turns out to be two complementary—dialogical, antagonistic; in other words, dynamic—components of a larger, more complex whole. As Merezhkovsky insists in his religious philosophy and fiction, apostasy is the other side, and not necessarily a dark one, of apostolic fidelity. The same is true of pagan roots and beliefs, into which idealistically minded apostates like Aleksandr Afanasiev used to delve, in search of the unholy grail of national (*narodnyi*) spirit, to emerge with treatises like *Poetic Views of the Slavs on Nature* (1865), which intellectuals and artists right up to Stravinsky and Roerich took as their handbook on paganism.[108]

Little wonder that, as the Ballets Russes enterprise went on, their librettos gravitated to *pagan* themes: in *The Firebird* (1910), the victory over Koshchei's kingdom was supposed to be read as an allegory of the Christianization of Rus'; Benois's *Petrushka* celebrated the Butter Week, a remnant of the pagan solar rite; and Stravinsky's conception (as described in a 1913 interview) of his *Rite of Spring*—a pagan ritual pure and simple— combined Easter-related ecclesiastic vocabulary ("holy resurrection") with a perhaps impromptu version of pagan lore: "In *The Rite of Spring*, I intended to express the Holy Resurrection of nature that is reborn into a new life, a complete, elemental resurrection, a resurrection of worldwide impregnation [*voskresenie zachatiia vsemirnogo*]."[109] The resurrection of impregnation! One imagines Pobedonostsev turning over in his grave at the thought.

Or take the first *Russian* ballet of the Ballets Russes, *The Firebird*, whose libretto was in part the brainchild of Aleksei Remizov and Sergei Gorodetsky, writers who routinely drew on and repurposed the pagan rituals of ancient Slavs. Central to *The Firebird* is the dance performed in the kingdom of Koshchei. In English, this is usually rendered as the "infernal dance," but its original Russian designation sounds more explicitly "pagan": *poganyi plias*. As mentioned above, the word *poganyi* has the same derivation as the English "pagan"; in modern Russian, it denotes "nasty" or "foul" rather than "pagan" (for which exists the neutral-sounding adjective *iazycheskii*) but still retains a certain "heathenish" or pagan echo. The phrase *poganyi plias*, moreover, was not devised by either Remizov or Gorodetsky; they borrowed it from Aleksandr Blok's article "The Poetry of Spells and Incantations" (1908), in which the poet speaks of, among other things, a folk interpretation of nature in winter (notably, in *The Firebird* Koshchei's kingdom is a realm of ice): "In this wind, which twists and turns on the roads, weaving pillars of snow, there dwells a demonic force.... In the whirling pillars, witches and devils arrange their infernal dances [*poganye pliaski*] and weddings."[110]

In this article, Blok runs against the tide. Poetry, as taught in schools, stored in books, or recited in salons, was normally thought of as an indoor thing, a part of *culture*. But here Blok dissociates the titular word "poetry" from culture and ascribes it rather to outdoor *nature*, complete with witches, winds, and whirling snow.[111] Fokine's logic is much the same. He thinks in terms of binaries. There are indoor phenomena that are considered "official,"

222 IMPOSSIBLE PROJECT

"imperial," "sacred," and "externally imposed"; on the other side of the door, however, out in *nature*, are things genuinely "Russian," "folk" (*narodnyi*), and "pagan." Much like Blok, who finds poetry in spells and incantations, Fokine reinterpreted the poetry of dance as it was performed on the Mariinsky stage—with its symmetrical battalions of tutus—as elemental, ecstatic, Dionysian choreographic bursts.

However, this Dionysianism and elementality do not mean that Fokine's apostasies were not handcrafted and deliberate; they were, no less than the orthodoxies he opposed. Modernist Russian "paganism" was an intellectual construct, often with an anticlerical motivation. Who, it would seem, could out-pagan Koshchei, the skeletal lord of the Russian (cold and icy) version of Hades? And yet there is reason to believe that, in choosing Koshchei as the antagonist of the Firebird, the ballet's librettists counted on his prior *political* reputation. A few years earlier, the same pagan demon (spelled Kashchei) was featured in Nikolai Rimsky-Korsakov's opera *Kashchei the Deathless*, which premiered in Moscow in 1902. In the revolutionary year of 1905, *Kashchei* was restaged in Petersburg by a troupe of students of the St. Petersburg Conservatory, from whose faculty, a few days before, its author had been dismissed for political liberalism.[112] The show was interrupted by police; as rumor had it, the character of Kashchei (whose name indeed derives from "boniness") had been made up to resemble the skeletally thin figure of Senator Konstantin Pobedonostsev, then still ober-procurator of the Holy Synod.[113] Appearances aside, Pobedonostsev did use the metaphor, as discussed in chapter 2, of "freezing" Russia to avert its democratic decay.

Political sentiments within the Ballet Russes differed, and changed as the times did. Artistically, as a composer Stravinsky was a radical, but when it came to taking political stances, he could be cagey. It may have been because of the political fraughtness of the Koshchei image that Stravinsky insisted on ending *The Firebird* with a scene in which the hero, Ivan, gets married and crowned as the new tsar.[114] (On the other hand, as Vladimir Propp tells us, the last—thirty-first—thing that invariably happens to male protagonists of Russian folk tales is that "[t]he hero is married and ascends the throne.")[115] Fokine was a democrat and an ardent supporter of the 1905 Revolution, and for his part Diaghilev hailed Nicolas II's abdication in February 1917 with enthusiasm. It was Diaghilev's idea, that fateful February, that Léonide Massine, who at the time danced the part of Ivan Tsarevich in *The Firebird*, instead of being crowned, should enter the stage waving a red flag.[116] While

BALLET AS A VERBAL ART 223

Fokine was no longer part of the Ballets Russes in 1917, the spirit of apostasy that fueled the enterprise saw its day of triumph.

But would Fokine, had he been asked, have approved this move? Politically, yes; artistically, hardly. Waving a flag was a direct appeal to the public, to its political sentiment. Addressing the public from the ballet stage was precisely what Fokine had opposed from day one of his creative career. I tend to think that coming out with a flag would be, in Fokine's eyes, tantamount to reviving the cult of the second foot position he so derided in *Petrushka.*

Catering to the public, soliciting applause, and other swaggery tricks that the *baletnye* were known for—Fokine the ballet artist was ashamed of these, and Fokine the apostate shamed his dancers for them. "Do not dance for the audience, do not show yourself, do not admire yourself," he instructed the male lead of his *Les Sylphides.* "On the contrary, you have to see, not yourself, but the ethereal Sylphides around you, look at them while dancing, admire them, reach for them."[117] Curiously, in a time when apostates of dramatic convention like Meyerhold were busy demolishing the invisible "fourth wall" separating players from the public, it was just such a wall that Fokine sought to erect—precisely because, in ballet, the fourth-wall convention had never been taken seriously to begin with. This was, once again, Fokine going against the tide. In this case, however, it also meant going against the tide of an already countertidal epoch—against the uprising that modernist artists around the world and across the arts waged against realist conventions.

No wonder that the neo-Noverrian strain in Fokine's choreographic philosophy found more skeptics than enthusiasts among proponents of the new art. In this respect Fokine's apostasy was, mutatis mutandis, akin to Tolstoy's. Tolstoy's bashing of art for betraying life co-occurred in time with, yet ran athwart, the currents of thought that proved productive among the young. If, in Tolstoy's view, Beethoven should have dropped writing music the moment he discovered he was deaf, or Baudelaire and Mallarmé should have paid more attention to reality than they did to words, the artists thus decried at least saw things from a standpoint complementary to Tolstoy's.[118] A symbolist poet, that is, would posit the existence of a higher reality (*realiora*) that was attainable only through poetry—that is, via words. An admirer of Beethoven could argue that being deaf to the sounds of the world afforded him access to the music of higher spheres. All this is rhetoric, a Tolstoyan might counter, but it might be countered to *this* that so was all Tolstoy's shaming of singers for singing and dancers for dancing.

224   IMPOSSIBLE PROJECT

Likewise, in an age when the arts, to use the phrase from formalist theory, were prepared to bare their devices, Fokine's lecturing on the artistic value of the fourth wall and the perils of the second position was bound to fall on deaf ears. *Pace* Tolstoy and Fokine, the early twentieth century was not the time to be ashamed of what one did in art. In particular, the stakes of realistic motivation had shrunk to virtually nothing. Levinson found Fokine's tendency to "cover" every dance, to find a piece of narrative motivation each time a character started dancing, not just aesthetically but even *ethically* misguided. In ballet, no one should be waiting for an excuse or permission to dance. Fokine, to Levinson, was too much of a Noverrian. In a 1911 critique of Fokine's devotion to storyline at the expense of dancing, Levinson laments *ballet d'action* as doctrinally requiring a ballet maker to scrabble around for narrative motives and effects. "[I]n his *Firebird*," claims Levinson, "Fokine felt compelled to reduce dances to a minimum; the few he kept are motivated with laborious duplicity [*so staratel'nym litsemeriem*]: the Firebird is allowed to dance because she is in flight; the captive princesses dance because they are playing a game of catch; even the 'infernal [*poganyi*] dance' performed by Koshchei and his minions is caused by coercive means: they dance because the Firebird enchants them to. And all this for the sole and only reason: so that it never occurs to balletgoers that dancers dance because this is *ballet*."[119]

Did Fokine's aversion to "naked" dance, his urge to cover it with whatever realistic motivation, stem from an inability to choose between Tolstoy and Terpsichore? Germinal to Fokine's apostasy, as we recall, was his encounter as a young man with Tolstoy's denunciatory "What Is Art?" The "elder" Tolstoy awoke young Fokine to the idea that what the "elder" Johansson had taught him to master and to worship was shameful. Lurking behind this self-narrative is the story of Eden, where Adam and Eve first learned they should be ashamed of being naked. Fokine's subsequent quest in ballet, as he himself makes clear and as Levinson cleverly confirms in his analysis of *The Firebird*, can be summarized as a desperate search for some literary motivation or other that might *cover* the shame. The shame of what? Of naked dances, someone like Levinson might have asked. Is it not dancing that you, the *baletnye*, are needed for? Remove the tale from *The Firebird* ballet, and it is still ballet. But take away the dances, and what are we left with? Three fiery feathers, Koshchei the Deathless, and other remains of the folktale's skeletal morphology.

A complementary way of reading Fokine's Eden story is to imagine *Tolstoy* as the serpent. In his later days, Tolstoy resolved to place himself, as a thinker,

BALLET AS A VERBAL ART   225

above art—above his own novels and, for that matter, above contemporary poetry, to say nothing of opera and ballet. Tolstoy and his young follower Fokine declare themselves ashamed of their métier. Their path is apostasy: sailing against the tide. Fine. Yet, as we recall from Legat's memoirs, there existed an alternative way of seeing things: to put what you do, your métier or vocation, above *yourself*—yourself as a thinker or dancer. Or as a thinker of dance.

Or, to rephrase this dilemma in terms of the religio-philosophical discourse in vogue in turn-of-the-century Russia: Which proved more productive for twentieth-century ballet? Was it apostasies like Fokine's or, to the contrary, the theodicy of classical dance developed by its apostles like Volynsky and Levinson and taken up and furthered by Kirstein? Or perhaps, in the historical course of twentieth-century ballet, the apostolic and apostatic successions coalesced?

Akim Volynsky, or Short Story Long

"M-me Bakerkina looked pleasing."[120] Critical reflection on ballet may sometimes seem a trivial matter—perhaps just a press writeup of what took place on a ballet stage last night (as, for instance, the Mariinsky coryphée Bakerkina would find, if she cared to open the morning paper and read what Skalkovsky had to say about her). But less obviously, ballet as a stage practice, as I intend to show in the final section of this chapter, can reflect theoretical reflections (pleonasm intended) on ballet. Ballet's history—or, to shift our perspective back in time, its future—was shaped as much by critics as by ballet's insiders. The outsider view on ballet became particularly productive in the early twentieth century, with Fokine trying to steer ballet in one direction and his critics, Levinson and Volynsky, in another—as everyone thought, the opposite from his.[121]

Fokine indeed saw Levinson and Volynsky as his sworn opponents. There was, however, a common denominator to everyone's concerns about ballet's survival. Ballet, it was felt, would go extinct if it had no meaning. The "keepers" and apostles of the classical school held their *battements*, *développés*, and other classical techniques as sacrosanct; even so, in a time when every item of the artistic legacy was being inventoried and assessed, no technique was exempt from the *why* test. Fokine sought meaning outside the pale of dance as such, in literary storehouses of fabular motivation. Volynsky's

226   IMPOSSIBLE PROJECT

and Levinson's idea, also taken up by Shklovsky, was different: rather than condemning ballet's *battements* as meaningless, to vest the "naked dance" with meaning.

As it turned out, it took an outsider to succeed in a venture of this sort. If you were one of the *baletnye*, you had long since made ballet's *battements* et cetera your own—so much so that it was nearly impossible to look at them afresh. Volynsky's signature way of enstranging choreographic techniques, which mesmerized many of his *baletnye* acquaintances, was to read symbolic, philosophical, even cosmogonic meanings into the minutest element of dance; Levinson's hermeneutics, on the other hand, was introverted, geometric, and body-specific; and the paradox-loving Shklovsky, rather than subordinating dance to pop-philosophy, as Duncan did, or to pedestrian plotlines, as did Fokine, held that the meaning and value of classical pas lay in their quality of being transrational, *beyond* meaning.

The main thing, to repeat, was that our three sages were unapologetic outsiders, external observers of ballet. Were Volynsky himself capable of executing a string of *battements*, his philosophy of dance would hardly have been heeded.

Volynsky, who came to ballet from literature—or, as he conceived it, fled literature, like Tolstoy fleeing his ancestral home, to ballet—was a man of the world, or, rather, many worlds and many words.[122] The letters housed in his sizable archive give the impression of a human hub of culture; he corresponded with virtually everyone, from Tolstoy to Karsavina. Having graduated with a law degree from St. Petersburg University in 1889, Volynsky was offered a teaching position in its Philosophy Department, on the condition that he (born Khaim Leybovich Flekser) convert to Russian Orthodoxy. He declined, opting for a less comfortable career as a literary critic. Initially, Volynsky wrote reviews primarily for Russian Jewish periodicals. His collection of rather denunciatory essays on the history of Russian literary criticism made a splash, albeit a mostly negative one; then came his *Book of Great Wrath*, on Dostoevsky, and another on Leonardo. Volynsky was omnivorous. He studied Russian and Byzantine icon painting; visited the autonomous monastic community on Mount Athos; was employed as a dramaturg at the Komissarzhevskaya Theater; edited Russian translations of Spinoza and Wagner; wrote about Rembrandt, Kant, Otto Weininger, Nikolai Fedorov, the Greek dithyramb, the Gospels; introduced and substantiated a subdivision of women into two types, "druidesses" and "amourettes"; was in charge of the Italian section of Maxim Gorky's "Global Literature" publishing

BALLET AS A VERBAL ART   227

project; and in Petrograd in the 1920s he founded and ran the School of Russian Ballet. Volynsky died in 1926, less than a year after the school was closed; those who knew him surmised he saw no reason to go on.

Such, in a nutshell, was Volynsky's intellectual biography, whose twists and turns, observers remark, were fueled by temperament more than intellectual consistency. Volynsky was notorious for his uncompromising tone and vitriolic language and his penchant for cultural iconoclasm. Somehow, Volynsky earned an utterly self-contradictory reputation: that of an ascetic, devoted solely to the life of the spirit ("[H]is one coat, which was long, black, and tightly buttoned, looked more like a monk's robe. It would not have been at all odd had he used a coarse rope as a belt"),[123] but also a ladies' man, whose name was linked with such celebrities as the journalist Liubov' Gurevich, the poet Zinaida Gippius, the dancer Ida Rubinstein, and the ballerina Olga Spesivtseva—a romantic "trail" to match his intellectual trajectory.[124]

A telling example is the saga of Volynsky's fractured friendship with Dmitrii Merezhkovsky and his wife, Gippius. Volynsky gained recognition in the 1890s as a leading critic and the de facto editor of the *Northern Herald* (*Severnyi vestnik*), a nest of the nascent symbolist movement in Russia. It was in this literary journal that Merezhkovsky's *Death of the Gods: Julian the Apostate*—the historiosophical novel mentioned above—was first published. True, Merezhkovsky's work came out heavily redacted by Volynsky, but no other venue previously approached by the author had even considered running so unorthodox a piece of prose. When in 1896, a year after *Julian the Apostate* appeared in Volynsky's *Northern Herald*, Merezhkovsky and Gippius planned a research trip to Italy in preparation for the second novel in Merezhkovsky's historiosophical trilogy, to be titled *The Resurrection of the Gods: Leonardo da Vinci*, they asked their friend—and, at the time, Gippius's romantic interest—Volynsky to join them. This would nearly cost Merezhkovsky his literary subject, Leonardo, and his wife. In the middle of the trip, Volynsky and Gippius's affair ended in a messy breakup. (It is hard to say whether the husband was in the know—but then, his and Gippius's was a famously unconventional marriage.) To make things worse, when the three returned to Russia, Volynsky refused to print Merezhkovsky's new novel in the *Northern Herald* and instead published his own essay on Leonardo, a germ from which Volynsky's monograph *Leonardo da Vinci* would soon grow.

Personal and romantic matters aside, it does seem significant that Volynsky in effect absconded with Leonardo. Some perceived the incident

228   IMPOSSIBLE PROJECT

as plagiarism, for, indeed, Volynsky's reflections on Leonardo's work and life saw print before Merezhkovsky's. But the case was more complex than that. Volynsky's was an uncommonly flammable intellect. If his reading of Leonardo was derivative of Merezhkovsky's, it was only so by contrast. The variance is of interest per se and can also help clarify Volynsky's later vision of ballet.

Per Merezhkovsky, the Italian Renaissance was all about the amalgamation of Christianity and ancient paganism—the titular *Resurrection of the Gods*. Following Nietzsche's teaching about the power of the Dionysian element in art, Merezhkovsky posits *John the Baptist* to be the central work in Leonardo's oeuvre. Central to Merezhkovsky's argument is the resemblance between Leonardo's depiction of St. John the Baptist and his portrayal (nowadays attributed to Leonardo's workshop) of Bacchus. The similarity of facial features and manual gesture between the Christian artwork and the tribute to the pagan pantheon is evident: wasn't Leonardo striving to merge Christianity and its pagan past? *The Resurrection of the Gods: Leonardo da Vinci* was part of Merezhkovsky's "Third Testament" project.

Volynsky could not have agreed less. In everything he said or did, he was a holist. To really believe in God or gods, he would insist, one had to wholly belong to one religion or another, otherwise the faith is compromised. There *is* a duality in Leonardo's work, but *pace* Merezhkovsky, this vitiates it. Volynsky's Leonardo is preternaturally talented as an artist but is fatally held back by his faith in reason, his individualism, and even his curiosity about dark forces, something Volynsky dubs Leonardo's "demonism." To the contrarian Volynsky, the true hero of the Italian Renaissance was Savonarola.[125] Individualism, typically considered the quintessential Renaissance virtue, was to Volynsky a vice, a deleterious attraction to the random and egoistic as opposed to the universal and eternal. The overdose of reason, which Volynsky diagnoses in Leonardo, impedes religious enthusiasm: "The spiritual man is [properly] irrational, ecstatic."[126] Reason begets decadence is the gist of Volynsky's charges against Merezhkovsky and Nietzsche, the idol of Volynsky's early days.

That our northern herald would critique Leonardo's flirtation with pagan antiquity and apotheosis of the intellect was one thing, but he even decried *The Last Supper*, the centerpiece of the artist's *religious* art, in a manner that Stanley Rabinowitz characterizes as "occasionally manic."[127] As befits a Savonarola, Volynsky is more oratorical than bookish; we can imagine him in that Milan church, perhaps with Merezhkovsky and Gippius at his

BALLET AS A VERBAL ART   229

side, addressing Leonardo's mural with one diatribe after another: "There is not a single figure in the painting imbued with unearthly ecstasy. It was not in Leonardo da Vinci's spirit to depict whole people of a new idealistic type."[128] Regard the disciples. Their hands are all gesture, but is there music or madness in what they express? "Faces, hands, poses—everything speaks, even shouts—and yet there is no music coming from the depths of the soul, no quiet strains in which random individual feelings and moods are transformed into something mysterious, eternal, universal. There is no religion in this painting. There is a living, earthly psychology unfolded in an entire range of human types, but not infused with divine madness."[129] To those familiar with Volynsky's subsequent ballet writings, his description of the tableside ensemble prefigures his censures of the Petersburg corps de ballet for failing to put *soul* into the dance: "Among the twelve disciples of Christ in *The Last Supper*, we find not a single figure embodying the martyrdom and sacrifice of the first centuries of Christianity. We do not sense in them that general mood that occasionally casts a whole group of heterogeneous characters in a single bright light, erasing their individual differences. It comes about precisely when people are seized by this or that religious impulse, when what is deepest and most universal in them comes to the surface."[130] In other words (more of the same, actually), in the painting,

> each apostle expresses his own individual feeling, without blending with anyone or resembling anyone else. In contrast to a universalizing religious ecstasy, the purely psychological mood, as depicted by the artist, brings about each individual nature in particular, each individual character in their limitations and singularities.... A work of genius artistically and psychologically, this painting cannot be called a religious-cum-poetic work. It is full of the luxury of scientifically developed notions and perceptions, but there is no higher, transcendent, religious transformation—no idealism. Over it blows the cold rationalism of Leonardo da Vinci, ready to turn all the mysteries of history into a naturalistic drama that is based on the struggle between irreconcilable aspirations.[131]

As said earlier, in his writings, Volynsky was passionate about—jealous of, enamored with—cultural icons. What attracted him to another was his own strongest characteristic: ardor. Born and raised Jewish, Volynsky nevertheless admired the unapologetically xenophobic Dostoevsky for his ferocity, religious and stylistic. On the other hand, Volynsky viewed Tolstoy—with

230   IMPOSSIBLE PROJECT

whom he corresponded—much as he did Leonardo: with a mix of admiration and disapproval, the latter because, in his teaching, Tolstoy stripped the Gospels of their marvels, thus *rationalizing* the Bible into a piece of mere ethical instruction.[132]

Volynsky's myriad intellectual interests—philosophy, history and historiosophy, literature, art, drama, "female typology," and, finally, ballet—might, despite their great variety, harbor a unifying thread: the quest for faith. While never having converted into the Christian faith, early on Volynsky grew infatuated with Jesus Christ. Tempted to convert, he consulted Tolstoy, monks of Mount Athos, even the archbishop of St. Petersburg. He could never commit to the decisive step of abandoning either Judaism or his love of Christ. In keeping with his self-sworn holism, Volynsky considered devoting himself to a major study on what he thought was the common, synthesizing source of Judaism and Christianity: the solar cult of Apollo. (Central to the polytheist pantheon, in the temple of Volynsky's ideas, the Apollo cult acquired monotheistic overtones.) According to Elena Tolstaia, Volynsky ultimately concluded that it was Judaism that had "preserved the greatest fidelity to this ancient universal revelation [of religion]."[133] Volynsky embodied what we might call Russian modernism's "postrational" turn; no matter the topic—Tolstoy, Dostoevsky, Nikolai Leskov, Leonardo da Vinci, or classical ballet—he wrote about the mystery of religion, whether openly or covertly under the nickname of "idealism."

To be sure, the notion of tracing an intellectual thread, so as to bottom-line an erratic life lived amid erratic times, may seem an *ignis fatuus*. In 1926, in his obituary of Volynsky, Boris Eikhenbaum emphasized the temperamental element:

> [H]e didn't write but rather ruminated, like a sorcerer, over ancient texts, studying the Gospels and ancient dance. He needed to prove something that no one believed. But it seemed very important, because it was fanatical and fantastical . . . . People related to him as if he were a statue preserved from antiquity, and sometimes treated him like an oracle. He was odd, helpless, and often pathetic, but when he spoke, it was transfixing, full of the incomprehensible, exotic passion of an Old Testament Jew who had survived all ages and civilizations—the passion . . . concentrated in one organ, the brain. The pulsating of this fanatical brain seemed to him and to others to be life.[134]

BALLET AS A VERBAL ART   231

But here again, the bottom line is indeed Volynsky's thriving on religious experience, which he associated with the transcendence of the individual and merging with the universal. Exodus, escape, ecstasy, communion—the ritual that transforms a sum of individual parishioners into one body of the congregation with Christ and Church, which transformation Volynsky saw as absent from Leonardo's depiction of its origin point, the Last Supper— these were his favorite words. "Ecstasy," or *ex-stasis*, that is, an escape from the stasis of one's separate self, was also how Volynsky conceptualized his sudden rebirth as a ballet critic.

Exeunt Omnes, Enter Ballet

What Volynsky found missing in the everyday cultural environment he found in ballet. Exactly when and how, we do not know. Unlike the *baletnye*, whose involvement with dance would date to the age of nine or ten, the earliest hard evidence of Volynsky's interest in ballet comes from 1911, when the already well-established cultural historian and champion of literary symbolism took the position of ballet critic for the *Stock Market News* (*Birzhevye vedomosti*). When Volynsky's new life began, he was nearing fifty and had never published a single line on ballet.

Of course, preparation for this new job did involve some prior investment of time. Volynsky's archive contains numerous notebooks, with detailed notes on steps and variations.[135] He began by sitting in on ballet classes (and possibly on rehearsals as well). He befriended Nikolai Legat and even tried exercising at the barre under Legat's guidance.[136] (Volynsky was said to be gaunt and clumsy.)

Volynsky's first writings on the subject evince a solid knowledge of ballet literature, which he must have devoted some time to studying. Even so, his "conversion" to ballet was surprising in intellectual circles, but also *un*surprising, in the sense that it seemed to exemplify the signature Russian act, and signature *symbolist* act, of "life-building" (*zhiznestroitel'stvo*). An act like this, to repeat, embodies Volynsky's favored figure of departure, *ex-stasis*, escape from one's former self. It also helped that, less than a year before, Tolstoy made *his* great departure, first from home and family, soon after from this life. Volynsky styled his as no less than a religious conversion, a stand-in, perhaps, for the official conversion to Christianity he contemplated

232　IMPOSSIBLE PROJECT

but never saw through; as the ballerina Vera Trefilova recalled, "[He] looked like a fanatic, whose enthusiasm for our art, which was new to him, had no limits, and whose passion for it was as exceptional as only a proselyte could have."[137] Volynsky's first (and long—five hundred lines) article on the topic, titled nothing less than "The Sacred Act [*Sviashchennodeistvie*] of Dance," published in the otherwise rather mundane *Stock Market News*, caused something of a sensation among ballet critics. "Volynsky comes to ballet criticism like a 'deus ex machina.' All lovers of literature of course know his major work, *Leonardo da Vinci*, and his . . . literary criticism," commented the balletomane Valerian Svetlov (later Trefilova's husband) in an article spanning two issues of the leading theater trade periodical *Theater and Art* (*Teatr i iskusstvo*). "His interest in Greek theater and literature is also known. His appearance on the scene of ballet criticism, however, has come as a complete surprise to those who follow the [current] theater."[138]

And an *unpleasant* surprise, at that. A sympathizer of Fokine, Svetlov in this piece slams Volynsky for bombast, vagueness, and arrogance. But as they say, there's no such thing as bad publicity. An expert provocateur, Volynsky knew that applying the epithet "sacred" to an art form like ballet would imbue his entry onto ballet's intellectual stage with maximum theatrical effect.

One theory—a conspiracy theory—linked Volynsky's sudden involvement in ballet with Kschessinska's feud with Fokine. With her clout at court and wealth, some remarked, Kschessinska could certainly afford a hit-job critic. But, it was further rumored, Volynsky eventually talked back, and the ballerina told off her supposed hireling, claiming he did not understand "a pig's navel" (*svinogo pupa*) about ballet.[139] Be that as it may, unlike Levinson, whose ballet criticism was the picture of Olympian objectivity, Volynsky invariably reviewed Fokine's productions vitriolically.

Indeed, from day one Volynsky would cuff Fokine in every other article, whether technically reviewing a production of his or not. (Usually not, for, unlike other critics, who would undertake seasonal voyages to Paris to monitor the current offerings of the Ballets Russes, Volynsky could not have cared less.) But he did have his reasons, and he laid them out clearly. He perceived Fokine's dramatization of ballet as an attempt to rationalize the irrational; this followed the same logic by which Volynsky faulted Leonardo's *Last Supper* for naturalizing that historic mystery into a mere tableside scene, and Tolstoy for demythologizing the Gospels. In effect, Fokine was caught in the line of fire Volynsky aimed at Nietzsche and the Russian Nietzscheans, idolators of apostasy like Viacheslav Ivanov or Merezhkovsky.[140] Fokine's, per Volynsky,

BALLET AS A VERBAL ART   233

was a "plebeian gamble on bacchanalianism [*vakkhichnost'*]"[141]—clearly, a shot at the Nietzschean Dionysus who was so in the air. In his *Preludes*, staged to the music of the Christian idealist Liszt, Fokine took up the visual style of Botticelli, a "refined pagan" (before, Volynsky specifies, his repentance and embrace of the teaching of Savonarola).[142] Long story short, Volynsky sensed the paganist turn in Fokine's system of choreographic values and slammed it as vociferously as he did all his other foes, living or dead.

The panoptic nature of Volynsky's writings constitutes both their power and their drawback. Traversing confessions, centuries, and arts, Volynsky would juxtapose wildly diverse phenomena and figures, ideals and heresies, with an audacity unique to turn-of-the-century Russian symbolists. What connection could there possibly be between Russian Orthodox icons and the body-colored tights worn by *baletnye* on stage? "To turn a person into an icon," reasons Volynsky in his 1904 *Book of Great Wrath* on Dostoevsky, "[the icon painter] must purify this person's features by getting rid of anything random"; only then will the work acquire "religious meaning."[143] About a decade later, Volynsky repurposed this argument, in support of tights. Whether stage dancers should wear tights was an ongoing debate, especially after 1904, when Duncan landed in Russia unashamedly barefoot and barelegged. When Volynsky entered the tights wars on the side of their defense (even insisting on them), it was not out of pudicity, as his religion-mindedness might imply, but rather owing to the artistic principle he had observed in Russian icons, which, he would have Duncan know, applied also to Greek sculpture. In his 1913 essay on this issue, Volynsky traces tights all the way back to the ancient Greek theater and emphasizes their religious nature. Why did the Greeks feel a need for them? Because they knew that the naked body is an individual body, and that even a "hint of individual psychology" would be perceived in the Greek theater as a profanation of the cult. Here the performer was expected to transform themselves into a being of a higher order, a god or hero, which presupposed the erasure of individual features, including the face, thus kept behind a mask. It was for the same reason that ancient performers were to refrain from everyday speech and were instead to "orate" like priests (in Christian churches as well). And the ancient orchestra, too, Volynsky would later add, functioned as a "liturgy," the "refraction of the body of an entire nation in honor of the gods."[144]

With Volynsky, analogizing is unstoppable. When, in the early 1920s, he again argued (and again with great vitriol) for the import of tights in ballet, he compared the tights-wearing body to Greek sculpture, recycling the

234 IMPOSSIBLE PROJECT

argument made in 1904 regarding the Orthodox icon: "These are bodies in general, universal bodies: nothing individual, no random features."[145] And so on. But one thought here stands out, as if to underscore Volynsky's awareness that his topic is ballet, a *wordless* art: "Persons here not only renounce personal interests, but also their individual language, in order to speak to the world in a language universal and eternal."[146]

Volynsky's fascination with the religious aspects of ancient Greek theater is not surprising in the modernist context. More unusual was his aim to repudiate Nietzsche. In 1907, he traveled with Ida Rubinstein to Greece in order to "determine" on the very spot "the connection between Christian liturgy and Hellenic ecstasy."[147] Together, the critic and the aspiring dancer came to the conclusion that Greek tragedy arose, not from Dionysian orgies, but from the Apollonian tradition, with its symmetry and discipline, especially the dithyramb, a folk genre of choral lyrics. According to his own origin story as a ballet writer, then, it was in Greece, with Rubinstein at his side, that Volynsky realized that, of all the extant arts, it was ballet that came the closest to ancient theater.[148]

A Theodicy for the Classical

Classical ballet, in Volynsky's view, was not silly—as Fokine, Tolstoy, and the progressive intelligentsia believed it to be—but rather *irrational*, in the same sense that religion was. Disregard the libretto, music, set designs— humdrum paraphernalia that embarrassed intellectuals, including Volynsky. What Volynsky espoused was that productions be stripped of individual traits—the conceptual equivalent, for ballet as an art form, of putting integrative tights on disparate dancers. Or revealing *the* face inside an icon. Pared of nonessentials, ballet becomes dance clear and pure: a bare variety of movements, like the life of any living matter. Plants blossom and wither, creatures crawl and fly, human beings fall and rise. If this sounds more poetic than terpsichorean, it's worth noting that turn-of-the-century Russia was a poetry-stricken culture.

To Volynsky, classical dance was an earthly vehicle for expressing things unearthly, much like religion: "Projecting itself in all directions, the [dancer's] body turns into a perceptible emanation of the spirit [*dostupnoe izluchenie dukha*]."[149] Unsurprisingly, cardinal among these directions was *upward*. Volynsky never tired of citing a verse (ascribed to Homer) describing the inspired Apollo as "rising on his toes, preparing for flight," which to Volynsky corroborated the ancient (ergo, universal) origin of dancing *sur les pointes*.[150] Likewise, Volynsky connected the "spiritual element" in balletic elevation (jumps and leaps) to Christ's transfiguration: "One always needs to ascend to a Mount Tabor in order to shine."[151]

Volynsky's dance teaching, or perhaps rather "preaching," hinged on the titular comparison made in that first (1911) essay on ballet, "The Sacred Act of Dance." Like religion, ballet is held to rely on the power of the practitioner's will, unlike modern dance, which celebrates organic spontaneity. As in the case of a religious adept, becoming a classical dancer requires physical sacrifice and asceticism. Classical dance students are disciples, not the kind misportrayed by Leonardo (mere realistic diners) but true apostles and martyrs of ballet. And like any religion, ballet endures on the basis of recurring congregations, whether onstage or in class; what is corps de ballet if not a choreographic iteration of the holy communion—a transformation of individuals into a single, ideally coordinated body?

With his intensely mythogenic mind, Volynsky was a prophet in search of a religion. The two he had been involved with till now, Judaism and Christianity, were too well-formed to need yet another prophet. Hitting upon ballet was a stroke of luck, for here was a cult without a language, creating which would be Volynsky's special gift. How many years it took him to prepare his Calvinistic takeover of ballet is an open question. He would always be a prophet distinctly located *not* "in his own country," but early on Volynsky had agents and informants among the *baletnye*. Aside from Kschessinska, Karsavina, and Spessivtseva, with whom he at times conversed or corresponded, an early source, it appears, was Nikolai Legat, who, as we recall from chapter 2, had been steeped in quasi-religious ballet lore from the time he stood at Christian Johansson's barre. Volynsky frequented Legat's own classes; often, their conversations ended up late at Legat's place. While we have nothing by which to reconstruct it, theirs was no doubt a two-way exchange: the dancer knew how to cut a figure; the writer, how to sharpen a phrase. One way or another, Volynsky provided what ballet's Apollonian self was in need of: theodicy, a verbal justification of its divine nature.

Legat needed an oracle like Volynsky, no less than Volynsky needed Legat. To resort, once again, to Noverre's grand synecdoche, in their symbiotic relationship Legat was the feet; Volynsky, the head and tongue. Key to their theodical alliance was how Fokine stood in relation to it. To recall, Legat and

236 IMPOSSIBLE PROJECT

Fokine were rivals. Early on, the Imperial Ballet found a problem in Fokine, who, as discussed above, showed himself to be an apostate, albeit also a talent the Directorate could ill afford to lose.

In terms of temperament, Legat could be as willful as Fokine (time and again, Teliakovsky rebuked both for insubordination), but he was less of a public speaker, and still less of a writer than Fokine, and never took a public stand against the Imperial Ballet. Nor did he feel the need to: a faithful disciple of Johansson, Legat the dancer, Legat the ballet master, and Legat the pedagogue felt called to shore up the old architecture of classical dance increasingly questioned by the likes of Fokine. And even had Legat been keen to speak out on something, he seemed to lack what Fokine and Volynsky had in spades: the audacity and stamina of natural-born speakers.

An excellent classical dancer, as was Fokine, as a ballet master Legat was Fokine's inverse. Like several young principal dancers at the Mariinsky in the early twentieth century (e.g., Samuil Andrianov, Viktor Semenov), and unlike such old-timers as Petipa, Lev Ivanov, or Gerdt, Legat was an uneven mime, reflecting the trend of the slow-but-sure success of Vsevolozhsky's drama-poor fairy tales. The only pantomime-heavy ballets to remain in the repertoire were time-proven pieces like *Esmeralda*, *Giselle*, and *The Pharaoh's Daughter*.

As a result, younger dancers had fewer occasions to practice miming on stage. As a choreographer, Legat was tremendous at staging stand-alone classical dance numbers, chiefly pas de deux and male variations. (Petipa, whose focus was the choreographing of female dancers, often left their counterparts in the care of Legat.)[152] But Legat's full-length ballets (*A Scarlet Flower*, *Puss in Boots*) came apart at the seams: the dances and dancers were exemplary but failed to add up as a coherent action.[153] The "old ballet" in its new iteration was losing the connective tissue previously furnished by the plot, ballet's once trusty verbal bolster. In modern academic parlance: ballet was turning into a signifier without a signified.

Which, in the discourse of older periods, meant the time was ripe for apostasy and for a commensurate theodicy. It was time, declared Fokine, for stories, ideas, poets, and painters to help ballets make sense. Even a composer like Stravinsky was expected to write music *about* things, whether a puppet or Russia's pagan past. On the other hand, Legat more than welcomed Volynsky and his prophetic zeal to reveal to the *baletnye* the meaning of what they were doing, the "sacred" poetics of the pointes—to infuse any who would listen with an Apollonian, apostolic *élan*.

BALLET AS A VERBAL ART   237

In ballet's cultural memory, Volynsky became imprinted as a man *writing*. "At the beginning of our acquaintance, [Volynsky] sat in on our dance classes—even now, I can see him sitting there, notebook in hand," recalled Legat in 1922 in a speech given at the celebration of the fortieth anniversary of Volynsky's writing career. "He wrote down everything he saw. . . . But he didn't just write down the movements; he decoded them, explained them, spiritualized them, moralized them. For instance, the simple *battement*, this simple kick of the leg, he called volitional [*volevoi*], while the soft, smooth [variety of] the *battement*—the *développé*—he called psychological, vegetal [*rastitel'nyi*]."[154] Kschessinska, recalls Legat, was thoroughly mesmerized: "'A blossoming *battement!*' [she] repeated enthusiastically."[155]

Spessivtseva, another speaker at the 1922 celebration, must likewise have been struck; as she addressed the hero of the day, "You translated for me all our ballet terms into the language of the will and of feelings. My whole soul was illuminated by your teachings on the classical clarity of dance. [To this day,] some of your definitions—that *attitudes* are chaste, that the *battement* is virtuous—resound in me like the echoes of a distant paradise [*otzvuki dalekogo raia*]."[156]

The distant paradise, no longer ours, was an apt metaphor for Spessivtseva to use. Like Adam in the Garden of Eden, in his heyday as a philosopher of ballet Volynsky was busy attaching words to things. With a key difference: in those days of creation, Adam gave names to God-created animals, whereas Volynsky did something of the opposite. The words, that is—*battement, sur les pointes, développé*—had been around for some time already, but until Volynsky, no one had had the audacity to say which "animal" meant what. Volynsky read higher meaning into a bunch of preexisting terms, which till now had only pertained to the motoric repertoire of classical dance. Under Volynsky's pen, a set of classroom commands blossomed into a sort of somatic philosophy. Gone was ballet's proverbial wordlessness, which was precisely how Volynsky understood the mission of a critic: "Every feature of any movement is, after all, only a symbolic sign. Steps on the floor . . . or jumps in the air . . . have a certain content, which criticism reveals and explains."[157] This was the essence of Volynsky's theodicy: in the beginning was the word; in the end, the word was given meaning.[158] Or, as the clever Levinson put it in his obituary, Volynsky's accomplishment as a ballet theorist was the "verbal transposition of a movement and its aesthetic exegesis."[159]

Most remarkable about Volynsky's input, however, was not that he infused ballet's vocabulary with philosophy but rather that the vocabulary thus

238 IMPOSSIBLE PROJECT

transformed wrought certain transformations in dancers themselves. Legat again: "It was as if I were reborn. With my conscience clarified, a source of new insights, new delights, [new] charms opened up. Our entire art came down to us from some Apollonian heights as if transfigured, illuminated [*prosvetlennyi*]."[160] In other words, Volynsky liberated ballet's language from muteness. This, I suspect, we owe to Volynsky being something of an actor sans stage, an everywhere oracle, like some peripatetic philosopher of old. Levinson again: "Volynsky wasn't so much an abstract thinker, stuck with books in his home; he was a born speaker, powerful, eloquent and magnetic [le *chrysostome*, le *magnetiseur*]."[161]

Nor was it, of course, that Volynsky had discovered some true and ultimate meaning of choreographic terms. Claims about the "volitional" nature of the *battement* (the foregrounding of "will" itself points to Kant and especially to Volynsky's beloved Schopenhauer) or about the *attitude* being a conveyor of "chastity" cannot be verified or refuted. Neither can theodicy, which serves rather solely to vindicate. If literal (theological) theodicy represents a vindication of worship, Volynsky's balletic theodicy was a vindication of practice. Whether because his exegeses gave dancers a shortcut from here to sublimity, or because the former abracadabra-like "entrechat" now acquired a saintly status akin to Church Latin or synagogal Hebrew, the fact was that Volynsky's barely readable scrabbles, his ramblings, helped ballet survive as surely as any patristic dilations have helped establish any religion. By the same token, the pragmatics of religious practice is akin to that of classical dance; both are *technically* "useless."

Whether Volynsky actually "vindicated" ballet is an open question. In any case, not only did he preserve his authority among devotees as an augur; he also managed, pragmatically and practically, to found and run for a whole five years, 1920 to 1925, an official, state-sponsored School of Russian Ballet—an unheard-of achievement for a ballet critic who had never himself performed a single pas on stage. Volynsky employed dance teachers of the highest caliber, including Agrippina Vaganova and Legat, but built the practice curriculum around his own classroom lectures on ballet's *theory*. He also published a book subtitled *An ABC* [*Azbuka*] *of Classical Dance*," recalling grammar school instruction. In his school's curriculum, the ABC of dance intertwined with exegesis. As a place where learning a language was held inseparable from professing a faith, Volynsky's ballet school resembled a yeshiva.[162]

BALLET AS A VERBAL ART   239

Not everyone among the *baletnye* fell as headlong under the spell of Volynsky's teaching as Spessivtseva or Legat, but, as befits a prophet, he had many in fear of his fulminations. Most of these were aimed at Fokine, whose neo-Noverrian poetics of ballet hinged, to Volynsky's mind, on mere *believability* rather than faith. And true to his self-image as a cultural prophet and to his earlier authorship of *The Book of Great Wrath*, Volynsky knew how to champion balletic faith over good works *vociferously*.

He was certainly vociferous when his friend and follower Karsavina defected to the Ballets Russes to star in Fokine productions. Reduced to tears by Volynsky's reaction, the prodigal daughter returned to her native fold of classical ballet.[163] Back in Petersburg, Karsavina publicly renounced the apostate in the *Theater Review* (*Obozrenie teatrov*): "[Fokine's] ballets, indeed, are detrimental to classical dances."[164]

Fokine believed Tolstoy, who did not believe in biblical miracles. Volynsky's *Book of Great Wrath* was about Dostoevsky, for whom the raising of Lazarus was a fulcrum of faith. Volynsky conceived of his mission as miracle-making, and in secular terms at least he seems to have succeeded. His "fanatical and fantastical" (Eikhenbaum) teachings raised dancers in their own eyes, and classical ballet in the eyes of the public. The transformation took a substantial amount of time and hundreds of reviews. "Volynsky argued that classical ballet is an art that comes down to us directly from ancient Greece, preserved in all its purity, in no way corrupted," wrote the poet and critic Georgii Adamovich in an obituary of Volynsky. Notably in Adamovich's telling, the reception of Volynsky's ideas slowly curve from rejection to recognition: "He was the first to speak of ballet as a great and high art. His pathos, at first, seemed inappropriate to the topic. His first articles on ballet were laughed at a lot—and in very different circles. Typical decadent ravings [*bred*]. Later, people saw that there was something very profound in these ravings."[165]

Enter Levinson

It is hard to say whether Volynsky's ideas would have been as productive for ballet's future as they proved, were it not for Levinson, another warrior resolved to fight for the same cause. Like Volynsky, Levinson was a polymath and polyglot, but their methods and instincts could not have been more different. By temperament, Volynsky was an oracle; Levinson, a scholar.

240   IMPOSSIBLE PROJECT

Volynsky's entree into ballet meant meeting and talking to as many dancers as he could; Levinson, rather than rubbing elbows with the *baletnye*, went to the library to explore the past and present of this art form that had captivated him since childhood.[166] Volynsky's first writing on ballet boldly referred to it as a "sacred act"; Levinson's first ballet-related book was a study of figures from Noverre to Blasis modestly titled *Masters of Ballet*. But both, the former as a visionary, the latter as a historian, in a sense coauthored the future of ballet.

And both, as it happened, began writing about ballet in the same year, 1911. Again, one showed up in the field with pomp, the other inconspicuously. A person of renown, Volynsky, as mentioned above, staged his passage from letters to dance as a resonant act, something of a conversion. Levinson, over twenty years Volynsky's junior (though not, as some assume, Volynsky's disciple),[167] in 1911 was a philology student who lived a five-minute walk from the Mariinsky, just across a canal.

Both Volynsky and Levinson became ballet regulars, but hardly in the loathsome sense of the *habitués* described by Khudekov in his 1870 novel.[168] Both came to ballet not for the dancer, but for the dance. Neither cared if Madame Bakerkina looked pleasing, and unlike ballet critics before them, neither belonged to an established balletomane community. What was innovative about their reviews was the pivot toward theory. Balletomanes like Khudekov and Skalkovsky had at times cited theory, but typically with the intent of reining in whatever novelty threatened to alter their preferred evening dish. Rather than digging up old tenets of Noverre, Volynsky and Levinson developed their theories (in fact, as will be seen, the same theory, with two faces) from scratch. To contemporaries, and to subsequent observers, the strangeness of their position lay in the fact that, each in his own way, Volynsky and Levinson strove to expose the newness of the old, or, as their own starry-eyed epoch might have put it, to see the light of the future in the past.

As discussed above, what could be called the "Levinson-Volynsky classical dance theory" emerged in response to the attempts of younger Noverrians (not to be confused with old-school ones like Khudekov and Skalkovsky) to reinstate narrative conventions that would "cover" naked dances.[169] Countering this, Levinson addressed a convention of a different order— the very basis of ballet as an art form. In Fokine's *Firebird*, for instance, do Koshchei and his minions need an extra excuse, other than their existence as ballet characters, to burst into dance? *Do not be ashamed of what you are,* came Levinson's not unexpected objection to plot-conscious productions like Fokine's.

At the same time, the new classical dance theory also responded to the *theoretical* discourse of proponents of plot: Fokine, Benois, and a multilanguage chorus of critics and balletgoers whose voices, amplified in seasonal accounts by Valerian Svetlov, brought home the foreign triumphs of the Ballets Russes. That technically this company's dancers were beyond reproach and that its choreography was innovative and varied went without saying, but foreign fans were equally wowed by the ironically exotic, self-reflective theatricality of the Ballets Russes spectacles. In the 1900s, Nikolai Evreinov, the future author of the self-mirroring stage play *The Main Thing*, espoused and popularized the idea that *the main thing about theater is theater*. Before *The Firebird*, and even before the founding of the Ballets Russes, Benois, in his programmatic essay of 1908, worried that, stripped of stories, ballet might relapse into what it had been before it became ballet—a ballroom: "Without a dramatic lining [*podkladka*], ballet loses its theatrical nature, becomes a ball. To remain theatrical, ballet needs to spin dancing bodies around some sort of a plot; it needs pantomime to do so."[170]

In this view, if you remove the pivot of the plot, the stage becomes a mere dance floor. Volynsky's and Levinson's answer to this was as minimalist and brilliant as was Meyerhold's to Evreinov. The pivot of the stage is not the plot or play, but the actor—in the case of ballet, the dancer. Do we still long for *pas d'action*? Per classical dance theorists, the only action worthy of enacting was "exercise" (*ekzersis*), the kernel of the classical—much as the *lazzi* and etudes in the mid-1910s, later transformed into biomechanical exercises, were for Meyerhold.

In ballet lore, the new cult of classical dance altered ballet's mental architecture. When Volynsky unabashedly shrank the "essence" of ballet to a set of context-free exercises, or when Levinson, without a shade of irony or disapproval, referred to classical dance as "gymnastics,"[171] they were relocating the heart of dance from the stage back to its original habitat, the classroom. It is fitting that, owing to his repute among higher-ups of the Paris Opera, Levinson acted as an informal adviser on matters pertaining to the dance school curriculum,[172] and just as fitting that the years Volynsky spent as head of the School of Russian Ballet in Petrograd were a culmination of his ballet life. In the ethos of twentieth-century modernism, the home of art was not where art was displayed—a gallery, a stage—but where it was made: the studio, the workshop, and, when it came to dance, the class.

242 IMPOSSIBLE PROJECT

To listen to classical dance theory, ballet's narrative apparatus—the miming of emotions, *pas d'action* in lieu of pas proper—was not just superfluous but even detrimental to the quality of dance. "Classical dances, by their very nature, cannot have any external meaning," asserts Volynsky in a 1915 essay titled, generically, "Classical Dances." "When subordinated to the tasks of pantomime, with its unavoidably prosaic content reminiscent of everyday reality, classical dances lose all their beauty and are reduced little by little to almost nothing."[173] In keeping with his antidrama stance, Volynsky would in his critical articles eulogize Vaganova, famous for her impeccable technique and notoriously helpless when it came to acting; in his view, this neglect of miming was to Vaganova's credit.[174]

Volynsky's pejorative epithet "prosaic" was pointedly chosen. In a sense, classical dance theory's disagreements with neo-Noverrians paralleled age-old debates on poetry and prose and on whether they have particular missions. Is poetry's job to convey stories to its readers or to transport them to worlds *beyond* narrative meaning, beyond the Earth? To defend the irrationality of dance, Volynsky resorted to the model of poetry. Levinson went one better. Not only did he deny dance a kinship with narrative prose; he questioned its purported affinity with *language* in general. In a 1927 article, Levinson argued that the Aristotelian formula of dance, boiled down here to the idea of "using dance as a substitute for words," has long deprived dance the status of an independent art, reducing it instead to a communicative means.[175] But dance, per Levinson, is an end in itself—any *use* of it is a *mis*use.

Volynsky was not, himself, a poet. But steeped in the cultural climate of his time, he championed the symbolist movement, which encouraged placing poetry above prose, or, for that matter, above language—the very words that constituted poetry's material. Words were but a vehicle to transport the reader, to use Viacheslav Ivanov's mot, *a realibus ad realiora*—from reality toward a higher reality.

Prose, by contrast, implied earthly ("prosaic") matters. Prose was understood as opposite to *form*. In the symbolist imagination, form was native to music, poetry, and crystal—and, in Volynsky's view, to classical dance, which, in its very crystalline form, is thus unsuited to prosaic subject matter. "If [we agree that] the form of ballet dance is ideal, then it follows that its theme has the same ideal character," states Volynsky in his foundational 1911 essay "The Sacred Act of Dance." "Prosaic needs do not dictate our body to assume an artful attitude," Volynsky goes on, and adds, in an unlikely solidarity

BALLET AS A VERBAL ART   243

with Russia's best-known hater of verse and ballet, "If we can't help but laugh alongside Tolstoy at the bombastic rhetoric of the old opera . . . we must likewise condemn as senseless and inappropriate the scrutinizing of our everyday concerns through the precious crystal of choreographic poetry."[176]

Given Volynsky's devotion to poetry over prose, it was only to be expected that he would value corps de ballet no less than stand-alone choreographic numbers. Versification terms like "verse" and "feet" are believed to derive from the ordered movements of ancient Greek choruses, which used to step rhythmically in sync with the verses recited. Also, in Volynsky's value system communal actions are by definition a step above individual ones; communities express the communal spirit, while individuals have only their own individual story to narrate. Individual psychology, according to Volynsky, is unfailingly prosaic—and this is what, in his view, places the supremely individualistic dancer Duncan *below* ballet: "[Duncan] will never go beyond personal feelings," he claimed after seeing her perform in January 1913. "The choreographic phrase [*tantseval'naia fraza*] performed without a verse meter, without poetic wording puts her dances at best at the level of refined prose."[177]

Duncan's refined prose—something like a *B*– on Volynsky's grade sheet— can reach the level of poetry only when she ceases to be *the* Duncan of dance and becomes part of ballet as a whole. Corps de ballet is a chorus that never falls apart: it can move only in unison or as a contrapuntal whole, whereby "strophes and antistrophes interact as in a dithyramb by Arion."[178]

Similar as their thoughts on classical dance were, Levinson's style of thinking was complementary—or, as Volynsky might have put it, *antistrophic*—to Volynsky's. Volynsky's was a spiritualizing and synthesizing mind; Levinson's, analytic and dissecting. In the above-quoted obituary, Levinson called Volynsky an *inquisiteur de l'exercice*, an exegete who never tired of connecting dancers' daily *pas d'élévation* or *battements développés* to organic metaphors like growing, crawling, or soaring.[179] Levinson belonged to the postsymbolist generation, many of whose members had had their fill of symbolic generalities; as such he was a more matter-of-fact thinker, inclined to take things apart rather than conjure them. And he was as averse to religious as to narrative motivations. To Volynsky, classical dance was beautiful by virtue of its relatedness to higher, invisible reality; to Levinson, the beauty of classical dance was immanent in dance as such: "Classical dance is, of course, not conditioned upon any external causal compulsion; it carries within itself its own *immanent* law, its own internal logic."[180]

244 IMPOSSIBLE PROJECT

Unlike Volynsky, who extolled classical dance for transporting us *a realibus ad realiora*, Levinson's main concern was how dance relates to practical, experiential, everyday *realia*. If walking and running are innate, natural ways of human locomotion, the virtue of classical dance is that it is a *made* thing—locomotion without practical need or destination. Per Levinson, "art is a ceaseless *deformation* of reality," hence "ballet is above all an *artificial* dance,"[181] in which the ballerina stands on her toes, rising "above the laws of balance, above earthly gravity, above the mechanical habits of everyday movement."[182] Levinson's interrogation of the meaning of dance, and his answer to the question thereof, echoes the Russian formalist approach to the give and take between language and poetry and, by extension, between walking and dancing. "Dance is constructed from movements that do not participate in one's everyday gait [*obyknovennaia pokhodka*]," wrote Eikhenbaum, crediting this thought to Shklovsky.[183] As Shklovsky himself put it, "Dance is walking constructed so as to be sensed [or experienced: *chtoby oshchushchat'sia*]."[184]

Like Noverre before him, Levinson envisioned classical dance theory as an act of wedging apart what had earlier seemed an indivisible whole. It was this logic—the logic of splitting, wresting dance as art from its mundane counterparts—that prompted Levinson to posit that, to be recognized as art, classical dance should distance itself from social dancing, as it indeed had managed to do by the late nineteenth century. Dancing *sur les pointes*—an *artificial*, nonutilitarian way of controlling your body—was not within the powers of a society lady. "Artifice [in ballet] has triumphed," exulted Levinson.[185]

Temperamental opposites, Levinson and Volynsky had one key thing in common: both saw what I am calling here "classical ballet theory" *not* as a theory but as a project. Indeed, as theorists of classical dance, neither was conservative or traditionalist, as ballet histories have tended to portray them; rather, they were modernist to the bone. To discover a stand-alone art form, or even a universal language, in the mix of old French *danse d'école* and Italian pointe technique of the late nineteenth century—this was a powerful modernist gesture ("decadent ravings," as Adamovich described the first impression made by Volynsky's discourse), akin to other "discoveries" of Russian modernism, like the reconsideration of icons as works of art, the celebration of sectarian glossolalia as a precursor to transrational poetry, or Russian futurists' fascination with shop signs. The daring tone of classical dance theory, of Volynsky's "great wrath" and Levinson's grand constructs,

BALLET AS A VERBAL ART 245

applied to an art form generally thought of as trifling at best—in private, the
director of the Imperial Theaters Teliakovsky referred to ballet as "a harem"
and deemed it harmful to children and the less-educated (*narod*)[186]—this all
sounded much like an avant-garde manifesto.

Historical evidence notwithstanding, Volynsky and Levinson alike held
pointe work to be the *ur*-phenomenon at the core of classical dance, due to
Kant's recognition of the upright posture as a distinct trait of the human build
and the human spirit. The verticality argument points to yet another factor
in the "discovery" of classical dance as an art: modernism's obsession with
geometry, from cubism to vorticism to constructivism. The straight lines
of classical corps de ballet may have reminded Fokine of parades and drills
of the "old ballet" (which is understandable, given his own experience with
such oppressive rectilinearity), but for those in the audience with modernist
sensibilities, this geometry might have looked modern, if not indeed avant-
garde, reminiscent of "The Black Square." It was Russian futurism, after all,
that came up with the "as such" and "by itself" argument to justify less than
intuitive art, like transrational poetry and nonfigurative painting. As with
poetry, so with ballet. The "dance-as-such" philosophy, which Volynsky
and Levinson advanced in 1911 so as to substantiate the inherent value of
classical dance, was soon to chime with Khlebnikov and Kruchenykh's
1913 manifestos "The Word as Such" and "The Letter as Such." And, to add
Malevich's suprematism to the equation, *form*-as-such. It was in the mindset
of the epoch that in order to build the new, one had to get back to one's ABCs.
Not unlike avant-garde endeavors across the arts, classical theory stripped
dance down to what it had always been conceived as in the classroom: the
pas per se, an element of geometry-in-motion.

Classical Repertoire: Enter Svetlov and Teliakovsky

If classical dance is a repertoire of pas, classical ballet is a repertoire of tales
and titles. And despite the "ageless" connotation of its designation, classical
repertoire is as recent a phenomenon as its choreographic counterpart.
While the two notions eventually converge (for us, classical dance and classical repertoire are but two sides of the same coin: classical ballet), the emergence of classical repertoire is a separate (and little-studied) story.

Broadly speaking, any theatrical repertoire involves a trade-off between
the venue and the viewer. A filmgoer is keen to avoid spoilers, and a clever

246 IMPOSSIBLE PROJECT

reviewer knows enough to protect their cherished nescience. ("I leave for you to discover" and "in ways that I didn't foresee and won't disclose" are just two of the critic Anthony Lane's recurring blinders.)[187] But classical repertoire draws on a different mindset. The distinction between the two is like that between sightseeing and coming home. Within the classical idiom, one does not *discover* a *Giselle*; one *returns* to *Giselle*, as one does to the Mariinsky or one's native St. Petersburg.

As said, none of the nineteenth-century titles that are nowadays canonized as classical were held sacred by nineteenth-century ballet lore. Rather, the opposite is true. What *was* venerated in the period criticism was a show's novelty value. "[F]or years, the same ballets have been shown to the same public," fulminated Skalkovsky in 1883 in response to the Directorate's decision to increase admission prices to the first two nights of every opening. "Who is going to pay triple price for a show bereft of innovation?"[188] For our ballet to roll on, what it needs is the rotation, not reiteration, of repertoire. Some twenty years later, in an interview already quoted in the first chapter of this book, the same Skalkovsky called *Giselle*—first staged in Paris in 1841, restaged by Petipa in Petersburg in 1887—a sixty-year-old "ramshackle affair" (*rukhliad'*). The same applies, per Skalkovsky, to the sexagenarian *Esmeralda* and supercentenarian *La Fille mal gardée*: "Inarguably, Petipa has talent, but has grown old, and is unable to come up with anything new."[189]

This interview dates to 1904. After Skalkovsky's death in 1906, the role of resident Jeremiah passed to Valerian Svetlov, the last of the Russian Noverrians, an admirer of the neo-Noverrian Fokine, and from early on, an apologist of errant Ballets Russes. Two of the angriest outbursts Svetlov would direct toward the Mariinsky repertoire were caused by a significant change in the ticketing system instituted by the last director of the Imperial Theaters, Vladimir Teliakovsky, ahead of the 1911–12 season.

Until 1911, in order to get into the Mariinsky, a balletgoer needed either a single-admission ticket or to be the fortunate holder of a prepaid season subscription (*abonement*). Neither format facilitated public access nor afforded the establishment much glory or money. Most open-market tickets fell into the hands of "scalpers" (*baryshniki*). The subscription system, too, was a mixed blessing. On the one hand, money up front did help the Directorate fund upcoming ballets; on the other, *abonements* enabled balletomanes to virtually monopolize Mariinsky seating, thus blocking entrance to nonregulars—which was especially embarrassing, given the

Imperial Theaters' noncommercial, educational charter adopted during Vsevolozhsky's directorship.

From contemporary lore, it would not be difficult to conjure, in the mind's eye, the lofty Mariinsky auditorium as glimpsed before the curtain goes up. The stalls and beau monde boxes and other prestigious seats are all occupied by subscription-holding balletomanes, and not just for the length of the season but virtually for life, and—given how these persons cherished their privilege—perhaps for the life of their descendants as well. The nonsubscribers are relegated to low-cost boxes and the uppermost balconies—the ironically termed abode of the "gods."

If we turn our gaze from the auditorium to the repertoire, we may notice a correlation between the two. The subscription system furnished the balletomanes with the lion's share not only of seats but also of shows. As we learn from Teliakovsky's 1924 *Reminiscences* (*Vospominaniia*), around the beginning of his directorship in 1901, forty of the total fifty ballets staged by the Mariinsky troupe were performed for subscribers.[190] These forty were the crème de la crème: they included all premieres and the classiest of the old or recently revived titles. The remaining ten consisted of matinees, several Christmas and Shrovetide festivities shows, and what could be called occasional balletry, for instance, the annual *benefis* for the corps de ballet.

Does ballet exist only in order to please balletomanes? Formed in the epoch dominated by Nekrasov, Tolstoy, and Saltykov-Shchedrin, the Russian public's attitude toward ballet might have remained forever lukewarm if not for a historical surprise: the success of Diaghilev's enterprise in Paris. The Ballets Russes triggered a surge of cultural curiosity about Russia; no longer seen as a realm solely of self-important literati, daredevil dancers were discovered there, in whose performances exoticism, experiment, and expertise converged. The new tide ricocheted back on Russia amplified by ballet lore—not least, Svetlov's ecstatic dispatches, replete with quotations of Russes-bewitched Western luminaries.

Could it be that, in the eyes of the West, the *baletnye* had gained the upper hand over those bearded bullies from belles-lettres? It seemed worth checking out. By the end of the 1900s, says Teliakovsky in *Reminiscences*, ballet was once again the talk of the town.[191] And, if such a phrase exists, the talk of the world. As the 1914 edition of Karl Baedeker's *Russia, with Teheran, Port Arthur, and Peking Handbook for Travellers* alerts potential tourists, "[T]he excellence of the Russian Ballet has been amply demonstrated both in other parts of Europe and in America."[192]

248   IMPOSSIBLE PROJECT

What all this entailed was that the caste of seasoned balletomanes would have to make room for an influx of newbies, both bigwigs and people from the street. This was what Teliakovsky's 1911 repatterning of attendance was about: to allow more people to see more shows. Enforced in the teeth of the balletomane lobby, Teliakovsky's reform was aimed not at abolishing subscriptions as a system (which democratic radicals had previously called for, to no avail) but rather to split the former—blanket—subscription into three alternating tiers. "Instead of the former forty shows, the Directorate would only allot ten shows per subscription, but, instead of a single subscription, balletgoers would be offered three smaller-scale ones," explains the former director of the former Imperial Theaters. "This way, the ten remaining ballets became available to non-subscribers."[193]

As Svetlov was quick to point out, the new template was fraught with a (probably unforeseen) threat to ballet's repertoire. To avoid the charge of favoritism and discrimination, Teliakovsky decreed that each echelon of the threefold contingent of subscribers be shown exactly the same set of ballets. This meant that every title formerly listed once or twice in a seasonal repertoire would now appear three times as often. And *this*, in turn, meant the diminishment of the repertoire's diversity.[194]

"Of new ballets, only one was performed: *Vernal Daydreams* [*Vesennie grezy*], a dispensable diminutive one-acter staged [by the ballet school faculty member Klavdia Kulichevskaia] to showcase the current graduates from the Ballet School,"[195] Svetlov alerted readers of *The Yearbook of the Imperial Theaters* in his overview of the 1911–12 season. Otherwise the repertoire was packed with time-proven staples: *Swan Lake* ran four times; *La Bayadère*, three times; *Giselle*, twice.[196]

What troubled Svetlov about the season in question was both the absence of new titles and a noticeable curtailment of the existing repertoire. Gone were not only certain old reliables (Svetlov could not have cared less about what he considered outdated junk) but also Fokine's recent—controversial, self-reflective, ironically stylized—*Le Pavillon d'Armide* from 1907. Also gone were some lovely tales that used to impart a sense of richness and variety to the Mariinsky offerings. Where was the Mariinsky repertoire headed?

Noverrians, as well as Noverre himself, have never been known to shy from expressing their displeasure with balletic developments in angry "Letters." The second of Svetlov's "Letters on Ballet," subtitled "On Ballet's Repertoire," opens with the following question: "Is it possible to sit through [Petipa's 1862] *Pharaoh's Daughter* for the one-hundred-and-forty-sixth time?"[197] Printed in 1911, Svetlov's letter warns of the impending mummification of the Mariinsky repertoire due to Teliakovsky's meddling with the subscription format. While the rich Imperial Ballet goes clad in rags (*vetosh'*), take a look at the Ballets Russes: "In the space of but three years, Diaghilev has spawned a massive ballet repertoire. They offer: *Carnaval, Le Spectre de la rose, Scheherazade, Petrushka, Narcissus, Cléopâtre, Sadko, L'Oiseau de feu, Chopiniana [Les Sylphides], [Le Pavillon d']Armide, Polovetsian Dances.* In preparation for the upcoming winter season are *Daphnis et Chloé, Le Dieu bleu, La Péri, Thamar,* and a number of other novelties of which I am not authorized to speak."[198]

Svetlov's angry list reads like a marquee, followed by a brief preview of coming attractions or, to use his pet word, "novelties" (*novinki*). Svetlov was, true enough, an insider of sorts in Diaghilev's circle and may very well have been "authorized" and "not authorized" to make various disclosures about it. But this very hinting at some unnamed "novelties" to come represents, I would emphasize, not so much the judiciousness of the reviewer ("I-leave-for-you-to-discover"), but the teaser of a nineteenth-century showman. The show, that is, the repertoire, must go on.

On the other hand, this was already a new century. The year, let us recall, was 1911. And it was from this year onward that many an old value started flipping. Enter Volynsky and Levinson, with their conviction that, whether it was Thamar or the Firebird dancing, what really mattered was the dance. Dance was ballet's sine qua non, and the rest of it—librettos, set design, costumes, even music—disposable adornments. The same logic applied to repertoire. Here, the more-the-merrier mentality was giving way to the sober mood of less-is-more. In Svetlov's eyes, Teliakovsky's subscription tinkering all but decimated ballet's repertoire; for the likes of Volynsky and Levinson, Teliakovsky brought it down to bare essentials. How many times can one sit through *The Pharaoh's Daughter*? As if answering a question Svetlov had asked rhetorically, in 1915 Volynsky wrote the following: "Provided it is performed artistically and technically well, classical dance, much like [classical] music, can be repeated endlessly before the public without tiring or even straining their nerves."[199]

At the time when Volynsky and Levinson turned their thoughts to ballet, the reduction of the Mariinsky repertoire was in progress. What the two thinkers did was to make a move that is arguably at the heart of any theodicy: to reconceptualize a bug as a feature. "In the life of our ballet theater," reasoned Levinson in 1918, "repertoire is a constant; its composition

250 IMPOSSIBLE PROJECT

is hardly ever updated."[200] This was what Svetlov, like Skalkovsky before him, had been harping on for years. For Levinson, however, repetitive repertoire was the order of the day. This statement on constancy comes, after all, in Levinson's review of *Raymonda*, which was sixth in the top-twelve list of most frequently performed ballets between 1900 and 1911.[201] With minor modifications, the canonical twelve, with the same *Raymonda* in the middle, remain what we call "classical ballets" to this day.

Classical ballet was *named* into being. If the name *classical*, when added to *dance*, wedded dance to classical statuary, the phrase *classical repertoire* conjured the additional element of classical *languages*. Adding a new title to the canon seemed as preposterous as opening up the linguistic corpora of ancient Greek or classical Latin to new texts. "The language of classical ballet is a mysterious cypher of sorts that has hitherto escaped cultural analysis," pronounced Volynsky in 1922.[202] It was precisely because Petipa, as Skalkovsky begrudged in 1904, had grown old and unable to come up with anything new that, under the pen of Volynsky, the veteran ballet master became a kind of Homer, a bard whose lines we ought to "analyze" and "decipher" instead of attempting to improve on or quarrel with them. Like Latin, classical dance remained alive on the strength of being dead. *Pace* Skalkovsky, repetition is a form of survival. It's another new century already, and *Giselle* is very much around.

A Lofty Shore: Enter Duncan, Shklovsky, Balanchine

Duncan's first visit to Russia in 1904–5 invigorated, as shown above, ballet lore and sparked a spirit of dissent in the *baletnye*. When, after a series of return visits, Duncan came to Russia (now Soviet) in 1921, she found the cultural climate significantly changed. In Petrograd, with its former Imperial Ballet-cum-school still standing and Volynsky's School of Russian Ballet already functioning, Duncan's arrival was anticipated with mixed emotions, as seen vividly in one piece of lore in particular: a magazine article by Shklovsky. Never before translated into English, the piece deserves being quoted in full:

On the Lofty Shore [Na vysokom beregu]
Of the two pictures we reproduce in this [1922] issue [of *Peterburg*], one is a photo of the great Russian danseuse Pavlova, the other, Yuri Annenkov's sketch depicting Isadora Duncan, who recently arrived in Moscow.

We cherish Isadora Duncan as our first love, the passion of our days of youth.

The arrival of Duncan is like the arrival of an ocean liner to the port of Petersburg.

No, better: amidst all that Moscow noise, Duncan's name is a note of global noise, and noisy Moscow gladly welcomes Duncan.

In Russia, Russian classical ballet has long been underrated.

It took Akim Volynsky's daring to speak of it, with a fervor previously reserved for speaking of Beethoven, Dostoevsky, and Leonardo.

Russian classical ballet is nonfigurative [or conventional, *usloven*].

Classical dance is not emotional; it does not depict a mood, nor does it illustrate anything.

This explains the shabbiness and ridiculousness [*ubozhestvo i nelepost'*] of old ballet librettos.

They were hardly needed. The classical pas exist and succeed one another according to internal laws of art.

Classical ballet is as nonfigurative [or conventional] as music. The dancer's body does not so much define the structure of the pas as serve as a self-hymn of [their] wonderful conventionalities [*sluzhit samoodoi iz prekrasneishikh uslovnostei*].

The epoch of Fokine was the age of classical dance's triumphant fall [*pobedonosnogo padeniia*].

Classical dance came close to becoming a character one.

New, deftly crafted librettos and psychologically motivated movements pushed ballet in the direction of pantomime.

This was as much of a decline, as if music had gone the way of onomatopoeia.

And, as often happens, the epoch of decline was also one of popularization.

Russian ballet spread all over the globe.

Masters of genius, like Pavlova or Pushkin, always emerge at the end, rather than the beginning, of an epoch.

A genius is a bad sign for descendants.

For all her talent, Duncan's dancing, convincing as it is, is infinitely inferior to, infinitely narrower than, the art we call classical dance.

Her dances can be understood; but great art can only be contemplated [*sozertsaemo*]. The beauty of the human body in motion, which Duncan's dances once manifested, and may manifest to this day, is below the kind of beauty inherent to classical dance.

252   IMPOSSIBLE PROJECT

The difference between the two is like that between a merely captivating story and a poem or story structured to be a literary work.

That Duncan's dances are "natural" and "sincere" is not to their credit.

"The proper place for sincerity is the marketplace," [Aleksei] Kruchenykh once said, and said it well.

Art requires artifice [*sdelannost'*].

Classical ballet is an infinitely more advanced art than Duncanism.

We in Petersburg welcome the arrival of the long-range ship *Isadora Duncan*, but we welcome her from a lofty shore.[203]

A literary critic and avant-garde theorist, Shklovsky was decidedly not a balletgoer, let alone a balletomane or ballet theorist. What inspired this piece was less in-person familiarity with dance performances than his reading of Levinson's and Volynsky's writings on classical ballet theory. The reference to ballet's "nonfigurative" or "conventional" nature and "artificiality" (*uslovnost'*, *sdelannost'*; literally, "madeness") clearly derives from Levinson's defense of classical ballet; Volynsky, whom Shklovsky credits here for "fervor," was Shklovsky's neighbor, interlocutor, and occasional backer. (Both resided, when this piece was written, in the House of Arts [Dom iskusstv], and it was Volynsky who, in 1916, accepted for publication in the *Birzhevye vedomosti* Shklovsky's piece on Oleksandr Potebnia's literary theory that later grew into his seminal article "Art as Device," from which the formalist theory would grow in turn.)[204] In effect, Shklovsky's rendering of Volynsky's and Levinson's ideas was but an exercise in rereading classical ballet theory in formalist terms.

In the run of history, Shklovsky's one-off foray into ballet lore would have considerable resonance, albeit with a delay of half a century or so. It so happened that Shklovsky's "On the Lofty Shore" caught the attention of young George Balanchine, a ballet school graduate whose devotion to dance ill matched, or so he thought, the disdain in which ballet was typically held among the avant-garde artists and poets he mixed with in the early 1920s, a cultural and psychological ambivalence captured and examined in Elizabeth Kendall's biographical study of the celebrated American ballet master's Russian years.[205]

The young Balanchine's exposure to the world of modernist art was due in part to his marriage to another aspiring dancer, Tamara Geva, the daughter of art collector and patron Levkii Zheverzheev. "Take Mayakovsky," explained Balanchine in an interview given to Solomon Volkov in New York in 1982.

BALLET AS A VERBAL ART 253

"I adored him, but he didn't pay any attention to me. He didn't understand a thing about ballet.... [Left-leaning] artists came to Zheverzheev's, had tea, talked. They mocked ballet: 'It's ludicrous,' 'no one needs it.'"[206] The more Balanchine became aware of the avant-garde experiments on stage or in verse, the more he felt his métier was falling behind.

Much like Fokine two decades before him, the young dancer Balanchine felt ashamed for his art, classical ballet.[207] Then came a "Eureka" moment: Shklovsky's backhanded welcome of Duncan. Balanchine, who met Shklovsky at the home of Yuri Slonimsky and heard him speak on art, was at first reluctant to buy into the zigzags of formalist thought. "It was difficult listening to Shklovsky, because he kept getting sidetracked," confessed Balanchine. "But his article on ballet was another matter. It was written like a poem. And it seemed very important right away.... Shklovsky was also a very progressive, very left person. But he wrote of the ballet with respect, not trying to kill it off. He explained why ballet didn't need complicated plots. And why you could dance without 'emotions.' And it was written clearly and simply—not like the muddled and verbose articles on ballet by Volynsky."[208]

In 1922, it was hardly possible to fathom how the ideas that Balanchine fished out of Shklovsky's "On the Lofty Shore" (which Shklovsky, in turn, had fished from the Levinson-Volynsky classical dance theory) would play out in Balanchine's future philosophy and practice of ballet. For someone feeling ashamed of classical ballet's figurativeness and emotionality, at a time when other—progressive—arts had already turned away from such old-fashioned qualities, Shklovsky's assertion that "[c]lassical dance is not emotional; it does not depict a mood, nor does it illustrate anything" sounded like an entry ticket to modernism. If Balanchine's neoclassicism would need any historical justification, Shklovsky's "Lofty Shore" fit the bill. And how productive ballet lore turns out to be! Shklovsky—a writer never inclined to sit still, now discoursing on poetry, now on cinema, now on the circus—could hardly have known that his very short essay of 1922 would become a theodicy for a whole late twentieth-century school of ballet.

* * *

We often hear and speak of great critics' great influence on art. Histories of Russian literature typically emphasize Vissarion Belinsky's impact on Russian prose of the 1830s and 1840s. (Although, scandalously, in 1896 Volynsky was the first to *decry* this impact.) Art historians explain that Botticelli's choice

254 IMPOSSIBLE PROJECT

of pictorial subjects hinged on the taste and ideas whispered into his ears by contemporary humanists like the poet and scholar Angelo Poliziano, and that the same Botticelli burned his paintings when brainwashed by Savonarola. And it is true that, key to Zucchi's contract with the Directorate of the Imperial Theaters in the early 1880s, and to Spessivtseva's invitation to dance *Giselle* at the Paris Opera, was the string-pulling of prominent critics—Skalkovsky and Levinson, respectively.[209] Some critics are heeded more than others and better know the backstage mechanisms of power to see their visions through.

Yet the power of lore discussed above is of a different, ballet-specific nature. Classical dance is often defined as a language without words. This definition is by no means wrong. Dancers and mimes do manage to bypass speech and yet communicate meaning. On another level, however, classical dance is never short of words, even if it is always short of meaning. This is where a mastermind of meaning-making like Volynsky comes in, conjuring a series of "Aha" moments among the *baletnye*. Who would have known that a body-related word like *développé* actually means "blossoming"? This is where Levinson comes in, explaining that the meaning of choreographic figures is relational rather than lexical; that *sautés*, *pliés*, and *jetés* pertain to the vertical and horizontal coordinates of space. And that the body is about geometry, not emotions.

Once promulgated by Volynsky and Levinson, ballet's theoretical apologia—the theodicy of classical dance as an independent art—proved useful to ballet in moments of crisis and would remain so throughout the twentieth century. Ballet, said to be in decline in fin-de-siècle Europe, had remained onstage in early twentieth-century Russia primarily for nonartistic reasons. One of these was the bureaucratic inertia of the Directorate of the Imperial Theaters (which not even Teliakovsky could surmount, despite still mulling the abolition of ballet as late as 1910);[210] another, the patronage of the grand dukes; yet another, the conservatism of court tastes; and so on. And there was always—at least, in the old days—ballet's relevance to the socially accepted culture of movement (bowing, kneeling, social dancing).

In the twentieth century, when much of this relevance was lost and the other reasons just mentioned fell away along with the empire itself in 1917, other processes were underway: the well nigh miraculous preservation of ballet in Bolshevik Russia,[211] its revival in France, and the adoption of the classical dance tradition in the United Kingdom, the United States, and Australia. And so on. The architects of these movements drew, directly or in a roundabout way, on the theories of Volynsky and Levinson. Fedor Lopukhov, the head of the Mariinsky Ballet in the 1920s, now mostly remembered as an avant-garde choreographer and as Balanchine's teacher, made the utmost use of Volynsky's and Levinson's arguments. It was Lopukhov who managed to keep (though not without edits and "updates") Petipa-staged ballets at the Mariinsky well after the October Revolution. Serge Lifar, a Ballets Russes alumnus and, starting in the early 1930s, head of the ballet company at the Paris Opera, heeded Levinson's exhortations that more classical ballets be included in the repertoire, which in the long run helped restore France's status as a ballet superpower.[212] Finally, Levinson's writings greatly influenced Lincoln Kirstein,[213] who eventually succeeded in convincing Americans they needed ballet not merely as a show but as an integral institution, complete with a school and a permanent company and stage—all of this under one helm, as used to be the case in Russia. We are used to thinking of ballet as a teaching "handed down" by foot—a podal-apostolic succession, as it were. My aim in this book has been to show how much the survival of ballet was and remains about *words*.

Epilogue

What is meant by "our," "national," or "native" ballet depends on who uses such a phrase, when, and where. As Levinson once remarked, "Asiatic in Paris, Russian ballet was [perceived as] occidental in Saint-Petersburg."[1] Apostates like Fokine (there were many among the *baletnye* who agreed with him on that) used the idea of "Russian" ballet as part of a decolonization effort, a rebellion, as it were, on the part of locals (Russians) against foreign domination (the French school). That this effort was eventually embodied in a French phrase, *Ballets Russes*, is ironic but also logical: foreign and imperial back home, insofar as its participants were concerned ballet arrived in Paris fully Russian. Ballet was no longer "imperial" or "classical"; it was *national*.

Diaghilev sided with national values and against classical dance throughout all twenty years of the complex trajectory of the Ballets Russes. When, in 1921, the company appeared to make peace with the "old ballet" and staged *Sleeping Beauty* (retitled *Sleeping Princess*) based on Nikolai Sergeev's notations,[2] Nijinska (who was extremely upset by the whole idea)[3] added the Russian dance of the three Ivans to the last act, and the likes of Bakst and Stravinsky insisted in the program that this French-themed ballet, first staged for an Italian star, was somehow inherently Russian.[4] About a month before his death in 1929, Diaghilev published an open letter in the London *Times*, in response to criticism calling Balanchine's choreography acrobatic:

> The classical dance has never been and is not today the Russian Ballet. Its birthplace was France; it grew up in Italy, and has only been conserved in Russia. Side by side with the classical dance there always existed the character or national dance, which has given the evolution of the Russian Ballet. I do not know of a single classical movement which was born of the Russian folk dance. Why have we got to take our inspiration from the minuet of the French Court and not from the Russian village festival? That which appears to you acrobatic is a dilletantic terminology for our national dance step. The mistake really, in fact, goes much deeper, because it is undoubtedly the

Impossible Project. Daria Khitrova, Oxford University Press. © Oxford University Press 2025.
DOI: 10.1093/9780197653081.003.0005

EPILOGUE 257

Italian classical school which has introduced into the dance the acrobatic elements. The coarsest acrobatic tricks are the toe-dancing, the "Double tours *en l'air*," next to the classical "Pirouettes en dehors," and the hateful "32 Fouettes [*sic*]" that is where acrobatics should be attacked. In the plastic efforts of Balanchine in *The Prodigal Son*, there are far less acrobatics than in the final classical *Pas de deux* of *Aurora's Wedding*.[5]

For all his collaborations with non-Russian celebrities, from Debussy to Picasso, Diaghilev thought of ballet primarily as a vessel to promote Russian art, whether visual or aural. Contrary to the popular narrative, he didn't think of ballet as some long-sought form of *Gesamtkunstwerk*; for Diaghilev, who had once trained to become an opera singer, what was missing from ballet was the human voice, and he kept theorizing this in his interviews[6] and wedding vocal and choreographic elements in many of his productions, from *Le Coq d'Or* and *Daphnis et Chloé* to *Les Noces, Romeo and Juliet, Ode*, and more. Nor did his ballet masters necessarily care about classical dance or even dance in general. After 1912, when Fokine was dismissed from the Ballets Russes as *passé* after just four seasons, his rebellion against the "old ballet" proved to be the gentlest of challenges compared to the approach of Diaghilev's other choreographers, from Nijinsky to Balanchine, which Valerian Svetlov, writing in 1933, summarized as "danceless ballet."[7]

It's no wonder that opposition to the "danceless" idea was brewing. It found expression in the writings of Volynsky and Levinson, who were both critical of Diaghilev's ballets, and on stage in Russia, where the Mariinsky company was unevenly divided. Many of its top-tier classical dancers remained loyal both to the classical idiom (that is, to Petipa's ballets, which continued to be performed at the Mariinsky with the help of Sergeev and his notations) and to their imperial service. (Of all the Mariinsky ballerinas at that time, only Karsavina joined Diaghilev's Ballets Russes as a permanent star, only, as we recall, to return and repent.) The October Revolution of 1917 forced most of the high-ranked dancers into emigration. Out of the ten early twentieth-century Mariinsky ballerinas, only one, Agrippina Vaganova, stayed.

It was not without a touch of anti-Diaghilev sentiment that this exodus was transformed into an opportunity to present the world with the crème de la crème of classical ballet. After years of collaboration, including on the 1921 *Sleeping Princess*, Léon Bakst grew so disappointed with Diaghilev that he openly came athwart the latter's cause by pushing the classical ballet agenda on the Paris Opera stage. Specifically, Bakst used his influential friend

258 IMPOSSIBLE PROJECT

Levinson to get Spessivtseva invited to star in *Giselle*, and also wrote and designed a number of Paris ballets himself. (Bakst died while working on one of those.)[8]

Most ballerinas who had emigrated, however, were now past their prime performing age. Without pensions and diamonds, and with their princely husbands now jobless and penniless, they turned to teaching.[9] For them, it was more than just an income; it was a mission, just as it had been for Petipa and Johansson decades earlier. The mission: to keep ballet afloat.

Thus the story of classical dance and its survival takes the form of two symmetrical cycles. Mocked in the aftermath of the French Revolution, the old good French school was religiously preserved in the Russian Empire by the likes of Didelot, Petipa, and Johansson. When the Russian Empire came to an end, many of the dancers who fled Russia took up the role of guardians of the classical school.

Inadvertently, classical dance changed its passport in the process. The new *baletnye* referred to the dance *they* had preserved as either Russian or classical ballet, not the French school. It was in their studios, most notably those of Kschessinska, Preobrajenska ("Préo," to her students), and Egorova, that the new generation of Russian ballet dancers was brought up, starting with famous "baby ballerinas" (Tamara Toumanova, Tania Riabouchinska, and Irina Baronova), who remained on stage well after World War II, then taught, as did their pupils, into the twenty-first century. With the imperial social hierarchy now irrelevant, young people from the former aristocracy (Toumanova), the business elite (Riabouchinska), and the Jewish community (David Lichine), were eager to join the ranks of the *baletnye*. None of which was possible in the empire.

With the empire now gone, the sharp distinction between the "imperial" and the "Russian" was erased as well. Mass nostalgia made good old classical dance as Russian as Pushkin's poetry or Tchaikovsky's music. In the process, ballet's reputation also made a U-turn: now being in ballet was a respectable profession, priced by many as the pride of Russian culture. A kept woman in Petersburg, Matilda Kschessinska became a princess in Paris (a hard-working royal, to feed her family, Kschessinska taught well into her nineties); Pavlova, according to Arnold Haskell, elevated ballet as a career in England.[10] Haskell, a critic who was instrumental in shaping the ballet tradition in Britain, came up with a magic formula about Russian ballerinas: "The strength of the Russian school lay in the fact that ballet was a vocation for life, because no one really retired and the tradition was never broken."[11] In 1939, a French critic defined Russian ballet in exile as "the Russian companies who run from capital to capital, carrying the flame of an art become religion."[12]

It is one thing to run from capital to capital, another to restore or establish a permanent ballet institution. For that, Sergeev and his notations came in handy: his 1924 revival of *Giselle* with Spessivtseva at the Paris Opera signaled the upcoming turn to classicism in French ballet of the 1930s. Next came the Royal Ballet, with its strategic choice to revive *Sleeping Beauty* from Sergeev's notations for its inaugural performance as the resident company of the Royal Opera House in 1946. The story of returning to life after near-death, an Easter-like resurrection of love and beauty, resonated in postwar Europe. No notation was needed for Balanchine's 1954 *Nutcracker*, a staple of the American Christmas ever since. From birth to death to resurrection, ballet had come full circle.

Notes

Introduction

1. All quotations from Noverre used in this book are from the first volume of his *Lettres sur les arts imitateurs en général et sur la danse en particulier* (an 1807 version of his 1760 *Lettres sur la danse and les ballets*).
2. Noverre, *Lettres*, 224.
3. Noverre, *Lettres*, 225.
4. Krasovskaia, *Russkii baletnyi teatr nachala XX veka, chast' 1*, 34 (emphasis added).
5. Krasovskaia, *Russkii baletnyi teatr vtoroi poloviny XIX veka*, 23 (emphasis added).
6. Lieven, *The Birth of the Ballets-Russes*, 63.
7. Krasovskaia, *Russkii baletnyi teatr vtoroi poloviny XIX veka*, 397.
8. Krasovskaia, *Russkii baletnyi teatr vtoroi poloviny XIX veka*, 338.
9. Krasovskaia, *Russkii baletnyi teatr vtoroi poloviny XIX veka*, 338. Volume 4 (1918) of Khudekov's work is preserved as an advance copy only. A useful sketch of Khudekov's biography and writings is found in Korshunova, *Mysl' o balete*, 121–29.
10. Krasovskaia, *Russkii baletnyi teatr vtoroi poloviny XIX veka*, 338.
11. Khudekov, *Istoriia tantsev*, 4:viii.
12. Khudekov, *Istoriia tantsev*, 4:23–24.
13. Khudekov, *Istoriia tantsev*, 4:153.
14. Krasovskaia, *Russkii baletnyi teatr vtoroi poloviny XIX veka*, 32.
15. Krasovskaia, *Russkii baletnyi teatr vtoroi poloviny XIX veka*, 5.
16. Krasovskaia, *Russkii baletnyi teatr vtoroi poloviny XIX veka*, 472.
17. Krasovskaia, *Russkii baletnyi teatr vtoroi poloviny XIX veka*, 496.
18. Krasovskaia, *Russkii baletnyi teatr vtoroi poloviny XIX veka*, 572.
19. Krasovskaia, *Russkii baletnyi teatr vtoroi poloviny XIX veka*, 575; see also the chapter on Italian dancers in Russia (560–93).
20. Noverre, *Lettres*, 146.
21. Skalkovsky, *Stat'i*, 285.
22. Skalkovsky, *Stat'i*, 285.
23. Pleshcheev, *Nash balet*, 31.
24. Pleshcheev, *Nash balet*, 32.
25. Krasovskaia, *Russkii baletnyi teatr nachala XX veka, chast' 1: Khoreography*, 236.
26. For the illuminating discussion of Soviet "symphonism," see Scholl, *Sleeping Beauty*, 64–100.
27. Krasovskaia, *Russkii baletnyi teatr nachala XX veka, chast' 2: Tantsovshchiki*, 7.
28. Krasovskaia, *Russkii baletnyi teatr nachala XX veka, chast' 2: Tantsovshchiki*, 7.
29. Krasovskaia, *Russkii baletnyi teatr vtoroi poloviny XIX veka*, 19.
30. Krasovskaia, *Russkii baletnyi teatr vtoroi poloviny XIX veka*, 483.
31. Krasovskaia, *Russkii baletnyi teatr vtoroi poloviny XIX veka*, 483.
32. Khudekov, *Istoriia tantsev*, 4:122.
33. Khudekov, *Istoriia tantsev*, 4:122. For the detailed discussion of the history of Zucchi's invitation to dance on the imperial stage in St. Petersburg, see Yakovleva, *Sozdateli i zriteli*, 72–81.
34. Stanislavski, *My Life in Art*, 130–31.
35. Krasovskaia, *Russkii baletnyi teatr vtoroi poloviny XIX veka*, 572.
36. Krasovskaia, *Russkii baletnyi teatr nachala XX veka, chast' 1: Khoreography*, 20.
37. Krasovskaia, *Russkii baletnyi teatr nachala XX veka, chast' 1: Khoreography*, 87.
38. Krasovskaia, *Russkii baletnyi teatr nachala XX veka, chast' 1: Khoreography*, 60.
39. Khudekov, *Istoriia tantsev*, 4: 121–22.
40. Krasovskaia, *Russkii baletnyi teatr vtoroi poloviny XIX veka*, 471.
41. With the treasurer share added in the 1880s.
42. Krasovskaia, *Russkii baletnyi teatr vtoroi poloviny XIX veka*, 32.

262 NOTES

43. Krasovskaia, *Russkii baletnyi teatr vtoroi poloviny XIX veka*, 113–14.
44. Pleshcheev, *Nash balet*, 32.
45. Slonimsky, *Mastera baleta*, 220. Recently, the back and forth between Petipa's choreographic choices and Khudekov's criticism has been usefully analyzed in Tikhonenko, "Tvorchestvo Mariusa Petipa v zerkale kritiki Sergeiia Khudekova"; Khudekov is also a recurring character in Nadine Meisner's masterful biography of Petipa.
46. McNeill, *Keeping Together in Time*, 133.
47. I am using the most recent (to my knowledge) translation by Maureen Needham (Needham, "Louis XIV and the Académie Royale de Danse, 1661," 180).
48. McNeill, *Keeping Together in Time*, 137.
49. Eikhenbaum, *Lev Tolstoy*, 149.
50. Cited in Veroli, "Serge Lifar as a Dance Historian," 108.
51. Scholl, *From Petipa to Balanchine*, 3.
52. Pleshcheev, *Sergei Lifar'*, 18. Pleshcheev was not the first to have commented on the propensity of Lifar's dance to mediate the traditional and innovative. See a detailed discussion of Sazonova's conception regarding Lifar's neoclassical choreography in *Prométhée* in Franko, *The Fascist Turn*, 68. Given Balanchine's uncredited input in this production, it is not surprising that the term would later stick to Balanchine's choreographic style.
53. Pleshcheev, *Sergei Lifar'*, 77.
54. Pleshcheev, *Sergei Lifar'*, 11–15.

Chapter 1

1. Skalkovsky, *Stat'i*, 211.
2. "Espece de danse de personnes masquées qui font certaines figures & postures en dansant, & qui representent quelque chose." All citations from *Dictionnaire de l'Académie française* are from the electronic edition available at https://www.dictionnaire-academie.fr/.
3. "Espece de danse de personnes masquées, accompagnée de figures & de postures qui represent quelque sujet particulier."
4. "Danse figurée, & concertée entre plusieurs personnes, qui représente quelque sujet particulier."
5. Noverre, *Lettres*, 340. "The physiognomy is a part of our self that is most useful for expression," Noverre argues in "Letter on Facial Expression and the Inconvenience of Masks," "so why eclipse it with a mask and thus give crude art the upper hand of nature?" (314).
6. "*Ballet pantomime*, ou simplement, *Ballet*, Pièce de théâtre où l'action n'est représentée que par les gestes et les attitudes des danseurs."
7. Arguably, the term "classical" has been imported into French and English by Russian émigré dancers and critics of the first half of the twentieth century.
8. Skalkovsky, *Stat'i*, 211.
9. Cited from the electronic edition available at https://www.merriam-webster.com.
10. Quoted in Glushkovsky, *Vospominaniia*, 165.
11. Beumers, Bocharov, and Robinson, *Alexandr Shiryaev*, 93.
12. Skalkovsky, *Stat'i*, 211.
13. Skalkovsky, *Stat'i*, 211.
14. Noverre, *Lettres*, 333.
15. Noverre, *Lettres*, 333.
16. Noverre, *Lettres*, 333.
17. Noverre, *Lettres*, 340.
18. Noverre, *Lettres*, 221.
19. Noverre, *Lettres*, 262.
20. Noverre, *Lettres*, 208.
21. Skalkovsky, *Stat'i*, 46.
22. Skalkovsky, *Tantsy*, 262.
23. Skalkovsky, *Stat'i*, 46.
24. Quoted in Boglacheva, *Peterburgskii balet*, 185.
25. Garafola and Souritz, "Chernota delaet roscherk v dushe moei," 405. As Sergei Konaev has established (446), the above quotation is an uncredited quotation from Valerian Svetlov's *Modern Ballet* (*Sovremennyi balet*).

NOTES 263

26. Mamontov, "Salambo," 6.
27. Mamontov, "Salambo," 5.
28. Mamontov, "Plastika," 1.
29. Ushakov, "Russkii teatr," 363.
30. Quoted in Krasovskaia, *Russkii baletnyi teatr vtoroi poloviny XIX veka*, 470–72.
31. See Skhlovsky, *Knight's Move*, 73.
32. Cited in Chapman, "Auguste Vestris," 14.
33. Chapman, "Auguste Vestris," 12.
34. Noverre, *Lettres*, 272.
35. Noverre, *Lettres*, 271–72.
36. Blasis, *Manuel*, 80. As a dancer and dance teacher, Blasis was swayed by his older contemporary, the classicist sculptor Antonio Canova, whose works are invoked more than once in Basis's *Manuel*; Canova's image of Terpsichore is featured on its frontispiece. Notably, Canova's studies of movement pivot around various dancing figures—Graces, Venus, and nameless dancers from Greek and Roman times—all captured in motion or in flight. On Canova and dance, see Capitani, "Künste des Raums, Künste der Zeit."
37. Radina, *Matil'da i Iosif Kshesinskie*, 379.
38. Chapman, "Auguste Vestris," 12.
39. Chapman, "Auguste Vestris," 12.
40. Noverre, *Lettres*, 330.
41. Slonimsky, *Klassiki khoreographii*, 83. Blasis: "The public, too, by an excess of indulgent applause or sheer ignorance sometimes swells the rabble of acrobatic dancers, who imagine they have reached the pinnacle of their art" (quoted in Chapman, "Auguste Vestris," 13).
42. Quoted in Chapman, "Auguste Vestris," 12.
43. See Chapman, "Auguste Vestris," 16–17.
44. Sveshnikova, *Peterburgskie sezony Artura Sen-Leona*, 80.
45. Petrov, "Teatral'naia letopis'," 67.
46. Glushkovsky, *Vospominaniia*, 192.
47. Glushkovsky, *Vospominaniia*, 164.
48. Balzac, *Théorie de la démarche*, 55–56.
49. Skalkovsky, *V teatral'nom mire*, 175.
50. Quoted in Sveshnikova, *Peterburgskie sezony Artura Sen-Leona*, 44.
51. Skalkovsky, *V teatral'nom mire*, 239.
52. Petrov, "Teatral'naia letopis'," 68.
53. Vazem, *Zapiski baleriny*, 82.
54. Quoted in Krasovskaia, *Russkii baletnyi teatr vtoroi poloviny XIX veka*, 102.
55. Pleshcheev, *Nash balet*, 266.
56. Skalkovsky, *Stat'i*, 343.
57. Vazem, *Zapiski baleriny*, 206–7.
58. *Bol'shaia Sovetskaia Entsiklopediia*, 41:567.
59. Blok, *Klassicheskii tanets*, 28–29.
60. Khudekov, *Istoriia tantsev*, 4:65.
61. Khudekov, *Istoriia tantsev*, 4:65.
62. Khudekov, *Istoriia tantsev*, 4:130.
63. Khudekov, *Istoriia tantsev*, 4:132.
64. Khudekov, *Istoriia tantsev*, 4:132.
65. Khudekov, *Istoriia tantsev*, 4:133.
66. Khudekov, *Istoriia tantsev*, 4:189.
67. Pleshcheev, *Nash balet*, 268.
68. Vazem, *Zapiski baleriny*, 162.
69. See Skalkovsky, *Stat'i*, 438.
70. Vazem, *Zapiski baleriny*, 207.
71. Nor did they have means to do so. According to Skalkovsky, to be able to rise *sur les pointes*, one had to use expensive Italian footwear; Russian ballet shoes used by coryphées were not suited for pointework. See Skalkovsky, *Stat'i*, 308.
72. Blok, *Klassicheskii tanets*, 29.
73. Blok, *Klassicheskii tanets*, 328.
74. Krasovskaia, *Zapadnoevropeiskii baletnyi teatr*, 101. For a detailed study of the editorial history of Noverre's *Letters*, see Pappacena, "Noverre's *Lettres Sur La Danse*."
75. Noverre, *Lettres*, 333.

264 NOTES

76. Noverre, *Lettres*, 336.
77. Skalkovsky, *Stat'i*, 44.
78. Skalkovsky, *Stat'i*, 44.
79. Pleshcheev, *Nash balet*, 270.
80. Pleshcheev, *Nash balet*, 271–72.
81. Pleshcheev, *Nash balet*, 268.
82. Noverre, *Lettres*, 125.
83. Noverre, *Lettres*, 136.
84. Noverre, *Lettres*, 253.
85. See Fokine, *Memoirs*, 49–50.
86. Rappaport, "Teatral'naia letopis'," 383.
87. Quoted in Sveshnikova, *Peterburgskie sezony Artura Sen-Leona*, 150.
88. Quoted in Boglacheva, *Peterburgskii balet*, 115.
89. *Entsiklopedicheskii slovar'*, IIa (4):800.
90. Nelidova, *Pis'ma o balete*, 50; intially published in 1893 in *Artist* magazine.
91. Krasovskaia, *Russkii baletnyi teatr vtoroi poloviny XIX veka*, 637.
92. Nelidova, *Pis'ma o balete*, 51.
93. Skalkovsky, *Stat'i*, 301.
94. Noverre, *Lettres*, 256.
95. Noverre, *Lettres*, 6, 10.
96. Quoted in Pappacena, "Noverre's *Lettres Sur La Danse*," 18.
97. Noverre, *Lettres*, 156.
98. Pappacena, "Noverre's *Lettres Sur La Danse*," 21.
99. Noverre, *Lettres*, 11.
100. "Mr. Didelot's ballets are filled with vivid imagination and exceptional charm. One of our romantic poets found more Poetry therein than in the entire French literature" (Pushkin, *Polnoe sobranie sochinenii*, 6:191).
101. Noverre, *Lettres*, 153.
102. Garafola, "Introduction," xiii. Current billing practice ("*The Sleeping Beauty* by Tchaikovsky") foregrounds music; at the same time, the balletic text sine qua non remains, of course, choreography (*The Sleeping Beauty* by Petipa); one could also point to an epoch in early twentieth-century ballet in which the physiognomy of a ballet was largely defined by the choice of a set or costume designer.
103. Vazem, *Zapiski baleriny*, 53.
104. Quoted in Boglacheva, *Peterburgskii balet*, 71. When Rappaport was reviewing the ballet, he was apparently unaware that the opera had been written after, not before the ballet, which premiered in Paris in 1827.
105. *Sistematicheskaia rospis'*, 384.
106. Quoted in Ruprecht, "The Romantic Ballet and Its Critics," 178.
107. Skalkovsky, *Stat'i*, 226.
108. Saltykov-Shchedrin, *Sobranie sochinenii*, 7:117.
109. Petipa, *Puteshestvuiashchaia tantsovshchitsa*.
110. Skalkovsky, *V teatral'nom mire*, 125.
111. The dance class setting as a framing device for dancing has been also used in, among others, *A Marriage during the Regency*, *The Wilful Wife*, and *L'Ordre du Roi*.
112. See Wiley, *Tchaikovsky's Ballets*, 40, 326.
113. Quoted in Boglacheva, *Peterburgskii balet*, 175. Technically, the letter was addressed to Sergei Khudekov.
114. Pleshcheev, *Nash balet*, 147.
115. Quoted in Boglacheva, *Peterburgskii balet*, 79.
116. Skalkovsky, *Stat'i*, 259.
117. Vazem, *Zapiski baleriny*, 64.
118. Wiley, *Tchaikovsky's Ballets*, 358.
119. Skalkovsky, *V teatral'nom mire*, 148.
120. Quoted in Boglacheva, *Peterburgskii balet*, 363.
121. Teliakovskii, *Dnevniki, 1901–1903*, 60–61.
122. Teliakovskii, *Dnevniki, 1913–1917*, 531.
123. Fokine, *Memoirs*, 46.
124. Fokine, *Memoirs*, 46. The last sentence translated from the Russian original of Fokine's memoir (Fokin, *Protiv techeniia*, 57).

NOTES 265

125. Fokine, *Memoirs*, 46–47.
126. Fokine, *Memoirs*, 130.
127. Fokine, *Memoirs*, 131.
128. Quoted in Boglacheva, *Peterburgskii balet*, 71.
129. Nekhendzi, *Petipa*, 124.
130. See, for instance, Pavlova extolling the Imperial Theaters for ignoring the cost of productions as well as the box office for the sake of the high quality of art (*Novoe russkoe slovo*, July 28, 1929).
131. See Skalkovsky, *V teatral'nom mire*, 221–22; Khudekov in Wiley, *A Century of Russian Ballet*, 251. Pleshcheev, writing in the late 1890s, expressed hope that ballet would get his second day a week back (Pleshcheev, *Nash balet*, 558).
132. Quoted in Skalkovsky, *V teatral'nom mire*, 221.
133. Skalkovsky, *V teatral'nom mire*, 221.
134. Skalkovsky, *V teatral'nom mire*, 222.
135. Skalkovsky, *Stat'i*, 112.
136. Skalkovsky, *Stat'i*, 101.
137. Skalkovsky, *Stat'i*, 102.
138. Skalkovsky, *Stat'i*, 116.
139. Skalkovsky, *Stat'i*, 33.
140. Pogozhev, *Proekt*, 2:189. See also Pleshcheev, *Nash balet*, 558–59.
141. *Ezhegodnik imperatorskikh teatrov: Sezon 1891–1892 gg.*, 31.
142. *Ezhegodnik imperatorskikh teatrov: Sezon 1891–1892 gg.*, 27–30.
143. Skalkovsky, *V teatral'nom mire*, 33.
144. Skalkovsky, *Stat'i*, 361.
145. Filosofov, "Zametki," 68.
146. For illuminating analyses of Petipa's management of the Imperial ballet, see Garafola, "Russian Ballet in the Age of Petipa"; Garafola, "Introduction"; Meisner, *Marius Petipa*; Yakovleva, *Sozdateli i zriteli*.
147. Beumers, Bocharov, and Robinson, *Alexandr Shiryaev*, 94.
148. See, for instance, an 1897 trade press article hinting at authoritarian methods and even corruption in Petipa's management of the company: F[edorov], "Baletnye nedorazumeniia."
149. Dunaeva, "Zagadochnyi avtograf Mariusa Petipa," 11.
150. Among recent scholarship on the subject, see, for instance, Pouillaude, *Unworking Choreography*, and Pakes, *Choreography Invisible*.
151. Nekhendzi, *Petipa*, 121.
152. Skalkovsky, *Stat'i*, 209.
153. Skalkovsky, *Stat'i*, 229.
154. Pleshcheev, *Nash balet*, 351.
155. Skalkovsky, *Stat'i*, 220.
156. Nelidova, *Pis'ma o balete*, 12.
157. Benois, "Beseda o balete," 100.
158. Benois, "Beseda o balete," 100.
159. Skalkovsky had to explain to his readers in 1893, apropos a ballet performed by "aristocratic amateurs," "Dancing is both easy and difficult. Everybody dances, more or less, but to be able to dance in a correct way, and with lightness and glamour that are so caprivating on stage, one must study for around ten years" (quoted in Pleshcheev, *Nash balet*, 455–56).
160. Chistiakov, *Metodicheskoe rukovodstvo*, 113.
161. Chistiakov, *Metodicheskoe rukovodstvo*, 27.
162. Fokine, *Memoirs*, 52.

Chapter 2

1. Levinson, *Ballet Old and New*, 1.
2. Krasovskaia, *Russkii baletnyi teatr vtoroi poloviny XIX veka*, 13.
3. Krasovskaia, *Russkii baletnyi teatr vtoroi poloviny XIX veka*, 9–10.

266 NOTES

4. Krasovskaia, *Russkii baletnyi teatr vtoroi poloviny XIX veka*, 87–89. Krasovskaia's disparaging portrayal of Saint-Léon has been challenged recently by Alisa Sveshnikova in her compelling monograph on the ballet master (see her critique of Krasovskaia in *Peterburgskie sezony*, 16–18). See also Yakovleva, *Sozdateli i zriteli*, 57. At the same time, it is important to keep in mind that it was Krasovskaia who first used Saltykov-Shchedrin's and Nekrasov's satires in ballet scholarship. Since then, these have been analyzed by Yakovleva (*Sozdateli i zriteli*, 33–45) and in the 2010 dissertation by Rouland, *Choreography in Conversation*.
5. See Sveshnikova, *Peterburgskie sezony*, 11; Yakovleva, *Sozdateli i zriteli*, 40–41.
6. Vazem, *Zapiski baleriny*, 57.
7. Quoted in Sveshnikova, *Peterburgskie sezony*, 138.
8. Saltykov-Shchedrin, *Sobranie sochinenii*, 6:398.
9. Saltykov-Shchedrin, *Sobranie sochinenii*, 6:398.
10. Saltykov-Shchedrin, *Sobranie sochinenii*, 6:402.
11. Saltykov-Shchedrin, *Sobranie sochinenii*, 5:462.
12. Saltykov-Shchedrin, *Sobranie sochinenii*, 5:153, 6:399.
13. Saltykov-Shchedrin, *Sobranie sochinenii*, 7:122.
14. Saltykov-Shchedrin, *Sobranie sochinenii*, 5:435.
15. Saltykov-Shchedrin, *Sobranie sochinenii*, 5:202.
16. More on this in Khitrova, *Lyric Complicity*, 52–54.
17. Saltykov-Shchedrin, *Sobranie sochinenii*, 6:204.
18. Saltykov-Shchedrin, *Sobranie sochinenii*, 6:204.
19. Saltykov-Shchedrin, *Sobranie sochinenii*, 6:204.
20. Saltykov-Shchedrin, *Sobranie sochinenii*, 6:204.
21. Quoted in Saltykov-Shchedrin, *Sobranie sochinenii*, 6:632.
22. Saltykov-Shchedrin, *Sobranie sochinenii*, 6:632.
23. Saltykov-Shchedrin, *Sobranie sochinenii*, 5:34. "By the water" means in the last rows next to a backdrop; on the origin of this phrase, see chapter 3, page 179.
24. Saltykov-Shchedrin, *Sobranie sochinenii*, 6:185, 212.
25. Saltykov-Shchedrin, *Sobranie sochinenii*, 6:200.
26. Saltykov-Shchedrin, *Sobranie sochinenii*, 6:200.
27. Saltykov-Shchedrin, *Sobranie sochinenii*, 5:202.
28. Quoted in Pleshcheev, *Nash balet*, 505.
29. Quoted in Petrov, *Russkaia baletnaia kritika*, 33.
30. Saltykov-Shchedrin, *Sobranie sochinenii*, 5:202.
31. Saltykov-Shchedrin, *Sobranie sochinenii*, 5:202.
32. Krasovskaia, *Russkii baletnyi teatr vtoroi poloviny XIX veka*, 10–14, 673.
33. Saltykov-Shchedrin, *Sobranie sochinenii*, 7:118.
34. Saltykov-Shchedrin, *Sobranie sochinenii*, 7:116.
35. See Meisner, *Marius Petipa*, 117, 122–23.
36. On the traits common to Nekrasov's "Ballet" and Saltykov-Shchedrin's political philosophy, see Makeev, *Nikolai Nekrasov*, 162–64.
37. Sveshnikova, *Peterburgskie sezony*, 175.
38. Nekrasov, *Polnoe sobranie stikhotvorenii*, 2:208. The English translation with minor corrections is from Meisner, *Marius Petipa*, 117–18.
39. Nekrasov, *Polnoe sobranie stikhotvorenii*, 2:209.
40. Talioni, *Deva Dunaiia*, 15.
41. Quoted in Makeev, *Nikolai Nekrasov*, 162.
42. Vazem, *Zapiski baleriny*, 194.
43. Krylov, *Basni*, 213.
44. Nekrasov, *Polnoe sobranie stikhotvorenii*, 2:201.
45. Pleshcheev, *Nash balet*, 41–42, 522, 536, 545, 552.
46. Nekrasov, *Polnoe sobranie stikhotvorenii*, 2:209.
47. Saltykov-Shchedrin, *Sobranie sochinenii*, 5:202.
48. Egorov, *Zhizn' i tvorchestvo Yu. M. Lotmana*, 54.
49. Krasovskaia, *Russkii baletnyi teatr vtoroi poloviny XIX veka*, 673.
50. See Volkov, *Balanchine's Tchaikovsky*, 60.
51. Chistiakov, *Baletoman*, 6 (bold font in the original).
52. Tolstoy, *Resurrection; What Is art?; The Christian Teaching*, 2:141.
53. Tolstoy, *War and Peace*, 404.

NOTES 267

54. Tolstoy, *War and Peace*, 404.
55. Tolstoy, *War and Peace*, 405.
56. Tolstoy, *War and Peace*, 438.
57. Tolstoy, *War and Peace*, 451.
58. Eikhenbaum, *Lev Tolstoy*, 558.
59. Tolstoy, *War and Peace*, 454.
60. Tolstoy, *War and Peace*, 451.
61. Tolstoy, *War and Peace*, 451.
62. Tolstoy, *War and Peace*, 452.
63. Tolstoy, *War and Peace*, 451.
64. Tolstoy, *War and Peace*, 453–54.
65. Tolstoy, *War and Peace*, 453.
66. Tolstoy, *War and Peace*, 453.
67. Tolstoy, *War and Peace*, 450.
68. Saltykov-Shchedrin, *Sobranie sochinenii*, 5:202.
69. Svetlov, "Pis'ma o balete [1915]," 62.
70. On possible prototypes of Tolstoy's fictional opera, see Buckler, *Literary Lorgnette*, 97, 234.
71. Tolstoy, *War and Peace*, 261–62. Tolstoy apparently didn't know that the pointes were not yet around.
72. Tolstoy, *War and Peace*, 501.
73. Tolstoy, *War and Peace*, 501.
74. Tolstoy, *War and Peace*, 501.
75. See Rouland, *Choreography in Conversation*, 82.
76. Tolstoy, *War and Peace*, 498, 499, 500.
77. Tolstoy, *War and Peace*, 502.
78. Tolstoy, *War and Peace*, 498–99.
79. Tolstoy, *War and Peace*, 501. I restore the original French in the dialogue.
80. Shklovsky, "Art as Device," 163.
81. Tolstoi, *Polnoe sobranie sochinenii*, 13:832, 10:329.
82. Tolstoi, *Polnoe sobranie sochinenii*, 13:833.
83. Tolstoi, *Polnoe sobranie sochinenii*, 10:330.
84. Tolstoi, *Polnoe sobranie sochinenii*, 13:833.
85. Tolstoi, *Polnoe sobranie sochinenii*, 10:330.
86. A fragment from Tolstoy's earlier *Childhood* shows that Tolstoy, of course, knew his dancing pas and even knew how to enjoy them: "How sweet Sonichka Valakhin was when she danced a French quadrille opposite me, with the awkward young prince! . . . How naively she made *jeté-assemblé* with her tiny feet! . . . I boldly made *chassé en avant, chassé en arrière, glissade. . . .* All that is standing vividly before my eyes, and I still hear the quadrille from *The Maiden of the Danube*, to the sounds of which it all took place" (*Childhood; Boyhood; Youth*, 96).
87. Lotman, *Structure*, 63–64.
88. Tolstoy, *Childhood; Boyhood; Youth*, 35.
89. Tolstoy, *Childhood; Boyhood; Youth*, 33–34.
90. Tolstoy, *Childhood; Boyhood; Youth*, 34.
91. Tolstoy, *Childhood; Boyhood; Youth*, 35.
92. Saltykov-Shchedrin, *Sobranie sochinenii*, 7:117.
93. Quoted in Shklovsky, "Art as Device," 164.
94. Tolstoy, *Resurrection*, 168.
95. Saltykov-Shchedrin, *Sobranie sochinenii*, 5:202.
96. Skalkovsky, *Stat'i*, 305.
97. Skalkovsky, *Stat'i*, 296.
98. Skalkovsky, *Stat'i*, 327.
99. Skalkovsky, *Stat'i*, 338.
100. Nekrasov, *Polnoe sobranie stikhotvorenii*, 2:195–200. See also Krasovskaia's analysis in her *Russkii baletnyi teatr vtoroi poloviny XIX veka*, 12–13. For a detailed discussion of the real-life prototypes of Nekrasov's "Parable," see Gin, "Geroi i ego prototip," 138–42.
101. Nekrasov, *Polnoe sobranie stikhotvorenii*, 2:200.
102. For more on Vsevolozhsky, see the recent monograph by Gurova, *Vsevolozhsky*, as well as Meisner, *Marius Petipa*, 189–229.
103. Boborykin, "Direktor-Artist," 2.

268 NOTES

104. Boborykin, "Direktor-Artist," 2.
105. See Pogozhev, "Siluety teatral'nogo proshlogo,"122; Gurova, *Vsevolozhsky*, 82, 84.
106. See Khitrova, *Lyric Complicity*, 52–57.
107. Dolgorukov, *Povest' o rozhdenii moem*, 1:58.
108. Dolgorukov, *Povest' o rozhdenii moem*, 1:58.
109. Boborykin, "Direktor-Artist," 2.
110. Quoted in Khitrova, *Lyric Complicity*, 55.
111. Sarcey, *Adolphe Dupuis*, 19.
112. Boborykin, "Direktor-Artist," 2.
113. Sarcey, *Adolphe Dupuis*, 19.
114. Skalkovsky, *Stat'i*, 97.
115. Ch., "K voprosu o reforme frantsuzskogo teatra," 1.
116. Skalkovsky, *Stat'i*, 62. If we believe Petipa's (not always credible) memoirs, this disaster of a revival resulted in a disappointment on the part of the emperor and subsequent removal of Kister. See Petipa, *Russian Ballet Master*, 57–58.
117. Skalkovsky, *Stat'i*, 62.
118. Skalkovsky, *Stat'i*, 148.
119. Noverre, *Lettres*, 375.
120. Gaevsky, "Vremia Vsevolozhskogo," 35.
121. Ponomarev, "I. A. Vsevolozhsky," 32.
122. Ponomarev, "I. A. Vsevolozhsky," 26.
123. Skalkovsky, *Stat'i*, 229.
124. About this and other Hermitage ballets of Petipa and Vsevolozhsky, see Scholl, *From Petipa to Balanchine*, 32–34.
125. Ponomarev, "I. A. Vsevolozhsky," 31.
126. Belova, "Gipnoz Vatto."
127. See a monograph on the subject: Meisel, *Realizations*. Closer to the history of Russian ballet, see Khitrova, "Case of *The Dying Swan*," 223.
128. Krasovskaia, *Russkii baletnyi teatr vtoroi poloviny XIX veka*, 221–22.
129. *Vseobshchii kalendar' na 1879 god*, 413.
130. See Scholl, *From Petipa to Balanchine*, 15.
131. Pogozhev, "Siluety teatral'nogo proshlogo," 64.
132. Quoted in Pogozhev, "Siluety teatral'nogo proshlogo," 75.
133. Pogozhev, "Siluety teatral'nogo proshlogo," 75.
134. Boborykin, "Direktor-Artist," 2.
135. Pogozhev, *Proekt*, 1:17, italics mine.
136. Zimin, "Features," 305.
137. Pleshcheev, *Nash balet*, 319.
138. See Frame, *St. Petersburg Imperial Theaters*, 41.
139. Frame, *St. Petersburg Imperial Theaters*, 40–41.
140. Pogozhev, "Siluety teatral'nogo proshlogo," 223.
141. For a detailed account of the "Italian opera craze" in Russia, see Buckler, *Literary Lorgnette*, 36–56.
142. Nabokov, "Teatral'nyi Peterburg," 246–47.
143. For Khudekov grumbling about it, see Wiley, *Russian Ballet*, 251.
144. Quoted (from the memoirs of playwright Petr Gnedich) in Ippolitov, *Tuzy, damy, valety*, 148.
145. Aleksandr Aleksandrovich, "Dnevnik, 1880 g."
146. Wortman, *Scenarios of Power*, 260–62.
147. Pobedonostsev, "Rech o konstitutsii," 104–5.
148. Wortman, *Scenarios of Power*, 303.
149. Wortman, *Scenarios of Power*, 256.
150. Manfred, *Obrazovanie russko-frantsuzskogo soiuza*, 322.
151. Vazem, *Zapiski baleriny*, 144.
152. For detailed analysis of the creation of *Sleeping Beauty*, see Scholl, *Sleeping Beauty*, 1–29.
153. Quoted in Wiley, *Lev Ivanov*, 135.
154. The story was originated by E. T. A. Hoffmann, but Vsevolozhsky and/or Petipa used its French adaptation by Alexandre Dumas. See Krasovskaia, *Russkii baletnyi teatr vtoroi poloviny XIX veka*, 460. About the libretto's authorship, see Meisner, *Marius Petipa*, 230.
155. For a detailed analysis of *Night and Day*, see Galkin, "Ot baleta s vykhodami do baleta-feerii," and Grutsynova, "Noch i Den."

NOTES 269

156. Petipa, "Libretto baleta 'Noch i Den,'" 293.
157. Petipa, "Libretto baleta 'Noch i Den,'" 293.
158. The idea of using a "church-head" backdrop, this time painted by Aleksandr Golovin, was revived in the 1910 ballet *Firebird*, whose story, too, had to do with the struggle of darkness and light.
159. See Grutsynova, "Noch i Den,'" 323; Skalkovsky, *Stat'i*, 130.
160. Pleshcheev, *Nash balet*, 329.
161. See Galkin, "Ot baleta s vykhodami do baleta-feerii," 300–307.
162. This principle was described in Russian Formalist theory. See Tynianov, *Permanent Evolution*, 267–82.
163. Meisner, *Marius Petipa*, 207.
164. Pleshcheev, *Nash balet*, 331, 329.
165. Singing had been part of the historical-allegorical ballet *The Triumph of Russia, or Russians in Paris* (1814), staged in Petersburg to celebrate the victory over Napoleon; it would remain wedded to dancing in *Zhemchuzhina* (*The Pearl*), a ballet staged to celebrate the coronation of Alexander's successor, Nicholas II, in 1896. See Galkin, "Ot baleta s vykhodami do baleta-feerii," 304; *Ezhegodnik imperatorskikh teatrov: Sezon 1895–96 gg.*, 387.
166. Galkin, "Ot baleta s vykhodami do baleta-feerii," 299.
167. Balanchine and Mason, *101 Stories*, 394.
168. See Morrison, *Bolshoi Confidential*, 132.
169. Pogozhev, "Siluety teatral'nogo proshlogo," 216.
170. See Ippolitov, *Tuzy, damy, valety*, 176–77.
171. Pogozhev, *Ekonomicheskii obzor*, 38–39.
172. Pogozhev, *Ekonomicheskii obzor*, 38–39.
173. Pogozhev, *Ekonomicheskii obzor*, 41–42.
174. Pogozhev, *Ekonomicheskii obzor*, 41–42.
175. For a detailed account of Zucchi's arrival in St. Petersburg, see Fedorchenko, "Virginia Zucchi."
176. Quoted in Boglacheva, *Peterburgskii balet*, 240.
177. Boglacheva, *Peterburgskii balet*, 246.
178. Quoted in Pleshcheev, *Nash balet*, 381.
179. Pleshcheev, *Nash balet*, 381.
180. Khudekov was against the "Italian invasion" in general. See Wiley, *Russian Ballet*, 271.
181. Pleshcheev, *Nash balet*, 351.
182. Benois, *Moi vospominaniia*, 1:312.
183. Quoted in Scholl, *Sleeping Beauty*, 46.
184. Benois, *Moi vospominaniia*, 1:166.
185. Quoted in Boglacheva, "Sud'ba ital'ianskoi Terpsikhory," 27.
186. Quoted in Scholl, *Sleeping Beauty*, 46.
187. Laroche, "P. I. Tchaikovsky," 164.
188. Khudekov, *Istoriia tantsev*, 4:155–56.
189. Quoted in Scholl, *Sleeping Beauty*, 46. (I made a few minor corrections to this translation.)
190. Laroche, "Spiashchaia krasavitsa," 176.
191. Laroche, "Spiashchaia krasavitsa," 176.
192. Dostoevsky, *Polnoe sobranie sochinenii*, 27:192.
193. Quoted in Polunov, *Pobedonostsev*, 61.
194. See Ippolitov, *Tuzy, damy, valety*, 45–46.
195. Pobedonostsev, *Pis'ma*, 2:130.
196. Ippolitov, *Tuzy, damy, valety*, 45–47.
197. Scholl cautions that the diplomatic warmup culminating in the Russo-French rapprochement only really got going after *Sleeping Beauty*'s 1890 premiere (*Sleeping Beauty*, 31–33), but it seems significant that prior to this the Russian emperor was decidedly anti-Prussian and thus, especially after the Franco-Prussian War of the early 1870s, disposed toward all things French. On Alexander's anti-Prussian position, see Wortman, *Scenarios of Power*, 257.
198. Perrault, *Fairy Tales*, 16.
199. On poetry about Dagmar's arrival in Petersburg, see Leibov, *Liricheskii fragment Tiutcheva*, 107.
200. Quoted in Wiley, *Tchaikovsky's Ballets*, 200.
201. Radina, *Matil'da i Iosif Kshesinskie*, 409.
202. Benois, *Moi vospominaniia*, 220.

270 NOTES

203. "The round of balls, breakfasts, and receptions that lasted from New Year's until Lent demonstrated the staying power of the monarchical order in Russia" (Wortman, *Scenarios of Power*, 303).
204. Pokrovsky, *K. P. Pobedonostsev*, 266.
205. Pobedonostsev, *Moskovskii sbornik*, 188.
206. Another Coronation entertainment of 1883, aimed at popular audiences, was an "allegorical procession" called "Spring." See Wortman, *Scenarios of Power*, 278.
207. If we believe Grand Duke Aleksandr Mikhailovich, Pobedonostsev once said to Nicholas II, "I know that the existing regime can only be maintained if the country is held in a frozen state. The slightest wind of spring—and everything will collapse" (Aleksandr Mikhailovich, *Kniga vospominanii*, 147).
208. Translation quoted (with minor revisions) from Cronin, *Disenchanted Wanderer*, 166.
209. Amfiteatrov, *Sobranie sochinenii*, 6:596–97.
210. Ippolitov, *Tuzy, damy, valety*, 21. Less convincing is Ippolitov's alternative suggestion, that the Sleeping Beauty of the caricature was supposed to refer to Alexander III (42).
211. Ippolitov, *Tuzy, damy, valety*, 42.
212. Ippolitov, *Tuzy, damy, valety*, 21.
213. Ippolitov, *Tuzy, damy, valety*, 21, 40–41.
214. Blok, *Polnoe sobranie sochinenii*, 5:45.
215. Frame, *St. Petersburg Imperial Theaters*, 115.
216. In his reading of the ballet, Poel Karp emphasized the vulnerability of the court (*Polveka s baletom*, 2:89–90).
217. Pokrovsky, *K. P. Pobedonostsev*, 48.
218. Tchaikovsky, *Dnevniki*, 249.
219. Nekhendzi, *Petipa*, 132; Petipa, "Libretto baleta 'Noch i Den,'" 292.
220. Pokrovsky, *K. P. Pobedonostsev*, 48.
221. See Chernov, *Voina i "tret'ia sila,"* 23–26.
222. Scholl considers Lopukhov's story apocryphal, on the grounds that the throne scene is absent from Nikolai Sergeev's notation (Scholl, *Sleeping Beauty*, 109). But, as Lopukhov specifies, it was precisely Sergeev who cut it from the ballet after the 1905 Revolution (Lopukhov, *60 let v balete*, 225).
223. Blok, *Polnoe sobranie sochinenii*, 5:176.
224. Nil'sky, *Zakulisnaia khronika*, 250–51.
225. This conviction has been recently challenged in Pouillaude, *Unworking Choreography*, and Pakes, *Choreography Invisible*.
226. Hegel, *Aesthetics*, 2:721–27.
227. Volynsky, *Ballet's Magic Kingdom*, 102–4.
228. Needham, "Louis XIV," 180–81.
229. Louis, *Lettres patentes du Roy*, 5.
230. Fokine, *Memoirs*, 70. Vitale Fokine's translation adjusted in accordance with the original (Fokin, *Protiv techeniia*, 77–78).
231. Fokine, *Memoirs*, 70.
232. Legat, *Story of the Russian School*, 40.
233. Fokine, *Memoirs*, 42.
234. Kirstein, *Movement and Metaphor*, v.
235. Legat, *Story of the Russian School*, 14.
236. Fokine, *Memoirs*, 24.
237. Matthew 1:2–17.
238. Fokin, *Protiv techeniia*, 327.
239. Kirstein, *Movement and Metaphor*, 39.
240. Legat, *Story of the Russian School*, 14.
241. Legat, *Story of the Russian School*, 25.
242. See Lotman and Uspenskii, "Echoes."
243. John 3:8.
244. The value of historical mythoi is not so much in their factual veracity as in their formative power for the teaching. Scholars on the "quest for the historical Jesus," as Albert Schweitzer put it, may ask whether John rendered what Jesus actually said, or perhaps ascribed his own adage to the teacher, but this is not necessarily of interest to the believer. Likewise, the intrinsic benefit the movable dance mythos presents for this study resides mainly in its ideological impact.

NOTES 271

245. See Homans, *Apollo's Angels*, 1–9.
246. McAndrew, "Bournonville," 155.
247. Legat, *Story of the Russian School*, 14.
248. Legat, *Story of the Russian School*, 14–15.
249. See McAndrew, "Bournonville," 155.
250. Auger, *Physiologie du théâtre*, 1:330.
251. Börne, *Briefe aus Paris*, 1:162.
252. Jarrasse, *Deux Corps*, 9–29.
253. Jarrasse, *Deux Corps*, 594.
254. Hugo, *Works*, 3:8–9.
255. Hugo, *Works*, 3:15.
256. Hugo, *Works*, 3:15.
257. Hugo, *Works*, 3:9.
258. Hugo, *Works*, 3:9.
259. Hugo, *Works*, 3:21.
260. Guest, *Gautier on Dance*, 53.
261. These figures come from Inna Skliarevskaia's excellent monograph on what she calls "the Taglioni myth" (*Taglioni*, 27, 33–34).
262. We don't know whether this gesture was part of original choreography of *Giselle*, but, to me, the fact that, regardless of when it was introduced, the gesture remains canonical to this day signals that the *imitatio Christi* was not foreign to the ballet's narrative.
263. Jarrasse, *Deux Corps*, 646, 650–51.
264. Quoted in Kantorowicz, *King's Two Bodies*, 7.
265. Kantorowicz, *King's Two Bodies*, 13.
266. Kantorowicz, *King's Two Bodies*, 302–3.
267. A dramatic actor, Alekseev, who graduated from the Drama Department of the Imperial Theater School in Petersburg, wrote, "[T]he heads of the school didn't care much about educating future actors, but their religious feelings were developed actively and diligently" (quoted in Fomkin, *Dva veka "teatral'noi" tserkvi*, 95). In 1900, one reviewer wrote about the Imperial School in Moscow, only slightly exaggerating: "[T]hey teach two things there: dances and Orthodox faith [*zakon Bozhii*], and so they [its graduates] don't even know how to spell" (quoted in Korshunova, *Mysl' o tantse*, 77). It is worth keeping in mind that in the ballet departments of both imperial theater schools dance was a basis of the curriculum, not an extracurricular activity on top of other schooling.
268. The Imperial School charter gives the number of prayers to be read or sung by the ballet school students daily as six, before and after every meal (Borisoglebskii, *Proshloe baletnogo otdeleniia*, 1:327).
269. See Dunaeva, "Pis'ma T. P. Karsavinoi k V.Ya. Svetlovu," 305. A scanned copy of Gerdt's church marriage certificate is available online at https://forum.vgd.ru/file.php?fid=503601&key= 808045805.
270. See Geva, *Split Seconds*, 290.
271. See Fomkin, *Dva veka "teatral'noi" tserkvi*, 109, 281. According to Aleksei Fomkin, the author of a book-long study of the theater-school church, the volume of religious teaching in the school had been increasing throughout the nineteenth and early twentieth century (82).
272. Skalkovsky, *Stat'i*, 361.
273. Kirstein, *By With To and From*, 126.
274. Sontag, "Dancer and the Dance," 336.
275. Sontag, "Dancer and the Dance," 337.
276. As explained in the now classic anthropologic study of the meaning of "clean" and "unclean" animals in the Bible. See Douglas, *Purity and Danger*, 51–71.

Chapter 3

1. Adler, "Preface," 834.
2. Adler, "Preface," 835.
3. Many memoirists agreed on that. See, for instance, Legat's recollections in Nekhendzi, *Petipa*, 242.

272 NOTES

4. Noverre, *Lettres*, 140.
5. Quoted in Skalkovsky, *Stat'i*, 394.
6. In the mid-nineteenth century, such was the case not only with ballerinas like Elena Andreianova (see Bakhrushin, *Istoriia russkogo baleta*, 101) but also with rank-and-file orchestra musicians (see Ginzburg, *Istoriia violonchel'nogo iskusstva*, 128). Hard to say when the practice ceased, but according to Borisoglebsky's evidence in *Materialy*, as the twentieth century set in, dancers, as a rule, served their twenty years without additions. Still, the ethos of gratitude persisted: as late as the 1910s, each of the recent graduates of the Imperial School was supposed to thank the emperor personally for their education, as, one after another, they were introduced to him. (This follows from the unpublished memoirs of Olga Spessivsteva, held in the Manuscript Section of the Theater Museum in St. Petersburg, f. 81).
7. Khudekov, *Baletnyi mirok*, 13.
8. Fokine, *Memoirs*, 38.
9. Fokine, *Memoirs*, 38.
10. Khudekov, *Baletnyi mirok*, 19. A scanned copy of the novel with a contemporary's indications in pencil of real-life prototypes (including the list of married dancers) is available online: http://lib.sptl.spb.ru/ru/nodes/3646-hudekov-s-n-baletnyy-mirok.
11. Khudekov, *Baletnyi mirok*, 19.
12. Khudekov, *Baletnyi mirok*, 222.
13. See Liamina and Samover, "*Bednyi Joseph*," 314.
14. Khudekov, *Baletnyi mirok*, 125.
15. Khudekov, *Baletnyi mirok*, 223.
16. Boborykin, *Sobranie*, 6:249.
17. Time, *Dorogi iskusstva*, 65.
18. Fokin, *Protiv techeniia*, 54. The epigraph wasn't included in the English translation.
19. Fokin, *Protiv techeniia*, 58.
20. Fokin, *Protiv techeniia*, 55.
21. Fokin, *Protiv techeniia*, 62.
22. Fokin, *Protiv techeniia*, 61.
23. Fokin, *Protiv techeniia*, 61.
24. Tolstoy, *Resurrection; What Is Art?; The Christian Teaching*, 2:141.
25. Tolstoy, *Resurrection; What Is Art?; The Christian Teaching*, 2:136.
26. Tolstoy, *Resurrection; What Is Art?; The Christian Teaching*, 2:143.
27. See Radina, *Matil'da i Iosif Kshesinskie*, 402.
28. Skalkovsky, *Stat'i*, 303.
29. Zozulina and Mironova, *Peterburgskii balet*, 59.
30. Lotman, "Teatr i teatral'nost'," 282.
31. Lotman, "Teatr i teatral'nost'," 281.
32. Quoted in Zakirov, *Osnovy*, 7.
33. See Wiley, *Lev Ivanov*, 128–29.
34. See Meisner, *Marius Petipa*, 33.
35. Skalkovsky, *Stat'i*, 288.
36. Skalkovsky, *Stat'i*, 361.
37. Benois, *Moi vospominaniia*, 1:310.
38. Noverre, *Lettres*, 268.
39. Noverre, *Lettres*, 360–61.
40. See more on this in chapter 1 of this study.
41. Krasovskaia, *Russkii baletnyi teatr vtoroi poloviny XIX veka*, 134.
42. Gautier, *Voyage en Russie*, 1:251.
43. Pleshcheev, *Nash balet*, 405.
44. Pleshcheev, *Nash balet*, 405.
45. See Petrov, *Russkaia baletnaia kritika*, 258.
46. Petrov, *Russkaia baletnaia kritika*, 258.
47. Quoted in Fedorchenko, "'Nestor' russkogo baleta," 39.
48. Fedorchenko, "'Nestor' russkogo baleta," 39.
49. Okunev, *Dnevnik*, 1:144.
50. Radina, *Matil'da i Iosif Kshesinskie*, 386.
51. Preserved among the letters from Fedor Lopukhov to Yuri Slonimsky, Central City Archive of Literature and Arts of Saint-Petersburg. F. 137. Op. 1. No. 266, 78–79.

NOTES 273

52. Radina, *Matil'da i Iosif Kshesinskie*, 414–17.
53. Potemkina, "Pis'ma V. F. Nizhinskogo B. V. Asaf'evu," 481–82.
54. See Souritz, *Soviet Choreographers in the 20s*, 155.
55. Tolstoy, *Resurrection; What Is Art?; The Christian Teaching*, 2:277–78.
56. A telling comparison: Skalkovsky's book on ballet had only one print run; his *On Women: Old and New Thoughts* went through eleven. See Yakovleva, *Sozdateli i zriteli*, 69.
57. Yakovleva, *Sozdateli i zriteli*, 71.
58. Nelidova, *Pis'ma*, iii.
59. Nelidova, *Pis'ma*, 11.
60. For the most recent of many scholarly works on the subject, see Yushkova, "Isadora Duncan's Dance in Russia."
61. Kasatkina, *Aisedora*, 30.
62. Duncan, *Der Tanz*, 25.
63. Kasatkina, *Aisedora*, 54.
64. Fokin, *Protiv techeniia*, 57.
65. Fokin, *Protiv techeniia*, 303.
66. See Beaumont, *Michel Fokine*, 146.
67. See Fokine, *Protiv techeniia*, 396–99. This version of the letter comes with cuts, as does the one Martin printed in the *New York Times* on November 15, 1931. The typescript of Vitale Fokine's English translation with his father's remarks in the margins is preserved at the St. Petersburg Theater Library and available online at http://lib.sptl.spb.ru/ru/nodes/789-pismo-k-martinu-dzhonu-o-vliyanii-aysedory-dunkan.
68. On Stanislavsky's influence on Fokine, see Garafola, *Diaghilev's Ballets Russes*, 19–24.
69. Svetlov, "Pis'ma o balete [September 1911]," 703.
70. Benois, *Khudozhestvennye pis'ma*, 456.
71. Saltykov-Shchedrin, *Sobranie sochinenii*, 7:127.
72. For detailed analyses of the choreography of *Petrushka*, see Garafola, *Diaghilev's Ballets Russes*, 23–30; Scholl, "Fokine's *Petrushka*."
73. Fokine, *Memoirs*, 49.
74. Fokine, *Memoirs*, 49.
75. Fokin, *Protiv techeniia*, 59.
76. Garafola, *Diaghilev's Ballets Russes*, 37.
77. *Zhizn' iskusstva*, April 24, 1923, 10.
78. Teliakovskii, *Dnevniki Direktora Imperatorskikh teatrov, 1909–1913*, 269.
79. Fokin, *Protiv techeniia*, 323.
80. Levinson, "O 'Petrushke' Benois," 58.
81. Bakhtin, *Rabelais and His World*.
82. See Khudekov's account of this tradition in Wiley, *A Century of Russian Ballet*, 254.
83. Garafola, *Diaghilev's Ballets Russes*, 37.
84. Many of his pupils had vivid memories of Cecchetti's cane; see, for instance, Karsavina, *Theatre Street*, 279–81.
85. *Zhizn' iskusstva*, November 26–28, 1920, 3.
86. *Zhizn' iskusstva*, November 26–28, 1920, 3.
87. Fokin, *Protiv techeniia*, 229.
88. Lopukhov, *Khoreograficheskie otkrovennosti*, 66.
89. Nijinska, *Early Memoirs*, 118.
90. Khudekov, *Baletnaia kritika*, 2:125.
91. Khudekov, *Baletnaia kritika*, 2:125.
92. Benois, *Moi vospominaniia*, 2:367.
93. This follows from Nikolai Sergeev's choreographic notation of *The Fairy Doll*, preserved in Houghton Library at Harvard University, MS Thr 245, (13), box 3.
94. Nijinska, *Early Memoirs*, 118.
95. See Konechnyi, "Kakuiu arlekinadu videl Aleksandr Benois?"
96. Khudekov, *Baletnaia kritika*, 2:116.
97. Benois, *Moi vospominaniia*, 1:291. Benois must have misremembered: balagany were moved from Admiralty Boulevard to Field of Mars in 1873 (see notes of L. V. Andreeva and G. G. Pospelov, 2:640–41). See also Kennedy, "Shrovetide Revelry," 55–61.
98. *Rech'*, February 10, 1917.

274 NOTES

99. "One thing I must share with you is that classical dance is heading toward total decline," confessed Christian Johansson in an interview given to the *Petersburg Gazette* in 1902. "Some people, I am told, are trying to bring something called 'decadence' to dance. . . . A 'decadent' revival of *Don Quixote* is what they are planning to show at the *benefis* performance dedicated to [the sixtieth] anniversary [of my teaching career]. . . . From those familiar with the Moscow version of *Don Quixote*, I know that its 'originality' consists in the realism of its staging. The scene in the tavern, they say, is striking in its mass-scale movements. . . . For instance, different dances are performed at the same time. In a word, showiness is put above beauty [*bol'she pogoni za effektami, chem za krasotoi*], and the triumph of realism brings the downfall of classicism." *Peterburgskaia gazeta,* January 1, 1902.
100. Khudekov, *Baletnaia kritika,* 2:125.
101. Benois, *Khudozhestvennye pis'ma,* 462.
102. The complementary relationship between Fokine's political stance and his artistic views are captured in Garafola's chapter aptly titled "The Liberating Aesthetics of Michel Fokine" in *Diaghilev's Ballets Russes,* 8–49.
103. For the most detailed discussion of this ballet, including his literary source, see Morrison, "The Origins of *Daphnis et Chloé.*"
104. Levinson, *Bakst,* 91.
105. For the discussion of these productions, see Medvedkova, *Bakst,* 209–19.
106. Medvedkova, *Bakst,* 213.
107. Teliakovskii, *Dnevniki Direktora Imperatorskikh Teatrov, 1901–1903,* 316.
108. Taruskin, *Stravinsky,* 880–88.
109. Quoted in Vershinina, *Rannie balety Stravinskogo,* 139. For a detailed analysis of the Ballets Russes's turn toward Slavic mythology, see Shevelenko, *Modernizm kak arkhaizm,* 224–63.
110. Blok, *Sobranie sochinenii,* 5:38.
111. See Taruskin, *Stravinsky,* 849.
112. See Garafola, *Diaghilev's Ballets Russes,* 3, 29.
113. See Sargeant, "*Kashchei the Immortal,*" 29–30.
114. Fokine, *Memoirs,* 159.
115. Propp, *Morphology,* 63.
116. Homans, *Apollo's Angels,* 330.
117. Fokine, *Memoirs,* 132.
118. Tolstoy, *Resurrection; What Is Art?; The Christian Teaching,* 2:214–19, 253–54.
119. Levinson, "O novom balete," 18.
120. Skalkovsky, *Stat'i,* 296.
121. The legacies of both critics have enjoyed siginificant attention on the part of ballet scholarship. Volynsky's selected ballet writings have been republished by Galina Dobrovol'skaia in Russian (Volynsky, *Stat'i o balete*) and in the volume translated and edited by Stanley Rabinowitz in English (Volynsky, *Ballet's Magic Kingdom*), followed by a volume dedicated to Volynsky's writings on women, including ballerinas (Rabinowitz, *And Then Came Dance*). Joan Acocella and Lynn Garafola made a notable contribution to ballet scholarship in their volume of Levinson's dance-related essays from the 1920s, *André Levinson on Dance.* Levinson's French ballet writings were more recently analyzed in detail in books by Mark Franco, *The Fascist Turn* and Ilyana Karthas, *When Ballet Became French.*
122. See two recent book-length studies of Volynsky's legacy: Tolstaia, "*Bednyi rytsar'*"; Kotel'nikov, *Russkii Agasfer.*
123. Quoted in Volynsky, *Stat'i,* 16.
124. See Rabinowitz, *And Then Came Dance,* 39–62.
125. Volynsky, *Leonardo da Vinci,* 55–57.
126. Quoted in Kotel'nikov, *Russkii Agasfer,* 195.
127. Rabinowitz, *And Then Came Dance,* 15.
128. Volynsky, *Leonardo da Vinci,* 384.
129. Volynsky, *Leonardo da Vinci,* 383.
130. Volynsky, *Leonardo da Vinci,* 384–85.
131. Volynsky, *Leonardo da Vinci,* 385–88.
132. See Tolstaia, "*Bednyi rytsar',*" 116.
133. Tolstaia, "*Bednyi rytsar',*" 550.
134. Eikhenbaum, "Iz vpechatlenii," 45.

NOTES 275

135. See, for instance, RGALI. F. 95. Op.1. Ed. khr. 24 and 58.
136. See N. G. Legat, "Myslennyi tantsovshchik," RGALI. F. 95. Op. 1. Ed. khr. 1106, 1.
137. *Segodnia* (Riga), August 1, 1926.
138. Svetlov, "Pis'ma o balete [October 1911]," 762.
139. Leshkov, *Parter i kartser*, 237. There may be some truth to this. Volynsky himself recounted how, after he had hinted quite delicately (which was not typical of him) in a review of a Kschessinska performance that it was better to exit the stage in the prime of one's life (she was forty-three at the time), his fellow dance critics greeted him at the theater with the rumor that he had already been fired from the newspaper, which he found entirely plausible (but which turned out to be nothing but a rumor). See Volynsky, "Feia Olen'ego parka," 10–11. Volynsky probably relied on Kschessinska in some way—which is unsurprising, given the enormous power she wielded in anything having to do with ballet, including the press.
140. See *Birzhevye Vedomosti*, March 9, 1915.
141. *Birzhevye Vedomosti*, March 11, 1913.
142. *Birzhevye Vedomosti*, April 6, 1913.
143. Volynsky, *"Kniga velikogo gneva,"* xxx.
144. *Birzhevye Vedomosti*, January 15, 1913.
145. Volynsky, *Ballet's Magic Kingdom*, 103. (I use this translation with minor corrections.)
146. Quoted in Tolstaia, *"Bednyi rytsar,"* 488.
147. Tolstaia, *"Bednyi rytsar,"* 345.
148. See Gollerbakh, "Zhizn' A. L. Volynskogo, 26 (a biographical sketch based on the author's conversations with Volynsky. See also Kotel'nikov, *Russkii Agasfer*, 227–28". Whether we can believe Volynsky here is a serious question. Legat, for instance, recalled that he met Volynsky in 1906 through Kschessinska and that, at the time, he already showed an interest in ballet. See N. G. Legat, "Myslennyi tantsovshchik," RGALI. F. 95. Op. 1. Ed. khr. 1106, 1.
149. Volynsky, *Kniga likovanii*, 32.
150. Volynsky, *Ballet's Magic Kingdom*, 83.
151. Volynsky, *Ballet's Magic Kingdom*, 150.
152. Legat, *The Story of the Russian School*, 39.
153. See Krasovskaia, *Russkii baletnyi teatr nachala XX veka, chast' 1: Khoreography*, 100–106. One glorious exception was Legat's *Doll Fairy* (1903), co-choreographed with his brother Sergei.
154. Legat, "Myslennyi tantsovshchik," 1. Legat's speech, like Spessivstseva's, was published in *Neboskreb*, a "newspaper" whose only issue was exclusively dedicated to Volynsky's celebration. See Tolstaia, *"'Bednyi rytsar,"* 496–97.
155. Legat, "Myslennyi tantsovshchik," 1.
156. Quoted in Tolstaia, *"'Bednyi rytsar,"* 498. In Spessivsteva's archive, her speech is preserved written down in Volynsky's hand. Whether or not it means that he authored it remains an open question.
157. *Birzhevye Vedomosti*, October 31, 1913.
158. See Gaevskii, *Dom Petipa*, 153–54.
159. *Comoedia*, October 17, 1926.
160. Legat, "Myslennyi tantsovshchik," 2.
161. *Comoedia*, October 17, 1926.
162. For a detailed analysis of Judaic sources of Volynsky's ballet theory, see Bing-Heidecker, "The Godseeker."
163. Tolstaia, *"'Bednyi rytsar,"* 383.
164. Quoted in Zozulina, Mironova, *Peterburgskii balet*, 182.
165. Quoted in Tolstaia, *"'Bednyi rytsar,"* 382–83.
166. See Acocella and Garafola, *André Levinson on Dance*, 12–13.
167. For instance, French-Russian ballet critic André Shaikevitch, quoted in Franko, *The Fascist Turn*, 242.
168. True, Volynsky had an affair with a ballerina. A chivalrous myth about Volynsky's unrequited love for Spessivtseva still circulates in ballet literature. However, their correspondence, held in the ballerina's papers at the Theatre Museum in St. Petersburg, suggests that there was in fact a full-fledged affair, if not a civil marriage between the two; one possible reason for their breakup was Spessivtseva's insistent demands that the marriage be officially registered. She may not have known that by the time the two met, Volynsky was already married; the family he had started as a very young man he had left behind in his native city of Zhytomyr, Ukraine.

276 NOTES

In any case, Volynsky could not have been a typical balletomane "sugar daddy" even had he wanted to; he never had enough money.

169. For this dichotomy traced to our day, see Acocella and Garafola, *André Levinson on Dance*, 1–2.

170. Benois, "Beseda o balete," 110–11.

171. Levinson, *Ballet Old and New*, 78. Volynsky scolded those critics who railed against *fouettés* and gymnastics, arguing that *fouettés* were part of the ancient theater. *Birzhevye Vedomosti*, November 4, 1913.

172. Famously, Levinson's push against Dalcroze classes at the Opera led to their abolition in 1925. See Garafola, *Legacies*, 127. Amusingly, none other than Khudekov, who remained in Russia, greeted his colleague on this success. We know it from Pleshcheev's article in *Segodnia*, March 6, 1928. See also Levinson's detailed plan for the classical dance instruction in the school of Opera addressed to the Opera's director, Jacques Rouché, and published in *Comoedia*, February 2, 1925.

173. *Birzhevye Vedomosti*, February 23, 1915. See also his article from March 31 of that year on the results of Fokine's reforms, the mixing of ballet and "everyday drama." As Volynsky saw it, drama did not win out, but it did manage to make a victim of dance: "First of all, in the works of the new master, [dance] has lost its own character of expressive speech of a specific type of artistic content. Ecstasy, purely aesthetic, which is so similar in terms of the tremor of the strings resounding in it to the ecstasy of the moral and the religious," gave way to eroticism: "a prosaic corporeality without lines, without ovals, without singing groupings." In Volynsky's view, Fokine had made a "leap from the ideal to the real," which was a leap in the wrong direction.

174. See Rabinowitz, *And Then Came Dance*, 143–46.

175. Acocella and Garafola, *André Levinson on Dance*, 77.

176. Volynsky, *Ballet's Magic Kingdom*, 5; the title of the article and some quoted passages have been slightly altered to better match the Russian original (Volynsky, *Stat'i o balete*, 41).

177. *Birzhevye Vedomosti*, January 9, 1913.

178. Volynsky, *Stat'i o balete*, 94.

179. *Comoedia*, October 17, 1926.

180. Levinson, *Staryi i novyi balet*, 220.

181. Levinson, *Staryi i novyi balet*, 223–24.

182. Levinson, *Staryi i novyi balet*, 133.

183. Eikhenbaum, "Problemy kinostilistiki," 15.

184. Shklovsky, *Sobranie sochinenii*, 274.

185. Levinson, *Staryi i novyi balet*, 225.

186. Teliakovskii, *Dnevniki, 1903–1906*, 339; Teliakovskii, *Dnevniki, 1913–1917*, 435.

187. *New Yorker*, January 29, 2024; February 16, 19, 2024.

188. Skalkovsky, *Stat'i*, 150.

189. Skalkovsky, *Stat'i*, 361.

190. Teliakovskii, *Vospominaniia*, 432–33.

191. Teliakovskii, *Vospominaniia*, 433.

192. Baedeker, *Russia*, xxix.

193. Teliakovskii, *Vospominaniia*, 434. Lower on the same page, Teliakovsky specifies that, in the long run, the balletomanes won the ten shows back, thus regaining the former balance. For more on the vagaries of ballet marketing before and after the two 1917 revolutions, see Frame, *The St. Petersburg Imperial Theaters*, 66–79.

194. See Svetlov, "Balet," 101.

195. Svetlov, "Balet," 101.

196. Svetlov, "Balet," 101.

197. Svetlov, "Pis'ma o balete [September 1911]," 703. The figure Svetlov chose for his hyperbole was not arbitrary. It was an in-joke reference to Skalkovsky's boast of having seen *Little Humpbacked Horse* for 146 times (Skalkovsky, *V teatral'nom mire*, vii).

198. Svetlov, "Pis'ma o balete [September 1911]," 704.

199. *Birzhevye Vedomosti*, April 16, 1915.

200. *Zhizn' iskusstva*, November 5, 1918.

201. According to the statistical sample furnished by Murray Frame in his *St. Petersburg Imperial Theaters*, 115. Here, in descending order, is the list of the most frequently performed ballets between 1900 and 1911: *The Hump-Backed Horse, The Sleeping Beauty, Swan Lake, La*

NOTES 277

Bayadère, Paquita, Raymonda, The Awakening of Flora, Don Quixote, The Nutcracker, Le Corsaire, La Fille mal gardée, and *Giselle.*

202. *Zhizn' iskusstva,* May 23, 1922.
203. Shklovsky, *Sobranie sochinenii,* 411–12.
204. *Birzhevye Vedomosti,* December 30, 1916. Earlier that year, Volynsky became editor of the literary department in *Birzhevye Vedomosti;* see Aleksandrov, "A. L. Volynsky," 61–64.
205. Kendall, *Balanchine and the Lost Muse,* 147–65.
206. Volkov, *St. Petersburg,* 291, translation slightly amended.
207. See Khitrova, "Balanchin pered ot'iezdom."
208. Volkov, *St. Petersburg,* 291–92.
209. On Skalkovsky and Zucchi, see Yakovleva, *Sozdateli i zriteli,* 72–81. Levinson's involvement in the invitation of Spessivtseva follows from the fragments of Léon Bakst's letters to her, quoted in Bespalova, *Bakst v Parizhe,* 214–24; Shouvaloff, *The Art of* Ballets Russes, 133.
210. Teliakovskii, *Dnevniki, 1909–1913,* 211–12.
211. On ballet's survival under the Bolsheviks, see Ezrahi, *Swans of the Kremlin,* 10–29.
212. Karthas, *When Ballet Became French.*
213. See Acocella and Garafola, *André Levinson on Dance,* 20–21.

Epilogue

1. Levinson's maxim is quoted in Franko, *The Fascist Turn,* 95. One should not confound Levinson's reference to *le ballet russe* with the name of Diaghilev's company; here, Levinson has in mind the Russian ballet in general.
2. For the brief history behind the notations, see Scholl, *Sleeping Beauty,* viii.
3. See Garafola, *Diaghilev's Ballets Russes,* 124.
4. Ballets Russes Souvenir Program, *The Sleeping Princess,* n.p. Just ten years earlier, Diaghilev refused to consider staging *Sleeping Beauty* as it was, in his opinion, a "féerie franco-italienne" (see McDonald, *Diaghilev Observed,* 28).
5. *Times,* July 13, 1929.
6. For Diaghilev, "[t]he [opera-]ballet 'Coq d'Or' is an example of the right direction.... The right combination of spectacle and voice, which will not shock the eye, is yet to be made.... At present the ballet has partly reached that stage.... But the voice is not included. The problem before us is to engage every organ of the body sensible to art, every sense which reacts" (quoted in Roberts, *Nijinsky,* 58).
7. *Vozrozhdenie,* August 29, 1933.
8. See Bespalova, *Bakst v Parizhe,* 214–24; Shouvaloff, *The Art of* Ballets Russes, 133.
9. While it is not an easy task to list all Russian ballet émigrés who became influential teachers, some more than deserve being footnoted: Yulia Sedova, Vera Trefilova, Serafina Astafieva, Nikolai Legat, Pierre Vladimiroff, Felia Doubrovska, Anatole Viltzak, Anatole Oboukhoff, not to mention, of course Nijinska, Fokine, and Balanchine. For recollections of their pupils (and those of countless other Russian ballet teachers), see Meylac, *Behind the Scenes at the Ballets Russes.* Even former ballerinas who weren't teaching full time in studios and ballet schools often engaged in pedagogy otherwise; even Spessivtseva, after twenty years in a mental institution, wrote a ballet technique manual.
10. Haskell, *Balletomania,* 104.
11. Haskell, *Balletomania,* 282.
12. Quoted in Franco, *The Fascist Turn,* 101.

Bibliography

Acocella, Joan, and Lynn Garafola, eds. *André Levinson on Dance: Writings from Paris in the Twenties*. Hanover, NH: Wesleyan University Press, 1991.

Adler, Alfred. "Preface to *The Diary of Vaslav Nijinsky*." *Archives of General Psychiatry* 38, no. 7 (1981): 834–35.

Aleksandr Aleksandrovich. "Dnevnik, 1880 g." *Rossiiskii Arkhiv* 6 (1995): 344–57.

Aleksandr Mikhailovich. *Kniga vospominanii*. Moscow: Sovremennik, 1991.

Aleksandrov, Aleksandr. "A. L. Volynsky—sotrudnik i redaktor gazety 'Birzhevye vedomosti' v 1911–1917 gg. (po arkhivnym materialam)." *Russkaia literatura* 2 (2022): 55–66.

Amfiteatrov, A. V. *Sobranie sochinenii*. 10 vols. Moscow: Intelvak, 2002.

Auger, Hyppolite. *Physiologie du théâtre*. 3 vols. Bruxelles, 1840.

Baedeker. *Handbook for Travellers: Russia, with Teheran, Port Arthur, and Peking*. 1914; New York: Arno Press, 1970.

Bakhrushin, Yuri. *Istoriia russkogo baleta*. Moscow: Sovetskaia Rossia, 1965.

Bakhtin, Mikhail. *Rabelais and His World*. Translated by Helene Iswolsky. Bloomington: Indiana University Press, 1984.

Balanchine, George, and Francis Mason. *101 Stories of the Great Ballets*. New York: Doubleday, 1989.

Ballets Russes Souvenir Program: *The Sleeping Princess*. London: Alhambra Theatre, 1921.

Balzac, Honoré de. *Théorie de la démarche*. Paris: Didier, 1853.

Beaumont, Cyril W. *Michel Fokine and His Ballets*. London: Dance Books, 1996.

Belova, Yulia. "Gipnoz Vatto: 'Tableaux vivants' Ivana Vsevolozhskogo." *Nashe Nasledie* 102 (2012): 132–41.

Benois, Aleksandr. "Beseda o balete." In *Kniga o novom teatre*, 95–122. St. Petersburg: Shipovnik, 1908.

Benois, Aleksandr. *Khudozhestvennye pis'ma 1908–1917, gazeta "Rech'."* Peterburg. Vol. 1: *1908–1910*. St. Petersburg: Sad iskusstv, 2006.

Benois, Aleksandr. *Moi vospominaniia*. 2 vols. Moscow: Nauka, 1990.

Bespalova, Elena. *Bakst v Parizhe*. Moscow: Buksmart, 2016.

Beumers, Birgit, Victor Bocharov, and David Robinson, eds. *Alexandr Shiryaev: Master of Movement*. Pordenone: Le Giornate del Cinema Muto, 2009.

Bing-Heidecker, Liora. "The Godseeker: Akim Volynsky and Ballet as a Jewish Quest." In *Oxford Handbook of Jewishness and Dance*, edited by Naomi M. Jackson, Rebecca Pappas, and Toni Shapiro-Phim, 311–37. Oxford: Oxford University Press, 2022.

Blasis, Carlo. *Manuel complet de la danse: Comprenant la théorie, la pratique et l'histoire de cet art depuis les temps les plus reculés jusqu'à nos jours*. Paris: Roret, 1830.

Blok, Aleksandr. *Polnoe sobranie sochinenii i pisem*. 20 vols. Moscow: Nauka, 1997–.

Blok, Aleksandr. *Sobranie sochinenii*. 8 vols. Moscow: Khudozhestvennaia literatura, 1960–63.

Blok, Liubov'. *Klassicheskii tanets: Istoriia i sovremennost'*. Moscow: Iskusstvo, 1987.

Boborykin, Petr. "Direktor-Artist (Iz lichnykh vospominanii)." *Russkoe slovo*, October 31, 1909, 2.

Boborykin, Petr. *Sobranie romanov, povestei i rasskazov*. 12 vols. St. Petersburg: Marks, 1897.

Boglacheva, I. A., ed. *Peterburgskii balet. Tri veka: khronika. Tom III: 1851–1900*. St. Petersburg: Akademiia russkogo baleta, 2015.

280 BIBLIOGRAPHY

Boglacheva, I. A. "Sud'ba ital'ianskoi Terpsikhory: Virginia Zucchi v zerkale russkoi pressy." In *Zapiski Sankt-peterburgskoi teatral'noi biblioteki*, edited by Pavel Dmitriev, Vol. 8/9, 9–64. St. Petersburg: Baltiiskie sezony, 2010.

Bol'shaia Sovetskaia Entsiklopediia. 51 vols. Moscow: Bol'shaia Sovetskaia Entsiklopediia, 1949–58.

Borisoglebskii, Mikhail. *Proshloe baletnogo otdeleniia peterburgskogo teatral'nogo uchilishcha*. 2 vols. Leningrad, 1938–39.

Börne, Ludwig. *Briefe aus Paris*. 2 vols. Hamburg, 1832.

Buckler, Julie. *The Literary Lorgnette: Attending Opera in Imperial Russia*. Stanford: Stanford University Press, 2000.

Capitani, Lucia. "Künste des Raums, Künste der Zeit: Canova und der Tanz." In *Canova und der Tanz*, edited by Volker Krahn, 96–106. Berlin: Staatliche Museen zu Berlin, 2016.

Ch. "K voprosu o reforme frantsuzskogo teatra." *Sufler*, May 23, 1882.

Chapman, John V. "Auguste Vestris and the Expansion of Technique." *Dance Research Journal* 19, no. 1 (Summer 1987): 11–18.

Chernov, Viktor. *Voina i "tret'ia sila."* Petrograd, 1917.

Chistiakov, A. *Baletoman*. St. Petersburg: Kaspari, 1870.

Chistiakov, A. *Metodicheskoe rukovodstvo k obucheniiu tantsam v sredne-uchebnykh zavedeniiakh*. St. Petersburg, 1893.

Cronin, Glenn. *Disenchanted Wanderer: The Apocalyptic Vision of Konstantin Leontiev*. Ithaca, NY: Cornell University Press, 2021.

Dolgorukov, Ivan. *Povest' o rozhdenii moem…* 2 vols. St. Petersburg: Nauka, 2005.

Dostoevsky, Fedor. *Polnoe sobranie sochinenii*. 30 vols. Moscow: Nauka, 1972–90.

Douglas, Mary. *Purity and Danger: An Analysis of Concepts of Pollution and Taboo*. London: Routledge, 2003.

Dunaeva, Natalia. "Pis'ma T. P. Karsavinoi k V. Ya. Svetlovu." In *Teatral'noe nasledie*, edited by Pavel Dmitriev, Vol. 1, 299–353. St. Petersburg: Giperion, 2005.

Dunaeva, Natalia. "Zagadochnyi avtograf Mariusa Petipa." In *Iz istorii russkogo baleta: Izbrannye siuzhety*, 9–19. St. Petersburg, 2010.

Duncan, Isadora. *Der Tanz der Zukunft (The Dance of the Future): Eine Vorlesung*. Leipzig: Eugen Diederichs, 1903.

Egorov, Boris. *Zhizn' i tvorchestvo Yu. M. Lotmana*. Moscow: Novoe literaturnoe obozrenie, 1999.

Eikhenbaum, Boris. "Iz vpechatlenii." in *Pamiati A. L. Volynskogo*, edited by P. Medvedev, 44–46. Leningrad: Vserossiiskii soiuz pisatelei, 1928.

Eikhenbaum, Boris. *Lev Tolstoy: Issledovaniia. Stat'i*. St. Petersburg: Fakul'tet filologii i istorii iskusstv SPbGU, 2009.

Eikhenbaum, Boris. "Problemy kinostilistiki." In *Poetika kino: Perechityvaiia "Poetiku kino,"* edited by Roza Kopylova, 13–38. St. Petersburg: RIII, 2001.

Entsiklopedicheskii slovar'. 86 vols. St. Petersburg: I. A. Efron, 1891.

Ezhegodnik imperatorskikh teatrov: Sezon 1891–1892 gg. St. Petersburg, 1893.

Ezhegodnik imperatorskikh teatrov: Sezon 1895–96 gg. St. Petersburg, 1897.

Ezrahi, Christina. *Swans of the Kremlin: Ballet and Power in Soviet Russia*. Pittsburgh, PA: University of Pittsburgh Press, 2012.

Fedorchenko, O. A. "'Nestor' russkogo baleta: Nikolai Osipovich Gol'ts, 1800–1880." *Vestnik Akademii Russkogo Baleta im. A. Ya. Vaganovoi* 1 (2018): 33–41.

Fedorchenko, O. A. "Virginia Zucchi v teatre sada M. V. Lentovskogo 'Kin' grust" (leto 1885 goda)." In *Peterburgskie teatry, kotorykh net*, edited by Susanna Filipova, Vol. 1, 7–124. St. Petersburg: Levsha, 2019.

Fedorov, N. F. "Baletnye nedorazumeniia." *Teatr i iskusstvo* 26 (1897): 470–71.

Filosofov, Dmitrii. "Zametki." *Mir iskusstva* 12 (1902): 68.

Fokin, Mikhail. *Protiv techeniia*. Edited by Galina Dobrovol'skaia. Leningrad: Iskusstvo, 1981.

BIBLIOGRAPHY 281

Fokine, Michel. *Memoirs of a Ballet Master*. Translated by Vitale Fokine. Boston: Little, Brown, 1961.

Fomkin, Aleksei. *Dva veka "teatral'noi" tserkvi*. St. Petersburg: Akademiia Russkogo Baleta im. A.Ia. Vaganovoi, 2003.

Frame, Murray. *The St. Petersburg Imperial Theaters: Stage and State in Revolutionary Russia, 1900–1920*. Jefferson, NC: McFarland, 2000.

Franko, Mark. *The Fascist Turn in the Dance of Serge Lifar: Interwar French Ballet and the German Occupation*. New York: Oxford University Press, 2020.

Gaevskii, Vadim. *Dom Petipa*. Moscow: Artist-Rezhiser-Teatr, 2000.

Gaevskii, Vadim. "Vremia Vsevolozhskogo." In *Siluety teatral'nogo proshlogo: I. A. Vsevolozhsky i ego vremia*, edited by Arkadii Ippolitov, 32–36. Moscow: Kuchkovo pole, 2016.

Galkin, Andrei. "Ot baleta s vykhodami do baleta-feerii: Zhanrovaia priroda koronatsionnogo spektaklia 'Noch i Den.'" In *Balety M. I. Petipa v Moskve*, edited by M. K. Leonova and Yu. P. Burlaka, 293–308. Moscow: Progress-traditsiia, 2018.

Garafola, Lynn. *Diaghilev's Ballets Russes*. New York: Oxford University Press, 1989.

Garafola, Lynn. "Introduction." In "The Diaries of Marius Petipa." Special issue of *Studies in Dance History* 3, no. 1 (Spring 1992): i–xxiii.

Garafola, Lynn. *Legacies of Twentieth-Century Dance*. Middletown, CT: Wesleyan University Press, 2005.

Garafola, Lynn. "Russian Ballet in the Age of Petipa." In *The Cambridge Companion to Ballet*, edited by Marion Kant, 151–63. Cambridge: Cambridge University Press, 2007.

Garafola, Lynn, and Elizaveta Souritz. "'Chernota delaet roscherk v dushe moei.' B. F. Nizhinskaia. Dnevnik (1919–1922): Traktat 'Shkola i Teatr Dvizhenii' (1918–1919)." In *Mnemozina: Dokumenty i fakty iz istorii otechestvennogo teatra XX veka*, edited by Vladislav Ivanov Vol. 6, 297–450. Moscow: Indrik, 2014.

Gautier, Théophile. *Voyage en Russie*. 2 vols. Paris: Charpentier, 1867.

Geva, Tamara. *Split Seconds*. New York: Harper and Row, 1972.

Gin, M. M. "Geroi i ego prototip (zametki o stikhakh Nekrasova)." In *Nekrasovskii sbornik*, edited by Nikolai Bel'chikov et al., Vol. 4, 126–44. Leningrad: Nauka, 1967.

Ginzburg, L. *Istoriia violonchel'nogo iskusstva: Kniga vtoraia*. Moscow: Muzgiz, 1957.

Glushkovsky, Adam. *Vospominaniia baletmeistera*. Leningrad: Iskusstvo, 1940.

Gollerbakh, Erik. "Zhizn' A. L. Volynskogo." In *Pamiati A. L. Volynskogo*, edited by P. Medvedev, 11–28. Leningrad: Vserossiiskii soiuz pisatelei, 1928.

Grutsynova, Anna. "Noch i Den': 'Datskaia muzyka' Ludviga Minkusa." In *Balety M. I. Petipa v Moskve*, edited by M. K. Leonova and Yu. P. Burlakas, 309–44. Moscow: Progress-traditsiia, 2018.

Guest, Ivor, ed. *Gautier on Dance*. London: Dance Books, 1986.

Gurova, Ia. Iu. *Ivan Aleksandrovich Vsevolozhsky i ego sovremenniki*. St. Petersburg: Rodnye prostory, 2016.

Haskell, Arnold. *Balletomania: An Updated Version of the Ballet Classic*. London: Penguin Books, 1977.

Hegel, Georg Wilhelm Friedrich. *Aesthetics: Lectures on Fine Art*. 2 vols. Edited by Thomas Malcolm Knox. Oxford: Oxford University Press, 2015.

Hugo, Victor. *The Works*. 24 vols. Translated by Geoge Burnham Ives. Boston: Little, Brown, 1909.

Ippolitov, Arkadii. *Tuzy, damy, valety: Dvor i teatr v karikaturakh I. A. Vsevolozhskogo iz sobraniia V. P. Pogozheva*. Moscow: Kuchkovo pole, 2016.

Jarrasse, Bénédicte. *Les Deux Corps de la danse: Imaginaires et représentations à l'âge romantique*. Pantin: Centre national de la danse, 2017.

Kantorowicz, Ernst. *The King's Two Bodies: A Study in Medieval Political Theology*. Princeton, NJ: Princeton University Press, 2016.

Karp, Poel. *Polveka s baletom*. 2 vols. St. Petersburg: Lema, 2018.

282 BIBLIOGRAPHY

Karsavina, Tamara. *Theatre Street.* London: Dance Books, 1981.

Karthas, Ilyana. *When Ballet Became French: Modern Ballet and the Cultural Politics of France, 1909–1939.* Montreal: McGill-Queen's University Press, 2015.

Kasatkina, T. S., ed. *Aisedora: Gastroli v Rossii.* Moscow: Artist-Rezhiser-Teatr, 1992.

Kendall, Elizabeth. *Balanchine and the Lost Muse: Revolution and the Making of a Choreographer.* New York: Oxford University Press, 2015.

Kennedy, Janet. "Shrovetide Revelry: Alexandre Benois's Contribution to *Petrushka.*" In *Petrushka: Sources and Contexts,* edited by Andrew Wachtel, 51–65. Evanston, IL: Northwestern University Press, 1998.

Khitrova, Daria. "Balanchin pered ot'ezdom (po materialam arkhiva Slonimskogo)." In *Omnia Praeclara Rara,* edited by Natalia Yakovleva, 129–38. St. Petersburg: Chistyi list, 2023.

Khitrova, Daria. *Lyric Complicity: Poetry and Readers in the Golden Age of Russian Literature.* Madison: University of Wisconsin Press, 2019.

Khitrova, Daria. "The Case of *The Dying Swan*: The Performative Evolution of a Dance." In *Russian Performances: Word, Object, Action,* edited by Julie Buckler, Julie Cassiday, and Boris Wolfson, 218–26. Madison: University of Wisconsin Press, 2018.

Khudekov, Sergei. *Baletnaia kritika i proza.* 3 vols. St. Petersburg: Akdemiia russkogo baleta, 2020–22.

Khudekov, Sergei. *Baletnyi mirok: Zhivye kartinki.* St. Petersburg: Peterburgskii listok, 1870.

Khudekov, Sergei. *Istoriia tantsev.* 4 vols. St. Petersburg: Peterbugskaia gazeta, 1913–18.

Kirstein, Lincoln. *Movement and Metaphor: Four Centuries of Ballet.* New York: Praeger, 1970.

Kirstein, Lincoln. *By With To and From: A Lincoln Kirstein Reader.* New York: Farrar, Straus and Giroux, 1991.

Konechnyi, Al'bin. "Kakuiu arlekinadu videl Aleksandr Benois v ploshchadnom balagannom teatre?" *Literaturnyi fakt* 5 (2017): 225–35.

Korshunova, N. A. *Mysl' o tantse: Kritika i moskovskii balet nachala XX veka.* St. Petersburg: Renome, 2019.

Kotel'nikov, V. A. *Russkii Agasfer: Akim Volynsky kak myslitel' i kritik kul'tury.* St. Petersburg: Vladimir Dal', 2023.

Krasovskaia, Vera. *Russkii baletnyi teatr ot vozniknoveniia do serediny XIX veka.* Leningrad: Iskusstvo, 1958.

Krasovskaia, Vera. *Russkii baletnyi teatr vtoroi poloviny XIX veka.* St. Petersburg: Lan' and Planeta Muzyki, 2008.

Krasovskaia, Vera. *Russkii baletnyi teatr nachala XX veka, chast' 1: Khoreography.* St. Petersburg: Lan' and Planeta Muzyki, 2009.

Krasovskaia, Vera. *Russkii baletnyi teatr nachala XX veka, chast' 2: Tantsovshchiki.* St. Petersburg: Lan' and Planeta Muzyki, 2009.

Krasovskaia, Vera. *Zapadnoevropeiskii baletnyi teatr: Ocherki istorii.* Leningrad: Iskusstvo, 1981.

Krylov, Ivan. *Basni.* Moscow: Akademiia Nauk SSSR, 1956.

Laroche, Herman. "P. I. Tchaikovsky, kak dramaticheskii kompozitor." In *Ezhegodnik imperatorskikh teatrov: Sezon 1893–94 gg. Appendix 1,* edited by Anatolii Molchanov, 81–182. St. Petersburg, 1895.

Laroche, Herman. "Spiashchaia krasavitsa." In *Sobranie muzykal'no-kriticheskikh statei,* vol. 2, 171–180. Moscow: Gosudarstvennoe muzykal'noe izdatel'stvo, 1922.

Legat, Nicolas. *The Story of the Russian School.* Translated by Paul Dukes. London: British Continental Press, 1932.

Leibov, Roman. *"Liricheskii fragment" Tiutcheva: Zhanr i kontekst.* Tartu: Tartu Ülikooli Kirjastus, 2000.

Leshkov, Denis. *Parter i kartser: Vospominaniia ofitsera i teatrala.* Edited by T. L. Latypova. Moscow: Molodaia gvardiia, 2004.

Levinson, André. *Bakst: The Story of Leon Bakst's Life.* New York: Brentano, 1922.

Levinson, André. *Ballet Old and New.* Translated by Susan Cook Summer. New York: Dance Horizons, 1982.

BIBLIOGRAPHY 283

Levinson, André. "O novom balete." *Apollon* 9 (1911): 16–29.

Levinson, André. "O 'Petrushke' Benois." *Dom iskusstv* 1 (1921): 57–59.

Levinson, André. *Staryi i novyi balet: Mastera baleta.* St. Petersburg: Planeta muzyki, 2008.

Liamina, Ekaterina, and Natalia Samover. *"Bednyi Joseph": Zhizn' i smert' Iosifa Viel'gorskogo.* Moscow: Yazyki russkoi kul'tury, 1999.

Lieven, Peter. *The Birth of the Ballets-Russes.* New York: Dover, 1973.

Lopukhov, Fedor. *60 let v balete: Vospominaniia i zapiski baletmeistera.* Moscow: Iskusstvo, 1966.

Lopukhov, Fedor. *Khoreograficheskie otkrovennosti.* Moscow: Iskusstvo, 1972.

Lotman, Iurii M., and Boris A. Uspenskii. "Echoes of the Notion 'Moscow as the Third Rome' in Peter the Great's Ideology." in *The Semiotics of Russian Culture,* edited by Ann Shukman, 53–67. Ann Arbor: University of Michigan, 1984.

Lotman, Jurij. *The Structure of the Artistic Text.* Translated by Ronald Vroon. Ann Arbor: University of Michigan, 1977.

Lotman, Yuri. "Teatr i teatral'nost' v stroe kul'tury nachala XIX veka." In *Izbrannye stat'i v trekh tomakh,* vol. 1, 269–86. Tallinn: Aleksandra, 1992.

Louis XIV. *Lettres patentes du roy, pour l'établissement de l'Académie royale de danse en la ville de Paris.* Paris, 1663.

Makeev, Mikhail. *Nikolai Nekrasov: Poet i Predprinimatel'. Ocherki o vzaimodeistvii literatury i ekonomiki.* Moscow: Maks Press, 2009.

McAndrew, Patricia. "Bournonville: Citizen and Artist." *Dance Chronicle* 3, no. 2 (1979): 152–64.

McDonald, Nesta. *Diaghilev Observed by Critics in England and the United States, 1911–1929.* New York: Dance Horizons, 1975.

McNeill, William H. *Keeping Together in Time: Dance and Drill in Human History.* Cambridge, MA: Harvard University Press, 1995.

Mamontov, Sergei. "Salambo." *Russkoe slovo,* January 12, 1910.

Mamontov, Sergei. "Plastika i stsena." *Russkoe slovo,* January 28, 1910.

Manfred, Al'bert. *Obrazovanie russko-frantsuzskogo soiuza.* Moscow: Nauka, 1975.

Meisner, Nadine. *Marius Petipa: The Emperor's Ballet Master.* New York: Oxford University Press, 2019.

Meylac, Michael. *Behind the Scenes at the Ballets Russes: Stories from a Silver Age.* Translated by Rosanna Kelly. London: I. B. Tauris, 2018.

Morrison, Simon. *Bolshoi Confidential: Secrets of the Russian Ballet from the Rule of the Tsars to Today.* New York: Norton, 2016.

Morrison, Simon. "The Origins of *Daphnis et Chloé* (1912)." *19th-Century Music* 28, no. 1 (2004): 50–76.

Nabokov, V. D. "Teatral'nyi Peterburg: Vos'midesiatye gody." In *O tiur'me, Anglii, bol'shevistskom perevorote: Vospominaniia,* 246–48. Moscow: Yurait, 2019.

Needham, Maureen. "Louis XIV and the Académie Royale de Danse, 1661: A Commentary and Translation." *Dance Chronicle* 20, no. 2 (1997): 173–90.

Nekhendzi, A., ed. *Marius Petipa. Materialy, vospominaniia, stat'i.* Leningrad: LGTM, 1971.

Nekrasov, Nikolai. *Polnoe sobranie stikhotvorenii v trekh tomakh.* 3 vols. Leningrad: Sovetskii pisatel', 1967.

Nelidova, Lidiia. *Pis'ma o balete.* Moscow: I. N. Kushnerev, 1894.

Nijinska, Bronislava. *Early Memoirs.* Translated and edited by Irina Nijinska and Jean Rawlinson. Durham, NC: Duke University Press, 1992.

Nil'sky, Aleksandr. *Zakulisnaia khronika, 1856–1894.* St. Petersburg: Obshchestvennaia pol'za, 1900.

Noverre, Jean George. *Lettres sur les arts imitateurs en général, et sur la danse en particulier.* 2 vols. Paris: L. Collin, 1807.

Okunev, N. P. *Dnevnik moskvicha.* 2 vols. Moscow: Voennoe izdatel'stvo, 1997.

Pakes, Anna. *Choreography Invisible: The Disappearing Work of Dance.* Oxford: Oxford University Press, 2020.

284 BIBLIOGRAPHY

Pappacena, Flavia. "Noverre's *Lettres Sur La Danse*: The Inclusion of Dance among the Imitative Arts." *Acting Archives Essays Review Supplement* 9 (April 2011): 1–25.

Perrault, Charles. *Fairy Tales*. Translated by A. E. Johnson. New York: Dover, 1969.

Petipa, Marius. "Libretto baleta 'Noch i Den.'" In *Balety M. I. Petipa v Moskve*, edited by M. K. Leonova and Yu. P. Burlaka, 285–92. Moscow: Progress-traditsiia, 2018.

Petipa, Marius. *Puteshestvuiushchaia tantsovshchitsa*. St. Petersburg, 1865.

Petipa, Marius. *Russian Ballet Master: The Memoirs*. Translated by Helen Whittaker. New York: Macmillan, 1958.

Petrov, Oleg. *Russkaia baletnaia kritika vtoroi poloviny XIX veka: Peterburg*. Ekaterinburg: Sfera, 1995.

Petrov, Vasil'ko. "Teatral'naia letopis." *Teatral'nyi i muzykalnyi vestnik* 8 (1859): 67–69.

Pleshcheev, Aleksandr. *Nash balet (1637–1899): Balet v Rossii do nachala XIX stoletiia i balet v Sankt-Peterburge do 1899 goda.* St. Petersburg: Planeta Muzyki, 2009.

Pleshcheev, Aleksandr. *Sergei Lifar': Ot starogo k novomu*. Paris: Dom Knigi, 1938.

Pobedonostsev, Konstantin. *Moskovskii sbornik*. Moscow: Sinodal'naia tipografiia, 1896.

Pobedonostsev, Konstantin. *Pis'ma k Aleksandru III*. 2 vols. Moscow: Novaia Moskva, 1926.

Pobedonostsev, Konstantin. "Rech o konstitutsii." *Russkii Arkhiv* 5 (1907): 103–5.

Pogozhev, Vladimir. *Ekonomicheskii obzor desiatiletiia Imperatorskikh S.-Peterburgskikh teatrov posle reformy 1882 g.* St. Petersburg, 1892.

Pogozhev, Vladimir. *Proekt zakonopolozhenii ob imperatorskikh teatrakh.* 3 vols. St. Petersburg, 1900.

Pogozhev, Vladimir. "Siluety teatral'nogo proshlogo." In *Siluety teatral'nogo proshlogo: I. A. Vsevolozhsky i ego vremia*, edited by Arkadii Ippolitov, 119–238. Moscow: Kuchkovo pole, 2016.

Pokrovsky, Mikhail, ed. *K. P. Pobedonostsev i ego korrespondenty: Pis'ma i zapiski*. Vol. 1. Moscow: Gosudarstvennoe izdatel'stvo, 1923.

Polunov, Aleksandr. *Pobedonostsev: Russkii Torkvemada*. Moscow: Molodaia gvardiia, 2017.

Ponomarev, E. "I. A. Vsevolozhsky (Ocherk ego khudozhestvennoi deiatel'nosti)." In *Ezhegodnik imperatorskikh teatrov: Sezon 1899–1900 gg.*, edited by Sergei Diaghilev, 25–32. St. Petersburg, 1900.

Potemkina, S. B. "'. . . Smeias' nazyval sebia baletmeisterom': Pis'ma V. F. Nizhinskogo B. V. Asaf'evu." In *Mnemozina: Dokumenty i facty iz istorii otechestvennogo teatra XX veka*, edited by Vladislav Ivanov, Vol. 6, 481–88. Moscow: Indrik, 2014.

Pouillaude, Frédéric. *Unworking Choreography: The Notion of the Work in Dance*. Oxford: Oxford University Press, 2017.

Propp, Vladimir. *Morphology of the Folk Tale*. Translated by Laurence Scott. Austin: University of Texas Press, 2008.

Pushkin, A. S. *Polnoe sobranie sochinenii*. 17 vols. Leningrad: AN SSSR, 1937–59.

Rabinowitz, Stanley. *And Then Came Dance: The Women Who Led Volynsky to Ballet's Maguc Kingdom*. Oxford: Oxford University Press, 2019.

Radina, M. P., ed. *Matil'da i Iosif Kshesinskie: Dnevniki, pis'ma, vospominaniia*. Moscow: GTsTM im. Bakhrushina, 2018.

Rappaport, Mavrikii. "Teatral'naia letopis." *Teatral'nyi i muzykalnyi vestnik* 40 (1859): 382–84.

Roberts, Mary Fanton. "Nijinsky, the Great Russian: His Art and His Personality." *The Craftsman* 31, no. 1 (October 1916): 52–64.

Rouland, Natalie Joan. "Choreography in Conversation: The Imperial Ballet and Russian Literature, 1851–1905." PhD diss., Stanford University, 2010.

Ruprecht, Lucia. "The Romantic Ballet and Its Critics: Dance Goes Public." In *The Cambridge Companion to Ballet*, edited by Marion Kant, 175–83. London: Cambridge University Press, 2007.

Saltykov-Shchedrin, M. E. *Sobranie sochinenii v 20 tomakh*. Moscow: Khudozhestvennaia literatura, 1965–77.

BIBLIOGRAPHY 285

Sarcey, Francisque. "Adolphe Dupuis." In *Comédiens et comédiennes*, 1–24. Paris: Librairie des bibliophiles, 1884 (separate pagination).

Sargeant, Lynn. "*Kashchei the Immortal*: Liberal Politics, Cultural Memory, and the Rimsky-Korsakov Scandal of 1905." *Russian Review* 64 (January 2005): 22–43.

Scholl, Tim. "Fokine's *Petrushka*." In *Petrushka: Sources and Contexts*, edited by Andrew Wachtel, 41–50. Evanston, IL: Northwestern University Press, 1998.

Scholl, Tim. *From Petipa to Balanchine: Classical Revival and the Modernization of Ballet*. London: Routledge, 1994.

Scholl, Tim. *Sleeping Beauty, a Legend in Progress*. New Haven, CT: Yale University Press, 2004.

Shevelenko, Irina. *Modernizm kak arkhaizm: Natsionalism i poiski modernistskoi estetiki v Rossii*. Moscow: Novoe literaturnoe obozrenie, 2017.

Shklovsky, Viktor. "Art, as Device." Translated by Alexandra Berlina. *Poetics Today* 36 (2015): 151–74.

Shklovsky, Viktor. *Knight's Move*. Translated by Richard Sheldon. Normal, IL: Dalkey Archive Press, 2005.

Shklovsky, Viktor. *Sobranie sochinenii*. Vol. 1: *Revolutsiia*. Edited by Ilya Kalinin. Moscow: Novoe literaturnoe obozrenie, 2018.

Shouvaloff, Alexander. *The Art of Ballets Russes: The Serge Lifar Collection of Theater Designs, Costumes, and Paintings at the Wadsworth Atheneum, Hartford, Connecticut*. New Haven, CT: Yale University Press, 1997.

Sistematicheskaia ropspis' knigam, prodaiushchimsia v knizhnom magazine Aleksandra Il'icha Glazunova v Moskve. St. Petersburg: I. I. Glazunov, 1867.

Skalkovsky, Konstantin. *Stat'i o balete, 1868–1905*. Edited by Natalia Dunaeva. St. Petersburg: Chistyi list, 2012.

[Skalkovsky, Konstantin]. *Tantsy, balet, ikh istoriia i mesto v riadu iziashchnykh iskusstv*. St. Petesrburg: A. S. Suvorin, 1886.

Skalkovsky, Konstantin. *V teatral'nom mire: Nabliudeniia, vospominaniia i rassuzhdeniia*. St. Petersburg: A. S. Suvorin, 1899.

Skliarevskaia, Inna. *Taglioni: Fenomen i mif*. Moscow: Novoe literaturnoe obozrenie, 2017.

Slonimsky, Iurii. *Klassiki khoreographii*. Moscow: Iskusstvo, 1937.

Slonimsky, Yuri. *Mastera baleta: K. Didlo, Zh. Perro, A. Sen-Leon, L. Ivanov, M. Petipa*. Moscow: Iskusstvo, 1937.

Sontag, Susan. "Dancer and the Dance." In *Reading Dance*, edited by Robert Gottlieb, 334–39. New York: Pantheon Books, 2008.

Souritz, Elizabeth. *Soviet Choreographers in the 20s*. Translated by Lynn Visson. Edited by Sally Banes. Durham, NC: Duke University Press, 1990.

Stanislavski, Constantin. *My Life in Art*. Translated by J. J. Robbins. [New York]: Theatre Arts Books, 1948.

Sveshnikova, Alisa. *Peterburgskie sezony Artura Sen-Leona, 1859–1870*. St. Petersburg: Baltiiskie sezony, 2008.

Svetlov, Valerian. "Balet." In *Ezhegodnik imperatorskikh teatrov: 1912*, 24, 99–105. St. Petersburg, 1912.

Svetlov, Valerian. "Pis'ma o balete [September 1911]." *Teatr i iskusstvo* 38 (1911): 703–5.

Svetlov, Valerian. "Pis'ma o balete [October 1911]." *Teatr i iskusstvo* 41 (1911): 762–64.

Svetlov, Valerian. "Pis'ma o balete [1915]." *Teatr i iskusstvo* 4 (1915): 61–63.

Talioni, Filippo. *Deva Dunaiia: Pantomimnyi balet v dvukh deistviiakh i chetyrekh kartinakh*. St. Petersburg: Glazunov, 1837.

Taruskin, Richard. *Stravinsky and the Russian Traditions: A Biography of the Works through Mavra*. Berkeley: University of California Press, 1996.

Tchaikovsky, P. I. *Dnevniki*. Moscow: Gosudarstvennoe izdatel'stvo, 1923.

Teliakovskii, Vladimir. *Dnevniki Direktora Imperatorskikh Teatrov, 1901–1903. Sankt-Peterburg*. Moscow: Artist-Rezhiser-Teatr, 2002.

286 BIBLIOGRAPHY

Teliakovskii, Vladimir. *Dnevniki Direktora Imperatorskikh Teatrov, 1903–1906. Sankt-Peterburg.* Moscow: Artist-Rezhiser-Teatr, 2006.

Teliakovskii, Vladimir. *Dnevniki Direktora Imperatorskikh teatrov, 1909–1913. Sankt-Peterburg.* Moscow: Artist-Rezhiser-Teatr, 2016.

Teliakovskii, Vladimir. *Dnevniki Direktora Imperatorskikh Teatrov, 1913–1917. Sankt-Peterburg.* Moscow: Artist-Rezhiser-Teatr, 2017.

Teliakovskii, Vladimir. *Vospominaniia.* Leningrad: Iskusstvo, 1965.

Tikhonenko, Snezhana. "Tvorchestvo Mariusa Petipa v zerkale kritiki Sergeiia Khudekova (po materialam periodicheskikh izdanii XIX veka)." *Kul'tura i iskusstvo* 10 (2018): 64–72.

Time, Elizaveta. *Dorogi iskusstva.* Moscow: VTO, 1965.

Tolstaia, Elena. *"Bednyi rytsar'": Intellektual'noe stranstvie Akima Volynskogo.* Moscow: Mosty kul'tury, 2013.

Tolstoi, Lev. *Polnoe sobranie sochinenii.* 90 vols. Moscow: Khudozhestvennaia literatura, 1935–58.

Tolstoy, Leo. *Childhood; Boyhood; Youth; The Incursion.* Translated by Leo Wiener. London: J. M. Dent, 1905.

Tolstoy, Leo. *Resurrection.* Translated by Aline P. Delano. New York: T. Y. Crowell, 1911.

Tolstoy, Leo. *Resurrection; What Is art?; The Christian Teaching.* Translated by Leo Wiener. 2 vols. London: J. M. Dent, 1905.

Tolstoy, Leo. *War and Peace.* Translated by Aylmer Maude and Louise Maude. Norton Critical Edition. New York: W. W. Norton, 1996.

U[shakov], V[asilii]. "Russkii teatr." *Moskovskii telegraf* 28, no. 15 (1829): 357–72.

Vazem, Ekaterina. *Zapiski baleriny Sankt-Peterburgskogo Bol'shogo teatra, 1867–1884.* Moscow: Iskusstvo, 1937.

Veroli, Patrizia. "Serge Lifar as a Dance Historian and the Myth of Russian Dance in *Zarubezhnaia Rossiia* (Russia Abroad) 1930–1940." *Dance Research* 32, no. 2 (2014): 105–43.

Vershinina, Irina. *Rannie balety Stravinskogo.* Moscow: Nauka, 1967.

Volkov, Solomon. *Balanchine's Tchaikovsky: Interviews with George Balanchine.* Translated by Antonina V. Bouis. New York: Simon and Schuster, 1985.

Volkov, Solomon. *St. Petersburg: A Cultural History.* Translated by Antonina V. Bouis. New York: Simon and Schuster, 1995.

Volynsky, Akim. *Ballet's Magic Kingdom: Selected Writings on Dance in Russia, 1911–1925.* Edited and translated by Stanley Rabinowitz. New Haven, CT: Yale University Press, 2008.

Volynsky, Akim. "Feia Olen'ego parka." *Zhizn' iskusstva* 34 (1924): 9–11.

Volynsky, Akim. *Kniga likovanii: Azbuka klassicheskogo tantsa.* St. Petersburg: Planeta muzyki, 2008.

Volynsky, Akim. *"Kniga velikogo gneva": Kriticheskie stat'i.—Zametki.—Polemika.* St. Petersburg: Trud, 1904.

Volynsky, Akim. *Leonardo da Vinci.* St. Petersburg: A. F. Marks, 1899.

Volynsky, Akim. *Stat'i o balete.* Edited by Galina Dobrovol'skaia. St. Petersburg: Giperion, 2002.

Vseobshchii kalendar' na 1879 god. St. Petersburg: Goppe, 1879.

Wiley, Roland John, ed. *A Century of Russian Ballet: Documents and Eyewitness Accounts, 1810–1910.* Oxford: Clarendon Press, 1990.

Wiley, Roland John. *The Life and Ballets of Lev Ivanov: Choreographer of The Nutcracker and Swan Lake.* Oxford: Clarendon Press, 1997.

Wiley, Roland John. *Tchaikovsky's Ballets: Swan Lake, Sleeping Beauty, Nutcracker.* Oxford: Clarendon Press, 1985.

Wortman, Richard. *Scenarios of Power: Myth and Ceremony in Russian Monarchy from Peter the Great to the Abdication of Nicholas II.* Princeton, NJ: Princeton University Press, 2006.

Yakovleva, Yulia. *Sozdateli i zriteli: Russkie balety epokhi shedevrov.* Moscow: Novoe literaturnoe obozrenie, 2017.

Yushkova, Elena. "Isadora Duncan's Dance in Russia: First Impressions and Discussions, 1904–1909." *Journal of Russian American Studies* 2, no. 1 (2018): 15–43.

BIBLIOGRAPHY   287

Zakirov, Aidar. *Osnovy stsenicheskogo fekhtovaniia.* Moscow: VGIK, 2013.
Zimin, I. V. "Features of Finacing of Imperial Theatres in the Context of the Formation of the Budget of the Imperial Court (the Second Half of the XVIII–Early XX Centuries)." In *Marius Petipa: Empire of Ballet, from Rise to Decline,* edited by T. T. Burlakova and Yu. V. Domanskii, 301–9. Moscow: GTsTM im. Bakhrushina, 2021. (Russian original on 291–300).
Zozulina, N. N., and V. M. Mironova, eds. *Peterburgskii balet. Tri veka: Khronika.* Vol. 4: *1901–1950.* St. Petersburg: Akademiia russkogo baleta, 2015.

Index

For the benefit of digital users, indexed terms that span two pages (e.g., 52–53) may, on occasion, appear on only one of those pages.

Figures are indicated by an italic *f* following the page number.

abolition of serfdom, 79–86
Académie Royale de Danse, 31
Acis et Galatée, 28
Adler, Alfred, 177–78
Adlerberg, Aleksandr, 123
Adventures of Peleus, 28–29
Aksakov, Ivan, 84–86
Alexander I, 185–86
Alexander II, 82, 132
  assassination of, 123, 138, 150–52
Alexander III, 111, 123, 126–28, 129–30, 131, 133, 139, 142–44, 147–48, 150–51
Alexandrinsky Theater, 66–67, 111, 112–13, 219–20
Anchor (Iakor'), 49
Apollo and Daphne, 28, 53

Bakerkina, Nadezhda, 109, 225
Bakst, Léon, 209*f*, 210, 211, 212*f*, 213*f*, 214*f*, 219–20, 256, 257–58
balagan, 211–16
Balaganchik, 211–14
Balanchine, George, 20, 62, 72–73, 132–33, 250–55, 256, 259
baletnye (ballet professionals), 153, 158, 161, 168–69, 173, 196–97, 223, 247, 254, 256, 258
ballet
  linguistic policy, 125–26
  military, 16–17, 20, 35–36, 74, 75, 95, 185–87, 188, 245
  politics of, 82–86, 139, 150–52, 159–61, 162–63, 164, 165, 170–71, 175–76, 219–20, 222–23
  religion, 234–39, 258–59
  Christianity, 168–70, 171, 172–76, 258
  paganism, 220–21, 222
  Romantic turn, 166–68, 171–72, 217
  as Russian, 208, 211, 215–16, 250–52, 254–55, 256–57, 258–59
  as verbal art, 131–32, 197–98, 208, 237–38, 242–43, 250, 254
ballet d'action, 48–50, 51, 56–57, 131, 224
ballet lore, 2–3, 5, 9, 10, 15–16, 21, 22, 32–33, 38, 44–45, 56, 77, 86–87, 95, 108, 122, 127–28, 132–41, 152–58, 164–65, 175, 181, 241, 247, 250, 252, 254

balletomanes, 3–5, 14–15, 17, 19, 35, 39–40, 42–43, 44, 46, 64–65, 67, 68, 73–74, 86–87, 95, 109, 130–31, 161, 196–97, 246–48
ballets-féeries, 8–9, 20, 122, 128–29, 130–32, 133–35, 137–38, 141, 142–44, 148, 150–51. *See also Sleeping Beauty*
Ballets Russes, 23, 196–97, 207, 216, 221, 247, 248–49, 256
Bathyllus and Pylades, 1, 7, 8, 16, 17
Bayadère, La, 55, 56, 248
Beauchamp, Pierre, 24
Beaumont, Cyril, 19
Bekefi, Alfred, 217–18
belle danse, 163–64, 166, 167, 172. *See also* Classical dance
Bells of Corneville, 147*f*, 147–48
benefis, 67, 117, 247
Benois, Aleksandr, 10–11, 73–74, 118, 137, 142–44, 186–87, 196–97, 200*f*, 202*f*, 203*f*, 204*f*, 211–16, 215*f*, 217, 221, 241
Bezobrazov, Nikolai, 3, 6, 32, 135, 137
Blasis, Carlo, 24, 33, 34–35, 54, 118, 154–55
Blok, Aleksandr, 148–50, 152, 211–14, 221–22
Blok, Liubov, 31, 41–42, 45–46
Bluebeard, 68, 109
Boborykin, Petr, 6, 108–9, 111, 112–13, 114, 117, 123–24, 139–40, 182–83
Bocharov, Ivan, 49
Bolshoi Theater, 30, 102–3
Borkh, Aleksandr, 78, 110
Bournonville, Antoine, 40, 159–60, 163, 165
Bournonville, August, 40, 56, 57, 159–60, 163
Brianza, Carlotta, 6–7, 43, 50
British Ballet, 19
Butterfly, 44

Camargo, Marie, 17, 120
Cecchetti, Enrico, 6–7, 44–45, 205*f*, 206*f*, 207
Cellarius, Heinrich, 54
Chapman, John V., 33–34, 35
character dance, 25–26, 27–29, 39–40, 47, 55, 65, 90–91, 100, 132, 167, 171–72, 217–18, 251, 256–57
Chistiakov, Aleksandr, 95–96, 101–2, 130

290 INDEX

classical ballet, 16–17, 18, 21, 28–30, 41, 42, 45, 57, 60, 67, 153–57, 196–97, 234–35, 239, 244–46, 249–52, 253, 257–58, 259. *See also* classical dance
classical dance, 11, 19, 23–25, 30–31, 39, 40, 43, 57, 78–79, 153–58, 160–61, 165, 171–72, 173–74, 175–76, 186–87, 208, 216–18, 240–41, 242, 243–44, 249, 250–52, 253, 254–55, 256–57, 258. *See also* classical ballet
Conservatoire, Le, 56
Coppélia, 23, 210–11
Corsaire, Le, 44
Cyprian Statue, or Pygmalion, 38, 133
czárdás, 27–28, 90–91, 217–18

Dal', Vladimir, 87–89
"danceless ballet," 257
danse d'école. See classical dance
danse en action, 48–50, 51, 56–57, 131, 224
danse noble, 33, 35–36, 40, 44, 47, 155, 161, 162, 163, 165, 217. *See also* Classical dance
Dauberval, Jean, 70–71
defamiliarization. *See* enstrangement
Dell'Era, Antonietta, 43, 50
de Valois, Ninette, 19
Diaghilev, Sergei, 19, 20, 61, 68, 118, 175–76, 222–23, 247, 249, 254–55, 256–58
Didelot, Charles-Louis, 10, 19, 24–25, 28, 29, 35–36, 37, 40, 52, 53, 57, 62–63, 65, 68, 189–90
Directorate of Imperial Theaters, 3, 13–15, 37, 39–40, 60, 62–64, 66, 67, 69, 70, 71–72, 73, 109–10, 111, 116–17, 123–24, 125, 128–29, 133–35, 137–38, 181, 185, 188–89, 191, 246, 253–54
Director of Imperial Theaters. *See* Directorate of Imperial Theaters
Dolgorukov, Ivan, 112, 113
Dolin, Anton, 19
D'Or, Henrietta, 44
Dostoevsky, Fedor, 81, 82, 157, 229–30, 239
drambalet, 11
Drigo, Riccardo, 60, 61, 62
Duncan, Isadora, 192, 193–94, 219–20, 243, 250–55
Duport, Louis, 32–33, 98, 102–3, 104
Dupuis, Adolphe, 112–14

Eikhenbaum, Boris, 17–18, 99, 230, 244
Elsler, Fanny, 68
emancipation of the serfs. *See* abolition of serfdom
enstrangement, 104–8, 196–97
Esmeralda, 8–9, 67–68, 135, 138, 246
Eugene Onegin, 92–93
Evreinov, Nikolai, 241
Excelsior, 131

fairy ballets. *See* ballets-féeries
Fairy Doll (Feia kukol), 209f, 210–11, 212f, 213f, 214f, 215–16

Fantasy ballets. *See* ballets-féeries
Fatherland's Son (Syn otechestva), 49
Ferraris, Amalia, 38, 43
Fiametta, 49
Fille mal gardée, La, 70–72, 135, 246
Filosofov, Dmitrii, 68
Firebird, 221, 222–23, 224
Fokine, Michel, 10–11, 16–17, 20, 39, 45–46, 50, 60–62, 76, 79, 118, 157–58, 159–60, 175–76, 180, 183–84, 192, 194–96, 197–206, 208, 215–26, 232–33, 235–36, 239, 248, 254–55, 256, 257
Fossano. *See* Rinaldi, Antonio

Garrick, David, 47
Gautier, Théophile, 37–38, 54, 55, 168–69, 188
Gedeonov, Stepan, 109, 117
Gerdt, Pavel, 6–7, 68, 72, 116, 121f, 186–87
Gippius, Zinaida, 227
Giselle, 27–28, 54, 55, 67–68, 167, 188, 246, 248, 257–58, 259
Glushkovsky, Adam, 35–36
Gogol, Nikolai, 82
Golden Fish, 54–55, 86–87, 95, 106
Gol'ts, Nikolai, 188–89
Gorsky, Aleksandr, 29, 186, 215–16
Grand ballet, 67–68, 128–29, 185, 186, 208
Grantzow, Adèle, 38–39
Graziella, 29, 109

Hermitage Theater, 118–20
Hertel, Peter Ludwig, 70–71, 72
Hugo, Victor, 167–70

Imperial Ballet, 63–64, 69, 185, 217–18, 235–36, 250
Imperial Russian Opera, 125
Imperial Theaters. *See* Directorate of Imperial Theaters
Imperial Theater School, 35, 39, 112, 157, 172, 173, 183–84, 185, 186, 190, 217–18, 248
Ippolitov, Arkadii, 145–48
Istomina, Avdotia, 57
Ivanov, Lev, 6, 12, 13–14, 37, 72

Jason et Médée, 53
Johansson, Anna, 163
Johansson, Christian, 40, 86–87, 157–58, 159–60, 161, 163

Kantorowicz, Ernst, 170–71, 172
Karsavina, Tamara, 183, 201f, 239, 257
Khudekov, Sergei, 3–5, 6–7, 12–13, 16–17, 42–44, 46, 56, 78, 87, 95, 137–38, 142–44, 180–82, 188–89, 196–97, 210, 211–14, 216
Kiaksht, Georgii, 197–98
Kiaksht (Kyasht), Lidia, 183
King's Command, 54, 117

INDEX 291

Kirov Theater. *See* Mariinsky Theater
Kirstein, Lincoln, 159–60, 174, 218, 254–55
Kister, Karl, 78, 109, 110, 114–16, 122–23, 189
Krasovskaia, Vera, 2–7, 8–9, 11–12, 13–14, 19, 31–32, 46, 77–78, 89, 94, 95, 96–97
Krylov, Ivan, 92–93, 94
Kschessinska, Matilda, 44, 60, 75–76, 164, 198–99, 204–7, 232, 258–59
Kshesinsky, Felix, 75–76, 217–18
Kshesinsky, Iosif, 33, 142–44, 190, 191

Ladyzhensky, Petr Nikolaevich, 84–86
Lancret, Nicolas, 119*f*
Laroche, Herman, 137–39
Legat, Nicolas (Nikolai) 157–58, 161–62, 163–65, 173, 207, 231–32, 234, 235–37
Legnani, Pierina, 6–7, 44, 75–76, 119–20
Leontiev, Konstantin, 145
Levinson, André (Andrei), 11, 45–46, 77, 175–76, 207–8, 219, 224, 239–45, 249–50, 252, 254–55, 256, 257–58
Lifar, Serge, 18–20, 254–55
Little Humpbacked Horse, 95, 101, 132, 150–51, 188–89, 208
Lopukhov, Fedor, 152, 190, 254–55
Louis XIV, 16–17, 23, 48, 64, 74, 75, 129–30, 142, 151, 156–57

Magic Pills, 128–29, 131–32
Maiden of the Danube (La Fille du Danube), 92, 116
Maikov, Apollon, 82–83
Mamontov, Sergei, 29–31
Manzotti, Luigi, 131
Mariinsky Theater, 2–3, 4, 13–14, 30, 43, 61, 66–67, 73, 126, 137–38, 150–51, 183, 186–87, 203–4, 246–47, 248, 249–50, 254–55, 257
Markova, Alicia, 19
masquerade, 22, 46–48
mazurka, 27–28, 75–76, 217–18
McNeill, William H., 16–17
Merezhkovsky, Dmitrii, 218–21, 227–28
Meyerhold, Vsevolod, 211–14, 241
Miasoedov, Grigorii, 82–83
Mikhailovsky Theater, 112–14
Minkus, Ludwig, 72
Muravieva, Marfa, 49, 68, 79–80, 108

Naiad and the Fisherman, 83, 86–87, 89, 94, 105, 106, 174–75
National dance. *See* character dance
Nekrasov, Nikolai, 77–78, 79, 82, 89–95, 96–97, 99, 101–2, 105–6, 110–11, 216
Nelidova, Lidiia, 50–51, 72–73, 78, 192–93
Nicholas I, 185–86
Night and Day, 129–31, 133, 141–42
Nijinska, Bronislava, 29, 204–7, 210–11, 256
Nijinsky, Vaslav, 20, 45–46, 72–73, 177–78, 191

Nil'sky, Aleksandr, 153, 174–75
Noverre, Jean-Georges, 1–2, 4, 7–11, 14, 15, 16–17, 20, 22–23, 24, 25–28, 29, 31, 32–35, 40, 46–53, 56–57, 62–63, 68, 70, 116–17, 125, 159–60, 166, 179, 187, 194, 195, 244, 248–49
Nutcracker, 6, 8–9, 32, 75, 117, 129, 138, 259

Orphan Theolinda, or the Sprite of the Valley, 79–80
Ostrovsky, Aleksandr, 126

pantomime, 8, 9, 11, 23, 27, 31, 35, 48–50, 52, 53, 54, 188, 194, 236, 241, 251
pantomimi, 1, 7, 15
Paquita, 59, 65–66
Pavillon d'Armide, Le, 196–97, 217, 248
Pavlova, Anna, 20, 60–62, 250, 258–59
Perrault, Charles, 142–44, 148
Perrot, Jules-Joseph, 10, 35, 53, 72, 83, 86–87, 101–2, 133
Petipa, Maria, 49, 57–58, 68, 89–91, 90*f*, 92, 94, 96, 108, 187–88
Petipa, Marius, 5, 12, 16, 19, 20, 24–25, 28–29, 30, 33, 38, 40, 44, 48–49, 52, 54, 55, 56, 57–64, 68–70, 71, 72–74, 86–87, 89–90, 125, 128–29, 133, 151, 236, 248–49, 250, 257
Petrov, Vasil'ko, 35, 37, 38–39, 43, 78
Petrushka, 197–98, 200–3, 202*f*, 203*f*, 204*f*, 205*f*, 207–8, 210, 211, 215*f*, 215–16, 221
Pharaoh's Daughter, 21, 23, 60, 71–72, 248–49
Pleshcheev, Aleksandr, 3, 5, 10–11, 14–15, 19–20, 31, 38–39, 42–43, 44, 45, 47–48, 57, 72, 93, 124–25, 130, 135–37, 188
Pobedonostsev, Konstantin, 127, 128, 138–41, 140*f*, 142–48, 147*f*, 150–51, 167, 218, 219, 222
Pogozhev, Vladimir, 123, 124–25, 133–35
pointe, 41–46, 68–69
polonaise, 97–98
Ponomarev, Evgenii, 117, 119–20
Preobrajenska, Olga, 60, 61–62, 121*f*, 196–97, 204–7, 258
Prisoner of the Caucasus (Kavkazskii plennik), 52
Pushkin, Aleksandr, 52, 54, 89, 92–93, 95
Pushkin, Vasilii, 113

Radina, Liubov', 79–80
Rappaport, Mavrikii, 49, 53, 63
Raymonda, 6, 68–69, 249–50
Réveil de Flore, Le, 28–29
Rinaldi, Antonio, 26–27, 28–29, 32–34
Rite of Spring, 221
Robaudi, Vincenzo, 72
Roller, Andreas, 109
Rosati, Carolina, 58
Roxana, the Beauty of Montenegro, 60
Rubinstein, Anton, 123–24
Ruses d'Amour. See Trial of Damis
Russification. *See* ballet, linguistic policy

292 INDEX

Saburov, Andrei, 110
Saint-Léon, Arthur, 29, 35, 39, 49, 54–55, 58, 79–80, 87, 89, 96, 101, 132, 133, 210–11
Salammbô, 29–30
Saltarello, or Passion for Dance, 55
Saltykov-Shchedrin, Mikhail, 54–55, 77–78, 79–84, 85–89, 90–91, 93, 94–95, 96–97, 99, 101–2, 105, 106, 108, 116, 174–75, 197
Salvioni, Guglielmina, 106
School of Russian Ballet, 250
Scribe, Eugène, 53
sculptural style in dance, 12, 18–19, 24–25, 33–34, 49, 51, 154–55, 233–34, 264n.90
serfdom, 81, 82–138, 188. *See also* abolition of serfdom
Sergeev, Nikolai, 70, 170, 256, 259
Shaikevitch, André, 18–19, 240
Shakhovskoi, Aleksandr, 83–84, 85–86
Shiriaev, Aleksandr, 24–25, 69
Shklovsky, Viktor, 11, 32, 104, 107, 187, 244, 250–55
Skalkovsky, Konstantin, 3, 5, 6, 9–11, 13–15, 21, 23–25, 28–29, 30, 32, 37, 38, 39–40, 45, 46, 47–48, 50–51, 54, 55, 58, 59, 64–66, 67–68, 71–72, 95, 109, 114–17, 137, 173–74, 186–87, 192, 225, 246, 250
Sleeping Beauty
   ballet, 6, 8–9, 21, 55, 58–59, 64, 66–67, 68–69, 75, 87, 117, 128–29, 132–33, 137–38, 141–44, 143f, 145–48, 146f, 150–51, 152, 259
   film, 150
   Sleeping Princess, 256, 257–58
Slonimsky, Yuri, 16, 34–35, 253
Sobeshchanskaia, Anna, 120
Socialist realism. *See drambalet*
Sokolova, Evgenia, 59–60, 71–72
Somnambule, La, 53
Spessivtseva, Olga, 237, 253–54, 257–58, 259
Staats, Leo, 164, 173
Stanislavsky, Konstantin, 11, 12–13, 191–92, 195–96
Stravinsky, Igor, 208, 215–16, 221, 222–23, 236
subscriptions (*abonementy*), 246–47, 248
Surovshchikova-Petipa, Maria. *See* Petipa, Maria
Sveshnikova, Alisa, 35
Svetlov, Valerian, 101–2, 196, 231–32, 245–50, 257
Swan Lake, 6, 12, 23, 56, 64, 68–69, 248
Sylphide, La, 23, 41, 165–66, 168–69
Sylphides, Les, 61, 216–17, 223
symphonism, 11–12, 13–15, 23, 66

Taglioni, Filippo, 57–58, 70–71, 92, 116
Taglioni, Marie, 10, 17, 20, 35, 41–42, 57–58, 68, 92, 167, 168–69, 181

Taglioni, Paul, 70–72
Talisman, 188, 198–99, 204–7
Tchaikovsky, Petr, 8–9, 12, 13–14, 58–59, 73, 126, 137–38, 141
Teliakovsky, Vladimir, 60, 73–74, 198–99, 220, 244–50, 254
Thaw (political), 11
Tolstoy, Leo, 6, 17–18, 77–78, 79, 96–97, 99–102, 105–8, 151, 183–84, 218, 229–30, 239
   Childhood: 105–6
   The Power of Darkness: 139
   Resurrection: 107
   War and Peace: 97–105, 106
   "What is Art?": 183–84, 185, 191–92, 195–96, 224–25
Travelling Danseuse, 55
Trial of Damis, 118–20
Trubetskoi, Ivan, 38, 133, 135
Tsar Kandavl (Le Roi Candaule), 47–48, 66–67
Tulipe de Haarlem, La, 37

Ulanova, Galina, 41–42

Vaganova, Agrippina, 2–3, 41–42, 65, 242, 257
Valts, Karl, 109, 120, 129–30
Varlamov, Konstantin, 95, 101–2, 111
Vazem, Ekaterina, 38–39, 40, 44–45, 47–48, 53, 58–59, 79–80, 92, 116, 128–29
Vergina, Aleksandra, 47–48, 92
Vernal Daydreams (Vesennie grezy), 248
Vestris, Auguste, 32–35, 159–60, 173–74
Vestris, Gaetano, 173–74, 175
Vigel', Filipp, 113
virtuosity, 12–13, 20, 32–33, 35, 37, 39–40, 43, 44, 45, 68, 74
virtuozki. See virtuosity
Vivandiere, La, 37–38
Vizentini, Alberto, 54
Voltaire, 51, 52, 54–55, 112, 113
Volynsky, Akim, 11, 45–46, 175–76, 225–45, 249–50, 252, 254, 257
Vsevolozhsky, Ivan, 20, 69, 78–79, 87, 111–13, 114, 115f, 116–17, 118–25, 126, 128–29, 131, 132–33, 134f, 135, 136f, 139–48, 140f, 143f, 146f, 147f, 150–52, 191, 236, 246–47

Watteau, Jean-Antoine, 119–20

Zambelli, Carlotta, 39–40
Zéphire et Flore, 28
Zucchi, Virginia, 6, 8–9, 12–14, 21, 23–24, 25, 28, 43, 59, 65–66, 68, 71–72, 117, 125–26, 135–38, 136f, 139–41, 186–87, 253–54